Competition in International Business

The Columbia University Center for Law and Economic Studies

COMPETITION IN INTERNATIONAL BUSINESS

Law and Policy on Restrictive Practices

Edited by
Oscar Schachter
and
Robert Hellawell

1981
COLUMBIA UNIVERSITY PRESS
NEW YORK

Oscar Schachter is Hamilton Fish Professor of International Law and Diplomacy, Columbia University.

Robert Hellawell is Professor of Law, Columbia University.

Library of Congress Cataloging in Publication Data
Main entry under title:

Competition in international business.

Includes bibliographical references and index.
1. Restraint of trade.   2. International business enterprises—Law and legislation.
3. Technology transfer—Law and legislation.
I. Schachter, Oscar, 1915–   . II. Hellawell, Robert.

K3850.C65	343'.0723	81-3856
ISBN 0-231-05220-0	342.3723	AACR2

Columbia University Press
New York   Guildford, Surrey

Copyright © 1981 Columbia University Press
Printed in the United States of America

Clothbound editions of Columbia University Press books are Smyth-sewn and printed on permanent and durable acid-free paper.

Contents

◈

Preface   vii

Part 1. Transnational Corporations and Restrictive Business
Practices   1

Analysis of Restrictive Business Practices by
Transnational Corporations and Their Impact on
Trade and Development   N. T. Wang   3

Commentary   L. H. Bloom   22

Commentary   G. K. Helleiner   27

Discussion   34

Part 2. Restrictive Business Practices Affecting
Transfer of Technology   39

Control of Terms and Conditions for International
Transfers of Technology to Developing
Countries   Douglas F. Greer   41

Restrictive Business Practices in the
International Transfer and Diffusion
of Technology   Sigmund Timberg   84

Commentary   Walter Glass   139

Commentary   Ingo Walter   143

Commentary   Louis T. Wells, Jr.   160

Discussion   165

Part 3. Cartels and Cartel-like Practices   177

Economic and Political Characteristics of Cartel
and Cartel-like Practices   *Robert E. Smith*   179

International Cartels and Their Regulation   *James A. Rahl*   240

Commentary   *David G. Gill*   277

Commentary   *G. C. Hufbauer*   283

Discussion   286

Part 4. Mergers, Acquisitions, and Joint Ventures   291

Merger Control in Western Europe: National
and International Aspects   *Kurt Markert*   293

Appendix: Federal Cartel Office Guidelines on
Domestic Effects Within the Meaning of Section
98(2) of the Act Against Restraints of
Competition in the Case of Mergers   332

Commentary   *Mark R. Joelson*   335

Commentary   *W. F. Mueller*   344

Discussion   352

Part 5. International Codes of Conduct
          and Conventions   359

The Seeking of a World Competition Code:
Quixotic Quest?   *Joel Davidow*   361

Appendix: The Set of Multilaterally Agreed Equitable
Principles and Rules for the Control of Restrictive
Business Practices   404

Commentary   *Timothy Atkeson*   416

Commentary   *Samuel Wex*   422

Discussion   426

Contributors   429

Index   433

Preface

◆

This book was stimulated by recent efforts of governments in the United Nations to establish a code of conduct on restrictive business practices affecting international trade and development. The very idea of a worldwide code—an international antitrust law—may seem fanciful when we think of national policies on competition. Many economies are centrally planned and state directed. Many other countries consider it reasonable for private business to agree on prices or an allocation of markets. Even governments that profess and, to some degree, legislate adherence to free market principles are deeply ambivalent about restrictions and combinations in restraint of trade; in many sectors they deliberately depart from the ethos of a competitive system. Moreover, in a period when international economic relations are characterized by increased protectionism and preferential arrangements, an international code against restrictive practices hardly seems to fit the times.

Yet, despite these inauspicious conditions, a code on restrictive business practices was adopted in the United Nations in 1980. It was accepted by the three major groups of states: the industrial market economy countries, the developing countries of the Third World, and the socialist states of Eastern Europe. To be sure, the code does not purport to be legally binding and it has significant exceptions. It envisages only rudimentary procedures for international fact finding and surveillance of compliance. On the other hand, the code furnishes a political basis and a stimulus for enforcement through national legislation and administrative action. It remains to be seen how effective it will be in practice.

Still, the fact that the code was adopted attests to the persistence of views that anticompetitive practices are harmful to international trade and economic development. Most governments, especially those of developing countries, tend to see their countries as victims in some respects of foreign business enterprises using economic power to the detriment of national industry and well-being. In recent years, this concern has centered on multinational corporations. They have been perceived as engaged in cartel-like arrangements or as misusing their control of technology by restrictive practices in the transfer of such technology.

The papers in this book address these problems. Five major subjects are dealt with:

(1) restrictive business practices of transnational companies;
(2) restrictive practices affecting transfer of technology;
(3) cartels and cartel-like practices;
(4) mergers, acquisitions, and joint ventures; and
(5) international codes and guidelines.

Each of these subjects is examined in papers commissioned by the editors on behalf of the Columbia University Center for Law and Economic Studies. The authors are either economists or lawyers who have made distinguished contributions to the field and are internationally recognized experts. All of them have had experience in government or international organizations. In addition to the principal papers, the book includes short written commentaries on each paper. These commentaries present diverse viewpoints. Several of them are by executives or counsel of multinational companies. Others are by economists, government officials, and legal scholars. The book also includes summaries of observations made by participants at a conference held in November 1979 to discuss the papers. That conference had a spirited and wide-ranging intellectual discussion. It brought out the diversity of views and the complexity of issues relating to restrictive practices. One conclusion to be drawn is that there is ample room as well as a need for more empirical data and deeper analysis of the problems raised. Another is the desirability of, indeed the necessity for, interdisciplinary studies and analysis from different points of view. Clearly, this is an area in which economics, law, political science, business and public administration have much to contribute. There is also an important role for the practical and experienced corporate executive, legal counsel, and government official. It was gratifying to observe at the conference that persons with these varied backgrounds were able to carry on a mutually understandable and illuminating discussion of the issues.

Advice in planning the book and conference was furnished by several of the contributors. We would like particularly to note our debt to the late

Professor Corwin Edwards, whose work in the field of international regulation of cartels and restrictive practices has left a deep imprint on present thinking. Professor Edwards participated in the planning of the book and conference; unfortunately he died before he could prepare his own contribution. Moving tributes were paid to him at the conference.

The editors are grateful for the support of Professor Lewis Kaden, the Director of the Columbia University Center for Law and Economic Studies, and for the invaluable assistance of the Assistant Director, Marie Castro. Mrs. Anna Ascher merits many thanks for her expert editing.

Oscar Schachter
Robert Hellawell

Competition in International Business

I

TRANSNATIONAL CORPORATIONS
AND RESTRICTIVE
BUSINESS PRACTICES

Analysis of Restrictive Business Practices by Transnational Corporations and Their Impact on Trade and Development

N. T. Wang

INTRODUCTION

Restrictive business practices have received great attention in current discussions. At the intellectual level, the growth of transnational corporations has raised the question of their implications for the market structure. Where the activities of transnational corporations predominate, the atomistic competitive model hardly appears applicable. A large body of studies has emerged to document that transnational corporations owe their existence to market imperfections and that they in turn engage in numerous practices in restraint of competition.[1]

At the governmental and intergovernmental level, the attention focused on restrictive business practices is a necessary counterpart of the general concern about the pervasive effect of transnational corporations. Whether in connection with conditions for foreign direct investment, with the import of technology, with regional integration, or with a general code of conduct, specific reference to restrictive business practices is called for.[2] At the national level, many countries have introduced new laws or administrative machinery to deal with restrictive business practices. In the United States, a national Commission for the Review of Antitrust Laws and Procedures has been established.[3] The United Nations has declared itself ready to negotiate and adopt "a set of multilaterally agreed equitable principles and rules for the control of restrictive business practices . . . having adverse effects on international trade, particularly that of developing countries and in the economic development of those countries. . . ."[4]

In a rare display of unanimity, different schools of thought take it more or less for granted that restrictive business practices have an adverse impact on trade and development. The judgment is implicit in the terms used to describe their "restrictive," "predatory," or "discriminatory" nature, and the "abuse" or "collusion" that they involve. The mesmerizing effect of semantics is well illustrated by a recent incident at the United Nations in which an international civil servant innocently characterized the Organization of Petroleum Exporting Countries (OPEC) as a cartel. The term infuriated the OPEC members and their supporters: they claimed it was derogatory and particularly inappropriate for an international civil servant who should maintain an objective posture. He was forced to retract it, for how could a "cartel" be viewed in a positive light!

The negative connotation is often built into the very definition in international discussions. Witness the United Nations resolution just cited. Restrictive business practices by definition have adverse effects on trade and development.

The purpose of the present paper is to raise fundamental questions about costs and benefits and to go behind the facade of diplomatic niceties. The first task is to attempt to distinguish the act from the effect. It will be shown why this distinction is sometimes difficult to make. Moreover, the same act may have very different effects on different parties, from different perspectives and under different circumstances. A great amount of fine tuning is thus necessary. As a result, the ultimate solution is far less certain than is suggested by the conventional wisdom.

The apparent consensus in international discussion of restrictive business practices should be interpreted in a similar light. Typically, international negotiations deliberately skirt the difficult but fundamental questions. Matters of serious controversy are rightly passed over in silence lest they hinder general progress and poison the atmosphere.

An international consensus reached under such circumstances should not give a false sense of security. It is no more than a modest beginning on an arduous long march.

The central thesis of this paper is that the impact of restrictive business practices of transnational corporations cannot be properly analyzed without reference to the basic nature of these corporations and their capabilities, nor can it be understood in isolation from the circumstances in which the practices take place and their differential incidence. The inescapable conclusion that arises from these complex considerations is an equally complex set of policy implications. The simple logic that restrictive business practices are bad and should therefore be regulated or eliminated begs the question of how a balance can be struck between trade-offs. The following pages will demonstrate these considerations.

THE SCOPE AND THE CAUSAL LINK

A common cause of confusion about the impact of restrictive business practices is the fuzziness of a number of basic issues. First, what is the scope of these practices? Second, why concentrate on the restrictive business practices of transnational corporations? Third, what is their impact and on whom?

WHAT ARE RESTRICTIVE BUSINESS PRACTICES?

The fundamental concept underlying restrictive business practices is restraint of competition. The precise definition often varies with different philosophies and purposes. For the purpose of government regulation and control, where the emphasis is on the injurious effect, the definition is usually broad and the rule of reason applies in determining whether certain behavior constitutes a restrictive business practice. Where stress is laid on the prohibition per se of certain practices, the various types or forms are defined in greater detail even though a specific list of such practices may be presented as no more than illustrative in order to avoid loopholes. In international negotiations, the scope generally reflects the concerns of the governments in question. At the United Nations, the Third Ad Hoc Group of Experts on Restrictive Business Practices reached general agreement on their scope in terms of the following: [5]

1. participating in or otherwise purposely strengthening the restrictive effects of cartel(s), such as:
   a. agreements fixing price as to exports and imports;
   b. collusive tendering;
   c. market or customer allocation arrangements;
   d. allocation by quota as to sales and production;
   e. collective action to enforce arrangements—e.g., by concerted refusals to deal;
   f. concerted refusal of supplies to potential importers; and
   g. collective denial of access to an arrangement, or association, which is crucial to competition; and

2. unjustifiably fixing the prices at which goods exported can be resold in importing countries.

The group further identified as restrictive business practices abuse of a dominant position of market power in the shape of:

1. predatory behavior towards competitors, such as using below-cost pricing to eliminate competitors;
2. discriminatory (i.e., unjustifiably differentiated) pricing or terms or conditions in the supply or purchase of products or services, or excessive pricing of products and services;
3. mergers, takeovers, joint ventures or other acquisitions of control, whether of a horizontal, vertical, or conglomerate nature; and
4. the following, when not designed to ensure the achievement of legitimate business purposes, such as quality, safety, adequate distribution, or service:
   a. partial or complete refusals to deal on the enterprise's customary commercial terms;
   b. making the supply of particular products or services dependent upon the acceptance of restrictions on the distribution or manufacture of competing or other products, or imposing restrictions concerning where, or to whom, or in what form or quantities, the products supplied may be resold or exported; and
   c. making the supply of particular products or services dependent upon the purchase of other products or services from the supplier or his designee.

The developing countries as a group have expanded the list to include such practices as territorial allocation and transfer pricing. These are of particular interest to these countries, especially with regard to their exports or revenues. They are, moreover, difficult for them to deal with.

It is evident from this long list of restrictive business practices that the impact varies in accordance with the specific practice in question. For instance, the impact of simple price fixing is different from that of discriminatory pricing. Standard microanalysis shows that discriminatory pricing generally leads to larger outputs than under simple monopoly pricing and hence to an improved allocation of resources. At the same time, it enhances the monopoly power of the discriminator, and redistributes the income of the discriminated against.[6] The impact of transfer pricing on stated profits and government revenue depends on the incentives for shifting tax payments or avoiding exchange and remittance controls. These incentives are likely to be stronger in developing countries. Moreover, the machinery for monitoring transfer pricing practices is inadequate because of the lack of domestic administrative capabilities and cooperation with tax authorities in the countries in which the transnationals are based.[7]

WHY TRANSNATIONAL CORPORATIONS?

While it is generally acknowledged that all enterprises may from time to time engage in restrictive business practices, the focus on those of transnational corporations reflects the particular concern about the latter, following their phenomenal growth and increasing importance.

There is therefore general agreement that the impact of restrictive business practices by transnational corporations deserves special attention. The definition of transnational corporations is, however, a controversial issue in itself. It is significant that both the United Nations Centre on Transnational Corporations and the Organisation for Economic Co-operation and Development have maintained that it is possible to carry on practical work without a precise definition, notwithstanding urgings to the contrary by the Cartesian-minded.[8] The main reason for avoiding a clear-cut definition is political, for a number of countries, notably the socialist states and several developing countries, insist that their enterprises should not be lumped together with those of monopoly capitalism. A consensus cannot be reached if a formal decision must be taken on the definition. From a substantive point of view, different definitions may very well be adopted for different purposes. For example, the definition for purposes of national regulation may vary from the definition to be used in an international code of conduct; the definition for a general code may be different from that for international standards of accounting and reporting.[9] For present purposes, the term *transnational corporations* may be understood in the broad sense offered by the Group of Eminent Persons[10] and be used interchangeably with multinational enterprises or multinational corporations.

The special relevance of transnational corporations to restrictive business practices is fairly evident. These corporations are frequently so powerful and large in size that possibilities of dominance and abuse are ever present. Furthermore, they are often found to engage in oligopolistic practices. They operate across national boundaries and are thus outside national jurisdiction and effective control.

For the same reason, however, the questions of whether restrictive business practices arise because corporations are large and concentrated or because they are transnational are hardly separable. Certainly, incentives for price discrimination, restraint on entry, or stable relations within the group exist in any oligopolistic situation. Their scope and opportunities are enlarged in transnational operations, partly because the relative size and degree of concentration are accentuated across the borders and partly because they are less noticed or noticeable. In some cases, as in transfer pricing, transnationality is certainly a determining factor, for incentives to shift stated profits within a nation do not usually exist.

The crucial question is not, however, whether transnationals may engage in restrictive business practices, but to what extent such practices are distinguishable from normal transnational practices, and whether, when an ever-expanding net is cast against restrictive business practices, the very rationale of transnational corporations is also impaired.

It is the contention of this paper that the difficulty of separating much of the normal practice of transnationals from those practices deemed to be restrictive poses a real dilemma. First, there are numerous ways in which transnational corporations amass power. They engage in vertical as well as horizontal integration. They also engage in diversification, product differentiation, advertising campaigns, and the creation of new technology. [11] These activities across national boundaries strengthen their power and are less subject to domestic antitrust scrutiny.

Second, many intracorporate transactions veiled in business confidentiality may achieve the same effect as restrictive business practices. For instance, the allocation of export markets to affiliates appears to be perfectly rational since one should not expect an affiliate of a transnational corporation to compete with another affiliate of the same corporation. Similarly, the pricing of technology and information in a way that permits maximization of group profits deviates from the arm's-length pricing rule. [12] Insistence on the arm's-length rule may be of questionable efficacy, apart from the practical consideration of whether an arm's-length price exists for such articles as intermediate products to be processed by affiliates.

Third, the very organization of transnational corporations is increasingly amorphous. These corporations may form group companies or strategic groups. Many of these groups have much in common with those in Japan or Korea where the relationship is often informal. [13] As a result, no explicit agreement on cartel types of activity is needed to pursue common policies in restraint of competition.

On the other hand, as long as modern technology requires vast scales of investment and operation, locational advantages exist because of proximity to market or natural resources, and major and minor innovations occur constantly, there is a positive rationale for transnational corporations together with the oligopolistic characteristics, even if all artificial barriers between nations are removed.[14] These corporations will continue to be large and powerful. Many of them will be integrated or diversified and will form alliances across national borders. The dividing line between what is an abuse and what is not, what is inimical to efficiency and what is not, is blurred. This lack of clarity is likely to increase as new and ingenious patterns of behavior are devised to circumvent regulations against restrictive business practices.

WHAT IMPACT AND ON WHOM?
The ultimate test thus rests on an assessment of the impact. Proper assessment of the impact, however, is hampered for many reasons. First, theoretical analysis often calculates the welfare loss of monopolistic practices as aberrations from pure competition, on a set of restrictive assumptions including the absence of scale economy and innovation. Such analysis is instructive from a pedagogical point of view, but the question arises whether the ideal state is a suitable or fair standard of comparison for practical policy purposes.

Second, the usual assumption of *ceteris paribus* in partial analysis is especially unrealistic since restrictive business practices are often part of the arsenal of transnational corporations in their internalization[15] and strategy of competition among a few. As was pointed out earlier, no formal agreement or collusion is needed in market allocation if a transnational corporation conducts its business through its own branches. Indeed, one of the reasons why many U.S. firms shy away from joint ventures may be to avoid possible infringements of U.S. antitrust regulations.[16] Similarly, no formal association need be organized if the chief executives maintain informal communications through breakfast meetings, games of golf, and so forth, or adopt such predictable reaction patterns as "follow the leader." Moreover, the impact cannot be isolated from the overall institutional and policy framework, as will be demonstrated later.

Third, trade and development are in themselves very broad concepts. Many identifiable restrictive business practices refer to export restrictions by subsidiaries of transnational corporations. Yet, the impact on trade cannot be evaluated by simply asking how much export would take place if the restrictions were removed. The question must also be asked whether such facilities will exist at all in the host country.

The assessment of a net trade effect must take into account the entire package. If foreign direct investment by transnational corporations is a vehicle for overcoming trade barriers, it is an alternative to trade, but the net effect on trade is a combination of trade displacement by foreign production and trade creation through capital flow, including exports of plant and equipment from the home to the host country and subsequent intracompany transactions. Moreover, the trade creation effect differs from industry to industry. It is likely to be higher for direct investment in raw materials or components than for export industry of the home country. The question is then whether certain restrictive business practices are a necessary cost or ingredient in the package. [17]

The assessment of the development effect is even more complex, and there is certainly no one-to-one correspondence with the trade effect. For instance, if development effect is narrowly defined as aggregate income effect, restrictive business practices are almost by definition output- and income-reducing as compared with pure competition. If development is conceived in terms of distribution as well, and through the various determinants such as capital, technology, innovation, and risk, the simple causal relationship evaporates. There are real questions: for example, whether innovations are ever introduced without some form of actual restraint of entry. There are also serious concerns about ruinous competition, especially in developing countries. When entry is relatively easy, each new entrant, not knowing of the impending activities of the others, assumes a larger share of the market than is feasible. The bandwagon effect thus results in high risk and bankruptcy rates, which must be painfully corrected through the process of natural selection and reduction in numbers.

Finally, the uneven distributional impact in trade and development evidently applies to countries also. The impact on the host country is not the same as on the home country. Nor is it necessarily a zero-sum game—in the sense that the loss of the host country is the gain of the home country, and vice versa. Consequently, there may be a net global gain or loss. These considerations are discussed in the following section.

THREE PERSPECTIVES

An evaluation of the impact of restrictive business practices depends further on whether a national or a global view is taken. In most countries, a national view is implicit in the relevant laws and regulations. The object of most of these measures is to protect the interest of the citizens. The nationalist orientation is clearest in antitrust laws that exempt export cartels. The reasoning is simply that though foreigners may be adversely affected, the national interest will not. Indeed, the argument can be pushed further and export cartels used to foster the national interest, though at the expense of others.[18]

The nationalistic approach assumes, however, that other countries are either unable or do not consider it worthwhile to retaliate. The assumption holds true more or less if the country that adopts this beggar-thy-neighbor policy is capable of molding the policies of the others, or, paradoxically, if it is relatively insignificant. An example of the former case is control of the trade and tariff policies of colonial or semi-colonial territories by the metropolitan power. Illustrative of the latter are relatively small countries whose actions may be ignored by the others, at least temporarily, so that the tail does not wag the dog. On the other hand, the policies of a relatively large country sometimes take into account the possible reaction of others, so that the nationalistic approach is tempered by global considerations.

THE VIEW FROM THE HOME COUNTRY

From the national viewpoint of the home country, what is good for its transnational corporations is not necessarily good for the country, since the global strategies of a transnational corporation do not necessarily coincide with the country's strategies. Restrictive business practices are not an exception. They may, for example, strengthen the monopolistic power of the corporation at home in conflict with domestic antitrust objectives. They may involve collusion with foreigners at the expense of home country consumers and shift revenue from the home country to the host country.

Yet, the traditional view that domestic enterprises should be encouraged or protected, even in connection with restrictive business practices, generally prevails. This is especially the case in relations with foreign countries where reciprocity is lacking. Consequently, restrictive business practices of transnationals in developing countries tend to be tolerated by developed home countries. An analysis of the provisions on restrictive business practices of the European Economic Community in agreements with developing countries shows, for example, that they tend to be extremely limited in scope and applicability.[19] The growing importance of business relations between the East and the West has prompted a number of market economy countries to encourage collective corporate action to emulate and deal with state trading companies.

The resurgence of neo-mercantilism in some home countries has also meant that strong transnational corporations are considered necessary for maintaining or strengthening their competitive position in the world market. In a curious twist of the mercantilist logic, even foreign export cartels are sometimes encouraged to take group action and establish voluntary export quotas for selected goods in order to protect declining industries or labor groups in the home country. In such cases, the interest of the consumers is clearly ignored. Indeed, consumers rarely constitute strong lobbying groups for political action as compared with other special interest groups.

The above further illustrates the possible divergence between what is perceived as being of national interest and the real interest from the point of view of development or employment. Certainly, as far as trade relations between developed and developing countries are concerned, the latter are net importers. The restrictions on exports of the developing countries affect their import capacity and thus the exports of the developed countries. Moreover, in a dynamic economy with a large degree of openness among the developed countries, declining industries in the home country can hardly be successfully propped up for any length of time. The legitimate concern of adjustment problems must therefore be dealt with by other measures, including industrial, adjustment, and employment policies. The ostensibly positive effect of restriction of exports by transnational corporations in the developing countries on development of the home country assumes the absence of such policies and when these policies exist, the result may be the reverse.

THE VIEW FROM THE HOST COUNTRY
From the standpoint of the host country, especially a developing country, restrictive business practices of foreign-based transnationals are of special concern. In the first place, these transnationals are controlled from abroad. As noted earlier, they are often backed by foreign powers even though

their interests and those of the home country do not necessarily coincide. In the second place, these practices are often at odds with national enterprises, even though they may be in collusion with some local elite. Lastly, many of these practices are shrouded in secrecy and appear to be difficult to deal with. These considerations explain why the developing countries attach special significance to this issue in international discussions.

Yet, many developing countries take an ambivalent position on restrictive business practices. The reason is that they are confronted by a real dilemma. First, there is a dilemma between efficiency and antimonopoly. While the same dilemma exists in developed countries and is often recognized,[20] the difficulty of choosing is especially acute in developing countries. In the developed countries, large firms do not necessarily exhibit higher efficiency because the advantages of scale economy are sometimes offset or more than offset by diseconomies of size due to strain on communications, difficulties of coordination, and growth of bureaucracy. For the overwhelming majority of developing countries, however, the size of the economy is so small that it is frequently no larger than that of a medium-sized town in a developed country. In the process of modernization, there is little room for many firms to compete in the same industry. The inefficiencies of having, for example, five or six transnationals or even more operating in the automobile industry in many developing countries are clearly reflected in the high cost of automobiles. Governments that recognize the importance of scale considerations have frequently conferred monopoly power on transnationals operating in their countries by restricting entry and erecting new trade barriers. The restrictive business practices of transnational corporations are thus not only tolerated by but also a necessary result of governmental action.

Second, there is a dilemma between equal and discriminatory treatment of transnationals. Most developing countries are particularly concerned about possible restrictive business practices of foreign-based transnationals. They are less concerned about similar practices by domestic enterprises, private or state owned. The domestic firms may indeed serve as a countervailing force against the transnationals. For this reason, these countries generally wish to exempt their domestic enterprises from controls over restrictive business practices.

Apart from the general question of discrimination, it may be argued that what should be controlled is those practices that have adverse effects on trade and development rather than those of a particular origin. On the other hand, the promotion of national champions may stimulate competition with the transnational oligopolists (although the reverse may also be true). Moreover, virtually all nations, including those that subscribe to the principle of national treatment, permit some form of unequal treatment among nonequals. Furthermore, state enterprises may indeed be deliberately created monopolies, though subject to public control and their profit accruing to the state.

A related dilemma is between the need for a detailed assessment of impact and the capacity to make one. Because of the importance of scale economy, a blanket prohibition of restrictive business practices per se would inhibit efficiency. Yet, a detailed assessment implies the possession of fundamental information at the micro- and macro-levels, as well as the skill and administrative capacity to carry out the sophisticated exercises involved. These conditions are rarely met in developing countries.[21]

THE GLOBAL VIEW

Viewed from the global perspective, the key question is: in what way is world trade and development adversely affected by restrictive business practices? In theory, this is the general case which includes the special cases of the effect on various countries or social groups in the world. In practice, however, the global view is rarely taken, since policy making remains in the hands of nation-states.

Here, the artificiality of a comparison between an oligopolistic model and a purely competitive model is most evident. This is especially the case with developing countries. In many developing countries, the pure competitive model is neither feasible nor desirable. It is infeasible because these countries are mostly small economically and fragmented internally. Moreover, it is not even desirable because according to the well-known argument, infant industry needs trade barriers in order to benefit from a downward-sloping learning curve. The same argument may be extended to the case for nonreciprocity in tariff negotiations with the developed countries and preferential treatment in favor of developing countries. A further argument is illustrated by the tendency of benefits to be concentrated in a few relatively developed countries, following the removal of trade barriers within a regional group.

In the fragmented world of nation-states and existing restrictions on the movement of output and factors of production, the transnational corporations are in one way or another overcoming these barriers. Where there

are trade barriers, they may be largely overcome by foreign direct investment. It is true that foreign direct investment is often carried out by powerful giants. Nevertheless, this power may also be instrumental in overcoming numerous existing obstacles.

From the global perspective, a similar dilemma exists to that confronting
the developing countries. A global system must reconcile competition with
efficiency. Such a system may very well see giants and atomistic competitors coexisting, and the rules of the game deviate significantly from those
of pure competition.

SOME POLICY IMPLICATIONS

BEYOND CONSENSUS

Recent studies on restrictive business practices of transnational corporations have strongly reinforced the notion that they do, in fact, exist.[22]
Some of these practices are indeed deeply rooted in the very characteristics
of transnational corporations, which operate in an oligopolistic or monopolistic environment and, in turn, strengthen and nurture such environments.

These practices are generally regarded as unfavorable to trade and development. It is virtually an article of faith to orthodox economists that
monopoly is bad and competition is good. It is also axiomatic to radical
economists that transnational corporations, being the tools of capitalists
and capitalism, are exploiters and that their restrictive business practices
are confirmations of their abuses.

In international discussions on restrictive business practices, the chorus
of various schools of thought and interest groups appears deceptively har-
monious. In part, this harmony reflects a semantic bias, since anything
termed *restrictive* carries the connotation of artificiality and abuse. Even
the voice of business is cautious lest it incriminate itself, and restrictive
business practices are rarely admitted or defended.

The apparent consensus on restrictive business practices also reflects
the general approach in international negotiations. Difficult as these negotiations are, the practical way of achieving results in them and avoiding
impasse and glaring failure is to seek common ground. While this tactic is
perfectly appropriate in a world still very much divided, numerous key
issues are glossed over.

As long as restrictive business practices are taken to refer only to those of transnational corporations based in developed private enterprise economies, it is easy for all the developing and socialist countries to condemn them. The real question is whether similar practices of enterprises based in developing and socialist countries, whether domestic or transnational, private or state owned, should be exempted, and if so, which are qualified by what criteria, and who is to be the interpreter? Until these hard questions are answered squarely, the consensus that may be reached is severely limited.

FROM NEGATIVISM TO POSITIVISM

The foregoing analysis has demonstrated the complexity of the issues in question. The impact of restrictive business practices on trade and development is no longer axiomatically negative. As with most economic and social issues, the essence of policy making is choosing among options with all sorts of costs and benefits. The evaluation of these costs and benefits or trade-offs is in most cases imprecise. It is for this reason that policy making cannot be entirely relegated to technicians who claim to have precise solutions. Such solutions exist only if their restrictive assumptions are granted. But seemingly reasonable alternative assumptions frequently yield very different results.

In real world situations, many of the ideal competitive solutions are clearly untenable, especially in the case of present-day developing countries. Because of the smallness of many of these countries, compounded by the fragmentation of their internal economies and the bulky requirements of modern industry, a completely open economy is likely to be more destructive than creative, at least in the short run.

As a result, few developing countries have opted for the competitive solution for their own economies. Transnational corporations operating in these countries are likewise granted various privileges, including blockage of new entrants. This does not, of course, preclude numerous measures that the governments may adopt to curb the power of transnational corporations operating in their territories. In particular, such measures may be specially designed to alter the relative position of the national enterprises. Increasingly, the approach is shifting from the negativism of "thou shalt not engage in this or that practice" to the positivism of "thou shalt perform this and that" for development.

An important implication of the positivist approach is the need for a new negotiated package. I have argued elsewhere that the key concept here is not necessarily de-packaging of foreign direct investment of transnational corporations but its repackaging.[23] De-packaging, however appropriate it may be under certain circumstances, denies any use of the transnationals' unique capacity to put together a workable package. It should not be a general rule for many developing countries, where the critical shortage is not lack of specific technical expertise, some of which is already standardized and readily available in the market, but of the ability to combine all the essential ingredients in a working order. The cements and lubricants for the various components are often intangible and nontransferable. Moreover, there is no guarantee that the aggregate cost, including the use of scarce domestic skills, is lower in a de-packaged situation than in some form of package. This is not to suggest putting the clock back and insisting on the traditional package of foreign direct investment. Between the traditional package and de-packaging, there is a rich repackaging spectrum where capital, entrepreneurship, management, technology, finance, and access to markets may receive variable weights, including zero values. The most suitable combination in the new package would depend on the country's development objectives, the industry concerned and its technological characteristics, and the host country's bargaining position and administrative capacity.

The development objectives are significant because transnationals must contribute to the same objectives. Maintenance of a competitive society may, for example, be less important in a society where monopoly profits are effectively recouped by the state. In addition, differing industrial and technological characteristics require different treatment. For instance, industries involving nonrenewable resources or defense establishments may be unsuitable for a large degree of foreign involvement. For high technology industries, existing technologies acquired through de-packaging may rapidly become obsolete as new research and development yields new technologies. Finally, the ultimate test is in the relative bargaining position and the alternative options open to both parties. These conditions, in turn, depend on the analytical ability and administrative capability of the host country's bureaucracy. For effective bargaining implies knowledge of the opposite side of the bargaining table. Many governmental regulations and controls reflect what the government considers desirable or undesirable, without any notion of the possible reaction of the transnational corporations. Evidently, one can prohibit what is not wanted, but one can hardly force a transnational to do what is wanted. The hostage effect applies only in the short run to existing investors.

Given the administrative capability of the host country, a case-by-case analysis and treatment in bargaining must be approached with great caution. Considerable simplification of practical procedures and decentralization of decision making is called for. Even developed countries are rediscovering the need for economy in administration, quite apart from swings in the political pendulum. The most effective control may still be very little control. A balance must therefore be struck between broad-gauged measures and fine tuning. This balance can be better achieved by a concerted attack. Thus, the attack on restrictive business practices of transnational corporations should not be limited to antitrust action; it should come from many fronts. The multi-pronged attack should include a general code of conduct as well as specific arrangements for the conduct of transnational corporations. The general code could encompass many gray areas and resolve the perennial problem of whether a specific kind of behavior such as transfer pricing properly belongs among restrictive business practices. Specific arrangements might include reporting and disclosure requirements. Adequate disclosure could act as a deterrent to questionable behavior and could serve as a warning signal of possible unforeseen problems. These should be supplemented by trade and monetary measures, which are intimately related to restrictive business practices. For example, a most potent competitive force is actual or potential competition from abroad, provided it is not blocked by trade and monetary restraints.

THE FUTURE OF TRANSNATIONAL CORPORATIONS

The observations made have an important bearing on the future of transnational corporations. When transnational corporations are seen as the originators of restrictive business practices and the preoccupation is with drawing a narrower and narrower circle within which transnationals may operate, they may be restrained from doing wrong but their capacity to do the right things may also be severely restricted. An equally untenable position is to claim that transnational corporations always serve as agents of development. The key strategy is to maximize the net benefit rather than to eliminate negative effects at all cost. The doctrinaire answer is either that it is a contradiction in terms for transnationals to make a positive contribution to development or that such a contribution naturally ensues when the transnationals are left entirely alone. The present paper argues that the power of transnational corporations can be directed or redirected for the purpose of development, although an optimum set of policies is difficult to specify. Such direction, however, does imply an adjustment on the part of transnationals as well as a new approach by governments. Thus, the future of transnationals is not a replica of the traditional mode, nor are they on the road to extinction. Their future lies in a new role as one of the appointed agents of development. The definition, fulfillment, and monitoring of this role will occupy the energies of many generations to come.

NOTES

1. See C. P. Kindleberger, *American Business Abroad: Six Lectures on Direct Investment* (New Haven: Yale University Press, 1969); R. Vernon, *Sovereignty at Bay: The Multinational Spread of U.S. Enterprises* (New York: Basic Books, 1971); J. H. Dunning, *Trade, Location of Economic Activity and the Multinational Enterprise: A Search for an Eclectic Approach,* University of Reading, Discussion Papers on International Investment and Business Studies no. 29 (Reading, 1976); United Nations Conference on Trade and Development (UNCTAD), Restrictive Business Practices (New York: United Nations, 1971, TD/B/C.2/104/Rev. 1); UNCTAD, Restrictive Business Practices in Relation to the Trade and Development of Developing Countries (Geneva: United Nations, 1974, TD/B/C.2/119/Rev.2).

2. See United Nations, *The Impact of Multinational Corporations on Development and on International Relations,* ch. IX on competition and market structure (New York: United Nations, 1974, Sales no. E.74.II.A.5); United Nations Centre on Transnational Corporations, *National Legislation and Regulations Relating to Transnational Corporations* (New York: United Nations, 1976, Sales no. E.78.II.A.3); N. T. Wang, "The Design of an International Code of Conduct for Transnational Corporations," *Journal of International Law and Economics* (August–December 1975), 10:319–36.

3. For a summary of recent developments, see UNCTAD, Annual Report on Legislative and Other Developments in Developed and Developing Countries in the Control of Restrictive Business Practices, 1978 (Geneva: United Nations, 1978, TD/B/C.2/AC.6/15).

4. General Assembly Resolution 33/153 on a United Nations conference on restrictive business practices, 1978; UNCTAD Resolution 103(V) on restrictive business practices, 1978.

5. UNCTAD, Report of the Third Ad Hoc Group of Experts on Restrictive Business Practices on its Sixth Session (Geneva: United Nations, 1979, TD/B/C.2/AC.6/20). See also Report on its Fifth Session (Geneva: United Nations, 1978, TD/B/C.2/AC.6/18).

6. See F. M. Scherer, *Industrial Market Structure and Economic Performance* (Chicago: Rand McNally, 1970), pp. 258–59.

7. See N. T. Wang, "Code of Conduct and Taxation of Transnational Corporations," *Georgia Journal of International and Comparative Law* (1978), 8(4):809–22; United Nations, Tax Treaties Between Developed and Developing Countries: Seventh Report (New York: United Nations, 1978, ST/ESA/78).

8. United Nations Centre on Transnational Corporations, *Transnational Corporations in World Development: A Re-examination* (New York: United Nations, 1978, Sales no. E.78.II.A.5), pp. 158–70; Organisation for Economic Co-operation and Development (OECD), *Guidelines for Multinational Enterprises, National Treatment, International Investment Incentives and Disincentives, Consultation Procedures* (Paris: OECD, 1976), para. 8.

9. The Group of Experts on International Standards of Accounting and Reporting recommended that the list of minimum items for the enterprise as a whole should apply to transnational corporations that meet on a consolidated basis at least two of the following criteria: (1) total assets of over $U.S. 50 million; (2) net sales of over $U.S. 100 million; and (3) average number of employees, over 2,500 during the period. The group also recommended that the criteria for an individual member company should be set at the national level. United Nations Centre on Transnational Corporations, *International Standards of Accounting and Reporting for Transnational Corporations* (New York: United Nations, 1977, Sales no. E.77.II.A.17), pp. 47–48.

10. "Multinational corporations are enterprises which own or control production or service facilities outside the country in which they are based. Such enterprises are not always incorporated or private; they can also be co-operatives or state-owned entities." United Nations, *The Impact of Multinational Corporations*, p. 25.

11. See Alan M. Rugman, *International Diversification and Multinational Enterprise* (Lexington, Mass.: Lexington Books, 1979).

12. For an illustration, see Neil Hood and Stephen Young, *The Economics of Multinational Enterprise* (London: Longman, 1979), pp. 107–10.

13. Nathaniel H. Leff, "Industrial Organization and Entrepreneurship in Developing Countries: The Economic Group," *Economic Development and Cultural Change* (July 1978), 26(4):661–75.

14. The implication is that the oligopoly theory for explaining foreign direct investment is an overstatement and is incomplete.

15. Internalization refers to the allocation of resources, or the organization of transactions, within the firm (internally) rather than through the market in order to achieve lower cost. For elaboration of the concept, see P. J. Buckley and M. Casson, *The Future of Multinational Enterprise* (London: Macmillan, 1976).

16. C. Fred Bergsten, Thomas Horst, and Theodore H. Moran, *American Multinationals and American Interests* (Washington, D.C.: Brookings Institution, 1978), pp. 171–213.

17. See K. Kojima, *Direct Foreign Investment: A Japanese Model of Multinational Business Operations* (London: Croom Helm, 1978).

18. This is not to say that export cartels are necessarily in the national interest of the home country. See the view from the home country below. See also Robert Gilpin, *U.S. Power and the Multinational Corporation* (New York: Basic Books, 1975), pp. 169–97.

19. Michael Rom, "Restrictive Business Practices in European Economic Community Agreements with Less Developed Countries," *Journal of World Trade Law* (1978), 12(1):36–55.

20. In Canada, the proposed new Competition Board would be empowered to approve a merger that substantially reduces competition if it has brought about or there is a clear probability that it will bring about substantial gains in efficiency that save resources for the Canadian economy. In France, the Commission de la Concurrence is empowered to control mergers and related links among enterprises that result in a larger market share and do not bring in exchange a sufficient contribution to economic and social progress.

21. For an illustration of the problems, see, for example, UNCTAD, *Control of Restrictive Business Practices in India* (Geneva: UNCTAD, 1978, ST/MD/20).

22. See the works cited in John M. Connor, *The Market Power of Multinationals* (New York: Praeger, 1977), pp. 277–99.

23. N. T. Wang, *Taxation, Raw Materials, International Regimes,* Report of Working Group 1, The Carnegie Center for Transnational Studies (New York: Carnegie Center for Transnational Studies, 1975), p. 16; UN Centre on Transnational Corporations, *Transnational Corporations,* pp. 154–56.

Commentary

◆

L. H. Bloom

Under a very technical-sounding and weighty title, N. T. Wang has prepared a paper that happily deals with fundamentals more than technicalities. In reading it through the first time, I was reminded of a devastating experience in the Oregon style of debate which befell me in 1937 when the Massachusetts Institute of Technology was pitted against Pembroke. Working with the coach and my teammates, I had carefully prepared the questions for cross-examining my opponent so that whatever answer she gave, there was another question ready, until in the end she would be hopelessly trapped. We had the affirmative of the issue, and supposedly they had the negative. Much to our surprise, they twisted the issue around and took a position in favor of different measures that were stronger than those we advocated, rather than being opposed fundamentally to the proposition. Caught off guard, it was MIT rather than Pembroke which ended up in a shambles. Fortunately, the Wang paper was distributed in advance, or I would have been surprised again.

Why surprised? Because despite knowing that Wang did not always fully agree with the direction and form of the undertakings he was obliged to implement during his previous employment at the United Nations, I expected a more UN-like document. One seldom is altogether aware of all of the constraints which cause each of us to conduct ourselves as we do, whether in business, academia, or national or international civil service. Freed now of the constraints on an international civil servant, Wang in this paper fulfills an indispensable role of the academician in our society; he questions the basic assumptions on which so much of the current debate about transnational corporations—indeed, so much of the North–South dialogue—is based. Having raised questions, many in academia would have felt constrained to come up with answers, and quite possibly with answers highly skeptical of the role of transnationals. Wang has carefully avoided such a course. He has escaped from his constraints.

Lest those in the world of business conclude that I am entirely out of my mind and call out the fire brigade to deal with such a brash approval of Wang's analysis, let me assure you that like all business people, I, too, am the victim of some habitual constraints—and there are phrases here and there in the paper to which I reacted with dismay or frustration or defensiveness. The point is that the sum of what he says, to use his own words, moves "from negativism to positivism," and this I welcome and applaud.

The roster of contributors to this conference is replete with highly skilled professionals, and the participants will be treated to an ample supply of traditional economic and antitrust discussion of pure competition, economies of scale, market structure, monopoly power, and the like. Much of what will be said would have been included even if the word *international* had been omitted from the title of the conference. But there is danger in too readily adapting these time-honored analyses to a world in which there is a new vocabulary and in which old terms have new meaning. It is in this new world that transnational corporations now operate.

We are talking here about issues far different from such traditional ones as the interpretation of the Treaty of Rome and the extraterritorial effect of the U.S. antitrust laws. Based on much misinformation, lack of experience, fear, pride, and yearning for a better life for their peoples, the developing countries have sought much that is impossible, more that is impracticable, and a great deal that cannot achieve or is irrelevant to the results intended. Wang has listed those "restrictive business practices" on which "general agreement" has been reached as to inclusion in the UNCTAD code. But the Group of 77 originally proposed some forty practices for such inclusion, as well as a related but not identical forty for the Code on Technology Transfer. Naturally, the Group B countries and their industries reacted strongly, and the tug of war began in an atmosphere of bitter confrontation. Only patience has kept the discussions going—patience and the hope that out of dialogue might come greater mutual understanding of the problems faced by all concerned. In the center of the controversy stands the international civil servant, knowing that both the "77" and Group B must at least be prepared to tolerate a little longer his advocacy of what he sees as a compromise position, and often leaning towards the position of the UN majority whose rhetoric is the most vibrant and who can make his job intolerable if they are displeased. In this context, those who stand up for established legal and economic experience and understanding are seen as rigid, unfeeling, selfish, and condemned to oblivion under the "New International Economic Order."

Wang's analysis questions those value judgments. He suggests that one cannot assume that a "restrictive business practice" is necessarily bad—transnationals are not the only ones who engage in them, and governments may welcome, encourage, and reward them—and that transnational enterprises based in socialist countries may have no less and no better impact than those based in developed market economies. He focuses attention on the fundamental point that there are trade-offs, social and economic cost-benefit balances to be considered, differing situations leading to different impacts. In short, he brings the debate back to the real world.

Continuing in that real world, permit me to add a few other basic truths.

No two transnationals are exactly the same.

Generalizations about transnationals can only mislead.

No two countries are exactly the same; their needs, their resources, their environments differ.

No two UN agencies or other international organizations are exactly the same—they often engage in overlapping efforts—and do so in differing ways.

No transnational corporation is so big, so powerful, or so wealthy that it can prevent the government of the smallest developing country from adopting laws and regulations affecting right to invest, equity participation, taxation, industrial property rights, remittances, service fees—in short, just about everything that affects the viability of a business enterprise, including the right to take it all away and possibly to do so with limited or no provision for compensation. In this context, no transnational can have the oft-alleged "global strategy" but must instead constantly seek ways to operate in a variety of environments under a web of differing regulation and control. Yet some countries question the need to include in any code of conduct provisions on the obligations of governments, as well as those of transnational corporations, and on the applicability of established principles of international law.

On this last point, sadly, Wang's paper includes the old clichés. On page 7, he says: "These corporations are frequently so powerful and large in size that possibilities of dominance and abuse are ever present. . . . They operate across national boundaries and are thus outside national jurisdiction and effective control." This is only one of several places where an easy pejorative phrase slips into his presentation; but it is the one I simply could not let pass without putting it in proper perspective. In fact, the portion of his statement subtitled "The Global View" (p. 14 et seq.) does a good job of putting it right: "In the fragmented world of nation-states and existing restrictions on the movement of output and factors of production, the transnational corporations are in one way or another over-coming these barriers. . . . It is true that foreign direct investment is often carried out by powerful giants. Nevertheless, this power may also be instrumental in overcoming numerous existing obstacles. . . . A global system must reconcile competition with efficiency."

In the section entitled "From Negativism to Positivism," Wang does in-clude some proposals for action that merit thoughtful comment. Before turning to these, however, I cannot help but note the most candid and discouraging sentences in his entire piece. They appear in the introduc-tion, where he says: "Typically, international negotiations deliberately skirt the difficult but fundamental questions. Matters of serious contro-versy are rightly passed over in silence lest they hinder general progress and poison the atmosphere. An international consensus reached under such circumstances should not give a false sense of security."

Stated more bluntly, endless time is spent in dealing with minutiae and very little on substance. Is it any wonder that frustration grows, tempers become short, and confrontation takes over? Not only in international or-ganizations but in all deliberative political bodies the ability to examine together in an orderly and constructive way the problems and opportunities at hand and the alternative paths to mutually beneficial results is hope-lessly blunted by what is seen as political necessity.

So I welcome Wang's proposals, which seek to chart a positivist ap-proach for future cooperation between transnational corporations and de-veloping nations. Wang urges "a new negotiated package," stating that "the key concept here is not necessarily de-packaging of foreign direct in-vestment of transnational corporations but its repackaging." Recognizing the unique capacity of transnationals to put together a workable package, he seeks ways to alter the patterns of the past for the benefit of all con-cerned.

But I must complain once more that his agenda leans more toward the stick than toward the carrot. Even after saying that the "most effective control may still be very little control," he talks about "concerted attack,"

"attack on restrictive business practices of transnational corporations . . . from many fronts," and "multi-pronged attack," including "a general code of conduct as well as specific arrangements for the conduct of transnational corporations" ("reporting and disclosure requirements").

All of our experience causes us to be apprehensive about still more debate about codes, still more requests for disclosure of infinite and irrelevant detail in a format completely foreign to the ways in which business records are kept. Many—perhaps most—business managers have already become so weary of this game that they have elected to sit it out on the bench and devote themselves more directly to providing their shareholders with a reasonable return on their investment this year.

It takes very little thought to recognize that nothing could be more productive for the longer term prosperity of the industrialized West and its transnational corporations than the improvement of the standard of living in the huge potential markets of the Southern Hemisphere. If repackaging can be discussed in an atmosphere of mutual good will, with no zero-sum game implications, effort can be concentrated on the fundamental issues of matching the skills and resources of individual countries and companies in the developed world to those of individual countries in the developing world so that each sustains the other.

Before we can reach that euphoric state, it may be necessary for the developed nations, through their private sectors, to increase geometrically their assistance to developing nations in the areas of basic knowledge and understanding of the industrialization process, and in training their people in fields that will provide the necessary infrastructure for growth. There is some hope that the newly conceived and funded Institute for Scientific and Technological Cooperation could provide the instrument for setting such programs in motion; indeed, work is already under way in this direction as the United States follow-up to the Vienna conference. That conference in itself accomplished little, but if the U.S. preparation for it and follow-up from it can provide even a beginning for this mission, it will all have been worthwhile.

This is our response to Wang's seeking of a new negotiated package.

Commentary

G. K. Helleiner

N. T. Wang's paper has covered a lot of ground. In so doing, it has mixed up a number of issues which, at least for the purpose of conceptual clarity, are better kept separate. Its conclusions are therefore rather more general than necessary, and difficult to apply. Let me attempt to unravel a little what *is* certainly a complex and interconnected set of questions.

Let us agree at the outset that both national and world markets for goods and services are a very long way indeed from the frictionless world of competitive buyers and sellers interacting at arm's length with one another, so beloved both of crude economic theorists and, even more, of "pop" critiques of economic analysis. The world is ridden with "market imperfections" created by both private and governmental actions, and sometimes by nature itself. I hope that we also can agree that there is nothing "ideal" about a perfectly competitive world even if it could be attained, partly because of the well-known problems of "market failure," but more importantly because the Pareto "efficiency" which it can in special circumstances create does not allow for changes in income distribution. Where there is no government to pursue distributional objectives, as in the case of the *world* economy, this is a particularly damaging shortcoming; it is therefore especially necessary not to take at face value the frequent references to "efficiency" objectives at the *global* level (unless "efficiency at what" is clearly specified). The objectives of national or international regulatory (or other procompetition) policies ought to be to "improve" systemic economic performance in respect of a number of objectives, and specifically both Pareto "efficiency" (assuming distribution unchanged) and distribution itself.

Regulatory efforts and other government policies pursuing social interests are undertaken at present at the *national* level in respect of both restrictive business practices and transnational corporations. Efforts are now under way to develop *both* types of regulation and policy at the *world* level. While these various efforts at regulation and policy development to some degree overlap with one another, they all raise different issues; and they are undertaken by different government departments and in different international organizations. Each of the set of "empty boxes" in table 1.1 requires separate discussion.

NATIONAL REGULATION

Debates about the regulation of both restrictive business practices and transnational corporations at the *national* level have a long history. There are wide divergences of views and policies on these matters, and there is no need to detail them again here. The point is, however, that there does not exist a fully agreed framework of basic objectives or, equally important, policy instruments which would make it easy to develop further international cooperation in respect of either. Wang notes several strands of these debates, emphasizing elements which are of particular relevance to developing countries' own national policies.

A. RESTRICTIVE BUSINESS PRACTICES
On the subject of restrictive business practices, Wang notes that the small markets of most developing countries frequently require governmental support and protection for monopolistic producers who can take advantage of scale economies. In these circumstances the types of policies for the prevention of abuse of dominant positions of power are likely to look quite different from the provisions of U.S. or European antitrust laws. No doubt that is why laws regulating restrictive business practices are not frequently found or, if on the books, not vigorously applied in the smaller developing

TABLE I.I

	National Regulation/ Policy	International Regulation/ Policy
Restrictive business practices	A	D
Transnational corporate activity	B	C

countries. It could be useful nevertheless for us to review traditions, policies, and practices in such larger countries as India, Brazil, and Argentina in order to learn more of the roots of their likely approaches to the international regulation of these practices. If we did so, among the major debates which we would quickly find ourselves in is that over "national treatment" for foreign firms, an issue of importance to rich host countries as well as poor, but one that Wang has not mentioned. For the majority of developing countries, there will be increasing interest as development progresses in the control of restrictive business practices and the prevention of the abuse of power. Of critical importance, therefore, could be the details of the proposed model laws for developing countries which continue to be developed under UNCTAD auspices. (The much earlier model law on industrial property played a major role in the creation of national legislation in newly independent countries.) These have not been mentioned either. Perhaps it is because of his apparent lack of confidence in any such international discussions.

The asymmetry in national treatment of import and export cartels to which Wang properly calls our attention has important implications for the developing countries with which he is primarily concerned, and it is important to spell them out. The national antitrust laws of the industrialized countries can be employed, to some degree, so as jointly to remove the export-import asymmetry at least in respect of trade among themselves; each national policy's concentration on its own imports has the effect of controlling others' exports. But there is obviously no such countervailing policy in the developing countries, which have neither such laws nor adequate enforcement capacity. There is therefore a presumption, and a certain amount of supporting empirical evidence, that the unpoliced restrictive business practices of exporters from the industrialized countries will be exceptionally costly—in terms of both global Pareto efficiency and income distribution—in their sales to poor countries. This problem deserves more international policy attention than it has so far received.

B. TRANSNATIONAL CORPORATIONS

National policies towards transnational (or just foreign) corporations are a much more complex matter, because of the number of dimensions involved, the variety of types of enterprise, and the even smaller degree of consensus as to objectives or approaches. Our conference is not concerned so much with these issues as it is with restrictive business practices, so I say no more.

INTERNATIONAL REGULATION

C. TRANSNATIONAL CORPORATIONS

It is especially important to distinguish the issues which are under discussion at the international level. On the one hand, we have attempts to "rein in" the transnational corporations *qua* transnational corporations, through codes of conduct negotiated through the UN Centre on Transnational Corporations, the International Labour Office, the Organisation for Economic Co-operation and Development, or even through business organizations themselves such as the International Chamber of Commerce. These codes and discussions cover a wide range of issues and are intended to ease some of the problems created by the fact of competing national jurisdictions facing global actors.

D. RESTRICTIVE BUSINESS PRACTICES

On the other hand, there are attempts to develop regulations, codes, and the like in respect of particular *practices,* regardless of what types of firms or actors are engaged in them. The Technology Code of Conduct and the "principles and rules for the control of restrictive business practices" being developed under the auspices of the Technology and Manufactures Divisions, respectively, of the UNCTAD are in this latter category. Intergovernmental cooperation is bound to be required when attempts are made to transfer to the international sphere the objectives of various separate national policies in matters like restrictive business practices. Obviously, transnationals' activities account for major shares of the total activities to be regulated in these cases, but it is misleading to suggest that there is a *concentration* on the transnational corporations (cf. Wang, pp. 5, 18). To the contrary, there is a real possibility that much of their activity will not be subject to international surveillance at all. Nor does it make much sense in this context to worry overly about the *definition* of transnational corporations when what is at issue is a set of *practices,* rather than the behavior of particular institutions. "The real question" (p. 16) is actually much less the necessity of the *inclusion* of the practices of enterprises in developing or socialist countries than it is the possibility of the *exclusion* of major activities of the quantitatively much more important Western transnationals themselves, those relating to trade between parents and subsidiaries, or among subsidiaries of the same parent. The Group B position is, after all, that such intrafirm trade should be excluded from the application of the UNCTAD rules and principles relating to restrictive business practices. (The precise wording of the Group B draft is as follows: "The principles and rules for enterprises shall not apply to restrictions which are normally considered acceptable for the purpose of rationalization or reasonable allocation of functions between parent and subsidiary or among enterprises belonging to the same concern, unless amounting to an abuse of a dominant position of market power within the relevant market, for example, adversely affecting competition outside these enterprises.")

According to data from the Foreign Trade Division of the U.S. Bureau of the Census, 48.2 percent of total U.S. imports originated with foreign parties which were related by ownership to the importers in 1977. Intrafirm transactions are generally believed to account for even higher proportions of U.S. exports. The exclusion of intrafirm trade, it seems, would leave only about half of U.S. international trade subject to international jurisdiction at all. It is probably safe to assume that the extent of world trade which takes place on an intrafirm basis is more or less the same. The trade of socialist, other state, or developing countries' enterprises is obviously dwarfed by Western intrafirm trade in relative significance. The former trade *does* need some rules and principles, but let us retain some perspective.

The internalization of market transactions within private corporations, or what Oliver Williamson terms the replacement of markets by hierarchies, is what business expansion is all about. John Dunning has noted that there are extra reasons impelling firms to internalize international, as opposed to purely domestic, transactions. There is by now not only well-developed theory but also considerable evidence that intrafirm trade does not behave in the same fashion as trade which takes place at arm's length on markets—with respect to either volume, direction, or pricing. It seems likely that this divergence in performance is no less important than that between firms in competitive and in highly concentrated industries. Certainly, captive markets, tying, and transfer pricing abuses are unlikely to be conducive to maximizing global welfare.

Are the intrafirm trading practices of international firms that lead to results which differ significantly from those one would obtain on competitive arm's-length markets to be regarded as "restrictive business practices" for the purpose of international agreements on these practices? As Wang puts it, "many intracorporate transactions veiled in business confidentiality may achieve the same effect as restrictive business practices" (p. 8). Again, "no formal agreement or collusion is needed in market allocation if a transnational corporation conducts its business through its own branches" (p. 9). The private decisions of transnational corporations can clearly be of as great importance to trade flows as the public ones of governments in respect of tariffs, quotas, and voluntary export restraints. The GATT, which has taken keen interest in the latter governmental decisions, has devoted scant attention to the implications of the former private ones, although they govern just as much of world trade.

What is at issue, then, is the *convention*—it is no more than that—which views intracorporate activity as legitimately "veiled in business confidentiality," and subject to no external monitoring or control, in circumstances where there is reason to believe that restrictive practices may be found in them. Wang does not argue that such monitoring or control of intrafirm activity is illegitimate, but that they are unproductive. He argues that *quasi*-"restrictive business practices" are a "normal" (p. 7) and inherent part of transnational corporate activity. Since transnationals are potentially important "agents of development" (p. 19), one cannot seek to restrain them in this respect without losing the gains they can provide. "Love me, love my restrictive business practices," he seems to have the transnationals telling their host countries. This is essentially the same argument (although Wang has mercifully refrained from references to geese and golden eggs) which has always been made about attempts to regulate business activity in the social interest through appropriate "repackaging" (Wang's term) or otherwise. It is not clear to me that the control of restrictive business practices is any less important or more difficult than that of, say, corrupt practices. The inclusion of intrafirm or related-party trade in an agreement relating to restrictive business practices is so important, to my mind, that it would be worth trading off other controversial clauses (exceptions? differential treatment?) for its sake. It would also dispense with the difficult business of defining "subsidiaries" and "parents," and tend to generate more information about intrafirm transactions, which is still sadly lacking.

One last major undiscussed question is the most appropriate locus for decision making and the eventual means for administering international rules in respect of restrictive business practices. There is an obvious logic in having the GATT handle these issues along with the other codes for which it is now responsible, or, even better, to combine the current UNCTAD and GATT functions in a new (resurrected) International Trade Organization.

Discussion

◇

JAMES R. ATWOOD: G. K. Helleiner suggests there is empirical evidence that differential pricing in capital goods exists, and that it may be the result of export cartels. I'm not aware of any U.S. export cartels that deal in capital goods. Indeed, I think the evidence shows that export cartels don't work for complex differentiated products, but are effective only for homogeneous commodities.

Secondly, on the subject of intrafirm transactions, Helleiner suggests that by excluding this subject from the codes, we are excluding more than one-half of world trade. That way of putting it seems to me to exaggerate the matter. Take the U.S. domestic market, for example. Intrafirm transactions must account for the vast majority of economic activity in the United States. There can be a variety of intrafirm transactions on almost any product before you reach a market transaction. So is it really fair to say that excluding intrafirm transactions removes a vast portion of world trade from scrutiny?

G. K. HELLEINER: I suggest, at a minimum, that we should know a good deal more than we do about intrafirm transactions. I agree that there is a lot of internalized trade within nations that is not germane. But a high proportion of international trade, on which countries' policies are based, is on an intrafirm basis. The activities of the GATT relate to only half of the trade decisions that are made.

RICHARD S. NEWFARMER: I can only speak to the case of the international electrical industry, and particularly the International Electrical Association. As many of you know, this is a cartel mostly of Western European firms, although recent documents indicate that the Japanese have joined.

The company documents that we have indicate that when the cartel was successful, it often raised prices between 15 and 25 percent. Applying that margin to sales of that part of the electrical industry covered by the cartel results in a figure in the hundreds of millions of dollars, which is substantial. But the more general answer to the questions raised is simply that we do not know much about cartels. The kind of data I have for the electrical industry is rare indeed. Because of legislation in the United States, cartels have largely been driven underground—to the extent they exist at all. Most of us believe that they are not as prevalent as they once were.

JAMES A. RAHL: G. K. Helleiner also raised the matter of asymmetry. Is the point that the OECD nations, unlike developing countries, have antitrust laws and use them to protect their own economies against restraints imposed upon their imports by the export cartels of others? Developing countries, of course, cannot do this.

That analysis is sound only if the OECD countries attack each other's export cartels. But my impression is that they do not. As to the United States, I refer to a letter from the Department of Justice to Senator Kennedy stating that it is U.S. policy not to attack the export cartels of other nations if they are of the type that would be lawful under our laws, namely, under our Webb-Pomerene Act. Of course, our Webb-Pomerene Act is construed rather narrowly, and consequently there are export cartels that would not qualify under it. But my overall impression is that hardly anyone attacks anyone else's export cartels. So I'm not sure there is much asymmetry in practice.

HELLEINER: I think there is an analogy to speeding laws. They probably deter a lot of fast driving. The number of speeders you catch is not the test of the effectiveness of speeding laws.

WALTER A. CHUDSON: It certainly should be axiomatic in talking about developing countries that only about 8 or 10 of the 100 or 110 developing countries have a sufficiently large domestic market or a sufficiently promising export trade to have a strong bargaining position. These are the "NICs" in current lingo, the newly industrialized countries (Brazil, Korea, et cetera). They are quite able to practice a countervailing power play with respect to transnationals in a broad sense. They know what they want, more or less, and they have the capability of obtaining information on the world market about their alternatives. But the great majority of developing countries are not in that position and it is important to keep that in mind throughout our discussion.

SIGMUND TIMBERG: On the basis of the evidence I have read, I think there is a cartel problem with regard to about 1.5 percent of American foreign trade, and with regard to about the same small percentage of the foreign trade of West Germany (which requires registration) and the United Kingdom (whose Board of Trade knows what's happening). Until I hear some evidence to the contrary, I am satisfied that the "export cartel problem" is not one of the great issues.

BARRY E. HAWK: I agree that we're making mountains out of molehills about export cartels from the United States. I would like to add to what James Rahl said about U.S. enforcement against foreign export cartels. U.S. policy, as I understand it, is that we will not generally enforce against a foreign export cartel that would enjoy a Webb-Pomerene exemption under U.S. law. That is a major qualification, because a company loses its Webb-Pomerene exemption if it participates in an international cartel.

If there had been a U.S. electrical equipment manufacturer in the Brazilian situation—which I don't think has ever been suggested—and if the U.S. equipment manufacturer had had a Webb-Pomerene exemption, the manufacturer would have lost the exemption for participating in an international conspiracy.

SEYMOUR J. RUBIN: It doesn't seem to me that the developing countries are much concerned with export cartels or horizontal restrictive business practices. As Joel Davidow pointed out in his paper, concern with those matters is characteristic of the developed countries, which try to eliminate cartels, the division of dividing markets, and the like. The restrictions that concern developing countries, as I understand it, are market restrictions, those that allow production but not an export of a particular product, or those that arrange a market allocation by assigning a certain market to a particular subsidiary or a particular independent contractor. That is where the developing countries are pushing very hard. And that is the focus of debate.

JOEL DAVIDOW: I would like to make three comments: One is on the purposes of controlling restrictive business practices. Even in our own country there are many purposes. Certainly, we can say something about economic benefits, free markets, and free trade. But I think control of restrictive practices also represents a view that private cartelization is taking a governmental prerogative into private hands. In treating private cartelization as illegitimate, you preserve the idea that restraint of trade should at least be publicly accountable.

Secondly, United States control of restrictive business practices has popular roots. In addition to purely economic analysis, it contains the ideas that the strong should not oppress the weak, the little guy should have a chance in the market, and the newcomer should be treated well. The developing countries are the "populace" of today, looking for relief, as they see it, or a chance in the marketplace.

When the Group of 77 was first asked to define a "restrictive business practice," the words "competition" and "cartels" were never mentioned. What was mentioned was "abuse of a dominant position." Their concern was with abusive single-firm action in pricing or in dealing.

This concern is even clearer in the transfer of technology area. There they deal directly with the process of contract negotiation and say they want a combination of what we would call "restrictive business practice enforcement" and implementation of a rather general idea that in contracting, the stronger party should not lean too much on the weaker party—with regard to either what is promised or what is not promised or how payment is made.

Finally, I believe that the percentage of trade affected by intraenterprise dealing is a meaningless figure. It tells us nothing about the relevance of restrictive business practice analysis. If you treat intrafirm arrangements or transactions as if they were between competitors, then almost every management decision by a transnational complex is illegal. That is, if two leading competitors in the world market were to agree on what they would produce, where they would produce it, how they would produce it, and how they would advertise it, each one of those agreements would probably be illegal. Therefore, either you don't apply the normal rules to intraenterprise relations at all, or you only apply them in very special cases—refusals to deal, for example, or cases where the subsidiary is a joint venture between two or three competing companies.

2

RESTRICTIVE BUSINESS PRACTICES AFFECTING TRANSFER OF TECHNOLOGY

Control of Terms and Conditions
for International Transfers of
Technology to Developing Countries

Douglas F. Greer

INTRODUCTION

Plato was the first to distinguish between limited and unlimited goods. Limited goods, such as money and power, are scarce. More of them for one person means less for another. In contrast, unlimited goods are those whose possession by one does not preclude or diminish their possession by another. Knowledge and the appreciation of beauty were seen by Plato as having unlimited qualities because one's increased learning and one's enjoyment of a sunset do not prevent others from partaking of them. Sharing is not a necessity and distribution is not a problem for such goods.

Plato would thus be puzzled, or possibly appalled, by this paper's topic. On the one hand, a few advanced countries, steeped in knowledge, account for well over 90 percent of all expenditures on research and development, produce all but a rather trivial portion of the world's inventions and innovations, and consequently bask in the marvels of modernity. On the other hand, the vast majority of the world's countries and people live in such a low state that an overwhelming amount—perhaps well over 90 percent—of their technical knowledge must come from their more advanced brethren. The transfer of this knowledge is imbued with complexities and hindered by restraints. Sharing is a necessity, and distribution is a serious problem. It seems, then, that knowledge, or at least technical knowledge, is not the unlimited good Plato thought it was. It has become entangled with two limited goods, money and power. It has therefore also

I am indebted to Robert E. Smith for comments on a preliminary version of this paper.

come to be called commercial knowledge, as those who have it do not give it freely to those who do not.

Of the many issues technology transfers have inspired, two stand out: (1) the terms and conditions under which technology is transferred, and (2) the appropriateness of the technology in light of the special needs of the less-developed countries (LDCs). Both issues find mention below, but the chief purpose of this paper is to analyze terms and conditions. In particular, it has been argued, and evidence has been mustered to show, that the market in which technology is transferred from developed to less-developed countries does not even roughly approach the theoretically and ethically ideal world of perfect competition, where multitudes of well-informed buyers and sellers mutually and fairly benefit from free and voluntary exchange. Rather, argument and evidence indicate a situation closer to the following analogy: a solitary man is standing on a dock, coiled lifeline in hand, trying to extract a commitment of financial reward from a helpless stranger floundering in the surf below, even though the man poised to pitch the lifeline is a millionaire and the drowning man is only of modest means. Understandably, the terms and conditions emerging from this bargaining may seem exploitative to the man in the water because the amount he pays for his life could well be onerous to him, more than the sum necessary to move his potential savior to action, and incrementally trivial compared to the riches the savior already possesses.

The terms and conditions attaching to transfers of technology include price, which may take the form of royalties and ownership dividends as well as lump sum fees; the structure of ownership and management control; rules and requirements relating to exports; restrictions on fields of use; volume limitations; the sources and prices of purchased inputs; restrictions on distribution channels; quality control; the acquisition of competing technologies; rights to related new technologies; provisions for training local personnel; duration of the arrangements; and rights of use after termination of the agreement. Because circumstances have often put transferors of technology in a position not unlike that of the man on the dock, the terms and conditions actually arrived at have often been discriminatory and restrictive.[1] As a consequence, the label "restrictive business practices" has taken on expanded meaning. Moreover, several less-developed countries have instituted new policies to deal with these practices,[2] and proposals have been made for an international code of conduct to govern such practices.[3]

Of course, the perception of a problem and the prescription of remedies imply the application of certain value judgments. In turn, the intrusion of value judgments inevitably provokes disagreement as to what ought to be done, if anything. Thus, one seaside observer of our drowning incident may feel that the unbalanced bargaining presents no problem as long as in the end the soul in the water is saved. Conversely, another observer may be disgusted by even so much as a pause to discuss price. Still others may wish to specify details that variously define proper conduct depending on the circumstances; for instance, they may grudgingly allow the savior to dicker if he must risk his own life by swimming choppy waters to effect the rescue.

The cautious and qualified approach of this last position suggests that we recognize that the problem of technology transfers has its own diversities and complexities. Technical knowledge may be embodied in skilled labor or in physical goods. Other technical knowledge may be disembodied, taking the form of unpatented know-how or of legally protected patents or trademarks. For our purposes later in this paper, it is important to distinguish among "firm specific," "system specific," and "general" technology.[4] Firm specific technology is the bundle of practical and often unique knowledge that a firm accumulates to produce and market a particular product or line of products. System specific technology comprises the capabilities and equipment a firm develops for production techniques, such as welding and machining, that are common to numerous industries. General technology is nondetailed, fundamental knowledge that is readily available from technical journals, textbooks, equipment suppliers, and the like. Of the three types, it should be obvious that firm and system specific knowledge are typically proprietary; they sometimes constitute what may be called "core" technology, or that which gives the firm some degree of market power. Strictly speaking, general knowledge is not proprietary, although some enterprises are able to profit from assembling, translating, and selling such knowledge.

Aside from the various forms technical knowledge may take and the sundry ownership claims to it, there is additional diversity in the methods by which it may be transferred. Transfer may be accomplished by means of (1) direct investment in wholly owned subsidiaries or joint ventures, (2) licensing, (3) management and technical aid contracts, (4) turnkey projects, and (5) the installation and servicing of purchased equipment. All these methods imply some conscious and voluntary effort by the transferor to effectuate the transfer. In addition, of course, there are various forms of piracy, such as reverse engineering, industrial espionage, and patent infringement.

To state my own standards and value judgments at the outset, I think there is solid evidence that, if left unchecked, restrictive business practices do impose excessive and needless costs on the less-developed countries that receive technology. In short, there is a problem. I also think, however, that remedies to the problem would be lopsided and ultimately counter-productive if they focused solely upon expanding the rights and improving the treatment of the recipients. Adequate weight must be given to the interests of those transferring the technology and to the diversity of cir-cumstances surrounding transfers. In other words, an ideal policy would (1) improve the terms and conditions received by less-developed countries in obtaining transfers; yet (2) preserve an environment in which technol-ogy transfer is potentially profitable for the transferors; and (3) retain suf-ficient flexibility for both the transferor and transferee to negotiate an agreement tailored to the needs of each situation.[5]

The thesis of this paper is that official attempts to control the conduct of transferring parties cannot, in and of themselves, satisfactorily meet all three of the above criteria. Conduct control, as used in this paper, means the imposition of official constraints that prescribe certain limits to terms and conditions or prohibit certain terms and conditions altogether in order to boost the bargaining strength of the less-developed countries and their local firms. Such control constitutes the backbone of present LDC policies and proposed international codes of conduct. Mexico's law of 1972 typifies this approach, as is indicated by the following official summary:

> Contracts shall not be approved when they refer to technology freely avail-able in the country; when the price or counterservice is out of proportion to the technology acquired . . . ; when they restrict the research or technolog-ical development of the purchaser; when they permit the technology supplier to interfere in the management of the purchaser company or oblige it to use, on a permanent basis, the personnel appointed by the supplier; when they establish the obligation to purchase inputs from the supplier only or to sell the goods produced by the technology importer exclusively to the supplier com-pany; when they prohibit or restrict the export of goods in a way contrary to the country's interest; when they limit the size of production or impose prices on domestic production or on exports by the purchaser; when they prohibit the use of complementary technology; when they oblige the importer to sign exclusive sales or representation contracts with the supplier company covering

the national territory; when they establish excessively long terms of enforcement, which in no case may exceed a 10-year obligation on the importer company, or when they provide that claims arising from the interpretation or fulfilment of such contracts are to be submitted to the jurisdiction of foreign courts.[6]

Aside from administrative difficulties, such attempts at controlling conduct pose two main problems. First, there is ample opportunity for evasion, circumvention, and negation of the policy, especially by its primary targets, namely, large multinational enterprises. Second, to the extent conduct control actually increases the bargaining power of less-developed countries at the direct expense of transferors, it may be less than optimal in meeting the last two of the three policy criteria mentioned above. That is, conduct control may eliminate the dirty bath water, but it may endanger the baby as well. It may needlessly or excessively diminish the motivation of transferors and impose a rigidity on transactions that is inappropriate to the kaleidoscopic variety of circumstances created by technology's assorted forms, ownership structures, transfer methods, transferors, and transferees.

The word "may" qualifies these assertions because conduct control apparently does work fairly well under certain circumstances, which will be outlined later. Thus, this paper does not urge abandonment of the conduct approach. It calls instead for a substantial expansion of policy in order to achieve major modifications in the structure of the markets for technology transfers. In particular, it is argued that these markets can be made more competitive than they are now, and that greater competition will enhance the bargaining power of the less-developed countries without curbing the incentives of transferors and allowing the terms and conditions of transfer arrangements to ossify in some narrowly detrimental mold. To put it differently, structural policies, such as those that would increase the number of transferors or reduce the entry barriers facing new suppliers of technology, are highly desirable because they would make conduct controls more effective and reach adverse conditions currently left untouched by the conduct approach.

My advocacy of a structural approach can be loosely likened to the widespread advocacy of structural approaches to controlling oligopoly power in domestic U.S. industry. The Sherman Act's prohibition of price-fixing conduct produces the intended result of vigorous competition only when the underlying market structure forces firms to compete once they are deprived of the option of cartelization. However, if tight-knit oligopoly prevails, tacit collusion offers a viable alternative to explicit collusion for the achievement of maximal joint profits.[7] Thus, it is argued that prohibition of cartel-like conduct does little good in such cases. Structural modification by divestiture and dissolution is said to be more effective.

Of course, divestiture and dissolution, though perhaps desirable, are very remote possibilities in the international market for technology transfers. Numerous other structural policies are closer to reality, however, and these will be discussed in the last section of this paper. Meanwhile, it is incumbent upon me to support my asserted skepticism about conduct policies and my avowed faith in structural remedies. In particular, I must demonstrate linkages between structure and conduct in this market and then probe those linkages for policy implications. I shall do so by (1) outlining conditions on the transferor's side of the technology market; (2) specifying conditions among transferees; (3) viewing transferors and transferees together in hopes of delineating the circumstances to which conduct and structural policies are best suited; and (4) analyzing current conduct policies in some detail.

THE TRANSFERORS' SIDE OF THE MARKET

To speak of *a* market for technology is quite misleading. It suggests singularity and homogeneity when in fact there are thousands of separate markets offering knowledge on subjects as diverse as 100-megabit computer disks and harrow disks. Likewise and consequently, the suppliers range from IBM to farmers in the Peace Corps.

Following the guidance provided by industrial organization economics, this diversity may be reduced to manageable proportions if the available empirical evidence concerning transferors is categorized under three major components of market analysis, namely, basic conditions, structure, and conduct. Basic conditions may be thought of as characteristics that are either inherent in the traded item (such as product durability) or relatively impervious to easy manipulation by policy (as would be true of cost configurations). The major elements of structure, such as seller concentration, also tend to be stable over time, but they can be affected by private and governmental action. Conduct refers to the behavior, policy, and strategy of firms in the market as regards pricing, promoting, and producing the traded item. Amassed theories and evidence indicate substantial causal

TABLE 2.1
Outline of Transferor Characteristics

Characteristic	Monopolistic	Competitive
A. *Basic Conditions*		
1. Technology involved	Advanced, firm specific	System specific, general
2. Duration of transfer process	Long-term, substantial learning economies	Relatively short term
3. Type of product	Complex, differentiated, durable, income elastic	Simple, standard, usually nondurable
Examples	Computers, autos, aircraft, chemicals	Paper, leather products, textiles
4. Cost of transfer	High cost	Low cost
B. *Structural Conditions*		
5. Concentration	High concentration	Low concentration
6. Condition of entry	High barriers	Low barriers
7. Type of companies making transfers	Large, diversified, integrated MNCs	Relatively small firms, engineering companies
C. *Transferor Conduct*		
8. Export versus transfer	Exports preferred, then transfer	Transfers common, defensive motive
9. Transfer method	Direct investment	Licensing, turnkey
10. Purchase of intermediate inputs	Heavy importing	Few imports
11. Price elasticity of supply	Low	High
12. Form of competition	Nonprice rivalry	Price competition
13. Restrictive behavior	Restraints and price discrimination	Relatively few restraints

linkage among these components for conventional product markets, with the basic conditions heavily influencing market structure, and structure, in turn, affecting conduct.[8] Thus, it would be logical to expect a similar causal linkage in technology markets.

Table 2.1 summarizes the available evidence and the main inferences that can reasonably be drawn from that evidence. Following the lead of industrial organization economics once again, I have presented the evidence for two rather extreme cases, one labeled "monopolistic," the other "competitive." This format runs substantial risk of oversimplification because a continuum connects the two extremes, but it certainly aids analysis.

The reasoning behind many entries in table 2.1 is self-evident. Thus, by definition, an innovator stands alone for a while, so transferors from the computer industry, for example, which is grounded on truly advanced technologies, innately possess more monopolistic power than transferors from such industries as paper and textiles, which are relatively staid and conventional. Similarly, high concentration and high barriers to entry are common indicators of monopoly power, and those having such power are notorious for refraining from price competition in favor of nonprice rivalry. Still, the entries of table 2.1 depict monopolistic and competitive patterns that can be fully substantiated only by recourse to the empirical evidence, which amply includes the following.

TECHNOLOGY, PRODUCT TYPE, AND COMPETITION

Opportunities for technological advance vary across industries in accordance with product life cycles and the march of science. The amount of research and development (R&D) expenditure, expressed as a percentage of sales, more or less measures these interindustry differences because this outlay is positively correlated with R&D productivity. Thus, aircraft, electronics, motor vehicles, chemicals, computers, instruments, and machinery head any list of R&D spenders, with outlays amounting to 3 percent of sales and more. Indeed, these industries alone account for over 80 percent of all industrial R&D in the United States. In contrast, domestic R&D falls below 1 percent of sales in paper, textiles, lumber and wood products, and leather goods.[9] The same pattern holds for the R&D expenditures of foreign affiliates of U.S. manufacturing firms.[10]

Among those stressing the importance of technological types is Walter Chudson, who distinguishes between "conventional" and "high" technology. He finds the international supply of know-how for the former category to be "relatively competitive, even though the market is far from perfect." That is to say, "Many firms in many countries are prepared to supply the production technology."[11] Chudson counts shoes, textiles, cement, and paper in this class, the last of which he describes as follows: "A final example to be given here is in the important field of pulp and paper. . . . The technology, like that of cement, petrochemicals and a number of intermediate products—and the important industry of food processing also— is not proprietary in the narrow sense of being significantly patented or difficult of access. In fact the market of equipment suppliers appears rather competitive. Technology is relatively stabilized, though marginal adjustments may be made."[12]

In contrast, "high" technology industries are characterized by enormous "research and development expenditure, a large element of complex patented or non-patented proprietary technology, rapid and continuing technological change, high capital requirements, a stake in maximizing the profits or quasi-rents on this high technology, and product differentiation." Chudson therefore finds quite formidable bargaining positions for transferors of this technology: "the firms having the know-how are in a strong position and the host country is in a weak position." [13]

COSTS, TIME, AND COMPETITION

In the past a number of economists have maintained that the costs of transferring technology must be small because the knowledge already exists and can easily be communicated. However, David Teece has recently disabused us of this notion. He points out that major costs may arise from (1) preengineering technological changes, (2) the engineering of process and product designs, (3) the use of R&D personnel to solve unexpected problems during all phases of the transfer process, and (4) prestart-up training and operations "debugging." Teece's statistical analysis of a sample of specific transfers reveals that transfer costs are especially high when the technology involved is new or the transfer represents the first manufacturing start-up, and when there are few firms offering competitive, substitute technologies. [14]

Additional age and start-up experience reduce transfer costs for fairly obvious reasons. Age, even without transfer, results in greater stability in engineering designs, fewer unsolved problems, and a larger work force able to assist in any transfer. Start-up experience yields economies from learning by doing.

More interesting is Teece's explanation of why costs are inversely related to the number of firms utilizing the technology or "similar and competitive" technology. This variable apparently represents "the degree to which the innovation and the associated manufacturing technology is already diffused throughout the industry. The greater the number of firms with the same or similar and competitive technology, then the greater the likelihood that technology is more generally available, and can therefore be acquired at lower cost." [15]

Another major determinant of cost is the time taken to complete a given transfer. There is a substantial time-cost trade-off beyond that just noted, with total cost of the transfer process falling as transfer time is stretched, or rising as transfer time is compressed, very much like the time-cost trade-off that has been found for R&D itself. Costs rise with shorter time because haste leads to (1) multiple designs as a hedge against uncertainty, (2) more engineers at reduced productivity, and (3) greater coordination expense.[16]

MULTINATIONAL CORPORATIONS AND TECHNOLOGY TRANSFER

Theoretically, multinational corporations (MNCs) should be closely associated with transfers of advanced technology because ownership penetration of foreign markets should be predicated on some competitive advantage over native rivals, and command of advanced technology or product differentiation certainly provides that kind of competitive edge.[17] It is not surprising, then, that virtually all of the largest MNCs come from the most technologically advanced countries. Indeed, as of 1971, eight of the top ten and fifty-eight of the top one hundred multinational corporations were United States offspring.[18] By the same token, approximately 80 percent of all direct foreign investment emanating from the United States is made by three hundred multinational companies ranking among the country's top five hundred, and these five hundred account for the lion's share of all U.S. R&D expenditures and patents.[19] More specifically, it has been estimated that U.S. multinational corporations raked in 88 percent of all U.S. net international receipts for royalties, license fees, rentals, and management and service fees in 1966.[20]

Data for individual U.S. industries complete the pattern. Electronic computing equipment, machinery, transportation equipment, chemicals, drugs, and instruments account for a majority of U.S. direct foreign investments and for an immense portion of net royalties and fees from abroad, as well as for the bulk of domestic R&D expenditures. Conversely, the figures for textiles, apparel, paper, wood products, and major sectors of food processing amount to very little in all these respects.[21]

It is instructive to compare this U.S. portrait with data from Japan, a country ranked below the United States in overall technological attainment, at least in the past. Textiles, lumber, pulp, steel, and nonferrous metals could all qualify as having conventional technologies, and these few industries accounted for 56 percent of all Japanese direct foreign investment in 1970, as against only 11 percent for all U.S. direct foreign investment.[22] Correspondingly, it has been observed that a very substantial portion of Japanese transfers has entailed technology of no more than moderate sophistication.[23]

MARKET CONCENTRATION, ENTRY BARRIERS, AND THE MNCS

Absolute overall size probably has less influence on business conduct than relative size within specific markets. It is therefore significant that foreign affiliates of U.S. multinational firms tend to congregate in industries with above average concentration ratios. Such concentration has occurred in Europe [24] and, more pertinent to our investigation here, in less-developed countries as well. Conservative estimates for Brazilian manufacturing indicate that in 1968 four-plant concentration averaged 54 percent in those industries where three or four of the largest plants belonged to MNCs, while concentration averaged 39 percent where the largest plants belonged to domestic firms.[25] More detailed data for Mexican manufacturing are presented in table 2.2, which shows that 60.9 percent of MNC production was in markets where the largest four plants accounted for half or more of the market's total sales. In contrast, Mexican enterprises placed only 28.8 percent of their production in such highly concentrated markets. By inference and evidence, large MNCs are likewise associated with markets with above average entry barriers.[26]

CONDUCT, EXPORTS, AND OWNERSHIP CONTROL

Given complete freedom of decision making and low transportation costs, the typical large, technologically oriented multinational corporation would

TABLE 2.2

Mexico: MNC and Mexican Enterprise Share of Production by Degree of Market Concentration, 1970

Industries where the 4 largest plants produced	MNC output	Mexican enterprise output
75% or more	21.2	4.7
50–75%	39.7	24.1
25–50%	30.1	38.1
less than 25%	9.1	33.1
Total	100.0	100.0

SOURCE: Richard S. Newfarmer and Willard F. Mueller, *Multinational Corporations in Brazil and Mexico: Structural Sources of Economic and Noneconomic Power,* Report to the Subcommittee on Multinational Corporations of the Senate Committee on Foreign Relations, 94th Cong., 1st Sess. (1975), p. 61.

apparently prefer relatively centralized production plus exports to far-flung manufacturing and the extensive transfer of technology that such spread implies. On the other hand, contrasting conditions of more conventional technology, more competition, and relatively smaller firms are apparently more conducive to a dispersion of technology and manufacturing facilities. These structure-conduct divergences are suggested by both theoretical and empirical observations, including Raymond Vernon's now familiar theory linking product life cycles with trade and investment behavior,[27] the high technological content of U.S. exports,[28] the low technological content of U.S. imports,[29] and case studies of specific industries.[30] One major exception can be found in labor-intensive component manufacturing, or "offshore" assembly within vertically integrated MNCs, best illustrated by the electronics industry in Hong Kong, Taiwan, and Mexico.[31]

The penchant of the monopolistic firms in table 2.1 toward tight control is further revealed by their policy of "packaged" transfer: their technology moves abroad only as a part of direct investment in wholly owned subsidiaries, or to a lesser extent, in joint ventures. Competitive conditions, on the other hand, produce abundant "unpackaged" transfers via licensing, turnkey projects, and management contracts. Thus, Robert Stobaugh has shown that for relatively new advanced petrochemicals, direct investment accounted for 73 percent of all transfers, but for older mature petrochemicals, licensing accounted for 73 percent.[32] In addition, several studies have found that interindustry differences in ownership policy seem to be caused by differences in the extent both of competition and of the technological lead enjoyed by innovating firms. In particular, computer and pharmaceutical transfers have in the past been made primarily by means of direct investment, whereas in the more competitive industries of plastics and basic electronic goods the more common channel for transfers seems to have been licensing.[33] Similarly, a comparison of U.S. and Japanese direct foreign investment indicates that the former is concentrated more heavily in industries of advanced technology and in wholly owned, as opposed to partially owned, subsidiaries.[34]

Complementing these findings, copious evidence indicates that, within a given industry and generally, medium and small firms are less insistent on tying their transfers to direct investments and more willing to use licenses than large firms, in part because small firms lack the capital resources of large firms.[35] When large firms dealing in majority ownership are asked why they prefer that approach to transfer, they stress protection of their key assets: technology, brand names, and product quality.[36]

These facets of transfer conduct are perhaps best exemplified by the computer industry. The industry's smaller firms, such as Amdahl, Honeywell, Control Data, and Sperry Rand, have included liberal amounts of licensing and joint venturing in their transfer repertoire,[37] but IBM has not:

> IBM's specialized manufacture and interchange system has remained to this day under their full ownership and managerial control. IBM purchases materials and parts from suppliers with their own technology, but it shares its core technology with no one. A critical element in this global posture is the technological lead IBM has managed to maintain over would-be competitors. Other equally large companies in the automotive and consumer electronic fields, whose technological leads have been eroded by competing enterprises at home and abroad, have been edged out of certain product lines or now feel compelled to share technology in order to maintain segments of world markets.[38]

CONDUCT CONCERNING INTERMEDIATE INPUTS

As table 2.1 further indicates, monopolistic and competitive sectors differ in the extent to which MNC affiliate companies purchase intermediate inputs from their parent companies or from local and other outside sources. Table 2.3 presents some recent data for 50 Japanese MNCs that reveal tight control and extensive vertical integration in monopolistic sectors but more open-market purchasing in competitive sectors.[39]

TABLE 2.3

Percentage of the Value of Materials and Components Purchased from Parent Companies by Local Subsidiaries of 50 Japanese Manufacturing Enterprises

Industry	Percentage of intermediates purchased from parent
Precision machinery	78.7
Transportation	75.8
Electrical machinery	59.7
Ferrous and nonferrous metals	59.4
Chemicals	57.0
Nonelectrical machinery	47.5
Textiles	38.7
Paper and pulp	8.8

SOURCE: M. Y. Yoshino, *Japan's Multinational Enterprises* (Cambridge: Harvard University Press, 1976), p. 156.

OTHER CONDUCT

Data on still other aspects of conduct are sketchier and less systematic, but what they show conforms to the foregoing. Thus, data on foreign collaboration agreements in India, the Philippines, and Japan from periods preceding conduct control policies reveal that export restrictions, tie-in purchase clauses, and other such restraints were applied most frequently to pharmaceuticals, transportation equipment, electronic goods, and machinery. Conversely, textiles, foods, and beverages show much lower frequencies of restrictive clauses except when trademarks and product differentiation gave transferors substantial market power.[40] As Jack Baranson has remarked: "Within the corporate world, there are often considerable differences between hardliners who have a very restrictive set of policies regarding technology sharing with foreign enterprises and firms that have a more liberal policy of technology sharing with associated firms overseas. The former typically are technology leaders and have a strong market position, including financial resources to capitalize their technology assets— in contrast to firms that do not have a predominant market position."[41]

These findings suggest that monopolistic transferors of technology have relatively low price elasticities of supply, and competitive transferors relatively high elasticities. Differences in pricing behavior would follow accordingly, as is illustrated by Baranson's observations on the consequences of a sharp decline in world market power recently experienced by once dominant U.S. chemical companies:

> For U.S. product companies, the increased competition means that they no longer wield the same bargaining leverage in entering foreign markets on their terms or in withholding their technology. There are very few product areas where nearly equivalent technologies are not available from an alternative source. If one U.S. firm refuses to share its technology with a potential purchaser, it generally faces the prospect that equivalent technology will be obtained from an alternative source (American or foreign), and the holdout company in any event will face a new competitor supplied by another source.[42]

SUMMARY OF TRANSFERORS' SIDE

To recapitulate, the facts leave no doubt that market structure greatly influences conduct in this realm: relatively competitive structures produce less restrictive, less "packaged," and less reluctant seller conduct than monopolistic conditions. The evidence is not sufficiently refined to reveal the optimal structure, but perfect competition is not required. Fairly good results ensue when loose-knit oligopoly is coupled with no more than moderate barriers to entry. Indeed, the economics of technology transfer seem close enough to the economics of innovation and invention to suggest that loose-knit oligopoly and medium-sized firms might well produce the best conduct and performance in this area. Figure 2.1, which is adapted from F. M. Scherer's analysis of R&D behavior, illustrates this possibility.[43] The cost curve C depicts a time-cost trade-off, similar to that discussed previously. Each R function represents the present value of the total revenues that can be expected from the transfer in question. These revenues decline with the duration of a transfer for two reasons: (1) dispatching the transfer sooner rather than later allows the firm to reap the market's profit potential for a longer period; and (2) delay of the transfer raises the probability that the firm's rivals will gain an earlier and firmer foothold in the new market, which lowers the firm's share of the market's total profit potential. It is this latter effect that causes the revenue function of the oligopolist, R_o, to fall faster than the revenue function of the monopolist, R_m, because the chances of displacement by rivals is clearly greater for the oligopolist. By the same token, the revenue function for the purely competitive firm, R_c, has the steepest descent of all.

Profit is the vertical difference between revenue and cost, when revenue exceeds cost. It may be seen, then, that the monopolist will delay transfer much longer than the oligopolist (to T_m, as compared with T_o). On the

Figure 2.1 Optimizing the Speed of Technology Transfer

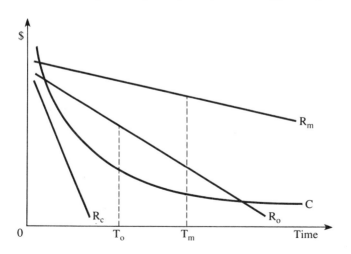

other hand, too much competition may be stifling, as the purely competitive firm of figure 2.1 would never be able to cover cost. Thus, vigor in transferring may be a nonlinear function of concentration, with mild activity where concentration is either very high or very low and fireworks somewhere in between, not too far from the low end. It is apropos that Frederick Knickerbocker has found just such heightened oligopolistic vigor in the timing of overseas direct investment and in the R&D intensity of U.S. multinational firms.[44]

THE TRANSFEREES' SIDE

Turning now to the other side of the coin, we can summarize the range of recipient circumstances in table 2.4, which again reduces the world's continuum to two extremes. At the fortunate end of the spectrum, the most advanced countries enjoy abundant technological capabilities; highly trained and well-informed work forces; diverse production experiences; lofty incomes per head; expansive home markets; relatively competitive commercial conditions; high domestic ownership of industry; relatively efficient, low-cost adoption of new technologies; and a large potential for self-reliance. A list of examples would surprise no one: the United States,

TABLE 2.4
Outline of Recipient Country Characteristics

Characteristic	Large capacity	Small capacity
1. Technical capability	High, self-sufficient	Low, dependent
2. Information level	Well informed	Poorly informed
3. Price elasticity of demand	High	Low
4. Products produced	Wide range, including complex manufactures	Narrow range, extractive
5. Income per head	High income	Low income
6. Size of home markets	Large and expansive	Small and thin
7. Concentration in home markets	Relatively low	Relatively high
8. Extent of foreign control of industry	Relatively low	Relatively high
9. Cost of receiving technology	Low cost, low risk	High cost, high risk
10. Intermediate imports	Few	Many

West Germany, Great Britain, France, and Japan. At the unfortunate other end of the spectrum, we find scores of countries enduring opposite characteristics in every particular, countries like Ethiopia, Burma, and Honduras. In short, these poor countries tend to have small, weak, specialized, and highly dependent economies, whereas the rich countries tend to have large, powerful, diversified economies with the capacity to generate their own sources of growth.[45]

The importance of this diversity is that it greatly affects two key factors on the recipient's side of the market: the capacity to absorb transfers and bargaining strength. The two are so closely related that to distinguish between them in detail is impossible, but some distinction may be helpful.

CAPACITY

Moving a kidney from one human to another seems more than plausible, but a transplant from a human to a hound stuns the imagination. A similar impression results from reading technical literature comparing the capacities of, say, the United States and Swaziland for receiving advanced technology. Successful technology transplants require vast and complex connections to the surrounding environment for transportation, communications, finance, fuel, trained personnel, component parts, and so on. The United Nations has scores of experts who produce reports with titles like "Factors Inhibiting the Indigenous Growth of the Fertilizer Industry in Developing Countries," and all these reports bear essentially the same message about capacity.[46]

On a more quantitative level, Teece demonstrates statistically that the more years of manufacturing experience the recipient of the transfer has accumulated and the larger the size of the recipient's market, the lower the total cost of a specific transfer.[47] A Swedish executive confirms the contribution of recipient experience:

> When it comes to transferring technology to a developing country—whether it is via a license agreement or technical know-how in running and administering an industrial process—we can generally state that the costs for our company to transfer such knowledge are much higher for a developing country than for an industrial country. The main reason for this is that the people in the developing country normally do not have the background that makes it easy for them to absorb and understand technical problems. We have also often found that they underestimate their difficulties. For us, this means that we have to put more people on these jobs than would have been the case in an

industrial country, and we nearly always have to keep them there for a much longer time than we intended. [48]

As for size, an Australian executive may have given us the best indication when he said, "The cost of servicing technical agreements in small volume markets tends to be high in terms of percentage on potential sales." [49]

Another measure of capacity is the proportion of sales accounted for by locally owned firms. In pharmaceuticals, circa 1970, this proportion was 20 percent for Pakistan, 56 percent for Portugal, 70 percent for Spain, and 85 percent for the United States. [50] In petrochemicals the proportion was 75 percent for less-developed countries involved in production and 96 percent for the United States. [51] Likewise, less-developed countries generally import a larger portion of intermediate inputs than developed countries do, which further discloses their relative incapacity. [52]

One upshot of divergent absorptive capacities is that, contrary to naive supposition, most transfers of technology do not flow from developed to less-developed countries at all; rather, they flow between already developed countries. In 1977, for instance, the United States received $2,193 million in royalties and license fees from abroad, $2,006 million, or 91.5 percent, from developed countries and only $177 million, or 8.1 percent, from less-developed countries. [53]

BARGAINING POWER

Absorptive capacity and recipient bargaining power are like cold weather and snow because the factors that create one necessarily create the other. Note first that countries with dazzling profit prospects for outside investors and transferors can use this attractiveness to secure favorable terms and conditions. Nearly all studies of the determinants of attractiveness conclude that a large gross national product, a rapid rate of economic growth, and a solid infrastructure prove to be the greatest inducements to direct foreign investment, and, as we have seen, most transferring is linked to direct investment. [54] The added bargaining power advancement brings may help to explain how Japan could reduce the royalty rates it pays on technology from the 7 to 10 percent range of the 1950s to the 2 to 4 percent range of today.

Risk is another factor. The economic inadequacies that shrink absorptive capacity likewise undermine political stability, stagger balance-of-trade accounts, and burden strained credit standings. All these consequences raise the risk that transferors, who are usually compensated over long time spans, will never collect their total due.[55] The adverse implications for a risky recipient's bargaining position need no elaboration.

An additional and extremely important variable on the recipients' side of the negotiating table is level of information. Some degree of ignorance is inevitable in anyone seeking to acquire knowledge; indeed, the inevitably uninformed state of buyers of information is perhaps the most frequently cited of all flaws in this market.[56] But some buyers are less informed than others, and this is the main point here. A Greek businessman, who could be speaking for all businessmen in less-developed countries, said it neatly: "Not having a thorough knowledge, it is impossible to make an estimate of what should be charged for the advanced technology or for the license permitting the manufacture of a product."[57]

Two noteworthy corollaries emerge from buyer ignorance. First, other things being equal, price elasticity of demand is probably an inverse function of the degree of ignorance: the more the ignorance, the less the elasticity. An "income effect" and a "substitution effect" determine elasticity. If a product takes a high portion of one's income, the price elasticity is likely to be high by reason of ability to pay. Given the low incomes of those most ignorant in the case at hand, it might appear that the income effect would make their demands elastic. But technology payments constitute a very small portion of the LDC's outlays, so their price elasticity is probably dominated by the substitution effect, and it is this latter effect that generates the inverse relationship. Almost by definition, a well-informed buyer of technology has a readily available and, at the margin, a relatively inexpensive substitute for what is offered by transferors of technology: namely, self-supply through R&D. His price elasticity will consequently be high. Conversely, self-supply to the uninformed buyer is neither convenient nor cheap, which implies a willingness to pay more than the well-informed buyer for the same technology. Actual estimates of elasticity for various transferees are not available for this market, but it does appear that less-developed countries do in fact pay more than their advanced brethren,[58] and an inverse relationship is evidently suggested by Taylor and Silberston's rather startling discovery that twenty-two technologically oriented British companies would be willing to pay no more than about three-quarters of one percent of their total combined R&D budgets to gain access to all the information contained in British patents, assuming such information was sold rather than publicly disclosed and was otherwise unavailable.[59]

The second corollary is that some of the knowledge possessed by a particularly well-informed transferee may be of great value to the transferor, in which case the well-informed transferee has a bargaining advantage that is denied the ill-informed transferee. Thus, for example, John Tilton reports that Europe's most technologically advanced electronics firms were able to acquire semiconductor know-how from American innovators more cheaply than their less knowledgeable European cohorts because the latter had "nothing to offer in exchange."[60]

SUMMARY OF TRANSFEREES' SIDE
The last several pages testify to heterogeneity on the transferees' side of the market, with some holding considerable monopsonistic or oligopsonistic power and others less well blessed. Moreover, by some paradoxical fate, those least in need of technology transfers, most elastic in their demands, and most capable of absorbing innovations are also the most powerful potential buyers. Adding to this power is the fact that relatively few countries command the most advantageous positions. The countries having opposite traits are competitively numerous, typically small, and individually weak, even though their governments now intervene to negotiate on their behalf.

TRANSFERORS AND TRANSFEREES TOGETHER

When now called upon to consider both sides of these markets simultaneously, a cynic with no more than static conditions in mind might argue that there really is no problem requiring the formulation of policy because, given the facts to this point, monopsonistic buyers should be dealing solely or primarily with monopolistic sellers, while competitive buyers should be dealing chiefly with competitive suppliers, and the free forces of the marketplace will enforce these tendencies, covering all situations in between. There is, of course, some truth to this argument, given the less-developed countries' limited capacity for monopolistically controlled advanced technology, and given the large degree of self-sufficiency advanced countries possess in areas of conventional technology. Indeed, evidence already presented suggests that the powerful and the weak tend to conduct the bulk of their technology commerce in separate circles.

Still, the cynic's view is too narrow, too simplistic, and too static. Unless the less-developed countries acquire technology that at any one point in time is somewhat beyond their technical capacity and easy budgeting, they will never gain substantial ground against misery. Indeed, most commentators take a view quite different from the cynic's. Failing to recognize the considerable benefits LDCs do win in the open market, they focus too narrowly on the IBMs and Gambias of the world, insistently declaring that the steep imbalance of bargaining power can only be righted by rigid governmental control of business conduct. Fortunately, the preceding two sections have prepared the way for a broader view, one encompassing nearly all buyer-seller combinations. Three questions now dominate the analysis: (1) When are terms and conditions least favorable to transferees? (Or, where do restraints of trade pose the biggest problem?) (2) Under what circumstances do conduct control policies work best? and (3) Under what circumstances would structural policies work best? We begin with the first.

WHEN DO ONEROUS TERMS AND RESTRAINTS ARISE?
Consider figure 2.2, which divides transferor and transferee relationships into a four-part matrix and thus oversimplifies once again. Transferors are characterized as being either monopolistic or competitive, and the traits associated with these designations, as outlined in table 2.1, are assumed to carry over here. Similarly, table 2.4 guides the two-part classification of transferees.

Thus, cell 1, with considerable power on both sides of the market, summarizes conditions likely to produce fairly balanced bargaining. Examples include General Electric's entry into a joint venture with France's

Figure 2.2 Four-part Summary of Transfer Markets

		Transferors' Side	
		Monopolistic	Competitive
Transferees' Side	Strong bargaining position	1. Balanced bargaining	2. Transferee has the upper hand
	Weak bargaining position	3. Transferor has the upper hand	4. Balance, and narrow bargaining range

TABLE 2.5
Share of Total Sales of Selected Manufacturing Industries Accounted for by Affiliates of U.S. Multinational Enterprises, 1970

(1)	France	W. Germany	(2)	France	W. Germany
Chemicals	12%	7%	Food	3%	4%
Rubber	6	11	Paper	8	2
Machinery	14	11	Primary metals	2	7
Elec. machinery	8	6	Textiles	0	1
Transportation equipment	8	25	Lumber	0	1
Instruments	20	25	Stone, clay, & glass	9	4
Averages	11%	14%	Averages	4%	3%
(3)	Brazil	Mexico	(4)	Prazil	Mexico
Chemicals	19%	20%	Food	3%	8%
Rubber	48	40	Paper	13	23
Machinery	34	63	Primary metals	12	38
Elec. machinery	24	52	Textiles	5	3
Transportation equipment	65	45	Lumber	1	2
Instruments	N.A.*	N.A.	Stone, clay, & glass	9	26
Averages	38%	44% ·	Averages	7%	17%

SOURCE: U.S. Congress, Senate, Report to the Committee on Finance by the U.S. Tariff Commission, *Implications of Multinational Firms for World Trade and Investment and for U.S. Trade and Labor* (Washington, D.C.: Government Printing Office, 1973), pp. 735–46.
*N.A. = Not available.

SNECMA to produce sophisticated jet engines, and Cummins Engine's license agreement assigning major manufacturing responsibilities to Komatsu of Japan.[61] Cell 2 represents cases where the balance of power rests with the transferee, such as Motorola's divestiture of its wobbly television business to Matsushita of Japan.[62]

The lower half of figure 2.2 summarizes the circumstances facing less-developed countries. Cell 3, where the transferor has the upper hand, is illustrated by IBM's refusal to enter India except on its own terms,[63] and by many lopsided bargains between LDCs and multinational pharmaceutical firms.[64] On the other hand, relatively competitive supplies of technology are made to the LDCs under the conditions of cell 4. Textiles and paper are typical of the commodities fitting this description, and Sweden and Japan have been among the major suppliers.[65]

If one could obtain a reliable index of price per unit of quality for traded technology, duly adjusted to account for all terms and conditions, theory and existing evidence would lead us to expect a relatively high price index for the transfers of cell 3, a relatively low price index for those of cell 2, and intermediate indexes for cells 1 and 4. Although the data necessary to construct such a price index will never be available, our earlier analysis of structure and conduct indicates that MNC ownership penetration of foreign markets can serve as a crude surrogate. Table 2.5 therefore presents percentage shares of total sales of U.S. multinational affiliates in 1970 by industry and by country following the format outlined in figure 2.2. Subjective judgment influenced the designation of industries as either monopolistic or competitive, and limited data dictated the choice of countries filling the top and bottom halves of the table, so this must be taken as no more than a very rough test of the importance of structural conditions and power relationships. Nevertheless, the results match expectations, with cells 3 and 2 containing the highest and lowest values, respectively, and the values of cells 1 and 4 lying in between.

It seems reasonable to surmise, then, that cell 3's circumstances produce the least favorable terms and conditions and the most frequent restraints of trade, which is unfortunate for the less-developed countries. Cells 1 and 4 also give rise to uneven terms and restraints, but much less frequently. In what amounts to an illustrative comparison of cells 3 and 4, Lawrence Wortzel has observed that restrictions are found in pharmaceutical license agreements covering simple tableting and packaging technology in LDCs, "but the restrictions put on the local firm become even more severe" in agreements on production of pharmaceutical chemicals, an area of more advanced technology where patents abound.[66]

WHEN IS CONDUCT CONTROL MOST EFFECTIVE?
It should be evident that conduct control policies probably work best against restraints associated with cells 1 and 4, for under those conditions the restraints are all, or largely all, that stand between the transferee and fairly good terms and conditions. Thus, a transferor of the cell 4 variety, expecting little profit from the sale of its standardized technology, may try to compensate by tying supplies of overpriced intermediate goods such as raw materials, parts, and components to the transfer of its technology.[67]

Or a naive transferee of the cell 4 variety may fall prey to debilitating export restrictions merely by failing to research thoroughly the supply alternatives. But prohibition of these restraints and screening procedures to uncover them are likely to win genuine relief for transferees without driving transferors away.

As for cell 3 of figure 2.2, which is most severely plagued by restraints and slanted terms, control policies may well tend to be unneeded, ineffectual, or unwise. These shortcomings will be discussed in detail in the next section of this paper. Briefly, however, conduct control would be largely unneeded when the transfer is part of an effort to produce for export, which is true of offshore assembly and much mineral extraction; in such cases successful world-market penetration by suppliers in LDCs is an objective the transferor hopes to achieve rather than avoid. (On the other hand, control might be needed here to assure local assimilation of the technology, and it might be unusually effective in such cases because the recipient country would draw some bargaining leverage from its special resource.[68])

As for ineffectiveness, conduct control may be evaded when, as is typical in this realm, the transfer is part of a larger package that includes direct foreign investment, intermediate inputs, and the like, for in such situations the transferor may impose tacit restraints or dodge specific controls by shifting the locus of restraint from one facet of the collaboration to another. The standard example is the use of transfer pricing to counter royalty rate ceilings.[69]

Finally, if effectual, controls can result in the withdrawal of technology. This result tests the wisdom of the conduct approach where, as in the case of cell 3, the supply alternatives are few. An Australian businessman explains: "Our company has recently canceled a proposed major expansion program in one Southeast Asian country because the conditions which the government of that country laid down on shareholdings and technical fees were such that the project had little prospect of returning an adequate return on the investment to the company that had to supply the technology and take the greater part of the risk."[70]

WHEN DO STRUCTURAL POLICIES WORK BEST?

Whereas conduct controls leave cell 3's conditions basically unchanged, successful structural policies have the effect of moving transactions from cell 3 toward either cell 1 (if change occurs primarily on the transferees' side) or cell 4 (if change occurs primarily on the transferors' side). In themselves, these changes should bring improvements. A beneficial by-product is that these alterations enhance the potency of existing conduct policies, which, as just noted, work best in realms 1 and 4.

Several strands of evidence from the transferors' side help make the case. First, second-tier, medium-sized firms rather than very top-ranked, large firms seem to be most eager to spearhead transfer operations in LDCs. The former firms apparently are large enough to fund such ventures, yet they are not so prominent that their incentives suffer. That is, relatively small transferors have the most to gain and the least to lose from upsetting the prevailing division of world business in their industry. For example:

1. The main innovating firm in the offshore assembly of semiconductor gadgetry has been Fairchild, the third largest firm in the U.S. industry, followed by Motorola, the second largest, and by Signatic, General Instruments, and Philco-Ford, all of which are even lower ranked in the industry.[71]
2. Chrysler has been notably flexible in accepting a minority interest in overseas undertakings in countries like Mexico, India, and Iran.[72]
3. Stobaugh found that in petrochemicals the vast majority of transfers were undertaken by nonproducing engineering firms and "followers," rather than by the originators of the technology.[73]
4. In the computer industry, Brazil, Iran, Romania, Mexico, and Venezuela have been the first LDCs to obtain major manufacturing operations, and the firms to be credited are Sycor, Control Data Corporation (CDC), and Honeywell.[74]

Perhaps it is no coincidence that medium-sized firms also have the best record of R&D performance in U.S. industries.[75]

Second, and by the same token, LDCs do well when dealing with firms from medium-ranked countries like Sweden, Japan, Switzerland, and Belgium. During the 1960s, the majority of Japanese transfers went to less-developed countries.[76] And businessmen from the medium-ranked countries stress price competition for the technology they extend to LDCs.[77]

Structural impact on the transferees' side can also be documented. Most crucially, abundant evidence indicates that remarkable benefits ensue from improved buyer information. More examples of this phenomenon turned up in studies by the Board of the Cartagena Agreement than can be cited here. A few must be mentioned, however, because they illustrate how concessions can be wrung even from mighty transferors:

> In a situation of this nature, the best course of action is to be able to demonstrate to the owner of the technique one wishes to obtain that one does not really need it, and this was precisely the strategy followed by the Japanese petrochemical industry whenever opportunity arose.
>
> In this way, for instance, during the 1950s, a Japanese company manufacturing rayon was one of the first to obtain a license to manufacture nylon using the Du Pont process, by demonstrating that it had developed a similar process that would allow it to manufacture nylon without infringing any of the patents protecting the Du Pont process.
>
> During the 1960s, the Japanese petrochemical industry introduced modifications and improvements for the most important tertiary petrochemical processes, which were originally imported, in order to improve its bargaining position with the holders of licenses for the original processes when they wished to increase their production volume (the object of which increase was often to be able to enter the international market).[78]

On a level more relevant to most LDCs, the Mexican Registry of Technology attempts to supply Mexican firms with information about technology trade. It obtains this information by reviewing collaboration agreements and exchanging information with other governments.

> In one case, a licensee in the chemical industry, which had negotiated a proposed \$4 million annual royalty down to \$2 million, was informed by the Registry that a similar technology could be obtained from a source in another country for a \$100,000 annual payment. Using this information, the licensee obtained a similar price from his original licensor. In another case, a licensee reported that a review of its licensing agreements led to a cancellation of several agreements which were no longer of significant benefit to the company.[79]

A second emergent empirical theme is that competitive pressures within LDCs seem conducive to the transfer of the most appropriate technology, if "appropriateness" is measured by labor-capital intensity.[80] Thus, structural conditions affect "quality" as well as "price."

CONDUCT REGULATION: THE SHORTCOMINGS

To condemn all conduct control would be foolish, but wisdom requires that we appreciate its limitations whenever they can be ascribed to structural conditions. In brief, the net benefits of conduct control diminish to the extent the structural features of cell 3 in figure 2.2 are realized. My pessimism may be illustrated by a brief analysis of several major areas of conduct control.

UNQUESTIONABLY GOOD CONDUCT POLICIES

Consider first several conduct policies of glowing general reputation but questionable effectiveness when faced with particularly noncompetitive structures: namely, prohibitions against (1) cartel activities, (2) the price fixing of products produced under transferred technology, (3) the continued duration of transferor's property rights, and (4) restrictions on transferee's R&D activities.

Prohibitions against international cartel conduct cannot be enforced by LDCs individually, and international codes of conduct are unlikely ever to grow enforcement teeth.[81] Not much can be expected when official timidity runs so deep as to preclude even the effective study of the extent of international cartel activity.[82] What is more, tacit collusion, the forte of tight-knit oligopolies, escapes cartel control.

As for the other prohibitions mentioned, all may be evaded by transferors who retain ownership and operating control within the LDCs through direct investment and vertical integration, two common characteristics of cell 3 transferors. Indeed, internal MNC control has often been so extensive as to raise occasional questions whether transfer has actually occurred.[83] In short, the larger the company, the bigger the problem.

ROYALTY RATE CEILINGS

Conventional theory of public utility regulation postulates that a price ceiling, when properly administered, can substitute for competition because it can reduce price, reduce profit, and increase output, and thereby move a monopoly in the direction of purely competitive performance. This theory might seem to justify the incorporation of ceilings on royalty rates in transfer agreements, but trade in technology is sufficiently different from the typical product market to prevent price controls from efficiently and effectively substituting for competition. There are, in particular, two features of technology trade that vitiate the theory: (1) transferors retain the right of refusal to sell (something denied regulated public utilities), and (2) the price elasticity of demand of transferees is inversely related to the costs and risks of transferring technology to them: i.e., the less the elasticity, the higher the cost and risk. Under these circumstances, sellers can easily exercise their market power by means of rejections and rationing if deprived of pricing freedom.

Price-ceiling regulation in the market for consumer credit provides the closest analogy, and elsewhere I have shown, using both theory and evidence, that the consequences for that market leave much to be desired.[84] Translating those findings into present relevance, one would have to conclude that ceilings on royalty rates probably do little to reduce the profits of transferors while most severely curtailing the supply of transfers to the very folks in greatest need of technology, namely, those with the highest costs and risks plus the least elastic demands. By analogizing further, it may also be deduced that more competitive seller-side structures would reduce rejections, boost technology supplies, lessen monopoly rents, and hold prices in check.

CONTROL OF TRANSFER PRICING

Apart from the foregoing problems, ceilings on royalty rates and other payment controls can be evaded by transfer pricing, which is made possible by technology's entanglement with direct investments and by the intrafirm product trade of MNCs. Pertinent here are two significant findings of Sanjaya Lall.[85]

First, the incidence of intrafirm trade and transfer pricing is most acute in research-intensive industries, in areas with advanced and firm specific technology, and in large, monopolistic firms—all of which obviously describes the sellers' side of cell 3.

Second, it is under just such circumstances that control of transfer pricing by regulation is most difficult. Its effective administration depends on the existence of competitively determined open-market prices against which the reasonableness of intrafirm prices may be compared. But if the open market in question is thin, noncompetitive, or intermittently nonexistent, as is usually the case under cell 3 circumstances, then LDC regulatory authorities are deprived of a proper standard for comparison. Once Lall adds further complications, he concludes, that, "in such a situation, it is impossible to define a transfer price which is correct in an objective sense. Reference to prices charged by the MNC in other markets, or by other firms which do not innovate, are not solutions."[86]

Lall's favored resolution of the difficulties is to replace direct regulation with LDC and MNC negotiation of the rate of return. But this recommendation really solves nothing; rather, it reminds us of hypothetical drownings. Technological imperatives admittedly limit what can be done structurally, but pursuit of as much competition as is feasible, coupled with negotiation, would seem to be the preferred course.[87]

PROHIBITIONS AGAINST TIE-INS AND PACKAGES

Tie-in clauses and package deals should not be flatly prohibited because at times such practices are procompetitive or especially helpful to the transfer process. Most obviously, quality control may justify a transferor's insistence that certain inputs used in the production process be acquired from designated sources. And a transferor's use of fairly comprehensive packages may be the most efficient way of completing transfers, particularly those going to transferees with scanty absorptive capacities. Several studies of collaboration arrangements indicate that the more comprehensive the package and the greater the degree of foreign ownership control, the more extensive the information and technology that are transferred.[88]

EXPORT RESTRICTIONS

It may seem that all export restrictions ought to be stamped out as being loathsomely burdensome to LDCs. But what about the Japanese electronics firm that reluctantly transfers technology to a firm in Singapore under no restrictions whatever except a ban on exports to Japan? Thus, the problem of transferor rejections crops up once again, though the benefits of the transfer as stated here may be quite generous to the LDC, even without the opportunity of serving the Japanese market.

There is also an echo here of impotent enforcement, perhaps not all to the bad. Thus, it is reported that "during the latter part of 1970 and the beginning of 1971, negotiations by the Colombian Comité de Regalías" succeeded in eliminating "100 per cent of the restrictive export clauses" in Colombia. Yet, the same account goes on to say that "the exclusion of clauses from the contract of a subsidiary does not mean that the practices involved will be abolished, since control through ownership could still dictate the same practices. As far as nationally owned firms are concerned, it is known that in some cases after such government intervention 'gentlemen's agreements' exist, extra-contractually, between licensors and licensees."[89]

To close this sobering list of shortcomings, mention should be made of administrative considerations. We are told on good authority that a lack of knowledge and experience has led Colombia's regulatory commission on royalty rates to be too lenient in some cases and too tight in others, "so permitting too high a cost to the economy or else deterring the inflow of technology."[90] It has also been observed that screening officials lack clear and consistent criteria, so that approval of any given project depends capriciously on the biases of particular reviewers.[91] Finally, and most discouragingly, we are told by LDC businessmen that they are less bothered and encumbered by the restrictions they suffer at the hands of technology suppliers than by the delays, paper requirements, and bureaucratic stumbling blocks imposed upon them by government regulators.[92]

THE STRUCTURAL APPROACH

Compared to conduct controls, structural remedies run less risk of reducing transferors' incentives and instilling rigidity. Yet they, too, have shortcomings. To the extent that technological imperatives determine structure, policy can have little effect. Moreover, where there is room for policy to maneuver, the countries with the most to gain, the LDCs, suffer the shortest jurisdictional reach vis-à-vis the MNCs. Still, there are possibilities.

LDC STRUCTURAL POLICIES

The number and variety of transferors would likely increase if LDCs modified their patent, trademark, and acquisition policies to reduce the barriers to entry confronting potential suppliers of technology. Neither Switzerland nor the Netherlands had patent systems during the latter half of the nineteenth century and first decade of this century, and according to Eric Schiff, who assessed the evidence provided by these countries, the absence of patents failed to paralyze industry in either. On the contrary, industry thrived.[93] Similarly, Japan was for many years between the world wars and for some time thereafter quite lax in respecting the patent rights of foreign enterprises. Its piracy by reverse engineering also seems to have paid off.[94] More recently, rapid development of Italy's pharmaceutical industry has been based on the absence of patents, a policy that did not block the movement of foreign capital and know-how into that country. According to the Board of the Cartagena Agreement: "The Italian market continued to attract foreign companies that were not only seeking means to protect their own market, but even wished to take advantage of the Italian policy of nonpatentability to profit by those held by other, rival companies, thus avoiding the payment of licenses. . . . Nonpatentability gave many international companies an opportunity to imitate products manufactured by competitors."[95]

Elsewhere I have given detailed justifications for abolishing patents in the LDCs.[96] Defenders of LDC adherence to the international patent system rebut by contending that relatively few transfers are grounded on patents and that MNC power has other, more important sources.[97] But these are not really defensive arguments at all, merely belittlings of the problem and questionable belittlings at that.[98]

More serious is the contention that piracy would sully the names of LDCs among MNCs, who insist on doing business in "probusiness" climates. This argument, however, ignores the experiences of Switzerland, the Netherlands, Italy, and Japan. To be sure, these countries have since returned to the "probusiness" fold because they have reached a stage of economic development at which conformity to patent conventions best suits their interests. This option would likewise be open to the LDCs in the future if they were now to withdraw patent protection from MNCs. Perhaps most telling in this regard is the almost magnetic draw East European Communist countries currently exert on many MNCs, despite the fact that not too long ago the same MNCs complained bitterly that those countries poached patents, stole secrets, and generally attempted to undermine the Western private enterprise system.[99] Short of total abolition, several changes in LDC patent systems could be made following the recommendations of Constantine Vaitsos; these changes could be considered a bare minimum of what is needed.[100] Then, too, abolition only for selected areas, such as pharmaceuticals and chemicals, might prove productive.[101] Weak patent protection for pharmaceuticals in Argentina has apparently stimulated the Argentine pharmaceutical industry.[102] Still another approach would be to grant patent protection only to medium and small firms, which have special needs for patent protection[103] and, as we have seen, generally serve the interests of LDCs better than giant firms.

Liberalization of trademark rights may also spur competition. A given trademark may have assorted owners around the world, as any particular trademark right is nation specific. However, competition between two owners of the same trademark is typically blocked by the fact that priority in any one country is held by the first claimant there. Thus, a firm holding trademark X in country A might want to transfer technology to country B in conjunction with its use of trademark X in B. The opportunity might be foreclosed, however, by another company's prior claim to X in B, a claim that company exploits solely by importing, without any transfer of technology. Were country B to persist in protecting the property right of the importing claimant, it would be closing the door to competition and opening self-inflicted economic wounds. Switching rights to the aspirant transferor would undermine traditional trademark law but yield appreciable benefits. Of course, the number of instances helped by such a liberalization would be limited. But the furor recently aroused by the legal liberalization of "parallel imports" in Europe and elsewhere suggests that the number of potential cases is far from trivial.[104]

Finally, we have what for lack of a better name might be called acquisition policies. All too often only one or a very few potential transferors of a given technology are approached by LDC companies and countries; those so selected usually have prior ties of some kind such as product import supply. A better strategy would rely as much as possible on competitive bidding that pitted numerous potential transferors against each other. Examples of competitive bidding's successful application include Yugoslavian copper,[105] Brazilian aircraft,[106] and telecommunications generally.[107] Indeed, the benefits of competitive bidding are especially evident in the case of telecommunications because the telephone and telegraph systems of advanced countries are government owned or otherwise monopolized and they choose to limit their sources of equipment to local manufacturers. By contrast, LDCs that have no local manufacturing industry to protect can acquire the equipment they need at cut-rate prices by international competitive bidding. And LDCs wishing to establish manufacturing capabilities have best done so by the same technique, acquiring complete plants at bargain prices. When competitive bidding is not feasible or efficient, acquisition policy could be devised to favor medium and small technology suppliers, a shift of policy that would simultaneously exploit the existing predilections of those firms and bolster their position relative to the dominant giants.

Whereas the foregoing policies would favorably influence structure on the transferors' side of the market, several further LDC policies would favorably affect the transferees' side. Most urgently, LDCs must give highest priority to developing technical expertise and business know-how so as to be able to bargain from a solid information base and thereby to increase the transferors' price elasticities of supply. Officials who screen collaboration proposals could concentrate more than previously on the acquisition and dissemination of information. Groups of LDCs could do more to pool their combined knowledge, exchanging information on technology sources, terms, and conditions. Individual LDCs could exploit further and encourage the expansion of international agencies dealing in technological matters, such as the Food and Agriculture Organization, the UN Industrial Development Organization, and the UN Conference on Trade and Development. The ultimate object is to heighten the sophistication of local businessmen and technicians, and to give those institutions responsible for implementing technology policy the capacity (1) to aid or conduct negotiations with native and foreign firms; (2) to have a thorough grasp of the technological problems involved in each investment project; (3) to ascertain the availability and real costs of native and foreign inputs, as well as the indirect commitments and restrictions involved in their acquisition; (4) to help identify the technology inputs to be imported and those that may be obtained in the country itself by "unpackaging" technology; and (5) to know all potential suppliers of a given technology and their terms and conditions.[108]

LDCs should likewise subsidize indigenous R&D to a greater extent than at present (and seek aid funds for that purpose). Such an effort not only will improve the LDCs' information base, but also can be tailored to attract transfers that would otherwise not occur. Thus, for example, a key element in Honeywell's decision to transfer computer technology to France through a joint venture with Compagnie Internationale pour l'Informatique was the French Government's heavy R&D funding of the collaboration.[109]

Regional integration of technology policy along the lines of the Andean Pact is an additional possibility, one that is widely advocated. Depending on the degree of integration, the reputed benefits to close intercountry cooperation include (1) added bargaining power vis-à-vis MNCs; (2) greater specialization in technological expertise without duplication across member countries; (3) the spread of fixed R&D costs over a larger economic base; and (4) production on scales large enough to match the production experiences of typical transferors. Of course, integration offers no panacea. Several attempts in this direction have failed miserably, and even the best suffer. A number of United States MNCs, for instance, claim to prefer investing in areas other than the Andean Common Market, the best such group to date, because of "the uncertainties and regulatory requirements in ANCOM."[110]

DEVELOPED COUNTRY POLICIES

Of seventy-six major U.S. multinational corporations surveyed by the Conference Board, six claimed to have invested in foreign countries partly because antitrust considerations prevented their vigorous expansion at home.[111] Separately, an extensive study of international diffusion of semiconductor technology concluded that the U.S. industry's competitive structure, which was due in part to antitrust constraints on American Telephone and Telegraph, contributed substantially to the rapid spread of semiconductor technology abroad.[112] These are just two examples of beneficial by-products stemming from the domestic application of antitrust policies in advanced countries.

Even though the LDCs have no direct impact on antitrust policy in the developed countries, they can certainly urge the adoption and diligent enforcement of policies having such favorable effects. These policies include:

1. Curbing international mergers that reduce the number of potential transferors in any given field. A recent instance fitting this description is the Federal Trade Commission's successful opposition to a merger between Bayer of Germany and Miles Laboratories of the United States.[113]

2. Abolition of advanced-country export cartels. Legalization of export cartels is popular enough to raise doubts that they will ever be abolished. Failing that, LDCs should vigorously oppose the legalization of collusion concerning transfers, which legalization has been proposed in the United States.[114]

3. Expansion of the international jurisdiction of the U.S. antitrust laws, such as would be gained by adopting an "affects commerce" standard for the Clayton Act instead of its present engaged-in-commerce standard.[115]

4. Greater collection and wider dissemination of information on restrictive practices at the international level.[116]

5. Relying more heavily on remedies that divest domestic monopolies of their large foreign subsidiaries. Precedent is provided in the United States by the *Alcoa* case, in which Aluminium Limited of Canada was severed from Alcoa. If the current *IBM* case ends by separating IBM-Europe and IBM-U.S., another example will emerge. Such remedies probably benefit the United States as well as the less-developed countries.[117]

Of late, there have also been a number of policies outside the antitrust realm that seem to have spurred competition. In particular, European governments are in various ways assisting their MNCs in competition against United States MNCs. The consequences include a marked decline in U.S. company control of Latin American industry and trade, with greater shares now going to British, Dutch, French, German, and Japanese companies. These results, in turn, suggest declining concentration and sharper vying for the privilege of indulging Latin America's technological needs.[118]

INTERNATIONAL STRUCTURAL POLICIES
Recent years have seen substantial progress toward an international Code of Conduct on the Transfer of Technology,[119] and we should not divert those efforts in pursuit of structural policies at the international level. Though limited, and perhaps even counter-productive in some particulars, a Code of Conduct will be a helpful first step. I seriously doubt whether additional steps in a structural direction could ever escape the realm of fantasy, so further space need not be spent on the subject here.

CONCLUSIONS

The terms and conditions attaching to transferred technology vary in accordance with assorted structural characteristics. When transferors and transferees are fairly evenly matched in market power, technical capability, and business acumen, we find rather balanced bargaining power which generates terms and conditions largely favorable to both sides of the collaboration. This is true for advanced technology as well as for conventional technology. Indeed, technology transfers are most common and fully refined between advanced countries, and the technology involved is often quite sophisticated.

Less-developed countries may be similarly situated as transferees when the technology in question is conventional and competitively supplied. However, much technology is neither conventional nor competitively supplied, in which cases LDCs scarcely have any bargaining power, unless they happen to be blessed with some particularly valuable resource such as oil or skilled low-wage labor. It is under such skewed circumstances that we find transferors most diligently retaining ownership control, earning especially lucrative profits, charging expensive royalties, tying in intermediate inputs, restricting exports, limiting fields of use, and imposing other assorted restraints of trade.

Because these adverse terms and conditions arise mainly from adverse structural circumstances, attempts to improve the lot of LDCs should focus mainly on structural remedies. Conduct controls also yield benefits, but they are most effective and least damaging when bargaining is fairly well balanced. Conversely, conduct controls are hampered when MNC transferors decisively have the upper hand, and certain peculiarities of the market may even make conduct controls counter-productive. In particular, controls may cut too severely into the profit incentives of transferors, which leads to rejections of transfer demands, and they reduce flexibility. Structural alterations that increase competition among transferors or build robustness among transferees do not share these faults.

NOTES

1. See, e.g., United Nations Conference on Trade and Development (UNCTAD), Restrictive Business Practices (New York: United Nations, 1971, TD/B/C.2/104/Rev.1).

2. For a recent review of laws in developed as well as less-developed countries, see UNCTAD, Control of Restrictive Practices in Transfer of Technology Transactions (Geneva: United Nations, 1978, TD/AC.1/17).

3. UNCTAD, An International Code of Conduct on Transfer of Technology (New York: United Nations, 1975, TD/B/C.6/AC.1/2/Supp.1/Rev.1).

4. George A. Hall and Robert E. Johnson, "Transfers of United States Aerospace Technology to Japan," in Raymond Vernon, ed., *The Technology Factor in International Trade* (New York: Columbia University Press, 1970), pp. 305–9.

5. Derived from Marcus B. Finnegan, "A Code of Conduct Regulating International Technology Transfer: Panacea or Pitfall?" *Hastings International and Comparative Law Review* (Spring 1977), 1:87.

6. Government of Mexico, *Law on the Transfer of Technology and the Use and Exploitation of Patents and Trademarks* (Mexico City, 1972), forward, p. 4.

7. Arthur G. Fraas and Douglas F. Greer, "Market Structure and Price Collusion: An Empirical Analysis," *Journal of Industrial Economics* (September 1977), 26:21–44.

8. F. M. Scherer, *Industrial Market Structure and Economic Performance* (Chicago: Rand McNally, 1970).

9. National Science Foundation, *Research and Development in Industry 1975* (Washington, D.C.: National Science Foundation, 1977), pp. 29–37.

10. Edwin Mansfield, "Technology and Technological Change," in John Dunning, ed., *Economic Analysis and the Multinational Enterprise* (London: Allen & Unwin, 1974), p. 166.

11. Walter A. Chudson, *The International Transfer of Commercial Technology to Developing Countries* (New York: United Nations Institute for Training and Research [UNITAR], 1971), p. 18.

12. *Ibid.*, pp. 16–17. When questioned, paper companies agree. By their admis-

sion, "The technology of the industry is basic and known around the world." J. Frank Gaston, "Why Industry Invests Abroad," in *The Multinational Corporation: Studies on U.S. Foreign Investment* (Washington, D.C.: U.S. Department of Commerce, 1973), 2:19.

13. Chudson, *International Transfer*, p. 19.

14. David Teece, "Technology Transfer by Multinational Firms: The Resource Cost of Transferring Technological Know-How," *Economic Journal* (June 1977), 87:242–61.

15. *Ibid.*, p. 249.

16. David Teece, "Time-Cost Tradeoffs: Elasticity Estimates and Determinants for International Technology Transfer Projects," *Management Science* (April 1977), 23:830–37.

17. Stephen H. Hymer, "International Operations of National Firms—A Study of Direct Foreign Investment," diss. Massachusetts Institute of Technology, 1960; Richard E. Caves, "International Corporations: The Industrial Economics of Foreign Investment," *Economica* (February 1971), 38:1–27.

18. United Nations Department of Economic and Social Affairs, *Multinational Corporations in World Development* (New York: United Nations, 1973, ST/ECA/190), pp. 130–33.

19. Development Centre of the Organisation for Economic Co-operation and Development (OECD), *Transfer of Technology by Multinational Corporations* (Paris: OECD, 1977), 2:157; Gaston, "Why Industry Invests," p. 5; Douglas F. Greer, *Industrial Organization and Public Policy* (New York: Macmillan, 1980), pp. 578–81.

20. U.S. Congress, Senate, Committee on Finance, *Implications of Multinational Firms for World Trade and Investment and for U.S. Trade and Labor,* 93d Cong. 1st Sess. (Washington, D.C.: Government Printing Office, 1973), p. 600. For related data, see Mansfield, "Technology and Change," p. 169.

21. United Nations, *Multinational Corporations*, p. 151, and Senate Committee on Finance, *Implications*, p. 601.

22. United Nations, *Multinational Corporations*, p. 151. See also M. Y. Yoshino, *Japan's Multinational Enterprises* (Cambridge, Mass.: Harvard University Press, 1976), pp. 92, 123.

23. Terutomo Ozawa, *Transfer of Technology from Japan to Developing Countries* (New York: UNITAR, 1971), pp. 31–38; Yoshino, *Japan's Multinational Enterprises*, pp. 69–73.

24. John H. Dunning, "Multinational Enterprises, Market Structure, Economic Power and Industrial Policy," *Journal of World Trade Law* (November–December 1974), 8:587–89.

25. Richard S. Newfarmer and Willard F. Mueller, *Multinational Corporations in Brazil and Mexico: Structural Sources of Economic and Noneconomic Power,* U.S. Congress, Senate, Report to the Subcommittee on Multinational Corporations of the Committee on Foreign Relations, 94th Cong., 1st Sess. (Washington, D.C.: Government Printing Office, 1975), p. 116.

26. Caves, "International Corporations," pp. 12–17.

27. Raymond Vernon, "International Investment and International Trade in the Product Cycle," *Quarterly Journal of Economics* (May 1966), pp. 190–207.

28. W. H. Gruber, D. Melita, and R. Vernon, "The R&D Factor in International Trade and International Investment of United States Industries," *Journal of Political Economy* (February 1967), 75:24–25; Vernon, ed., *The Technology Factor.*

29. Stephen Watkins and John Karlik, *Anticipating Disruptive Imports,* U.S. Congress, A Study for the Joint Economic Committee, 95th Cong., 2d Sess. (Washington, D.C.: Government Printing Office, 1978), especially pp. 8–10.

30. Lawrence H. Wortzel, *Technology Transfer in the Pharmaceutical Industry* (New York: UNITAR, 1971), p. 19.

31. G. K. Helleiner, "Manufactured Exports from Less-Developed Countries and Multinational Firms," *Economic Journal* (March 1973), 83:21–47.

32. Robert B. Stobaugh, *The International Transfer of Technology in the Establishment of the Petrochemical Industry in Developing Countries* (New York: UNITAR, 1971), p. 29.

33. Keith Pavitt, "The Multinational Enterprise and the Transfer of Technology," in John Dunning, ed., *The Multinational Enterprise* (New York: Praeger, 1971), pp. 68–70; Science Policy Research Center, University of Sussex, *The Transfer of Technology to Latin America* (Washington, D.C.: Department of Scientific Affairs, Organization of American States, 1972), pp. 64, 85–86.

34. United Nations, *Multinational Corporations,* pp. 151–52.

35. Testimony of Jack N. Behrman, in U.S. Congress, Senate, *International Aspects of Antitrust,* Hearings before the Subcommittee on Antitrust and Monopoly of the Committee on the Judiciary, 89th Cong., 2d Sess. (Washington, D.C.: Government Printing Office, 1966), pp. 197–98; Y. S. Chang, *The Transfer of Technology: Economics of Offshore Assembly, The Case of Semiconductor Industry* (New York: UNITAR, 1971), p. 21; Jack Baranson, *International Transfer of Automotive Technology to Developing Countries* (New York: UNITAR, 1971), p. 10; University of Sussex, *Transfer of Technology,* pp. 37, 65–66; and Stobaugh, *International Transfer,* pp. 33–35.

36. Yoshino, *Japan's Multinational Enterprises,* p. 155; Senate Committee on Finance, *Implications,* pp. 595–96.

37. Jack Baranson, *Technology and the Multinationals* (Lexington, Mass.: Lexington Books, 1978), pp. 69–94.

38. *Ibid.,* p. 148.

39. For further evidence, see Walter Chudson, *The Acquisition of Technology from Multinational Corporations by Developing Countries* (New York: United Nations, 1974, ST/ESA/12), p. 40.

40. UNCTAD, Restrictions on Exports in Collaboration Agreements in India (New York: United Nations, 1971, TD/B/389), p. 9, table 5, column (4); UNCTAD, Restrictions on Exports in Foreign Collaboration Agreements in the Republic of the Philippines (New York: United Nations, 1972, TD/B/388), p. 14; and University of Sussex, *Transfer of Technology,* p. 13. On the other hand, there is some evidence from Latin America indicating little difference between textiles and

other industries. See Constantine V. Vaitsos, *Intercountry Income Distribution and Transnational Enterprises* (Oxford: Clarendon Press, 1974), p. 56.

41. Baranson, *Technology*, p. 153.

42. *Ibid.*, p. 147. Baranson marshals much evidence from other industries to support this view, including the following:

> In deciding to participate in a transaction which will lead to a transfer of technology, Control Data Corporation considers: 1. The existence and availability of alternate sources of technology, and 2. the stage of technological development of the recipient. Ideally, if the buyer can procure the desired product and/or technology from other sources, CDC can discount most of the negative implications of its making the sale itself. . . . Because CDC has been faced with increased competition, market maintenance and market entry problems it has been encouraged recently to enter into relationships which involve a transfer of technology greater than that which normally takes place in the sale of equipment [pp. 93–94].

43. F. M. Scherer, *Industrial Market Structure*, pp. 366–68.

44. Frederick T. Knickerbocker, *Oligopolistic Reaction and Multinational Enterprise* (Boston: Graduate School of Business Administration, Harvard University, 1973), pp. 42, 53–100, 138–45.

45. See, e.g., Keith Griffin, "The International Transmission of Inequality," *World Development* (March 1974), 2:3–15.

46. See the publication list of the UN Industrial Development Organization (UNIDO). A drug report went so far as to classify countries explicitly into five levels of capacity: (1) countries with no pharmaceutical product manufacturing whatever (a surprisingly large number); (2) countries merely engaged in packaging and dosage formulation; (3) countries with modest backward integration into bulk manufacturing; (4) countries reaching a high level of self-sufficiency (like Spain and Argentina); and (5) countries with well-established drug industries. UNIDO Secretariat, *The Pharmaceutical Industries in the Second Development Decade* (New York: United Nations, 1969).

47. Teece, "Technology Transfer," pp. 251–55.

48. J. R. Basche, Jr. and M. G. Duerr, *International Transfer of Technology: A Worldwide Survey of Chief Executives* (New York: The Conference Board, 1975), p. 5. See also Jack Baranson, *Manufacturing Problems in India: The Cummins Diesel Experience* (Syracuse, N.Y.: Syracuse University Press, 1967).

49. Basche and Duerr, p. 4.

50. A. Cilingiroglu, *Transfer of Technology for Pharmaceutical Chemicals* (Paris: OECD, 1975), p. 40; *The Pharmaceutical Industry and the Third World* (Washington, D.C.: Pharmaceutical Manufacturers Association, 1979), p. 34.

51. Stobaugh, *The International Transfer*, p. 26.

52. See, e.g., Cilingiroglu, p. 45.

53. U.S. Department of Commerce, *Survey of Current Business* (August 1978), p. 23.

54. See, e.g., Oriye Agodo, "The Determinants of U.S. Private Manufacturing Investments in Africa," *Journal of International Business Studies* (Winter 1978), 9:95–107; H. J. Robinson and T. G. Smith, *The Impact of Foreign Private Invest-*

ment on the Mexican Economy (Menlo Park, Calif.: Stanford Research Institute, 1976), pp. 136–37; and Y. S. Hu, *The Impact of U.S. Investment in Europe* (New York: Praeger, 1973), pp. 54–57.

55. Basche and Duerr, *International Transfer of Technology*, p. 5.

56. See, e.g., Paul Streeten, *The Frontiers of Development Studies* (New York: Wiley, 1972), pp. 396–97.

57. Basche and Duerr, p. 7.

58. Ronald Muller, "The Multinational Corporation and the Underdevelopment of the Third World," in C. K. Wilber, ed., *The Political Economy of Development and Underdevelopment* (New York: Random House, 1973), pp. 135–36.

59. C. T. Taylor and Z. A. Silberston, *The Economic Impact of the Patent System* (Cambridge, Eng.: Cambridge University Press, 1973), p. 212.

60. John E. Tilton, *International Diffusion of Technology: The Case of Semiconductors* (Washington, D.C.: Brookings Institution, 1971), pp. 119, 149. For other examples, see Baranson, *Technology*.

61. Details on both may be found in Baranson, *Technology*.

62. *Ibid.*, pp. 103–5. An interesting case that falls somewhere between cells 1 and 2 is the confrontation between Texas Instruments and Japan. TI withheld its integrated circuit technology as a lever to obtain Japanese approval of a wholly owned subsidiary in that country, something contrary to standard Japanese policy at the time. However, Japanese firms succeeded in producing integrated circuits on their own, which undercut TI. TI's remaining trump card, patent foreclosure of the U.S. market to the Japanese, won for it a compromise settlement, "though most of the concessions were made by Texas Instruments." For details, see Tilton, *International Diffusion*, pp. 146–47.

63. P. B. Medhora, "Foreign Investment in India," in I. Litvak and C. Maule, eds., *Foreign Investment: The Experience of Host Countries* (New York: Praeger, 1970), pp. 280–302.

64. Cilingiroglu, *Transfer for Chemicals*; University of Sussex, *Transfer of Technology*; Vaitsos, *Intercountry Income Distribution*, pp. 42–65; and Sanjaya Lall, "The International Pharmaceutical Industry and Less-Developed Countries, with Special Reference to India," *Oxford Bulletin of Economics and Statistics* (August 1974), 36:143–72.

65. Chudson, *International Transfer*, p. 18; Yoshino, *Japan's Multinational Enterprises*, pp. 61–62; Ozawa, *Transfer from Japan*, pp. 5–6.

66. Wortzel, *Pharmaceutical Industry*, p. 25. Note also Daniel Chudnovsky's argument that the lot of Argentine drug firms improved with the decline in MNC drug innovation, in "The Challenge by Domestic Enterprises to the Transnational Corporations' Domination: A Case Study of the Argentine Pharmaceutical Industry," *World Development* (January 1979), 7:45–58.

67. See, e.g., Ozawa, *Transfer from Japan*, p. 12.

68. See, e.g., D. Babatunde Thomas, *Importing Technology into Africa* (New York: Praeger, 1976), pp. 134–75; and Gaston, "Why Industry Invests," p. 26.

69. For an example involving autos, see Baranson, *Automotive Technology*, p. 8.

70. Basche and Duerr, *International Transfer of Technology,* p. 139–44; Thomas, *Importing Technology,* pp. 171–72; W. A. Stoever, "Renegotiations: The Cutting Edge of Relations between MNCs and LDCs," *Columbia Journal of World Business* (Spring 1979), 14:10–11.

71. Chang, *Economics of Offshore Assembly,* pp. 40–41. See also Tilton, *International Diffusion.*

72. Baranson, *Automotive Technology,* p. 10; D. Germidis, ed., *Transfer of Technology by Multinational Corporations* (Paris: OECD, 1977), 2:12.

73. Stobaugh, *The International Transfer,* pp. 30–32.

74. Baranson, *Technology,* pp. 69–94.

75. Greer, *Industrial Organization,* pp. 576–91. Interestingly, the one major exception in domestic R&D is also the one major exception in transferring to LDCs, namely, Du Pont.

76. Ozawa, *Transfer from Japan,* pp. 5–6. India, for another example, transfers textile, wood, and other conventional technology.

77. Basche and Duerr, *International Transfer of Technology,* p. 4.

78. Junta del Acuerdo de Cartagena, *Technology Policy and Economic Development* (Ottawa: International Development Research Centre, 1976), p. 29. See also the TI case in note 62 above.

79. H. H. Camp, Jr., and C. J. Mann, "Regulating the Transfer of Technology: The Mexican Experience," *Columbia Journal of World Business* (Summer 1975), 10:113.

80. L. T. Wells, Jr., "Economic Man and Engineering Man: Choice of Technology in a Low Wage Country," *Public Policy* (Summer 1973), 21:39–42; L. J. White, "Appropriate Technology, X-Inefficiency and A Competitive Environment: Some Evidence from Pakistan," *Quarterly Journal of Economics* (November 1976), 90:575–89; and S. A. Morley and G. W. Smith, "Limited Search and the Technological Choices of Multinational Firms in Brazil," *Quarterly Journal of Economics* (May 1977), 91:263–87.

81. Joel Davidow and Lisa Chiles, "The United States and the Issue of the Binding or Voluntary Nature of International Codes of Conduct Regarding Restrictive Business Practices," *American Journal of International Law* (April 1978), 72:247–71.

82. Robert E. Smith, "Cartels and the Shield of Ignorance," *Journal of International Law and Economics* (June 1973), 81:53–83.

83. See, e.g., Germidis, ed., *Transfer of Technology by Multinational Corporations,* vol. I: Thomas, *Importing Technology,* pp. 134–75.

84. Douglas F. Greer, "Rate Ceilings, Market Structure, and the Supply of Finance Company Personal Loans," *Journal of Finance* (December 1974), 29:1363–82.

85. Sanjaya Lall, "Transfer Pricing and Developing Countries: Some Problems of Investigation," *World Development* (January 1979), 7:59–71.

86. *Ibid.,* p. 68.

87. For a general discussion of the inadvisability of substituting performance

regulation (or negotiation) for competitive structures, see Walter Adams, "The Case for Structural Tests," in J. F. Weston and S. Peltzman, eds., *Public Policy Toward Mergers* (Pacific Palisades, Calif.: Goodyear, 1969), pp. 13–26.

88. V. N. Balasubramanyam, *International Transfer of Technology to India* (New York: Praeger, 1973), pp. 23–25; Howard Davies, "Technology Transfer Through Commercial Transactions," *Journal of Industrial Economics* (December 1977), 26:161–75.

89. UNCTAD, Transfer of Technology (New York: United Nations, 1971, TD/107), paras. 38–39. See also Balasubramanyam, p. 87, for a discussion of ᵧgentlemen's agreements in India.

90. Sanjaya Lall and Paul Streeten, *Foreign Investment Transnationals and Developing Countries* (Boulder, Colorado: Westview Press, 1977), p. 148.

91. Francois J. Lombard, "Screening Foreign Direct Investment in LDCs: Empirical Findings of the Colombian Case," *Journal of International Business Studies* (Winter 1978), 79:66–78.

92. Balasubramanyam, *Technology to India*, pp. 88–89.

93. Eric Schiff, *Industrialization without Patents* (Princeton: Princeton University Press, 1971).

94. Ozawa, *Transfer from Japan*, p. 15; University of Sussex, *Transfer of Technology*, pp. 129, 135.

95. Junta del Acuerdo de Cartagena, *Technology Policy*, p. 20.

96. Douglas F. Greer, "The Case Against Patent Systems in Less-Developed Countries," *Journal of International Law and Economics* (December 1973), 8:223–66.

97. Lall and Streeten, *Foreign Investment Transnationals*, p. 69.

98. For data on the portion of transfers involving patents, see Greer, "Case Against Patent Systems," p. 243, and Germidis, ed., *Transfer of Technology by Multinational Corporations*, 1:228.

99. Josef Wilczynski, "Multinational Corporations and East-West Economic Cooperation," *Journal of World Trade Law* (May/June 1975), 9:266–86.

100. Constantine V. Vaitsos, "The Revision of the International Patent System: Legal Considerations for a Third World Position," *World Development* (February 1976), 4:85–99.

101. Mexico, for instance, recently replaced patents in certain areas with non-renewable investor's certificates, which permit the collection of royalties but deny control over licensing.

102. Chudnovsky, "The Challenge," p. 52.

103. F. M. Scherer, *The Economic Effects of Compulsory Patent Licensing* (New York: New York University, Graduate School of Business Administration Monograph Series in Finance and Economics, no. 1977–2, 1977).

104. Saul Jecies, "Encumbered Industrial Property Rights," *Antitrust Bulletin* (Spring 1976), 21:1–52; Ulrich Loewenheim, "Trademarks and Free Competition within the European Community," *Antitrust Bulletin* (Winter 1976), 21:727–49.

105. Junta del Acuerdo de Cartagena, *Technology Policy*, p. 32.

106. Baranson, *Technology*, pp. 34–38.

107. Germidis, ed., *Transfer of Technology by Multinational Corporations*, 2:222–26.

108. Junto del Acuerdo de Cartagena, *Technology Policy*, p. 50.

109. Baranson, *Technology*, pp. 85–88.

110. Germidis, ed., *Transfer of Technology by Multinational Corporations*, 2:110.

111. Gaston, "Why Industry Invests," p. 80.

112. Tilton, *International Diffusion*, pp. 170–71.

113. *Wall Street Journal*, August 17, 1979, p. 5. Another example is the EEC Commission's blockage of Continental Can's (U.S.) acquisition of Thomassen Drijver-Verblifa (Holland) in 1971.

114. U.S. Congress, Senate, *Export Expansion Act of 1971*, Hearings before the Subcommittee on Foreign Commerce and Tourism of the Committee on Commerce, 92d Cong., 2d Sess. (Washington, D.C.: Government Printing Office, 1972).

115. Antitrust Division, U. S. Department of Justice, *Antitrust Guide for International Operations* (Washington, D.C.: Government Printing Office, 1977), pp. 15–16.

116. Smith, "Cartels"; UNCTAD Secretariat, "Information Requirements for the Control of Restrictive Business Practices Originating with Firms of Developed Countries," reprinted in *Antitrust Bulletin* (Winter 1975), 20:833–85.

117. C. F. Bergsten, T. Horst, and T. H. Moran, *American Multinationals and American Interests* (Washington, D.C.: Brookings Institution, 1978), pp. 230–69.

118. "U.S. Power: The Multinationals," *Business Week*, March 12, 1979, pp. 74–82.

119. UNCTAD, An International Code; Finnegan, "A Code of Conduct"; Sigmund Timberg, "An International Antitrust Convention," *Journal of International Law and Economics* (December 1973), 8:157–84; Steven Chance, "Codes of Conduct for Multinational Corporations," *The Business Lawyer* (April 1978), 33:1799–1820.

Restrictive Business Practices in the International Transfer and Diffusion of Technology

Sigmund Timberg

I. INTRODUCTION

The primary purpose of this paper is to review and analyze those restrictions in technology-licensing arrangements [1] that impede the free flow and use of technology across national boundaries, restrain national and international trade, and adversely affect national economic development policies. The secondary objective is to see what legal machinery would most readily eliminate such objectionable restrictions.

As matters currently stand, the international transfer of technology is the result of thousands of licensing bargains reached between the possessors of the technology, which are usually located in the industrialized countries and are often multinational corporations, and its would-be recipients, located either in other industrialized countries or in the developing countries. Over the years, the developing countries (the so-called Group of 77) have taken the position that they and their nationals are the weaker parties to these bargains, and that the restrictive terms and conditions imposed upon them by the dominant possessors of the technology have been unduly unfair and restrictive and prejudicial to their economic development. For the past five years, the Group of 77 and the industrialized countries (the so-called OECD Group), with the participation of the socialist countries, have been negotiating a Code of Conduct that would eliminate licensing practices that restrict the international transfer and diffusion of technology along lines the developing countries regard as more conducive to their plans for national economic development and for a "New International Economic Order." They also seek protection from the imbalance and abuse of the power that they believe resides in the hands of the possessors of this technology. The licensing practices of which the developing countries complain overlap, to a surprisingly substantial extent, the licensing practices regarded as inimical to the antitrust and competition policies of the United States, the Common Market, the Federal Republic of Germany, Japan, and (as far as international trade is concerned) other members of the Organisation for Economic Co-operation and Development (OECD).[2]

The present status of these five-year-old negotiations is reflected in the latest draft of the Draft International Code of Conduct on the Transfer of Technology (UNCTAD Doc. TD/CODE TOT/14, dated March 28, 1979, which shall be cited henceforth as TOT). This Draft Code represents an emergent international consensus on a list of restrictive licensing practices, some twenty in number, that are considered (despite penumbral disagreements as to definition and coverage reflected in the draft) objectionable because they "unjustifiably restrain trade or adversely affect the international flow of technology, particularly as such practices hinder the economic and technological development of acquiring countries. . . ."[3]

There is still some disagreement over how the code is to be implemented. However, these differences, viewed in the larger context of international law and international relations, are unimportant when contrasted with the areas of substantive consensus. This international consensus is all the more remarkable when one considers:

1. the technical nature of the subject matters dealt with: patents, know-how, antitrust law, national development policy;

2. the conflicting interests involved: those of the patent and know-how owner in obtaining protection and compensation for his property rights and for his investment in research and development (R&D), and those of the technology-exporting and importing countries in obtaining adherence to their heterogeneous and largely uncoordinated national competition and economic development policies; and

3. the difficulties encountered in obtaining a satisfactory patent-antitrust interface even in a single country such as the United States, which has the longest legal history in this complex area of law and economics.[4]

This paper concerns countless individual licensing bargains that are necessarily dependent on their specific business and political milieu. The licensors and exporters of this technology, who currently control it, are part of a socio-economic-political system based on the fundamental premise that individual creative and competitive activity produces the most efficient and best economic results. The would-be recipients of the technology in the developing countries, for reasons unrelated to the technology-licensing process, are in a disadvantageous bargaining position. In these circumstances, the most that can be expected at the international level is the development of a code of conduct that will be acceptable to both sides as fair, because it eliminates licensing practices that unjustifiably restrict competition and national development.[5] There will be left to the final section (XIII) of this paper the considerations supporting the conclusion that the current version of the Draft Code of Conduct is approximating such an acceptable international consensus.

It should not be supposed, however, that the elimination of restrictive practices and conditions from international technology-licensing agreements will automatically bring about the procompetitive and developmental results desired by the international community. The adoption of the Code of Conduct may help in achieving such results, but the code's effectiveness in facilitating the international transfer, use, and diffusion of technology is dependent upon an understanding of the role and functioning of several other important economic and legal institutions, and their realistic treatment. These will be discussed in the next five sections of this paper.

Thus, the next section (II) will deal with the role of unpatented know-how in the international transfer and diffusion of technology and in national economic development. Unpatented know-how is important, even to licensees in the industrialized countries, because of the effect its use has on lowering the costs and improving the efficiency of production. In the case of the relatively unsophisticated technology largely needed by the developing countries, unpatented know-how is of overwhelming importance. Even if patent licenses are also required, know-how may be essential to the effective and economic utilization of the patents. The most imaginative patented inventions may not lead to the goals set by a country's competition or development policy, for these are meaningless unless they lead to commercial innovation. Know-how, of a kind that cannot be incorporated in a patent application, is an essential ingredient of innovation.

Section III describes the role of the Paris Union Convention of 1883, as amended, in facilitating the international diffusion and exchange of technology. With one recent exception,[6] national legal systems are responsible for the issuance and enforcement of patents, which are restricted in legal effect to the territorial boundaries of the issuing state. It is the Paris Union Convention that has converted these national, exclusionary patent systems into an international patent system that makes possible the international transfer, use, and diffusion of technology. The Paris Union also purports to legitimate and harmonize, from an international viewpoint, the provisions of national patent legislation for the compulsory licensing or revocation of patents held by foreign nationals that are not worked, or are inadequately worked, in the issuing state.

Section IV of this paper will set forth the unique significance in U.S. law and practice of trademarks and quality controls in obtaining consumer acceptance and market position for products, and suggests that they can therefore play a prominent role in achieving, for the Group of 77 countries, their objective of developing and expanding domestic and foreign markets.

Section V of this paper discusses what shall be called the "multi-layered bargain," which involves the international transfer, by the technology licensor, of capital, engineering skills, marketing, management, and practical expertise, and other resources needed, particularly in the case of developing countries, to make effective the use of the licensed technology and to promote its further diffusion.

Section VI deals with some of the special problems created by the existence of multinational or transnational corporations (MNCs). These problems arise primarily where the MNCs have dominant power or out of the fact that the parent corporation of an MNC frequently licenses technology to its wholly or partially owned subsidiary, rather than to an independent firm.

Section VII will comment on what seems to be the only other approach that has any substantial potential for correcting the bargaining imbalance between the technology-exporting and technology-importing countries, that of increasing the sophistication of the importers. This task, primarily one for private planners and government agencies, covers a wide variety of factors. These include:

1. the knowledge of all available sources of the various components required to develop and enhance the importing enterprise's production and marketing potential;

2. the rational selection of developmental priorities, having in mind both the resources and the needs of the importer's country;

3. the improvement of general educational levels within the country, so as to lay a proper basis for the use, diffusion, and control of the more technical licensed technology;

4. the strengthening of the country's infrastructure (transportation, electric power, etc.), so as to attract foreign technology; and

5. the realization of the extent to which low standards of living and thin markets necessarily limit the kinds of technology that can be effectively assimilated into the country's economy.

With this background, the paper devotes its next five sections to specific restrictive licensing practices. These are classified according to their effect primarily on: the use and diffusion of technology (section VIII); production under the license (section IX); the licensee's distribution system (section X); and royalties (section XI). These are all vertical restrictions, capable of producing harmful effects if imposed by a single licensor on a single licensee. Section XII deals with horizontal cartel arrangements, on whose objectionability there is genuine international consensus. [7]

The discussion of technology-licensing restrictions that are agreed to as being objectionable under the current draft of the Code of Conduct will enable us to ascertain the overall significance of the areas of procedural and definitional disagreement that remain. Coupled with the discussion in sections I to VII of this paper, it will also put us in a better position to evaluate the extent to which the adoption of such a code would improve the present, admittedly imperfect, system of technology transfer, use, and diffusion. This, as already indicated, will be the function of the concluding section XIII of this paper.

II. UNPATENTED KNOW-HOW AND INNOVATION

The international patent system may be defined as the aggregate of national laws and international treaties and conventions (from the Paris Union of 1883 to the Common European Patent Treaty of 1977) that provide for the granting of patents, and that body of national commercial law and business practices that provide for the licensing and assignment of the patents thus granted.

The international patent system plays an important role in the international transfer and diffusion of technology, particularly in those situations where a technologically sophisticated multinational corporation in an industrialized country licenses or assigns its foreign patent rights to an equally sophisticated MNC located in another country. But even in those cases where the suppliers and the recipients are both MNCs, primary importance attaches, after the basic patents in an industry have expired, to the transfer of the unpatented technology, the so-called know-how, of the licensor.

This know-how takes the written form of blueprints, drawings, specifications, formulas, manuals, memorandums, and letters. It takes the non-written form of visits by technicians to the plants and facilities of the acquiring enterprise, so that advice may be given on how to improve its operations. Or the experts and technicians of the acquiring enterprise may visit the plants and facilities of the technology transferor, so that they may have concrete visual evidence of the practical operation of the recommended know-how. Whatever form the know-how takes, it is usually the end product of years of industry experience and laboratory research and development.

Unlike patents, unpatented know-how has no statutory status. It is legally protected by rules of private (not public) law. Thus, the rules of contract law enable the courts to enforce confidentiality clauses, and other contractual obligations not to disclose trade secrets, that are imposed on employees, licensees, and contractors. Unpatented know-how is also protected by provisions of tort law designed to guard against industrial espionage and the breach of fiduciary relationships.[8] Unpatented know-how loses its protected character when it is no longer a trade secret and falls into the public domain.[9] Because of the especially intangible and elusive character of know-how, there are very few judicial precedents involving its use in contravention of antitrust or competition policy. However, the general assumption is that the licensing of know-how should follow the general antitrust rules applicable to the licensing of patents,[10] with the important reservation that certain monopoly rights inhere in a patentee that do not obtain in the case of the owner of know-how.[11]

The transfer of technology to inexperienced licensees or developing countries usually consists in preponderant measure (and often exclusively) of know-how or unpatented technology. The primary need of the developing countries is to develop low or medium technology industries in order to improve the basic living standards of their people.

Inventiveness and a national patent system that fosters and promotes inventiveness are important foundation stones for the building of an industrial economy, but will not by themselves create such an economy. A great deal more is needed before patents can be commercialized, and inventive concepts and technical ingenuity converted into a functioning industry. That *tertium quid* is the complex of business talents, practices, and procedures that fall under the heading of innovation.

Even in the United States there is concern that the domestic rate of growth of innovation is declining perceptibly, as contrasted with that of German and Japanese industry.[12] For the developing countries, whose primary concern is the introduction of industries and innovation rather than the rate of growth of established industries, innovation is even more vital. Any assessment of the impact of the international patent system on the international transfer of technology is valueless unless it can be assumed that the other factors involved in industrial innovation are present or can be made available.

In defining what is meant by innovation, reference may be had to W. Rupert MacLaurin's brilliant historical analysis of the technology of the radio industry,[13] in which he distinguishes among science, invention, and innovation. The work of the scientist, although basic to all inventions and all technology, is not patentable. A basic, or even an improvement, invention may result in the grant of a patent, but that grant means only that the patent is physically operable, not that it leads to a commercially viable product or process.[14] The ramified network of research and development and business practices and arrangements required to convert a patentable, but merely physically operable, invention into a commercial reality is what is known as innovation. Of the inventors described in MacLaurin's book, only Marconi can be classified as a business innovator, and he was aided by the resources of the British Navy, considerable financial backing, and the brains of the gifted lawyer-politician who later became Lord Chancellor of Great Britain and Viceroy of India.[15]

Innovation has been defined as "the total complex process by which an invention, or an idea, is brought to commercial reality for the first time."[16] John Copp, the former solicitor of one of the world's largest MNCs, which has licensed its technology broadly throughout the industrial and developing world, has defined innovation in the chemical industry as taking the following five forms:[17] (1) the invention of a new product; (2) the invention of a new and better process for making an existing product; (3) new uses for existing products; (4) minor improvements to manufacturing processes; and (5) minor improvements to processes that use the manufacturer's products.

The most immediate and obvious method for accomplishing innovation is research and development. It is especially significant in the pharmaceutical industry. John Dunning points out: [18] "The pharmaceutical industry is par excellence a science-based industry. It has spent, in proportion to its turnover, more on research and development than any other industry, except the aircraft and electronics industries, and no other industry employs a higher proportion of qualified staff."

Hoffman-LaRoche has reported that 11 percent of its total operating revenues is spent by its research division directly, and that, when hidden R&D costs in other Hoffman-LaRoche departments are taken into consideration, this figure would be raised to 16 percent. [19] A great deal of this research cost precedes production of the patentable invention. Statistics on pharmaceutical research show that only one commercially saleable compound emerges out of six thousand to ten thousand chemical syntheses. [20] None of this detail is intended to minimize the importance of patents; there is probably no industry that is more dependent, both for its technological advance and its economic viability, on the patent system. Also, a very high proportion of the costs of developing a drug product are those incurred in the clinical and toxicological testing of the drug so that it meets the standards of safety and effectiveness of the Food and Drug Administration or other regulatory agency whose clearance is required before the drug can be put on the market. [21]

The high cost of R&D is an important factor in the international transfer of technology. As pointed out by Copp: "It is always more profitable to manufacture yourself than to take a royalty for teaching someone else to manufacture." Because levels of expertise are low and workers are not well trained in the developing countries, technology transfers take longer and cost more in them than in the developed countries. [22] Firms with high R&D expenses located in the industrialized countries license their patents and know-how to the developing countries in the expectation that these costs will be recouped by royalties and that these royalties will be commensurate with the royalties that they receive from their licensees in the industrial countries.

The developing countries, with their low national incomes and balance-of-trade problems, frequently regard these royalty expectations as excessive. This is a recognized cause of tension between the technology-exporting and technology-importing countries. It may perhaps be suggested that, if the basic goal of the importing country is national industrial development, current balance-of-payment stringencies and low income levels should not be the decisive factor in defining acceptable royalty rates. The importing country should adopt a cost-benefit analysis that would take into account the long-term benefits in increased productivity, raised income levels, and improved living standards the technology would generate. And, if what we describe in section V as a multi-layered bargain is involved, the supplier, particularly if it has an equity participation in the importing enterprise, should consider as determinative whether its overall return from the multi-layered bargain is reasonable; the royalty rate for its technology would become a secondary consideration.

III. THE ROLE OF THE PARIS UNION

The essential core of the international patent system is the national patent systems of the individual countries. With the exception of the newly established system for the issuance of regional patents covering the nine European Common Market countries,[23] patents are issued by the Patent Offices of individual countries, are enforced according to the national legal system of the issuing state, and are restricted in legal effect to the territorial boundaries of the issuing state.[24] Taken by themselves, the national patent systems contribute to the industrial development of their respective countries, but they do not promote or facilitate the international diffusion and exchange of technology. On the contrary, the national patent systems have tended to be autarchic in nature, in that in practical operation they have favored domestic over foreign patentees.

The linchpin of the system for the international transfer of technology is the Paris Union Convention of 1883, as amended. Article 2 of the Paris Union requires member states to accord "national treatment" to foreign inventors. Under this principle of national treatment, nationals of foreign countries, or others who are domiciled or have effective industrial or commrcial establishments in a country, are guaranteed equality of treatment with the nationals of the country granting the patent.[25] The Paris Union is adhered to by some eighty countries, but the principle of national treatment is so important to the international diffusion of technology that it is followed by some countries that are not members of the Paris Union.

Several countries qualify the principle of national treatment by the "principle of reciprocity"; this also is true both of countries that are and are not members of the Paris Union.[26] Some of the countries that accord national treatment to foreign inventors require a foreign applicant for a patent to designate an agent for service of process or to designate a resident of the country to represent him in all matters pertaining to the patent application and in subsequent legal proceedings relating to the patent. This procedure is authorized by Article 2(3) of the Paris Union.

The practical working of the principle of national treatment is facilitated by another basic provision of the Paris Union (Article 4), which provides for the so-called right of priority. Under this right, an applicant for a patent that has filed a patent application in any one country may, for a period of twelve months after such filing, file a patent application in any other country recognizing the right of priority, and this subsequent filing will be dated back to the date of the first filing.[27] Several countries that are not members of the Paris Union also recognize the right of priority.

Another provision of the Paris Union that facilitates the transfer of patent rights from one country to another is Article 4 bis, which establishes the principle of the "independence of patents." Under this principle, the cancellation or expiration of a patent in one country of the Paris Union does not lead to the cancellation or expiration of a patent for the same invention in another member state of the Paris Union.[28]

The major substantive limitations imposed by the Paris Union Convention on the national patent systems of its member states are to be found in Article 5, which purports to limit the sanctions which national patent legislation may impose where the patent has not been worked at all, or has been insufficiently worked, in the country. But even this provision indicates the extent to which national legal systems control both the issuance of patents and their use after they have been issued. Under the patent laws of most countries of the world with patent systems (with the exception of the United States), provision is made for the compulsory licensing or revocation of patents in the event that there has been no, or inadequate, use of the patent within the country.[29] Article 5 of the Paris Union attempts to standardize, and render more lenient to the patentee, these national compulsory licensing and revocation procedures. It provides that revocation will be resorted to only if the compulsory license that has been granted does not suffice to prevent abuses resulting from nonuse of the patent. It also provides that an unused or inadequately exploited patent is not subject to compulsory licensing until three years after the date of its issuance, or until four years after the date of filing of the application (if the patent was issued within twelve months of filing), and that no patent should be subject to revocation until two years after the issuance of a compulsory license to an applicant. Important as these rules are considered to be, the national patent laws of some member countries of the Paris Union do not conform to the standard laid down in Article 5.[30]

Article 5 also prohibits the forfeiture of a patent on the ground of the importation into a country of patentable articles produced in other countries that are members of the Paris Union.[31] This provision safeguards the rights of patentees against xenophobic national legislation designed to prevent products made abroad under foreign patents from entering local markets.

In concluding this truncated account of the way the international patent system supplies a legal framework for the international *transfer* of patented technology, it should be noted that the principle of national treatment and the auxiliary provisions of the Paris Union do not give preferred status to nationals of the technology-exporting countries.[32] The developing countries, in their effort to accelerate domestic *use* and *control* of the transferred technology, have been pressing for revisions of the Paris Union that would give "preferential treatment" to their own nationals.[33] These proposals are not within the scope of this paper, but one practical observation may be made.

Purely apart from other economic and legal considerations, the enterprises of the industrialized countries tend to place their technology in countries that adhere to the fundamental principles of the national and international patent system, including those of the Paris Union. This is part of the "favorable climate" whose existence influences them to export their technology and invest their capital and other resources abroad. In the light of the relatively limited extent to which patented technology enters into the development planning of the Group of 77 countries, they should, in their own self-interest, be certain that proposed changes in the status quo will not be theoretical in nature and will in practice promote their development plans. Also, they would be well advised not to insist on changes that might lead the exporting countries to refrain from providing the developing countries with needed technology, capital, and other resources. As Douglas Greer pointed out in his paper, the market for transfers of technology to less-developed countries is a relatively small one;

Commerce Department figures on license fees and royalties received from abroad by U.S. firms for the year 1977 show $2,006 million, or 91.5 percent of the total, as coming from developed countries, contrasted with only $177 million, or 8.1 percent, from the developing countries.[34] The common goal of the international community is to stimulate larger flows of technology into the developing countries, and even psychological factors that would hinder such a flow should be avoided except when offsetting economic gains are a clear prospect.

IV. TRADEMARKS AND QUALITY CONTROLS

The countries that have been negotiating the Code of Conduct have agreed on what they mean by transfer of technology, which is defined as

> the transfer of systematic knowledge for the manufacture of a product, for the application of a process or for the rendering of a service and does not extend to the transactions involving the mere sale or mere lease of goods [TOT, p. 3, para. 1.2].

They are also in agreement that transfer of technology transactions involve:

> The assignment, sale and licensing of all forms of industrial property, except for trademarks, service names and trade names when they are not part of transfer of technology transactions [TOT, p. 3, para. 1.3(a)].

However, in light of two prohibitions desired by the Group of 77 and the socialist states, and disfavored by the OECD Group, it may be useful to restate the basic economic and legal assumptions underlying the classical U.S. view of trademarks and quality controls. The two prohibitions are paragraphs 16 and 17 of the current Draft Code:

16. [Use of quality controls]*/*** [35]

[Use by the supplying party of quality control methods or standards not needed or not wanted by the acquiring party, except]*/*** [to meet the requirement of a guarantee or]*** [when the product bears a trade mark, service name or trade name of the supplying party]*/***.

17. [Obligation to use trade marks]*/***

[Requirement to use a particular trade mark, service name or trade name when using the technology supplied]*/*** [; the supplying party, however, has the right to request that its name be mentioned on the product]***.

The two essential factors that enable any supplier to penetrate and expand the markets for its product are the price and quality of the product and its consequent acceptance by consumers. If the product is produced with the help of technology originating with and supplied by a third person, quality control by the latter supplier is indispensable to maintaining the product's reputation and consumer acceptance. Since the development of domestic and foreign markets and increased consumer acceptance of their products are objectives shared by the developing countries, they should favor, rather than oppose, quality control provisions in technology licenses, even if the product does not bear the trademark, service mark, or trade name of the supplying party. Likewise, from the standpoint of the supplier, the reputation of both its technology and its product will suffer if an inferior product is produced under technology it has supplied, even if there is no trademark or trademark-licensing arrangement associated with the use of the technology.

It is gratifying to note that developing countries seem to have accepted the premise, basic to the U.S. law of trademarks, that quality controls are appropriate to licensing arrangements involving trademarks or service marks. Since the U.S. concept of the function of a trademark differs from that of even the civil law countries in the OECD Group, it is worthwhile briefly to restate the U.S. law. Under that law a trademark is not recognized as an independent property right, and it cannot be assigned in gross, but only as part of a going business.[36] It represents the good will that has been built up as a result of the quality of the goods produced under the trademark. Trademark protection is thus part of the private law of fair competition. Trademarks protect consumers by giving them the assurance of quality that attaches to products coming from an established source and by preventing their being deceived by competitive products advertised as coming from that source.[37]

It is to prevent consumer deception that U.S. law holds trademark licenses invalid, unless the owner and licensor of the trademark exercises rigorous quality controls over its licensee by prescribing specifications for the goods and carrying out testing and inspection procedures to ensure that those specifications are in fact observed.[38] Moreover, as a commercial matter, the owner of a valuable and recognized mark will not risk the hurt to its reputation and that of its product by licensing the mark to a licensee that will not submit to adequate quality controls.

V. THE "MULTI-LAYERED BARGAIN"

In section II of this paper, it was shown that, important as the licensing of patents may be to the international transfer and diffusion of technology, there are many industrial areas where the significant technology is unpatented and arises from improvements in production, processing, product development, and use adaptation generated by years of industry experience and painstaking laboratory research and development. However, R&D may not be enough. In many cases, the new product or process covered by the patent is so revolutionary as to require the construction, start-up, and operation of expensive new plants or facilities. The technology involved in the construction and the subsequent operation of such facilities will consist mainly of designs, blueprints, manuals, formulas, and personal technical assistance, but additional patent rights may also have to be licensed.

The construction of new plants will also require capital financing and engineering resources. Typically, outside engineering firms will be called on for the engineering resources needed to construct the new facility. However, in the case of a developing country, the capital may have to be obtained from the transferor of the technology. The transferor of the technology needed to construct the plant, both patented and nonpatented, will have to continue supplying it for a period of time (five years is not uncommon) after the plant has started commercial operations. Inability to obtain necessary capital, engineering resources, and competent technical advice and administrative management will therefore constitute a barrier to the international transfer of technology, even when the host country is in a position to meet the royalty and other patent license requirements of the transferor.

Lowell W. Steele has thus summarized the major barriers to international technology transfer:

1. the investment barrier, arising out of lack of capital resources for building the needed plant or facility;

2. the local adaptation barrier, which involves adapting the product to the local market;

3. the adaptation barrier, which may involve rescaling or modifying the manufacturing process to meet local market needs or the local scale of production; and

4. the technical capacity barrier, caused by the rudimentary level of local technical capacity.[39]

Obviously, the international patent system, either in its present form or as some have proposed it be modified, can do nothing to remove these nontechnological barriers to technological transfer. Unless these barriers are overcome, the international patent system, by itself, is powerless to promote the industrial innovation and the national industrial development desired by the host country.

For either countries or enterprises that desire to make full-scale industrialized use of the imported technology, improved distribution patterns may be necessary. Thus, before the new, or more efficiently and cheaply produced, product can be marketed by the recipient of the technology, the potential of the market must be explored, which in some cases may involve advance testing. Moreover, to bring the product to the attention of industrial users and individual consumers, and to ensure effective marketing, advertising and promotion techniques may have to be utilized that involve the use of trademarks, copyrights, logotypes, and other forms of intellectual property. Such distributive and promotional techniques probably have been developed by the transferor of the patent rights and the industrial technology involved, and are not in the possession of the transferee.

It is only after the necessary R&D, capital outlays, engineering resources, local adaptation, and advertising and promotional efforts have been invested in patented inventions and improvements that the user of the inventions and improvements has met the prerequisites of innovation, that is, has produced a commercially viable product. When the technology importer not only enters into licensing agreements for patents and know-how, but also executes other agreements with the exporter covering the other necessary ingredients of commercial viability and innovation, the totality of such agreements will be referred to as a "multi-layered bargain." Such bargains are not within the purview of this paper, but three brief points concerning their relevance to the developing countries may be made.

Developing countries have a greater need for multi-layered bargains than industrialized countries. For the developing countries, the licensing of technology alone is of limited economic effectiveness, unless at the same time other vital factors of the production and distribution process are made available: physical plant and facilities, capital resources, marketing technology, management techniques, and the training of management, technical, and labor personnel. The cost, value, and impact of the technology transfer, patented or unpatented, cannot be realistically appraised on its own merits, but must be viewed as part of an overall economic package.

The technology exporter, the licensor of the patent rights and unpatented technology used in the production of a product, will in the usual case have innovated and brought that product into its home market, if not to some export markets. In such cases, it controls not only the technology, but also the other resources and factors needed to convert the technology into a commercial reality. The Draft Code forbids the exporter from using its technology as a lever to *require* the importer to enter into multi-layered bargains. But given the "unpackaging" that is the leitmotif of the code and increasing levels of commercial sophistication on the part of the importer, a multi-layered bargain may prove to be the cheapest and most convenient method of facilitating innovation and national development.

It has already been noted that the exporter of patented and unpatented technology expects royalties from the importing enterprise that will appropriately reward it, not only for the inventions it has patented but also for its R&D expense in developing the supporting unpatented know-how. Also, it was suggested that the host country importing the technology should weigh its royalty "cost" against the long-term contribution the technology makes to the overall economic development of the country, and that the exporter should consider the appropriateness of the royalty rate in terms of the total compensation he receives for the multi-layered bargain in which he has been involved. It remains only to make the additional point that, in the case of compensation from a multi-layered bargain, the importing country should take into account the overall long-term contribution to its economy made possible by the bargain in its totality, and place secondary emphasis on the specific contribution made by the licensed technology.

VI. THE ROLE OF THE MULTINATIONAL CORPORATION

It is generally recognized that the MNC has played a leading role in the development of patented and unpatented technology, particularly in the more technologically sophisticated industries, and that they are therefore important sources for those enterprises and countries desiring access to technology. Also, the large-scale financial, technological, marketing, and management resources and expertise available to the MNCs frequently put them in a position to furnish the necessary capital and the engineering, marketing, development, and promotional skills that may be required by the importing enterprises and countries.

It should not be thought, however, that an MNC necessarily has a monopoly on these technological and nontechnological resources and skills. Rather, except in the rare case of single-firm monopolies, there are multiple sources of such resources and skills: other MNCs, independent patent and know-how development companies, smaller firms that do not aspire to MNC status, international engineering firms (some quite large) that are in a position to build plants and facilities and provide follow-up services (and do so even for the MNCs), market research firms and other consulting organizations that produce feasibility studies and advice as to marketing and promotional programs and techniques, financial lending institutions and securities markets that are sources of needed capital.

It is generally considered to be in the public interest, in both the technology-exporting and technology-importing countries, that where there are competitive sources of capital services and skills, such sources remain available and not be unjustifiably foreclosed from access to the market. The motivation for prohibiting the specific restrictive licensing practices that will be examined later in this paper is therefore a dual one: that of the exporting countries in discouraging restrictive practices that restrain competition in the export of technology and of the additional capital and other resources,[40] skills, and services needed to make the technology commercially effective, and that of the importing countries in discouraging restrictive licensing practices that inhibit, restrain, or make more costly their national economic development.

The developing countries have no real problem with procuring all the requisite technology and associated resources, skills, and services from a single source such as the MNC, except when such procurement would inhibit, restrain, or make more costly their own development. They recognize that the availability of competitive sources operates to keep MNCs from unduly restraining trade or imposing overly high charges for their technology and other resources, skills, and services. This is why they so strongly favor the "unbundling" of these factors, but they have no inherent objection to multi-layered bargains, provided that they are offered without compulsion and freely accepted.

The MNC may at times be the only source of the components of the multi-layered bargain, but this factual state of affairs is not one which is susceptible of legal redress.[41] It is probable that the main constraint on furnishing technology, capital, and other services to the developing countries does not lie in anticompetitive agreements or in refusals to deal. Even oligopolistic enterprises want to find new outlets for their technology and to enter new markets, and will compete with each other to do so, provided that they are satisfied that these new outlets or markets will prove to be profitable and compensatory. What keeps the enterprises of the industrialized countries from taking advantage of their technology and entering new markets in the developing countries is the fear that such ventures will turn out to be costly and unprofitable. For these reasons an MNC, which has the financial resources to cope with risky ventures and the business knowledge needed to evaluate the nature and extent of the risks taken, frequently becomes the logical supplier of the technology or the package included in the multi-layered bargain.

Some MNCs take the position that their interests will not be adequately protected by licensing agreements with independent licensees and choose to exploit their technology by means of wholly owned subsidiaries or joint ventures. They regard an equity participation as necessary to compensate them for the economic risk that their investment will not be compensatory and to enable them to exercise proper controls over the use of their technology. Concededly, such a parent-subsidiary relationship raises difficult problems as to transfer pricing and the relative contributions of the technology-exporting and importing enterprises to the tax revenues of their respective countries, problems that do not arise in the case of the transfer of technology to an independent recipient. Such problems are not readily resolved by multinational negotiations and may, like double taxation problems generally, require bilateral country negotiations.

It is not within the province of this paper to probe in depth or detail the complex considerations bearing on the application of the proposed Code of Conduct to restrictions imposed by MNCs on their subsidiaries or, as the Draft Code puts it, "between commonly owned enterprises." However, it may be suggested that the reaching of a compromise between the industrialized and developing countries will be facilitated by disentangling the industrial realities from the ideological and linguistic matrix of the international debate that tends to obscure them.

A starting point is to recognize that the MNC's decision to allow its subsidiary to apply the MNC's technology to manufacturing operations in another country automatically achieves the following objectives implicit in the proposed code:

1. An unhindered international transfer of needed technology to the host country will have been accomplished.

2. The application of the technology to the manufacture of the product will be more effective than if it had been transferred to an independent enterprise.

3. In order to enhance the profitability of its operations, the subsidiary will do everything possible to develop its domestic market, including the adoption of the most effective production and marketing techniques and product adaptations designed for the particular market.

A host country is properly concerned that the MNC use local materials and other inputs in the production process. This does not necessarily conflict with any objective of the MNC. In fact, the MNC's decision as to where to locate its subsidiary may have been based on the availability of appropriately priced local inputs. Of course, where the local inputs are more highly priced than foreign inputs, the host country is faced with the political dilemma common to all countries: whether to subsidize its high-cost domestic producer or to help purchasers and consumers by making lower priced imports available to them.

Apart from their effect on costs of production, licensing practices have the potential for restraining the subsequent trade in the manufactured product. In this connection, reference can be had to the text proposed by the chairman of Working Party I as compromising the positions taken by the Group of 77 and the OECD Group:

> Practices and restrictions between commonly owned enterprises should be examined in the light of the rules, exceptions and factors applicable to all transfer of technology transactions. Such practices may be considered as not contrary to the provisions of this chapter when they are otherwise allowed and are of types normally acceptable for the purpose of rationalization or reasonable allocation of functions between parent and subsidiary or among enterprises belonging to the same concern unless amounting to an abuse of a dominant position of market power within the relevant market, for example unjustifiable restraint of the trade of a competing enterprise [TOT, p. 11, n. 22].

The quoted provision exempts from the application of the code practices "of types normally acceptable for the purpose of rationalization or reasonable allocation of functions between parent and subsidiary." Applying this exemption, for example, to the code's provision requiring the use of local personnel: if the productivity and distributive efficacy of the activity generated by the licensed technology are not to be drastically curtailed, initial control over the operations of the licensed activity should remain with persons having special expertise in production and distribution. Initially at least, as the Draft Code of Conduct recognizes, such expertise may not be available in most of the developing countries. However, it is in the self-interest of the MNC to develop such local technical and management talent. Moreover, the training and development of such local talent, and its placement in responsible managerial and operating posts, is one of the agreed purposes of the Draft Code.

On the other hand, the MNC, as the supplier of the technology, is obliged to act with proper regard for the "declared development policies and priorities" of the importing country and "to contribute substantially to the development" of that country. That obligation is currently spelled out in the Draft Code of Conduct as follows:

> Technology supplying parties when operating in an acquiring country should respect the sovereignty and the laws of that country, act with proper regard for that country's declared development policies and priorities and endeavor to contribute substantially to the development of the acquiring country. The freedom of parties to negotiate, conclude and perform agreements for the transfer of technology on mutually acceptable terms and conditions should be based on respect for the foregoing and other principles set forth in this Code [TOT, para. 2.2(viii)].[42]

There is no immediately apparent reason why the day-to-day specific production, distribution, promotional, and management activities of the subsidiary should conflict with the long-range development policies of the host country. In the first place, the host country usually reviews the license agreement to appraise its consistency with its own publicly held and publicly recognized development objectives. Second, if the market in which the subsidiary is involved is competitive, competition may be expected to prevent unreasonable price fixing and other undesirable restrictions of trade.

The Draft Code recognizes that at times the MNC's subsidiary may have "a dominant position of market power within the relevant market" and that this power may be abused, citing as an example "unjustifiable restraint of the trade of a competing enterprise." It is only in these situations that the code applies. The negotiating countries seem to be verging on acceptance of the doctrine of the "corporate entity,"[43] under which the internal relations between the MNC and its subsidiary are not subject to government review unless those internal practices and restrictions are the occasion for restraining trade or injuring third-party competitors. This approach seems to parallel the way in which the doctrine of "intracorporate" conspiracy has been applied in the United States.[44]

As for the MNCs, it should not be lightly assumed that they and their subsidiaries will not have the political wisdom to conduct the subsidiary's commercial operations in the light of the development expectations of the host country, already expressed in the Draft Code, and of the commercial demands of the domestic market. The host country always has strong sanctions at its disposal if these expectations and demands are not met.

VII. STRENGTHENING THE RECIPIENTS' INFORMATION BASE

The main complaint of the developing countries is the inequality of bargaining power between them and the possessors of the technology they desire. There are two ways of redressing this imbalance. One, to which the remaining sections of this paper are devoted, is to remove restrictive licensing conditions that would perpetuate or increase their competitive disadvantages in negotiating international technology transfers. The other, which will be discussed in this section, is to strengthen their bargaining position.

Most of the factors that contribute to the weak bargaining position of the developing countries are beyond their power to remedy, at least in the short run, because they relate to such factors as scarcity of natural resources, low standards of living, thin markets, undeveloped infrastructure, untrained labor, and low educational levels. But there is one remedy that lies within their control, and that is the accumulation of industrial information and general technical expertise that will increase their bargaining effectiveness.

As has already been indicated, there are many potential sources for the technology and the capital and other related resources and skills needed by the developing countries for the effective use and exploitation of technology. It would therefore be most advantageous for the developing countries to acquire a detailed knowledge of thse potential sources. Not all of the results of such knowledge would be as spectacular as the one noted in Greer's paper: a Mexican licensee in the chemical industry that had negotiated a proposed annual royalty of $4 million down to $2 million was informed by the Mexican Registry of Technology that similar technology could be obtained from a source in another country for an annual payment of \$100,000. On the basis of this information, the Mexican licensee obtained a similar price from the original licensor.[45] This case serves to illustrate the ability of a well-informed licensee to negotiate downward the cost of acquiring technology.

Another technique that is frequently used by industrial purchasers of technology in the industrialized countries could well be adapted to the situation of the developing countries. That is to obtain competitive bids from alternative suppliers of the technology and the other ingredients of the production process, and then negotiate with the supplier or suppliers most likely to satisfy the specifications of the licensee and the general economic and social policy requirements of the licensee's country.

One of the most important objectives of the Draft Code of Conduct under analysis is:

> To promote adequate arrangements as regards unpackaging in terms of information concerning the various elements of the technology to be transferred, such as that required for technical, institutional, and financial evaluation of the transaction, thus avoiding undue or unnecessary packaging [TOT, p. 5].

Three of the most significant licensing restrictions condemned by the Draft Code—the tying-in of the technology license to materials, services, and technology not desired by the licensee—are directed to the achievement of this unpackaging objective.

However, the unpackaging objective will be frustrated, and the legal unpackaging achieved by prohibiting restrictive tie-in licensing practices will be economically unproductive, unless a licensee is able to locate other sources of the materials, services, and technology he does not want to obtain from the original transferor. In view of the importance attached by the developing countries to economic self-sufficiency, the licensee within a developing country should, of course, be aware of domestic sources of materials, spare parts, services, and other industrial inputs. If those inputs are not available within the country, the costs to the licensee may be considerably reduced by taking advantage of the cheapest alternative foreign source of such inputs.

The foregoing observations all involve the acceleration of the learning process on the part of the licensees, technological institutions, and governments of the developing countries, and call for as complete a knowledge as possible of the technological and other problems involved in any new industrial development project. Basic to governmental planning in this area is the avoidance of projects unsuited to the needs and resources of the country. Such business and technical awareness is probably beyond the capacity of individual enterprises and requires the assistance of national and regional institutions that will be able to exchange information and bring relevant knowledge and expertise directly to the persons engaged in launching specific industrial projects.

The market for the international transfer of technology and related resources and skills on the seller's side is basically a competitive one. It is constrained largely by the inability of the developing countries to utilize effectively and to pay for the items they need. The patient and systematic building up of an information base that will enable them to exploit the competitive potential of this "sellers' " market may do more to rectify the imbalance in bargaining power than the elimination of restrictive "terms of trade" that is recommended in the balance of this paper. Any prediction as to the relative efficacy of either of these two approaches to rectifying the imbalance is necessarily speculative, but both approaches should be pushed to the maximum extent practicable.

VIII. LICENSING RESTRICTIONS AFFECTING USE AND DIFFUSION OF TECHNOLOGY*

1. GRANT-BACK PROVISIONS

Requiring the acquiring party to grant back to the supplying party, or to any other enterprise designated by the supplying party, an exclusive license for

* For purposes of convenience and timeliness, the license restrictions dealt with in this and the next five sections of this paper will be described as they are set forth in the latest Draft International Code of Conduct on the Transfer of Technology. Since the purpose of this paper is to describe the general area covered by the restrictive practice, rather than precisely to delineate and define the practice, reference will be made, where feasible, to the draft proposed by the chairman of Working Group I, which will be referred to as ch. draft. Where this is not feasible, a composite draft will be used, with the source of each element of the draft identified as follows:

Group of 77 (developing countries): *

Group B (OECD countries): **

Group D (socialist countries and Mongolia): ***

Since this paper was delivered, the countries negotiating the code have concluded a second conference in Geneva which, among other things, has produced agreement, or a closer approach to agreement, with respect to price fixing, tying arrangements and international cartel agreements (see pp. 111–13, 114–15, and 118–20 below). These restrictive licensing practices will be described as set forth in the amended text of chapter 4 of the TOT Code, as considered by a drafting group as of November 15, 1979.

improvements arising from the acquired technology, or transfer sole title to such improvements, without offsetting considerations or reciprocal obligations from the supplying party, or when such practice will constitute an abuse of a dominant market position of the supplying party; or requiring a non-exclusive grant-back without offsetting consideration or reciprocal obligations from the supplying party (when that practice will constitute an abuse of a dominant market position of that party) [TOT, p. 12, no. 1, ch. draft].

Exclusive grant-backs of the kind described in the first part of the above provision adversely affect the free flow of technology because they lead to a reduction in the inventive and innovative initiatives both of licensors and of licensees.[46] If the licensor is assured that all the inventive product of its licensee will flow back to it, the licensor's incentive to invent and innovate will be dampened. Similarly, the licensee will decide that there is no point in technological exertion on its part, since the fruits of its labors will revert to the licensor.

Patent grant-backs have been criticized on legal grounds as inconsistent with the rationale underlying the patent monopoly, in that they extend the licensor's original patent monopoly beyond its expiration date.[47] Also, regardless of whether grant-backs are exclusive or nonexclusive, they may, as is indicated in the quoted provision, tend to keep the licensor in a dominant or monopolistic position and thereby substantially lessen competition.[48]

That grant-back restrictions may also have adverse effects on national development policies is indicated by the fact that they are considered susceptible of abuse and therefore subject to control by the Andean Group of countries, Argentina, Brazil, Mexico, and Spain, as well as under the laws of the United States, the European Economic Community, and West Germany.[49] However, if the grant-back clauses are nonexclusive in nature and relate to improvements that fall within the scope of the technology granted by the licensor, and the licensor has entered into a similar undertaking to license any further improvements it may develop during the term of the agreement, they are not considered illegal.[50]

2. CHALLENGES TO VALIDITY

[Unreasonably]** requiring the acquiring party to refrain from challenging the validity of patents and other types of protection for inventions involved in the transfer or the validity of other such grants claimed or obtained by the supplying party, recognizing that any issues concerning the mutual rights and obligations of the parties following such a challenge will be determined by the appropriate applicable law and the terms of the agreement to the extent consistent with that law [TOT, p. 12, no. 2].

If licensees are required to refrain from challenging the validity of the patents under which they are licensed, they will have no incentive to invent or innovate within the industrial field embraced by those patents. Also, the unchallenged patents will remain as barriers to entry into the market of unlicensed third parties. It is something of a tribute to the extensive cultural diffusion of antitrust concepts that a practice that was not recognized as illegal by the United States Supreme Court until 1969[51] should have been branded as illegal under the law of the European Economic Community in 1975[52] and should be considered objectionable under the Draft Code.

3. RESTRICTIONS ON RESEARCH
[Unreasonably]**/*** restricting the acquiring party either in undertaking research and development directed to absorb and adapt the transferred technology to local conditions or in initiating research and development programmes in connexion with new products, processes or equipment [TOT, p. 13, no. 4].

4. RESTRICTIONS ON ADAPTATIONS
Restrictions which [unreasonably]** prevent the acquiring party from adapting the imported technology to local conditions or introducing innovations in it, or which oblige the acquiring party to introduce unwanted or unnecessary design or specification changes, if the acquiring party makes adaptations on his own responsibility and without using the technology supplying party's name, trade or service marks or trade names, and except to the extent that this adaptation unsuitably affects those products, or the process for their manufacture, to be supplied to the supplying party, his designates, or his other licensees, or to be used as a component or spare part in a product to be supplied to his customers [TOT, p. 13, no. 7].

These two restrictive licensing practices will be discussed together. While a licensor might well wish to "funnel back" to itself technological improvements or developments generated by its licensees, it is hard to believe that any licensor would wish to restrict a licensee from engaging in additional research, except as incidental to keeping the licensee from entering a field of use for which the licensee is not licensed. It is even more difficult to see why a licensor would restrict a licensee from adapting the licensed technology to local conditions, since the licensee's knowledge of local conditions is one of the main criteria for its selection and the financial impact of such adaptation would be to increase royalty revenues. In some situations, of course, restrictions on adaptations would be necessary to protect the licensor's reputation; such protection is afforded under a provision of the code by disassociating the licensor's name, trade name, or trade or service marks from the adaptation or innovation pioneered by the licensee. To a similar effect, the provision disallows adaptations that "unsuitably affect" the licensed products or processes.

Although restrictions upon the research activities of licensees might have the effect of restraining competition by preventing the licensee from developing new competitive technologies, the only litigated cases that readily come to mind involve horizontal agreements among patentees to exchange patented technology.[53] There have been situations where a restriction on the licensee's research has been ancillary to a program of preventing the licensee from using competing technology or from selling products not covered by the licensed technology, but these latter restrictions are designated as objectionable under another provision of the Draft Code (see p. 113 below).

5. RESTRICTIONS ON USE OF PERSONNEL

[Unreasonably]** requiring the acquiring party to use personnel designated by the supplying party, except to the extent necessary to ensure the efficient transmission phase for the transfer of technology and putting it to use or thereafter continuing such requirement beyond the time when adequately trained local personnel are available or have been trained; or prejudicing the use of personnel of the technology acquiring country [TOT, p. 13, no. 5].

This provision promotes the diffusion of imported technology. It is designed to remove restrictions on the licensee's use of local personnel after the "transmission [transition?] phase." The importance to national development policy of training and using local personnel is clear, and its desirability from the standpoint of the technology exporter has also been noted.

6. RESTRICTIONS AFTER EXPIRATION OF LICENSING ARRANGEMENT

Restrictions on the use of the technology of the country to which the technology was transferred after the expiration or termination of the arrangement, which extend beyond the legal protection of the relevant technology there [TOT, p. 15, no. 14, ch. draft].

This provision does no more than restate the correct practice, under contract law, following termination of a patent or know-how license arrangement, which is that the licensee is then free to use all the licensed information he has received under the license except that which is still protected by patent or by legally valid confidentiality or secrecy clauses. The negotiating industrial and developing countries express this prohibition in ways that differ from that contained in the chairman's draft, but both drafts appear to recognize that unpatented know-how which has entered the public domain or lost its secret character does not furnish a basis for collecting royalties or imposing other restrictions on the licensee. While the principles involved are clear, it is important that they receive international recognition because commercial licensing arrangements do not always accord with correct principles.

7. OBLIGATIONS FOR CONTINUING USE OF EXPIRED PROPERTY RIGHTS

Requiring payments or imposing other obligations for continuing the use of industrial property rights which have been invalidated, cancelled or have expired, recognizing that any other issue, including other payment obligations for technology, shall be dealt with by the appropriate applicable law and the terms of the agreement to the extent consistent with that law [TOT, p. 15, no. 13].

This uncontested provision recognizes an important principle, that the technology importer should be free to use licensed patents after they have expired and licensed know-how after it has lost its legally protected status.[54] Adherence to such a principle obviously facilitates the use and diffusion of the imported technology within the importing state, and leaves the licensee free to handle its marketing and distribution problems without outside direction. Desirable as this provision is from the standpoint of general principle, it is clear that it must be strictly limited to obligations incurred by the licensee for "continuing the use" of the expired industrial property rights, and cannot be applied to any other contractual obligations assumed by the licensee.

In addition, it may be noted that the developing countries favor, and the industrialized countries disfavor, a provision that would ban limitations on the use of technology already imported (TOT, ch. 4B, para. 20). Retention of the licensor's control over the use of licensed technology has certain legal and practical justifications.

On the legal side, field-of-use restrictions have not been successfully challenged even in the U.S. courts,[55] except where they have served as a device for dividing markets among the licensees. Such an allocation of markets is illegal under U.S. law [56] and would be contrary to a key provision of the code described later in section XII.

On the commercial side, there is no challenge to the proposition that the licensor may charge different royalty rates for different fields of application of the technology. Also, a licensee may be considered suitable for certain uses of the technology and not qualified for other, more sophisticated or more dangerous uses. Thus, a licensee qualified to produce a patented pesticide may not be qualified to produce a patented antibiotic drug, even if both products involve the same patented technology. Since all patent and know-how license agreements are bargains between the supplier and the recipient, it is not clear that the licensee's local economy will be seriously hurt if the licensor retains some control over the extent to which his licensee may use the licensed technology.

IX. LICENSE RESTRICTIONS AFFECTING PRODUCTION

8, 9, AND 10. TIE-IN RESTRICTIONS (UNDESIRED GOODS, SERVICES, AND TECHNOLOGY)

[Unduly]** imposing acceptance of additional technology, future inventions and improvements, goods or services not wanted by the acquiring party or [or unduly?]** restricting sources of technology, goods or services, as a condition for obtaining the technology required when not required to maintain the quality of the product or service where the supplier's trade or service mark or other identifying item is used by the acquiring party or to fulfil a specific performance obligation which has been guaranteed, provided further that adequate specification of the ingredients is not feasible or would involve the disclosure of additional technology not covered by the arrangement [TOT, p. 13, no. 9].

This is one of the most important provisions in the entire code because it carries out the code's fundamental purpose to promote the "unpackaging" of technology. It condemns three significant restrictive licensing practices: the tie-in of unpatented raw materials to the technology license, the tie-in of undesired services to the technology license, and the tie-in of undesired patents and know-how to the technology license.

The outlawing of tie-ins of goods (which include unpatented raw materials, spare parts, intermediate products, and capital goods) is in accord with the competition policy of most jurisdictions with functioning antitrust laws. In fact, such tie-ins were forbidden under the patent laws of the British Commonwealth countries and the United States even before consideration was given to their antitrust implications, because they were considered to fall outside the scope of the patent monopoly.[57] In the United States, West Germany and the European Common Market, such restrictions, except in unusual circumstances, are considered to violate the antitrust laws.[58] And they are quite repugnant to the developing countries, because they are considered to have detrimental consequences for national economic development policy and for the domestic economy.

These detrimental effects are summarized in the United Nations report, *The Role of the Patent System in the Transfer of Technology to Developing Countries,* as follows:

194. Most of the goods that are currently produced or planned for production in the developing countries are available on the world market from several sources, and potential purchasers of these products in the developing countries can buy them at world market prices. But when contractual agreements tie part or all of the inputs to a single source of supply, developing countries are deprived of the possibility of exploiting market opportunities and are faced with a price structure determined by the unique supplier. Tied-purchase provisions thus result in a monopoly control of the supply of equipment and other inputs by foreign enterprises, leading to what has come to be known as "transfer pricing", "transfer accounting" or "uneconomic output".

195. By reason of his exclusive position, the supplier is able to charge higher prices than for comparable equipment and other inputs that could otherwise be obtained elsewhere. Overpricing of inputs in this way constitutes a "hidden cost" of the transfer of technology which is much the same as that of aid-tying.

196. Tied-purchase clauses connected with the transfer of technology not only affect production costs through the overpricing of inputs but may have important indirect effects on the import substitution, export diversification and growth efforts of developing countries. When the source of supply is determined by the supplier, rather than by the receiver, of technology, a bias in favour of imports is only to be expected. Furthermore, since the imported technology itself originates in a developed country it is usually ill adapted to factor endowments and the availability of domestic resources in developing countries. Both these factors contribute to raising costs of production in developing countries and rendering the resulting product less competitive in world markets. The high cost of imported technology and inputs imposes a heavy burden on the balance of payments of developing countries. Together with reduced export possibilities, this affects adversely the rate of growth of the economy by preventing backward and forward linkages [footnotes omitted].[59]

There are also judicial precedents to the effect that the tie-in of unwanted services is inconsistent with antitrust policy.[60] The same is true of the "mandatory package licensing" of patients, i.e., the licensor's use of patents desired by the licensee to coerce the licensee into accepting patents he does not want, which is contrary to the antitrust jurisprudence of the United States and the European Economic Community.[61]

It may be noted in passing that the developing countries have favored including in the Code of Conduct a provision, which is disfavored by the industrial countries, that would forbid any license restrictions on the licensee's volume of production.[62] The reluctance of the United States and other industrial countries to curtail this right to restrict production volume is probably based on the legal proposition that such a right is within the patentee's legal monopoly. Fertile as United States law has been in curtailing the power of patentees to impose restrictive conditions on their licensees, the patentee's power to control the volume of the licensee's production has been upheld.[63] One may further speculate that the rationale underlying this power to control production rests on circumstances indigenous to the licensee's home territory, where the patentees frequently compete with their licensees. Presumably, firms licensing their patents to foreign licensees are usually happy to have the licensee produce quantities sufficient to meet the demands of the market it is expected to serve.

A different situation would exist if the volume restriction were imposed as a method of compelling the foreign licensee to restrict its production to quantities sufficient to meet the demands of its home market and to forgo exporting to foreign markets. But this contingency is taken care of by another provision of the code, discussed below, which forbids the imposition of unjustified export restrictions on licensees.

X. LICENSING RESTRICTIONS AFFECTING DISTRIBUTION

11. EXCLUSIVE DEALING ("TIE-OUT" CLAUSES)

Restrictions on the freedom of the acquiring party to enter into sales, representation or manufacturing agreements relating to similar or competing technologies or products or to obtain competing technology, when such restrictions are not needed for ensuring the achievement of legitimate interests, particularly including securing the confidentiality of the technology transferred or best effort distribution or promotional obligations [TOT, p. 13, no. 3, agreed text].

This provision is consistent with the rule of U.S. antitrust law that forbids the use of a patent license as a lever to prevent the licensee from using competitive technology or from manufacturing or selling competing products based on different technology.[64] This provision contains two safeguards for licensors. The first is that they may impose restrictions on the licensee with respect to such competing technologies or products where the restrictions are needed to secure the "best efforts" performance by licensees of their distributional and promotional obligations. The second safeguard is to permit such restrictions where needed to secure the confidentiality of the transferred information. It may be noted that the text of this important provision, a compromise between the freedom of the licensee and his obligation to the licensor that is not unfamiliar to the domestic U.S. scene, is not in dispute among the negotiating countries.

12. PRICE FIXING

[Unjustifiably]** imposing regulation of prices to be charged by acquiring parties in the relevant market to which the technology was transferred for products manufactured or services produced using the technology supplied [composite draft].

Restrictions regulating prices to be charged by acquiring party in the country to which the technology was transferred for products manufactured or services produced using the technology supplied, except when the acquiring party is not subject to competition in the relevant market [TOT, p. 13, no. 6, ch. draft].

This provision forbidding price fixing under technology licenses is important enough to warrant reproducing both the composite draft setting forth the positions of the negotiating countries, and the chairman's compromise draft. The developing countries are in favor of an absolute ban against price fixing under an industrial property license. On the other hand, the industrialized countries favor such a ban only where the price-fixing restriction is "unjustifiable" or the acquiring party faces competition in the relevant market for the product manufactured or the service rendered.

The position taken by the industrialized countries is opposed to that taken by the U.S. Justice Department in domestic U.S. litigation and probably by a majority of the antitrust bar,[65] both of which adhere to the view that the *General Electric* case of 1926,[66] which permitted vertical price fixing of this kind, is as a practical matter dead.[67] It would prohibit vertical price fixing in the one situation where it would be commercially stultifying, i.e., where the licensee's competitors are in a position to take away his customers by offering them lower prices. The provision doubtless testifies to the reluctance of the United States's OECD allies to adopt a per se prohibitory rule, particularly as far as the unsettled area of international trade and foreign industrial property licensing is concerned. Even in the United States, there are members of the patent bar who believe that the *General Electric* case still has some vitality. The United States cannot reasonably expect to embody a Sherman Act interpretation in an international agreement; it can only expect to have the agreement express procompetitive policies. From this standpoint, the draft language of both the OECD Group and the Group of 77 represents a long forward step.

13. EXCLUSIVE SALES OR REPRESENTATION AGREEMENTS
Requiring the acquiring party to grant exclusive sales or representation rights to the supplying party or any person designated by the supplying party, except as to sub-contracting or manufacturing agreements wherein the parties have agreed that all or part of the production under the technology transfer arrangement will be distributed by the supplying party or any person designated by him [TOT, p. 14, no. 8].

The text of this provision is not in dispute among the negotiating countries. It seems to represent a consensus that the selection by a technology exporter of a licensee in a foreign country usually carries with it the assumption that the licensee will take over the marketing and distribution of the licensed product. An exception is made, however, when the supplier desires to use local manufacturing resources to produce a product, but has its own distribution organization or plans for the product thus produced. Whatever the U.S. labor movement may think about Hong Kong, Taiwan, and South Korea, to name the leading "platform" countries that carry out such subcontracting arrangements for U.S. enterprises, there is no doubt that such arrangements make a substantial contribution to the economies of the host countries.

14. EXPORT RESTRICTIONS
[Unreasonable]** restrictions which prevent or [substantially]**/*** hinder export by means of territorial or quantitative limitations or prior approval for export or export prices of products or increased rates of payments for exportable products resulting from the technology supplied [, unless justified]**/*** [, for instance,]** [to prevent export of such products to countries where they are protected by the supplying party's industrial property rights]**/*** [or where relevant know-how has retained its confidential character]** [, or where the supplying party has granted]**/*** [an exclusive right]*** [a li-

cense]** [to use the relevant technology]**/*** [composite text; TD/CODE
TOT/20, p. 13].

Restrictions which prevent or substantially hinder export by means of territorial or quantitative limitations or prior approval for export or export prices of
products or increased rates of payments for exportable products resulting from
the technology supplied, except as to restrictions on exports of such products
to countries where the importation could be legally prevented by the supplying
party or where the relevant technology is licensed for production [TOT, p.
14, no. 10, ch. draft].

This is one of the most important provisions of the proposed Code of
Conduct from the standpoint of the developing countries, because it is
directed against restrictions which would prevent them from developing
their export potential. Such restrictions are felt by these countries to be a
most serious impediment to their efforts to industrialize their economies
and build up their foreign trade balances.

Both the chairman's draft and the composite draft of this restriction
recognize five main devices that are employed by technology suppliers to
"prevent or substantially hinder export": (1) territorial limitations; (2)
quantitative limitations; (3) the requirement of obtaining the supplier's
prior approval for export; (4) the requirement of obtaining the supplier's
prior approval for the export prices of products; and (5) increased rates of
payments for exportable products resulting from the technology supplied.
The specific enumeration of the devices used by suppliers to restrict exports gives teeth to this provision, reduces the need for provisions in the
code directed against territorial and quantitative limitations, and strengthens the provision against price fixing that has just been discussed.

American business should recognize that, were the negotiations on the
Code of Conduct to collapse, U.S. licensees would still be confronted, in
such significant markets as Argentina, Brazil, Mexico, and the Andean
Group countries, with national legislation forbidding restrictions on exports from those countries.[68] In the United States, contractual restrictions
on U.S. exports, even of products manufactured under U.S. patent licenses, have been considered by the Government to violate the Sherman
Act, unless covered by Webb-Pomerene export association immunity.[69] In
the European Economic Community, if they involved exports from one
country to any of the eight other countries of the Community, they would
be considered violations of Article 85 or 86 of the Rome Treaty.[70]

As is apparent from the composite draft of this provision, the OECD countries (with some surprising support from the socialist countries) are opposed to having the ban against export restrictions apply to export to countries where the supplier has a licensee producing under the relevant technology or possesses industrial property rights that would enable it to block the importation of the product. This would leave the supplier with a degree of discretion as to how to develop export markets that is consistent with generally prevailing competition policy. At the same time, it would leave the developing countries free to enter export markets where the technology is legally unprotected. Moreover, it should be pointed out that the Group of 77's position favoring broader export rights for licensees in developing countries could at most help those relatively industrialized developing countries that are already able to fully supply their domestic requirements and could be a disservice to those countries still attempting to realize their programs for self-sufficiency and import substitution.[71]

15. RESTRICTIONS ON PUBLICITY

Restrictions [unreasonably]** regulating the advertising or publicity by the acquiring party except where restrictions of such publicity may be required to prevent injury to the supplying party's goodwill or reputation where the advertising or publicity makes reference to the supplying party's name, trade or service marks, trade names or other identifying items, or for legitimate reasons of avoiding product liability when the supplying party may be subject to such liability, or where appropriate for safety purposes or to protect consumers, or when needed to secure the confidentiality of the technology transferred [TOT, p. 15, no. 12].

This provision, agreed on by the negotiating countries except as to one word, does not have much importance from the standpoint either of antitrust or national development policy. However, it does promote a climate of fair dealing by delineating, in rational and generally acceptable fashion, the areas in which the supplier of technology is justified in imposing restrictions on the licensee's advertising and publicity. The rest of the field is left to the discretion of the licensee, who is in a better position to appraise the effectiveness of advertising and promotion in reaching his local market.

XI. LICENSING RESTRICTIONS AFFECTING ROYALTY RATES

2. CHALLENGE TO VALIDITY (REPEAT)

[Unreasonably]** requiring the acquiring party to refrain from challenging the validity of patents and other types of protection for inventions involved in the transfer or the validity of other such grants claimed or obtained by the supplying party, recognizing that any issues concerning the mutual rights and obligations of the parties following such a challenge will be determined by the appropriate applicable law and the terms of the agreement to the extent consistent with that law [TOT, p. 12, no. 2].

This provision was discussed earlier as having an adverse effect on the use and diffusion of technology. Here it is sufficient to note that, regardless of whether the licensee is located in an industrial or in a developing country, a successful challenge of patent validity carries with it the important commercial consequence that the licensee (and others in the country similarly situated) is relieved from further royalty payments for the invalidated patent.[72]

16. PAYMENT AFTER EXPIRATION OF PROPERTY RIGHTS
Requiring payments or imposing other obligations for continuing the use of industrial property rights which have been invalidated, cancelled or have expired, recognizing that any other issue, including other payment obligations for technology, shall be dealt with by the appropriate applicable law and the terms of the agreement to the extent consistent with that law [TOT, p. 15, no. 13].

The effect of this uncontested provision, in leaving the technology importer free, without restrictive conditions or obligations, to use the licensed patent after it has expired or to use the know-how after it has lost its legally protected status, has already been noted. As to the demise of the obligation to pay royalties, the United States Supreme Court in 1964 held as a matter of patent law and without reference to antitrust considerations, that to require royalties to be paid on expired patents was per se illegal,[73] and other jurisdictions have followed suit.[74]

XII. INTERNATIONAL CARTEL ARRANGEMENTS

17 to 22. HORIZONTAL RESTRICTIONS ON TERRITORIES, QUANTITIES, PRICES, CUSTOMERS, MARKETS, AND ACCESS TO NEW TECHNOLOGY
Restrictions on territories, quantities, prices, customers or markets arising out of patent pool or cross-licensing agreements or other international transfer of technology interchange arrangements among technology suppliers which unduly limit access to new technological developments or which would result in an abusive domination of an industry or market with adverse effects on the transfer of technology, except for those restrictions appropriate and ancillary

to co-operative arrangements such as co-operative research arrangements [TOT, draft code as of November 16, 1979, p. 13, no. 11].

The Draft Code is directed primarily at vertical restrictions imposed by the technology suppliers on their licensees. This is the only provision of the Draft Code that prohibits horizontal restrictive agreements and arrangements or, as they are more popularly known, international cartels. It is especially important because it prohibits six kinds of licensing restrictions that adversely affect the transfer and use of technology, and restrain the production and subsequent trade and distribution of the products produced under the technology. They may impair potentials for national economic development as well.

A little history may prove helpful in understanding the large subject covered by a few lines of the proposed Draft Code. As a consequence mainly of legislative investigations commenced at the beginning of World War II by the United States, there was uncovered a massive amount of evidence showing how, in industry after industry, international cartels based on patent and process licensing agreements were adversely affecting the free flow and the levels of international trade and undermining the competition policies of the industrialized countries.[75] Later studies revealed that international cartels could also have harmful effects on the economies of the developing countries.[76] Shortly after World War II, efforts to develop international machinery for the prevention and control of international cartels (or, in alternative language, restrictive business practices affecting international trade) were initiated. These took the form of chapter V of the Havana Charter for an International Trade Organization, first proposed in 1946,[77] and a Draft Convention on Restrictive Business Practices developed by a ten-nation Committee of the Economic and Social Council, which started its deliberations in 1951 and made a unanimously favorable report to the ECOSOC in 1953.[78] In the post-World War II years, a number of countries developed new antitrust legislation.[79]

The specific proposals for international machinery to prevent and regulate international cartels never materialized, but they were part of the background (even as to language) that led to the adoption in 1957 of Articles 85 and 86 of the Rome Treaty,[80] which established a comprehensive system for the regulation and prevention of restrictive business practices affecting trade among the originally six, and now nine, member states of the European Economic Community. The establishment of the EEC coincided with growing international awareness that not only international cartels, but also MNCs possessing market power, could unreasonably restrain trade.[81] The rapid development of EEC antitrust law during the 1960s and 1970s established that arrangements by technology suppliers of any substance that interpose barriers to trade among the EEC's member states, whether of a horizontal or (where the supplier has a dominant position) of a vertical character, are prohibited by Articles 85(1) and 86 of the Rome Treaty. Such restrictions cannot be justified as an exercise of industrial property rights, but only under Article 85(3) of the treaty.[82]

In the United States, in a series of landmark court cases directed against international cartels, the six kinds of horizontally contrived restrictions covered by the provision in the Draft Code of Conduct were held to violate the Sherman Act, over the objection of defendants who claimed that they were participating in legally permissible patent and intellectual property licensing arrangements.[83] It has for a long time been accepted U.S. law that patent pools, cross-licensing agreements, and patent interchanges among competing firms are illegal if they impose unreasonable restraints on territories, quantities, prices, customers, markets, and the transfer and use of technology.[84]

The international consensus already reflected in U.S. and EEC antitrust law would be strengthened by the adoption of this provision by the international community as a whole, even if its adoption were not accompanied by enforcement machinery such as that of the United States and of the EEC.

XIII. IMPLEMENTATION OF AN INTERNATIONAL CONSENSUS

While, as noted earlier, the Draft Code of Conduct embodies a remarkable consensus on twenty-odd restrictive licensing practices that are branded as objectionable, there is disagreement as to the implementation of the code. Thus, the developing countries propose, with respect to any of these otherwise objectionable practices, that they be deemed valid if,

> based upon exceptional circumstances, the competent national authorities of the technology acquiring country decide that it is in its public interest and that on balance the effect on its national economy will not be adverse [TOT, p. 17, section C, ch. draft].

Even the socialist countries temper this exemptive provision with the further safeguard that the practice have "no substantial adverse effect on other countries" (*ibid.*).

The foregoing proposal is evidence of an understandable apprehension on the part of the developing countries that exceptional circumstances may arise that will justify a departure from the terms of the Code of Conduct. If the circumstances are truly exceptional and sporadic, the proposed code will continue to serve a useful purpose. But no country should be under any illusion but that arbitrary and unjustified applications of this escape hatch will destroy the Code of Conduct's acceptance and effectiveness, and every application of it will tend to weaken the code.

The industrial countries on their part are understandably skeptical that an inflexible and binding code can fairly and adequately cope with all the contingencies and public interest considerations that are likely to arise on the untidy and often turbulent international scene. This skepticism is reflected in their unwillingness to agree that the code shall have a binding character.[85] However, this unwillingness is no more conclusive that the Code of Conduct will not prove successful in practical operation than the reservation by the developing countries of the power to carve out exceptions to the code "in exceptional circumstances." An international agreement of the kind involved in the Draft Code of Conduct has a politically, psychologically, and morally obligatory aspect that is frequently lacking in more formal legally binding agreements. Publicity is a strong sanction in international affairs,[86] particularly when it involves parties that will be engaged continually in the process of international bargaining. It is not to be lightly assumed that even powerful MNCs will disregard with impunity a Code of Conduct approved by the international community, since these MNCs desire to project an image of fairness and responsibility, and the proposed code consists of provisions that have a wide acceptance in contemporary antitrust jurisprudence and promote a climate of fair and equitable dealing between licensors and licensees.

Moreover, for developing countries, the Code of Conduct will be a document that can be effectively used when they review and clear (as is the practice among many of the relatively advanced developing countries) international patent and know-how license agreements for their conformity with national development policy.[87] Similarly, the technology-exporting countries can look upon such a document as a help in applying and harmonizing their foreign economic policies with respect to the international transfer and use of technology. Finally, the MNCs should evaluate the

Draft Code of Conduct not on the basis of the extent to which it derogates from the full rights that they would like to have as the possessors of technology, but in terms of the power of national states to prescribe limitations on those rights that are far in excess of the moderate limitations imposed by the code.

By actual count, the Group of 77 and the OECD Group are agreed or virtually agreed on the language of six of the sixteen vertical licensing restrictions deemed objectionable under the Draft Code. The remaining ten and the six horizontal licensing restrictions condemned under the Draft Code would be banned by the Group of 77 without qualification, whereas the OECD Group would condemn them only where they are "unreasonable" or "unjustifiable."

It may be noted that there is no risk in the Group of 77's insistence on its more inflexible "per se" approach because it also insists on retaining the power to enter into restrictive licensing arrangements "in exceptional circumstances" (see p. 120 above). But history is probably the best justification for the OECD Group's insistence, on the basis of its longer experience with such problems, that certain restrictive licensing practices be condemned only when "unreasonable" or "unjustifiable."

There is probably no country as historically wedded as the United States to the concept that certain restrictive business practices are per se illegal. But when the Havana Charter and the 1953 Draft Convention on Restrictive Business Practices were supported by the United States and other countries, the one necessary concession that had to be made by the United States was that all restrictive business practices would be held invalid only on the basis of their demonstrated harmful effects.[88] Experience has demonstrated the wisdom of the U.S. courts, who early concluded that the Sherman Act, a statute on its face challenging all "restraints" on U.S. foreign and domestic commerce, was in fact directed only at "unreasonable" restraints.[89] Only two years ago, the United States Supreme Court unequivocally overruled a decision, reached by it only ten years earlier, that allocations of markets and customers vertically imposed by suppliers on their distributors and dealers were per se illegal, and decided that their legality should be adjudged by the "rule of reason."[90] Subsequently, the Supreme Court has ruled that the legality of two other restrictive practices that were argued to be per se antitrust violations, price fixing by a copyright pool and agreements not to compete by members of a professional association, should be decided on the basis of the "rule of reason."[91]

There is no rule more frequently enunciated than that tie-ins of unpatented materials to a patent license are per se violations of the antitrust laws when they affect an appreciable amount of trade,[92] yet there are cases where the U.S. courts, applying considerations of competition policy, have made exceptions to the per se rule and allowed tie-ins.[93]

As a practical matter, in view of the legal risks involved, enterprises that transfer technology will be most careful before concluding that an otherwise objectionable practice is "reasonable" or "justifiable." The primary consideration in an international agreement is good faith adherence to its spirit rather than the literal enforcement of its letter. In this light, the impressive consensus of agreement achieved by the Draft Code will not be substantially diminished if the longer experience of the OECD Group is taken into account and the cautious wording of "reasonably" and "unjustifiably" desired by them is retained.

There are linguistic imperfections in the proposed Code of Conduct that are unavoidable in any document drafted by an international committee. There are linguistic differences between versions of provisions favored by the Group of 77 and those favored by the OECD countries, differences that would be important if they constituted a national legislative mandate to be interpreted by brief writers for parties involved in national patent or antitrust litigation. However, in the context of a nonbinding international agreement expressive of an international consensus, and as a guideline to enterprises that wish to steer a fair and equitable course in the international licensing of technology (between the Scylla of extreme antitrust policy and the Charybdis of extreme development policy), these differences are relatively insubstantial.

Of course, the morally and politically compelling obligations of the Draft Code of Conduct cannot be equated with the legally enforceable obligations regarding restrictive business practices imposed by Articles 85 and 86, the antitrust provisions of the Rome Treaty establishing the European Economic Community. The Community is a political grouping with basically homogeneous economic, political, social, and cultural traditions. It was established in order to accomplish the procompetitive objective of eliminating all forms of barriers to trade, including restrictive business practices, among its member states. To achieve this purpose, those states surrendered their sovereign right to control and regulate trade to a supranational entity, in whose organs (the Commission, the Council of Ministers, the High Court in Luxembourg) and in whose administrative and judicial procedures they had confidence. There is no such homogeneity of tradition either among other industrial countries or among the developing countries, no such willingness on the part of states negotiating the Code of Conduct to surrender their sovereign powers, and no international institutions commanding the kind of respect accorded to those that have been established in the European Economic Community.

The true measure of the significance of the Draft Code of Conduct is the extent to which it is more effective than the Draft Convention on Restrictive Business Practices, drafted in 1953 by a representative but also largely expert committee consisting of the representatives of six industrial and four developing countries. That instrument dealt with the entire range of restrictive business practices, but it was limited, in jurisdiction and scope, to those engaged in by one or more commercial enterprises possessing "effective control of trade among one or more countries in one or more products . . . affecting international trade which restrain competition, limit access to markets, or foster monopolistic control, whenever such practices have harmful effects on the expansion of production or trade, in the light of the objectives set forth in the Preamble to this Agreement."[94]

The objectives set forth in the preamble were broader than, and somewhat different from, those set forth in the Draft Code:

1. To promote the reduction of barriers to trade, governmental and private, and to promote on equitable terms access to markets, products, and productive facilities;

2. To encourage economic development, industrial and agricultural, particularly in under-developed areas;

3. To contribute to a balanced and expanding world economy through greater and more efficient production, increased income and greater consumption, and the elimination of discriminatory treatment in international trade;

4. To promote mutual understanding and co-operation in the solution of problems arising in the field of international trade in all its aspects.[95]

Concerning the standard laid down in the 1953 Draft Convention, this writer has commented:

This was in retrospect a rather diffuse standard, incorporating economic and social assumptions and policies that are traditionally excluded from antitrust treatment by countries with developed antitrust systems. It led the United States to insist that the Convention leave individual countries like it free to enforce their own national statutes or decrees. The broad standards adopted by the U.N. Draft Convention concealed the lack of agreement among its members as to the purposes and aims of antitrust policy. This lack of comparability among national antitrust policies, legislation and enforcement procedures was the ground assigned by the U.S. State Department in 1955 for withdrawing the adherence of the United States to an agreement which it had sponsored in 1951.[96]

Enforcement of the 1953 Draft Convention was entrusted to the participating national governments. But it was provided, as a prelude to such enforcement, that a factual investigation would be undertaken by an international agency. That investigation was to take the form of an adversary procedure, with a member government filing a complaint against a restrictive business practice, either on its own behalf or on behalf of enterprises affected by the practice; a preliminary investigation by the agency's secretariat; and an opportunity for a hearing to be afforded in due course to the government of the national enterprise responsible for the restrictive practice.[97] It was the obligation of the member governments to present the complaint, conduct their own investigations, and make available to the international agency the reports and information requested by that agency.[98]

Implementation of the 1953 Draft Convention would have required, on a case-by-case basis:

1. the determination whether the enterprise or enterprises involved possessed effective control over the international trade in a product;

2. the determination whether the restrictive practice restrains competition, limits access to markets, or fosters monopolistic control;

3. the reconciliation of diverse, and at times conflicting, national viewpoints concerning the definition of "restraint of competition" and "monopolistic control";[99]

4. the determination whether the restrictive business practice in question has "harmful effects on the expansion of production or trade"; and

5. the determination whether the harmful effects "on the expansion of production or trade" might be counterbalanced by beneficial effects with regard to "economic development," "greater and more efficient production," or "the elimination of discriminatory treatment in international trade" (whatever the last-mentioned might mean), to list three of the other broadly worded objectives of the 1953 Draft Convention.

These difficult determinations were to be reached through an adversary, but nonjudicial, procedure, on the basis of evidence and information supplied by the governments that were attacking the restrictive business practice and by the governments of the enterprise or enterprises responsible for the practice. The progress of the Draft Convention in achieving practical guidelines for the international business community would have been glacial indeed, given the selective nature of such case-by-case enforcement, the complex and controversial nature of the policies and interests to be reconciled, the scope of the information to be evaluated, the dependence of the adversary procedure on information to be obtained from national governments largely without prior experience in collecting such information, and the necessarily slow tempo of international quasi-diplomatic proceedings.

By way of contrast, adoption of the Draft Code of Conduct will produce an international consensus that twenty or so restrictive licensing practices have harmful effects on the international transfer of technology and its subsequent use in production and distribution and should therefore be avoided.[100] This consensus will have been achieved in the especially difficult area where technology transferors and their licensees have differing expectations as to their respective rights and obligations, and in the face of the diverse economic, political, and legal systems and objectives of the negotiating countries. It is submitted that the progress of international law and the security of international technology transfers are better promoted by the kind of rule setting implicit in the Draft Code than in the case-by-case application of broad and, at times, irreconcilable standards to facts that can be developed only by protracted investigatory procedures, such as characterized the last effort, more than twenty-five years ago, to obtain a worldwide consensus through the 1953 Draft Convention.

A final word may be said concerning the interest of the American business community and the developing countries in political and economic stability, without which there can be no international trade and investment. The hard bargaining that has taken place over the Draft Code on the Transfer of Technology for the past five years is evidence that both sides of the bargaining table are concerned with entering into agreements for the transfer of technology and developing guidelines and rules that will reflect the competitive policies of the industrialized countries and the national development policies of the developing countries. Considering the possible alternatives in the international community, both the negotiating governments and their respective enterprises would be well advised to persist in the economic and political dialogue that has progressed so far and bring it to a fruitful close, even if, as is apparent, both sides will have to make concessions.

There are disruptive forces in the Third World with whom dialogue of this kind is not possible. A recent conference held by the United Nations Industrial Development Organization in New Delhi concluded with a somewhat Kafkaesque demand for $300 billion from the industrialized countries for the purpose of industrializing the economies of the developing countries.[101] This unilateral demand is a dead end, permitting no further dialogue, either political or economic. In the interests of the security of international transactions and of international relations, the dialogue on the Code of Conduct on the Transfer of Technology should continue and be pressed to a conclusion.

NOTES

1. The concern of this paper is not only with the licensing of patents and unpatented technology, but also with assignments and sales of technology. However, the great bulk of technology transfers take the form of licensing arrangements. Moreover, unlike licensors, assignors and sellers of technology are not as likely to impose conditions that raise problems under the national legal systems of the sellers and the purchasers of the technology.

2. Market dominance, at least under U.S., West German, and European Economic Community law, is a factor to be taken into account in appraising the antitrust legality of a licensing practice. Market dominance is a function of the market structure for a relevant product or process, and does not exist in the case of competitively structured industries and arguably in a number of oligopolistic industries. See Douglas F. Greer's paper in this volume, "Control of Terms and Conditions for International Transfers of Technology to Developing Countries." However, the issue of dominance is largely irrelevant from the standpoint of this paper, which proceeds from the premise, based on the competition policies of the United States and other industrial countries, that licensing restrictions may be objectionable even where imposed by nondominant licensors.

3. Draft International Code of Conduct on the Transfer of Technology (hereinafter referred to as TOT Code), UN Doc. TD/CODE TOT/14 (1979), p.11, n. 22 (draft of chairman of Working Party I).

4. Note the differing philosophies for reconciling the conflict between patent and antitrust law that are described in Sigmund Timberg, "Patents and Antitrust—Different But Compatible," APLA *Quarterly Journal* (Winter 1974), pp. 8–12.

5. See the last section of this paper on implementation. The situation here is

somewhat analogous to that of other areas involving international trade, where the primary law involved is the law of contracts and the basic contribution that can be made at the international level is to develop "terms and conditions" of trade.

6. The European Patent, see note 23 below.

7. The TOT Code and this paper deal only with international cartels based on patent and licensing arrangements, and not with OPEC or the quinine, dyestuffs, and beet sugar cartels successfully prosecuted by the European Economic Community, or the uranium cartel that has provoked such intense international protests and friction during the last few years.

8. *See* Roger Milgrim, *Trade Secrets* (New York: Mathew Bender, 1978), §1.09, pp. 1–42; E. I. du Pont de Nemours Powder Co. v. Masland, 244 U.S. 100 (1917); Kewanee Oil Co. v. Bicron Corp., 416 U.S. 470, 474–76 (1974); Imperial Chemical Industries, Ltd. v. National Distillers & Chem. Corp., 342 F.2d 737 (2d Cir. 1965) (bulk of information in public domain, yet trade secret); Speedy Chemical Products, Inc. v. The Carter's Ink Co., 306 F.2d 328 (2d Cir. 1962) (confidential relation may be implied); Wilkes v. Pioneer American Insurance Company of Fort Worth, Texas, 383 F.Supp. 1135 (D.S.C. 1974).

9. L. S. Donaldson Co. v. La Maur, Inc., 299 F.2d 412, 425 (8th Cir.), *cert. denied,* 371 U.S. 815 (1962); Wilson Certified Foods, Inc. v. Fairbury Food Products, Inc., 370 F.Supp. 1081, 1083–84 (D. Neb. 1974).

10. Restraints in international licensing agreements may be upheld if reasonably "ancillary" to the grant of the license, Shin Nippon Koki Co. v. Irvin Industries, Inc., 186 U.S.P.Q. 296 (N.Y. Sup. Ct. 1975); *cf.* A. & E. Plastik Pak Co. v. Monsanto Co., 396 F.2d 110 (9th Cir. 1968) (a domestic case). For the "reasonable ancillary restraints" defense to apply to know-how, the following conditions must be satisfied:

(1) the subject matter of the license is substantial, valuable, secret know-how;
(2) such restraint is limited to the "life" of the know-how; i.e., the period during which it retains its secrecy; and
(3) such restraint is limited to those products only which are made by use of the know-how.

186 U.S.P.Q. at 298.

11. A patent is a constitutionally protected monopoly, conferring on its owner, for the seventeen-year period following its issuance, the legal right to exclude any other person from practicing the patented invention, whether it be a product, process, or use patent. Antitrust difficulties arise, not from the prosecution of patent infringement proceedings, but from the presence of anticompetitive conditions in patent license agreements.

12. Under presidential direction, a U.S. governmental task force has been working on this problem, as well as an Advisory Committee on Industrial Innovation from the private sector, convened by and reporting to the Secretary of Commerce.

13. W. Rupert MacLaurin, *Invention and Innovation in the Radio Industry* (New York: Macmillan, 1949).

14. Sigmund Timberg, "Equitable Relief under the Sherman Act," *University of Illinois Law Forum* (Winter 1950), p. 647.

15. See H. Montgomery Hyde, *Lord Reading* (New York: Farrar, Straus and Giroux, 1967).

16. Alfred E. Brown, "Invention and Innovation—What's Ahead," in Marcus B. Finnegan and Robert Goldscheider, eds., *The Law and Business of Licensing* (New York: Boardman, 1977), 1:445.

17. John Copp, "International Licenses of Chemical Technology," in *ibid.*, 2:734.21.

18. John Dunning, *Science, Industry and the State* (1965), pp. 15–34, cited in Florian Von Oertzen, "Licensing Opportunities in the International Pharmaceutical Company," in *ibid.*, 1:506.155.

19. Von Oertzen, *ibid.*

20. *Ibid.*

21. Harold A. Clymer, "The Changing Costs and Risks of Pharmaceutical Innovation," ch. 6 in Joseph D. Cooper, ed., *The Economics of Drug Innovation* (1969), pp. 116, 117, 120.

22. Lowell W. Steele, "Barriers to Technology Transfer," in Finnegan and Goldscheider, *Law and Business of Licensing*, 2:734.62.

23. The European Patent Convention, which came into effect October 7, 1977, established a supranational entity, the European Patent Office, which is physically located in Munich and has the authority to issue a European Patent. However, the European Patent is effective only in those countries subscribing to the convention that have been designated by the patentee at the time it filed its European Patent Application. Moreover, a European Patent is to be construed and enforced according to national law.

24. Aluminum Co. of America v. Sperry Products, Inc., 285 F.2d 911, 925 (6th Cir. 1960).

25. See the report prepared jointly by the United Nations Department of Economic and Social Affairs, the United Nations Conference on Trade and Development (UNCTAD) Secretariat, and the International Bureau of WIPO, *The Role of the Patent System in the Transfer of Technology to Developing Countries* (New York: United Nations, 1975, Sales no. E.75.II.D6), p. 47. For this and succeeding footnotes, the reader interested in a fuller report on the Paris Union may wish to refer to an earlier UN report, bearing the same title and published in 1964 by the UN Department of Economic and Social Affairs, for which this author wrote the legal chapters. There are also economic approaches in the earlier report that the reader may find worth exploring.

26. United Nations, *Role of Patent System*, p. 9.

27. *Ibid.*, p. 44.

28. *Ibid.*

29. *Ibid.*

30. *Ibid.*, pp. 19 et seq.

31. *Ibid.*, p. 44.

32. In this respect, the structure of the international patent system is in marked contrast to what is known as the "minimum standard" of international law, which has been applied to the expropriation of foreign investments and has evoked so much criticism from the developing countries (particularly those in Latin America), because it discriminates in favor of foreign, and against domestic, nationals. See Georg Schwarzenberger, "The Principle and Standards of International Economic Law," in vol. 117, *Recueil des Cours,* Hague Academy of International Law, 1966-I (Leyden: Sijthoff, 1967), p. 78.

33. This standard, which authorizes preferential treatment for the nationals of the recipient countries and discrimination against the nationals of the supplying countries, is called by Schwarzenberger the "standard of equitable treatment." He justifies it on the same basis as do the developing countries, that it "may involve formal inequity and discrimination to attain substantive equality and justice on the level of community ethics." Regardless of how Schwarzenberger or other proponents of the "New Economic Order" would label these proposals for change, they are contrary to the position that for a century has been taken by the industrialized countries and the firms in those countries that are the primary exporters of technology.

34. See Greer, "Control of Terms," p. 58.

35. For an explanation of the asterisks in the quoted text, see the footnote on page 106 below.

36. 15 U.S.C. §1060; Mister Donut of America, Inc. v. Mr. Donut, Inc., 103 U.S.P.Q. 773 (C.D. Cal. 1967).

37. For the basic significance of the trademark as a source of origin, see Sigmund Timberg, "Trademarks, Monopoly and Restraint of Competition," *Duke, Law and Contemporary Problems* (1949), 14:326.

38. 15 U.S.C. §1127; Franchised Stores of New York, Inc. v. Winter, 394 F.2d 664 (2d Cir. 1968); Societe Comptoir de l'Industrie Cotonniere Etablissement Boussac v. Alexander's Dept. Stores, Inc., 299 F.2d 33 (2d Cir. 1962); E. I. du Pont de Nemours & Co. v. Celanese Corp. of America, 167 F.2d 484 (C.C.P.A. 1948).

39. Steele, "Barriers," in Finnegan and Goldscheider, eds., *Law and Business of Licensing,* 2:734.62.

40. While the official U.S. policy is to promote the international export of technology, note must be taken of the pressure for restricting the export of technology from the United States on the (to this writer most debatable) assumption that such exports materially increase U.S. unemployment. See Burke-Hartke bill, S. 2592, 92d Cong., 1st Sess. (1971), H.R. 10914, 92d Cong., 1st Sess. (1971); Stanley H. Ruttenberg, *Needed: A Constructive Foreign Trade Policy* (Washington, D.C.: Industrial Union Dept., AFL-CIO, 1971). For useful informational materials bearing on this labor-oriented approach, see Raymond Vernon, "International Investment and International Trade in the Product Cycle," *Quarterly Journal of Economics* (1966); 80:190–207; C. F. Bergsten, T. Horst, and T. H. Moran, *American Multinationals and American Interests* (Washington, D.C.: Brookings Institution, 1978);

Kent Hughes, *Trade, Taxes and Transnationals: International Economic Decision-Making in Congress* (New York: Praeger, 1979).

41. See Greer, "Control of Terms," p. 66.

42. Along similar lines is the language that was considered at the November 1979 meetings by the drafting group of Working Group 3:

> 4.3 While the provisions of this chapter are directed to transfer of technology transactions involving any Party, those arrangements, subject to 4.2, above, which are appropriate and ancillary to the nature of the economic interrelationship among affiliated enterprises, such as arrangements necessary for the rationalization or allocation of functions, are not intended to be precluded by the provisions of this chapter, unless amounting to an abuse of a dominant position of market power within the relevant market, for example undue restraint of the trade of a competing enterprise of the acquiring party's country.

The language of the proposed paragraph 4.2 of the draft code (chapeau) still further underscores the intention of the negotiators not to provide for governmental interference in individual transactions unless they have an overall adverse effect on the host country:

> 4.2. Practices listed are not contrary to this chapter if they are acceptable in accordance with exceptions stated herein or if, taking into account the relevant objective of this Code, they are otherwise justifiable or non-objectionable in an individual case in the light of all the relevant circumstances, including those prevailing at the inception of the agreement, in any case, if on balance the over-all effect of the transaction in the acquiring party's country would not be adverse.

43. See Adolf A. Berle, "The Theory of Enterprise Entity," *Columbia Law Review* (1947), 47:343–58.

44. See United States v. Yellow Cab Co., 332 U.S. 218 (1947); Kiefer-Stewart Co. v. Joseph E. Seagram & Sons, 340 U.S. 211 (1951); United States v. Timken Roller Bearing Co., 341 U.S. 593 (1941); Perma Life Mufflers, Inc. v. International Parts Corp., 392 U.S. 134 (1968); United States v. Citizens and Southern National Bank, 422 U.S. 86 (1975).

45. Greer, "Control of Terms," p. 66.

46. See United States v. Aluminum Co. of America, 91 F.Supp. 333, 410 (S.D.N.Y. 1950); United States v. General Electric Co., 82 F.Supp. 753, 815 (S.D.N.Y. 1949).

47. This was the basis on which exclusive grant-backs were held to be per se violations of the antitrust laws by Circuit Judge Learned Hand in Stokes & Smith Co. v. Transparent-Wrap Machine Corp., 156 F.2d 198 (2d Cir. 1946). This ruling was reversed by a five to four vote of the Supreme Court, 329 U.S. 637 (1947).

48. Cross-licensing of patents and grant-backs has been held to be an illegal method of enabling dominant enterprises to maintain a section 2 monopoly, United States v. General Electric Co. (Lamp case), 82 F.Supp. 753 (D.N.J. 1949); United States v. Aluminum Co. of America, 91 F.Supp. 333 (S.D.N.Y. 1950); or compet-

itors to fix prices, United States v. Line Material Co., 333 U.S. 287 (1949); or competitors to allocate fields of use among themselves, United States v. Associated Patents, Inc., 134 F.Supp. 74 (E.D. Mich. 1955).

49. United Nations, *Role of Patent System*, p. 24.

50. *See, e.g.,* Binks Mfg. Co. v. Ransburg Electro-Coating Corp., 281 F.2d 252 (7th Cir. 1960), *cert. denied,* 366 U.S. 211 (1961).

51. Lear, Inc. v. Adkins, 395 U.S. 653 (1969); Bendix v. Balax, 421 F.2d 809 (7th Cir. 1970), *cert. denied,* 399 U.S. 911 (1970), *on remand,* 321 F.Supp. 1095 (E.D. Wis. 1971) (Sherman Act violation), *reversed,* 471 F.2d 149 (1972), *cert. denied,* 414 U.S. 819 (1973); Troxel Mfg. Co. v. Schwinn Bicycle Co., 465 F.2d 1253 (6th Cir. 1972); W. L. Gore & Associates, Inc. v. Carlisle Corp., 381 F.Supp. 680 (D. Del. 1974). *But cf.* Congoleum Industries, Inc. v. Armstrong Cork Co., 366 F.Supp. 220 (E.D. Pa. 1973) ("no contest" clause unenforceable, but not misuse); Blohm & Voss A.G. v. Prudential Grace Lines, Inc., 346 F.Supp. 1116 (D. Md. 1972) (ditto).

52. AIOP-Beyrard, [1976–1978 Transfer Binder] Comm. Mkt. Rep. (CCH) ¶ 7801.

53. In two noteworthy cases, the Justice Department has attacked industry patent pools on the ground that they have restricted competition in research and development, United States v. Automobile Mfrs. Assn., [1969] Trade Cases ¶72,109 (consent decree); United States v. Manufacturers Aircraft Assn., [1976–1] Trade Cases ¶60,810 (consent decreee).

54. *See* Brulotte v. The Thys Co., 379 U.S. 29 (1965); Rocform Corp. v. Acitelli-Concrete Wall, Inc., 367 F.2d 678 (6th Cir. 1966); Prestole Corp. v. Tinnerman Products, Inc., 271 F.2d 146 (6th Cir. 1959), *cert. denied,* 361 U.S. 964 (1960); Pipkin v. FMC Corp., 427 F.2d 353 (5th Cir. 1970); Shields-Jetco, Inc. v. Tulsa-Jetco, Inc., 314 F.Supp. 1292 (D.R.I. 1970); *but cf.* Atlas-Pacific Engineering Co. v. Geo. W. Ashlock Co., 339 F.2d 288 (9th Cir. 1964).

55. Such limitations were held lawful in General Talking Pictures v. Western Electric Co., 305 U.S. 124 (1938); Sperry Products, Inc. v. Aluminum Co. of America, 171 F.Supp. 901 (N.D. Ohio 1959), *modified,* 285 F.2d 911 (6th Cir. 1960), *cert. denied,* 368 U.S. 890 (1961); Benger Laboratories, Ltd. v. R. K. Laros Co., 209 F.Supp. 639 (E.D. Pa. 1962), *aff'd per curiam,* 317 F.2d 455 (3d Cir. 1963), *cert. denied,* 375 U.S. 833 (1963); Chemagro Corp. v. Universal Chemical Co., 244 F.Supp. 486 (E.D. Tex. 1965); Armstrong v. Motorola, 374 F.2d 764 (7th Cir. 1967), *cert. denied,* 389 U.S. 830 (1967); Barr Rubber Products Co. v. Sun Rubber Co., 277 F.Supp. 484 (S.D.N.Y. 1967), *aff'd,* 425 F.2d 1114 (2d Cir. 1970), *cert. denied,* 400 U.S. 878 (1970).

56. Hartford Empire Co. v. United States, 323 U.S. 386 (1945). *See also* consent judgment entered against Farbenfabriken Bayer, [1969] Trade Cases ¶72,918; Donald Turner, "Patents, Antitrust and Innovation," *University of Pittsburgh Law Review* (1967), 28:151–60. Also, field-of-use restrictions present antitrust risks where imposed on resale of patented products; *see* Masters Corp. v. Burgess Industries, Inc., 450 F.Supp. 1195 (S.D.N.Y. 1978); Baldwin-Lima-Hamilton Corp. v.

Tatnall Measuring Systems Co., 169 F.Supp 1 (E.D. Pa. 1958); United States v. CIBA GEIGY Corp., [1976–1] Trade Cases ¶60,908 (D.N.J.).

57. *See* Motion Pictures Patents Co. v. Universal Film Mfg. Co., 243 U.S. 502 (1917). For the British Commonwealth legislation, see UN Economic and Social Council (ECOSOC), Official Records, 16th Sess., Supp. no. 11A, UN Docs. E/2379 and E/2379/Add.1 (1953), Analysis of Governmental Measures Relating to Restrictive Business Practices, p. 27, and the text of such measures in *ibid.*, Supp. no. 11B, passim.

58. International Salt Co. v. United States, 332 U.S. 392 (1947); International Business Machines Corp. v. United States, 298 U.S. 131 (1936).

59. United Nations, *Role of Patent System*, pp. 25–26.

60. United States v. Jerrold Electronics Corp., 187 F.Supp. 545 (E.D. Pa. 1960), *aff'd per curiam*, 365 U.S. 567 (1961).

61. Zenith Radio Corp. v. Hazeltine Research Inc., 395 U.S. 100 (1969), *over-ruling* Automatic Radio Manufacturing Co. v. Hazeltine, 339 U.S. 827 (1950); United States v. Loew's, 371 U.S. 38 (1962) (block booking of film-copyrights); American Securit Co. v. Shatterproof Glass Corp., 268 F.2d 769 (3d Cir. 1959), *cert denied*, 361 U.S. 902 (1959); Duplan Corp. v. Deering Milliken, Inc., 197 U.S.P.Q. 342, 384 (D.S.C. 1977). *But cf.* International Manufacturing Co. v. Landon, Inc., 336 F.2d 723 (9th Cir. 1964) (blocking patents).

62. "15. [Limitations on volume, scope, etc.]*/*** "[Unreasonable] *** [Restrictions on the scope, volume and/or capacity of production]*/*** [and/or field of activity]*."

63. United States v. E. I. du Pont de Nemours & Co., 118 F.Supp. 41 (D. Del. 1953), *aff'd*, 351 U.S. 377 (1964); Q-Tips, Inc. v. Johnson & Johnson, 109 F.Supp. 657 (D.N.J. 1951); Baldwin-Lima-Hamilton Corp. v. Tatnall Measuring Systems Co., 169 F.Supp. 1 (E.D. Pa. 1958), *aff'd*, 268 F.2d 395 (3d Cir. 1953), *cert. denied*, 361 U.S. 894 (1959).

64. National Lockwasher Co. v. George K. Garrett Co., 137 F.2d 255 (3d Cir. 1943); McCullough v. Kammerer Corp., 166 F.2d 759 (9th Cir. 1948), *cert. denied*, 335 U.S. 813 (1948); Park-in Theaters, Inc. v. Paramount-Richards Theaters, Inc., 90 F.Supp. 730 (D. Del.), *aff'd per curiam*, 185 F.2d 407 (3d Cir. 1950); Berlenback v. Anderson Thompson Ski Co., 329 F.2d 782 (9th Cir. 1964); Columbus Automotive Corp. v. Oldberg Co., 264 F.Supp. 779 (D. Colo. 1967); Stewart v. Mo-Trim, Inc., 192 U.S.P.Q. 410 (S.D. Ohio E.D. 1975), and cases cited therein. Also, a patentee may not restrict use or sale of unpatented products manufactured by patented process or apparatus, Cummer-Graham Co. v. Straight Side Basket Corp., 142 F.2d 646 (5th Cir. 1944), *cert. denied*, 323 U.S. 726 (1944); Barber-Colman Co. v. National Tool Co., 136 F.2d 339 (6th Cir. 1943); American Equipment Co. v. Tuthill Bldg. Material Co., 69 F.2d 406 (7th Cir. 1934); United States v. Studiengesellschaft Kohle, 426 F.Supp. 143 (D.D.C. 1976); Robintech, Inc. v. Chemidus Wavin, Ltd., 450 F.Supp. 823, 834 (D.D.C. 1978) (limitation on exports from United States).

65. *Cf.* the unsuccessful attacks on the *General Electric* case by the Antitrust

Division in United States v. Line Material Co., 333 U.S. 287 (1948), and in United States v. Huck Manufacturing Co., 227 F.Supp. 791 (E.D. Mich. 1964), *aff'd per curiam*, 382 U.S. 197 (1965).

66. United States v. General Electric Co., 272 U.S. 476 (1926).

67. *See* the erosion of the *General Electric* case in United States v. Line Material Co., 333 U.S. 287 (1948); Newburgh Moire Co. v. Superior Moire Co., 237 F.2d 283 (3d Cir. 1956); Tinnerman Products, Inc. v. Garrett Co., 185 F.Supp. 151 (E.D. Pa. 1960), *aff'd*, 292 F.2d 137 (3d Cir. 1961).

68. United Nations, *Role of Patent System*, p. 24.

69. The Justice Department has taken the position that patentees should rely on their rights to sue for patent infringement, and that contractual bans on exports are unjustified, see Antitrust Division, Department of Justice, *Antitrust Guide for International Operations* (Washington, D.C.: Government Printing Office, 1977), pp. 26–27; Joel Davidow, "United States Antitrust Laws and International Transfers of Technology—The Government View," *Fordham Law Review* (1975), 43:739. However, the courts have taken a more tolerant view by permitting such contractual restrictions where the product is covered by foreign patents, see Brownell v. Ketcham Wire & Mfg. Co., 211 F.2d 121 (9th Cir. 1954); Dunlop Co., Ltd. v. Kelsey-Hayes Co., 484 F.2d 407 (6th Cir. 1973), *cert. denied*, 415 U.S. 917 (1974). This judicial view has been attacked by many authorities as unsound, see Barry E. Hawk, *United States, Common Market and International Antitrust* (New York: Harcourt, Brace, Jovanovich, 1979), p. 211; Lawrence A. Sullivan, *Handbook of the Law of Antitrust* (St. Paul: West, 1977), pp. 538–39.

70. The EC Commission has disapproved, as contrary to the provision of Article 85(1), bans on the export of patented articles even to countries where the article has patent protection, see AOIP/Beyrard, [1976–1978 Transfer Binder] Comm. Mkt. Rep. (CCH) ¶7801; EC Commission, *Fifth Report on Competition Policy* (Brussels and Luxembourg: European Communities, 1976), p. 54; EC Commission, *Sixth Report on Competition Policy* (1977), pp. 83–84; EC Commission, *Seventh Report on Competition Policy* (1978), pp. 105–7; Breeder's Rights—Maize Seed, [Current Transfer Binder 1978] Comm. Mkt. Rep. (CCH) ¶10,083.

71. Argentina, Brazil, Mexico, and the Andean Group, the leaders in the drive for a complete ban on export restrictions, are undergoing a relatively rapid rate of industrialization and represent large markets by Latin American standards. But there are many smaller national markets and industries that could at this time accommodate only a single supplier.

72. Payments for unpatented know-how that does not relate to the invalidated patent are not affected by this provision.

73. Brulotte v. Thys Co., 397 U.S. 29 (1964).

74. *See* AOIP/Beyrard, [1976–1978 Transfer Binder] Comm. Mkt. Rep. (CCH) ¶7801.

75. U.S. Congress, Senate, *Patents*, Hearings before the Committee on Patents (Sen. Bone), 77th Cong., 1st Sess. (Washington, D.C.: Government Printing Office, 1942); U.S. Congress, Senate, *Scientific and Technical Mobilization*, Hearings

before the Subcommittee on Technological Mobilization of the Military Affairs Committee (Sen. Kilgore), 78th Cong. (Washington, D.C.: Government Printing Office, 1943–1944); U.S. Congress, *Investigation of the National Defense Program* (Sen. Truman), Hearings before a Special Committee Investigating the National Defense Program, 77th Cong., 1st Sess. to 79th Cong., 1st Sess. (Washington, D.C.: Government Printing Office, 1941–1945).

76. The most quoted research that led to the current drive of the developing countries to eliminate "tie-in" clauses and export restrictions is that of Constantine Vaitsos, who examined the policies followed by foreign companies in the pharmaceutical, rubber, chemical, and electronics industries in Colombia, and concluded that considerable overpricing and overcharging had taken place. See Louis Turner, *Multinational Companies and the Third World* (New York: Farrar, Straus and Giroux, 1973), pp. 52 et seq. For a survey of the various UNCTAD studies of a similar nature, see Sanjaya Lall, *Foreign Investment, Transnational Companies and Developing Countries* (London: Macmillan, 1977). This research proceeds on the premise that these abuses stem from the dominant market power of individual firms (whether or not they function as members of an international cartel), which in turn derives from their patents and technology. However, a recent book contains elaborate documentation that the companies engaged in the manufacture and international sale of electrical equipment have for decades operated an international cartel establishing prices and terms of trade for the sale of such equipment in developing countries. This cartel does not operate in the United States and the EEC countries, where it would clearly contravene the antitrust laws. See Barbara Epstein and Richard S. Newfarmer, *The Continuing Cartel: Report on the International Electrical Association,* reprinted as Committee Print 96–IFC 49 for U.S. Congress, House, Committee on Interstate and Foreign Commerce, 96th Cong., 2d Sess. (Washington, D.C.: Government Printing Office, 1980).

77. Reprinted in U.S. Department of State Publication no. 3206, Commercial Policy Series no. 114 (Washington, D.C.: Government Printing Office, 1948).

78. ECOSOC, Official Records, 16th Sess., Supp. no. 11, UN Doc. E/2380 (1953). Despite the favorable response of the committee and its endorsement by ECOSOC delegations from Sweden, Belgium, Norway, the Federal Republic of Germany, Turkey, and Yugoslavia, the Draft Convention was shelved by the Economic and Social Council when the United States, the original cosponsor with Sweden, withdrew its support on the ground that other countries had not reached the high plateau of U.S. antitrust enforcement. See Sigmund Timberg, "Restrictive Business Practices as an Appropriate Subject for United Nations Action," *Antitrust Bulletin* (1955), 1:411.

79. This movement already had considerable momentum at the time of the ECOSOC deliberations, ECOSOC, 16th Sess., Supp. no. 11A; Current Legal Developments in the Field of Restrictive Business Practices, ECOSOC, Official Records, 19th Sess., Supp. no. 3, UN Doc. E/2671 (1955); Sigmund Timberg, "Restrictive Business Practices: Comparative Legislation and the Problems That Lie Ahead," *American Journal of Comparative Law* (1953), 2:445–73. But it preceded

the adoption of national antitrust laws by other countries such as West Germany and Ireland, the strengthening of such laws in the United Kingdom and the Scandinavian countries, and even the adoption of antitrust legislation by countries such as Greece, Spain, Israel, and India. For such laws and their enforcement in the OECD countries, see OECD, *Guide to Legislation on Restrictive Business Practices* (Paris: OECD, looseleaf).

80. Giorgio Bernini, *La Tutela della Libra Concorrenze E I Monopoli* (Milan: Giuffré, 1963), 2:12–42.

81. The author was discussing the problems raised by "multinational corporations" as early as 1947, see "International Combines and National Sovereigns: A Study in Conflict of Laws and Mechanisms," *University of Pennsylvania Law Review* (1947), 95:575–620. But the two books that gave economic substance and depth to, and a broader public and political appreciation of, those problems were Raymond Vernon's *Sovereignty at Bay: The Multinational Spread of U.S. Enterprise* (New York: Basic Books, 1970) and Jean-Jacques Servan-Schreiber's *Le Defi Americain* (Editions Denoel, 1967) (known to English readers as *The American Challenge*).

82. Article 85(3) exempts agreements, decisions of associations, and concerted practices if:

1. the agreement contributes to improving the production or distribution of goods or to promoting technical or economic progress

2. consumers receive a fair share of the resulting benefits

3. the restrictions are indispensable to the attainment of the benefits, and

4. the parties are not afforded the possibility of eliminating competition in respect of a substantial part of the products in question.

83. United States v. Imperial Chemical Industries, 100 F.Supp. 504 (S.D.N.Y. 1951); United States v. National Lead Co., 63 F.Supp. 513 (S.D.N.Y. 1945), aff'd, 332 U.S. 319 (1947); United States v. General Electric Co. (Lamp case), 82 F.Supp. 753 (D.N.J. 1949); United States v. Bayer Co., 135 F.Supp. 65 (S.D.N.Y. 1955); United States v. Timken Roller Bearing Co., 83 F.Supp. 284 (N.D. Ohio 1949), aff'd, 341 U.S. 593 (1951) (trademark cartel).

84. Hartford Empire Co. v. United States, 323 U.S. 386 (1945); United States v. National Lead Co., 63 F.Supp. 513 (S.D.N.Y. 1945), aff'd, 332 U.S. 319 (1947); United States v. Vehicular Parking, Ltd., 54 F.Supp. 828 (D. Del. 1944); United States v. General Instrument Corp., 87 F.Supp. 157 (D.N.J. 1949); United States v. Besser Mfg. Co., 96 F.Supp. 304 (E.D. Mich. 1951), aff'd, 343 U.S. 444 (1952).

85. The contrasting positions of the Group of 77 and the OECD countries, with the socialist states supporting an interesting semantic straddle, are set forth in paragraphs (11) through (13) of the preamble:

(11) *Affirming* the benefits to be derived from a universally applicable Code of Conduct and that all countries should [ensure] */*** [encourage]** that their enterprises, whether private or public, [shall conform]*/***[follow]** in all respects to the provisions of this Code.

(12) [*Convinced* that an international legally binding instrument is the only form capable of effectively regulating the transfer of technology,]*

(13) [*Agree* on the adoption of this international legally binding Code of Conduct on the transfer of technology]*

[*Hereby set forth* the following code of conduct consisting of guidelines for the international transfer of technology:]**

[This universally applicable Code of Conduct on the international transfer of technology is established.]***

The preceding ten paragraphs of the preamble are agreed to.

86. International law, we have been reminded, "has been built up very largely on the mere research and opinion of learned writers," C. K. Allen, *Law in the Making,* 3d ed. (Oxford: Clarendon, 1939), p. 237. There would seem to be a much greater scope for international law, and sound international practice, if its source were the collective wisdom of the experts who have been negotiating the Code on the Transfer of Technology.

87. Japan, Mexico, and the Andean Group of countries are among those best known for their system of screening technology transfer agreements, but such screening is involved in any country that has currency exchange difficulties and therefore monitors the transmission of patent and know-how royalties abroad.

88. See Timberg, "Appropriate Subject," pp. 418 et seq.

89. Addyston Pipe & Steel Co. v. United States, 85 Fed. 271 (6th Cir. 1898), *aff'd,* 175 U.S. 211 (1899); Chicago Board of Trade v. United States, 246 U.S. 231 (1918).

90. Continental T.V., Inc. v. GTE Sylvania, Inc., 433 U.S. 36 (1977).

91. Broadcast Music, Inc. v. Columbia Broadcasting System, Inc., 441 U.S. 1 (1979), *rev'g* 562 F.2d 130 (2d Cir. 1977); National Society of Professional Engineers v. United States, 435 U.S. 679 (1978).

92. Northern Pacific Ry. Co. v. United States, 356 U.S. 1 (1956); United States v. Loew's, Inc., 371 U.S. 38 (1962); International Salt Co. v. United States, 332 U.S. 392 (1947).

93. United States v. Jerrold Electronics Corp., 187 F.Supp. 545 (E.D. Pa. 1960), *aff'd per curiam,* 365 U.S. 567 (1961); Dehydrating Process Co. v. A. O. Smith Corp., 292 F.2d 653 (1st Cir. 1961); *see* Electric Pipeline, Inc. v. Fluid Systems, 231 F.2d 370 (2d Cir. 1960). *See also* Jack Winter, Inc. v. Koratron Co., Inc., 375 F.Supp. 1 (N.D. Cal. 1974) (patentee entitled to evidentiary hearing).

94. ECOSOC, Official Records, 16th Sess., Supp. no. 11, pp. 12–13 (Art. 1.1).

95. *Ibid.,* p. 12 (preamble).

96. In "An International Antitrust Convention," *Journal of International Law and Economics* (1973), 8:175–76.

97. ECOSOC, Official Records, 16th Sess., Supp. no. 11, pp. 13–14 (Art. 3).

98. *Ibid.,* pp. 14–15 (Art. 5).

99. Subsequent experience has shown that the problems revolving around "mo-

nopolistic control" have been of relatively secondary significance to the antitrust law enforcement authorities of most countries with developed antitrust systems.

100. Since this paper was originally presented, the November 1979 negotiating session of the Draft TOT Code adjourned in some confusion and disarray because of the position taken by the socialist countries, evidently for the first time, that the code should not apply to governmental enterprises. Given the large-scale governmental involvement in industry in both the developing and the socialist countries, it is to be hoped that this position will be changed. Commercial coexistence in the international transfer of technology demands that the same rules apply to both governmental and nongovernmental transferors and users of technology.

101. See New Delhi Declaration and Plan of Action, issued February 8, 1980, contained in Report of the Third General Conference of the United Nations Industrial Development Organization, ID CONF.4/22 (April 11, 1980), at pp. 86–87, which reiterates a similar demand by the Group of 77 at Havana sometime earlier.

Commentary

<>

Walter Glass

Two items have come up in this morning's discussion on which I would like to comment before I go to my proper subject.

One of them is the continuing criticism of alleged misuse of transfer pricing by multinational corporations. As I understand it, the regulations of the Internal Revenue Service are going to put very stringent controls on transfer pricing in transfers between parent and subsidiary. But, as far as my own company is concerned, it has been an internal requirement for many years that transfers between departments of the company must take place substantially at market prices, among other things, because that is helpful in a proper evaluation of the performance of the business departments which make up our company. So, I suspect that there may not be such a deep, dark mystery to be revealed in this field after all.

I think the same is likely to be true with respect to the continuing suspicion of participation by American companies in an international electrical equipment cartel.

As everyone knows, we did have territorial agreements with counterpart companies in Europe and Japan that were entered into in the period between 1887 and 1910. These were terminated by agreement between the parties in the light of the *du Pont-ICI* case shortly after World War II.

The only one which we could not terminate because the other party was not willing to do so was made fully nonexclusive in the 1950s. And I, myself, negotiated the ultimate termination of that agreement in 1969, because the commercial and technical interests of the parties had become so divergent that even the nonexclusive technical agreements between the companies were no longer workable.

So, my feeling is—and I have been the responsible licensing counsel of our company for the contracts that deal with such matters—that the suspicions are misplaced.

Coming back to the regulations which are our subject, as a practical lawyer I should say that one of the issues which always concerns me is the question of style. And one of the things that makes it so difficult for companies to work enthusiastically with the United Nations development efforts is the tone of the discussions.

In Douglas Greer's paper there is the analogy of the drowning man who is being asked a high price for being given a rope with which to save himself. I say most of the people I know, multinationals or otherwise, who find themselves in that situation would hand the drowning man a rope, and even give him a drink after pulling him on board.

But the example is not an accurate analogy to the technology transfer process. In my own imaginative analogy, a company is approached by representatives of a developing country with a request that it train one of the world's great pianists. So you say: "Well, you know, there are the following steps you ought to take," and soon you find out that they really think that not only the pianist, but also the piano ought to be made in their country. So you discuss the question what it takes to make a piano. And then, when you point out that printed music will be needed, you get the response, "Aha, now you're trying to make us dependent in the software field." And so on, ad infinitum.

I must say that the charge that is often made that the industrialized countries have somehow willfully transferred inappropriate technology to developing countries is difficult for me to comprehend.

For instance, when you look at the struggle we have in our own country in determining the appropriate technology to develop energy sources, or when you look at the People's Republic of China and the convulsions it goes through in trying to determine what the appropriate technology ought to be at any particular time, these charges of willful wrongdoing seem to me to have no foundation in reality. This is not the world which is experienced by the executive working in this field.

As far as I can see from my observation and experience, the problem of transfer of technology, to the extent that industrial enterprises have the technologies that are wanted by the developing countries, reduces itself to a need for incentives to make the transfer effort—which is substantial—and to create better incentives on the receiver's side to make use of the information that is available.

The full complexity of the utilization process is only very partially understood. And to a significant extent, there is not very much the United States Government or multinational enterprises can do to change the incentive systems of the recipient countries.

Now as to the restrictive practices which have been talked about, again the tone of what is left of the Group of 77's proposals is not constructive.

For instance, there is a reference to a prohibition on restrictions on research by the recipient of the technology. Was there ever such a thing? I suppose Constantine Vaitsos must have found an agreement that had such a provision, but it is hard to imagine any practical purpose for it.

As for restrictions on adaptation, I cannot imagine that either, except perhaps in terms of a trademark license requiring certain standards of quality.

Restrictions on the use of local personnel, that strikes me as most astonishing of all. The search for qualified foreign personnel to be employed by the American company, or to be a business partner, is an effort most companies pursue very vigorously.

Part of the problem in this area is that what the developing countries really want is active support and assistance in making exports from their country. It is not a question of "restrictions" at all, and the discussion is therefore often beside the point, and in fact misleading.

And, I should point out from my own observation that where incentives to the transfer of technology are allowed to operate, there is active competition of remarkable intensity.

In looking at development examples we should not overlook Japan. Japan has purchased very substantial amounts of technology. Certainly, Japan is in no way a typical developing country, but it definitely had no difficulty in creating competition for the sale of technology.

Ten years ago, people in Europe were talking about the "American challenge," and the feeling that we were going to take over technologically. That tune is no longer played, and what we hear now when traveling in Europe is that the United States overestimates the policy concessions which can be obtained through control of technology, because the unique technological leadership position which existed immediately after World War II no longer exists.

In fact, when you look around in the United States, you find a new concern with a "Japanese challenge." The question is: What are they doing right that we're not doing? What has put us in the present situation?

There are no doubt many reasons. One of them may have been the effort to control the flow of technology where we no longer had the power to do so, as illustrated by the growing European influence in Brazil; one might note, incidentally, that this would seem to indicate a very active state of competition even in the very high technology fields that were at issue in that country!

Finally, I would like to make one specific point, and that is my concern with the thrust of the new regulations insofar as they make it a major objective to reduce compensation for the transfer of technology.

The general incentive problem is probably pretty well understood, but what I find particularly damaging—and that is a fine legal point—is the insistence on provisions which would make it unlawful to collect compensation for unpatented technology after it loses its "proprietary status." What we find here is that a concept developed as a legitimate expression of competition policy has become a device primarily aimed at price reduction. What I have in mind is this: It may be that, as in the old *du Pont/ICI* case, otherwise unlawful agreements were attempted to be justified by the utilization of unpatented technology, and the attachment of restrictions to that technology.

In examining the justification for a restriction, an antitrust enforcement agency might well wish to examine whether a technology has "trade secret" quality or is of a more common kind. But when it comes to the question whether someone can receive compensation for something which is no longer "proprietary," it is a very different matter.

Indeed, when this question came to the Supreme Court in the *Quick-point Pencil* case, the Court held that Mrs. Aaronson, the inventor of the key-ring device, was entitled to continuing compensation on the basis of a contract obligation, even though anyone who saw the device could imitate it and the design was therefore no longer proprietary.

This is an important principle, because the right to terminate an agreement when the information is no longer proprietary is a step in the direction of the constant renegotiation of agreements. In this it reflects what seems to be a tenet of the "New International Economic Order": the continuous renegotiation of agreements. A business manager who has the responsibility of setting a course for his enterprise obviously cannot accept such a principle of operation, and therefore cannot transfer technology or render services on this basis.

Commentary

◇

Ingo Walter

The paper by Douglas F. Greer, it seems to me, takes a rather constructive approach to the problem of technology transfers to the developing countries. It properly focuses on the bargaining context in which technology transfers take place, and on which all possible sources of market and non-market leverage are brought to bear.

In a static sense, developing countries want to import product, process applications, management, and marketing know-how that is in some sense "appropriate" to the local environment at the lowest available cost—if possible, for free. In a dynamic sense, they want to develop their own technological capabilities and the "external" benefits that may be associated with vigorous R&D efforts, while at the same time staying "plugged into" the state of the art in the rest of the world.

Multinational companies, by contrast, want to extract the largest profit they can from whatever market power proprietary know-how conveys upon them, which could be viewed as the discounted present value of differential returns attributable to such know-how, as they evolve through time. In other words, companies are interested not only in squeezing the last nickel of monopoly rents out of proprietary technology now, but also in making sure these rents keep coming in the years ahead. The two objectives are not always compatible. The capital markets keep management regularly informed of what they think of the prospects.

Putting the two sides together, we have what amounts to a classic bargaining situation in a positive-sum game. Each side wants to maximize its slice of a many-layered and growing cake. In their exertions, they can easily cause the cake to stop growing, or even shrink. Rational policies for both are defined jointly by what is likely to happen to their respective slices and the cake as a whole. Because of the amorphous nature and multiple conduits of international technology flows, rational policies are often hard to identify for either side. And our inability to come to grips with the equity issues involved often makes it nearly impossible to reach prescriptive conclusions from an outside perspective. Given the nature of the problem, it is hardly surprising that so much nonsense is written about technology transfer to developing countries by people who lack even rudimentary knowledge of what they are talking about. Fortunately, Greer's paper does not fall into this category.

INSTITUTIONAL COMPARATIVE ADVANTAGE AND TECHNOLOGY TRANSFERS

One can think about MNCs and technology transfer in terms of some sort of "institutional comparative advantage" in the real world, which corresponds roughly to classical notions of comparative advantage among nations. Arm's-length market transactions tend to be most efficient when there are many buyers, many sellers, low transactions costs, perfect information, instantaneous adjustment, homogeneous products, and similar characteristics, which make markets for stocks and bonds, wheat, pork bellies, and foreign exchange function so well. But these characteristics may not describe a great deal of international trade in electronic components or aircraft parts, and certainly not specific bits of hard or soft technology that may be in disembodied form or embodied in pieces of equipment, or in human beings who know something other people do not. Sometimes there are only a few buyers and sellers. Sometimes information or transaction costs are extremely high. And sometimes the buyers cannot tell the value of a piece of knowledge unless it is fully disclosed, whereupon (unless somehow protected) it obviously loses its value to the seller. And so one can perhaps view the role of *intrafirm* transactions within MNCs as surpassing the qualities of the marketplace in certain important respects. The social value of the MNC, in this view, is that it is more efficient than free markets as an institutional transactions medium, given the realities of international exchanges of goods and services in the modern world.[1] The key role of technology in conveying this institutional comparative advantage to intrafirm transactions over conventional market channels is clear.

If we accept the proposition that proprietary technology is a necessary part of the functioning of the modern international economy, then the MNC in one form or another is likely to be a prominent feature of the system in the years ahead. Given the complex nature of technology, the well-known "bundle" of MNC services (comprising capital, labor, management, and marketing know-how, access to markets and supplies, and entrepreneurship) may simply be the most efficient way to get it transferred. This hardly means it cannot be "unbundled," as indeed happens regularly through turnkey plants, management contracts, licensing, and the like. But it does mean that any unbundling has to be done with extreme care, especially in a dynamic context where the MNC parent-affiliate "umbilical" assuring continuous technological updates may be all-important.

It is easy to conclude, therefore, that the developing countries will have to continue to play the MNCs' game, in one form or another, if they are to succeed in harnessing technological change as an agent of economic growth. As Greer points out, the MNCs' game will continue to be played among the technologically advanced nations, where its value is clearly recognized, and its spread to the "newly industrializing" and Communist countries seems likely to intensify still further. If we therefore agree that developing-country *involvement* with MNCs cannot really be at issue, the conflict boils down to "terms and conditions," the price they must pay for multinationals' services. In this context, it may be instructive to view the problem from the perspective of MNC conflict management by using a behavioral "contingency" model that attempts to portray diagnostic and strategy-formation issues involved in multinational conflict management.[2]

Consider the schematic presented in figure 2.3. The term *cooperativeness* defines the extent to which a multinational enterprise is willing to help satisfy the concerns or interests of the other party(ies) in conflict. It can be viewed as a continuum, with very uncooperative behavior (hostile, distrustful, unhelpful, stubborn) and very cooperative behavior (friendly, trustful, helpful, complaisant) at the two ends of the scale. Increased cooperativeness implies greater sensitivity to the needs and desires of the other party. The term *assertiveness* defines the extent to which a multinational enterprise is willing to take a high profile in order to satisfy its own interests in a conflict. It, too, can be viewed as a continuum, extending from very unassertive behavior (passive, weak, lethargic, nonaggressive) at one extreme, to very assertive behavior (active, strong, vigorous, aggressive) at the other. Increased assertiveness implies greater initiative, persistent determination, and energetic pursuit of the firm's own ends, and typ-

Figure 2.3 Determinants of MNC Conflict Behavior

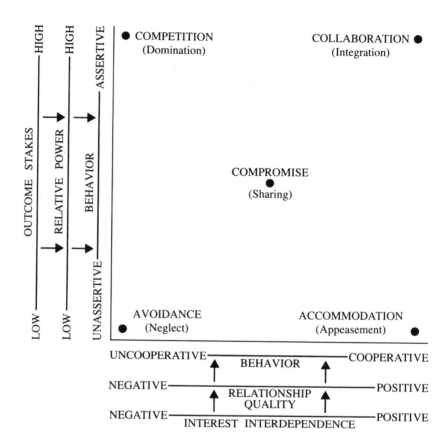

ically entails greater investment of organizational time, manpower, and other resources—qualities often embodied in a distinct managerial "style" of a particular firm.

There are, of course, many possible combinations of these two behavioral dimensions. Analytical emphasis can be given, however, to the five "pure" combinations, or behavioral "zones," corresponding to the corners and midpoint of the grid. *Competing* with the hope of achieving domination is assertive/uncooperative. *Avoiding* in order to neglect or withdraw from a conflict is unassertive/uncooperative. *Accommodating* for the purpose of appeasing the other party is unassertive/cooperative. *Collaborating* with the desire of fully integrating and satisfying the concerns of both parties is assertive/cooperative. *Compromise* in order to "split the difference" in bargaining represents an intermediate position in terms of both assertiveness and cooperativeness. In cases like technology transfer, multinationals regularly encounter conflict situations of a relatively pure form, in which the four variables combine and unambiguously suggest a corporate conflict-management position.[3]

DETERMINANTS OF ASSERTIVENESS

How assertive a firm wants to be in a given conflict situation appears to rest on the *stakes* the enterprise places on a given outcome, together with the relative *power* of the enterprise to bring about that outcome.

STAKES

The stakes of a multinational enterprise in any given conflict depend on the amount of perceived gain or loss associated with particular outcomes: stakes are high when a great deal can be won or lost. The factual determination of stakes is usually a very complex task and involves assessment of gains and losses, tangible and intangible factors, and short-term and long-term considerations, including the setting of precedents. Stakes can be subjectively estimated, but perhaps never rigorously defined in complete detail. Probably the most important factor in determining a multinational's stakes in a particular conflict outcome is its global strategy. A conflict outcome can be gauged according to its impact on (1) the corporate capabilities that underlie the company's strategy, (2) the economic basis of that strategy, and (3) the requirements for effective implementation of the strategy, such as degree of control. Conflict outcomes that weaken the heart of a strategy—damaging the firm's distinctive competence, competitive edge, or unique capabilities—are likely to be those management wants most to avoid, while outcomes that greatly strengthen the essential requirements for satisfactory pursuit of its corporate strategy are likely to be those the firm will most enthusiastically seek. Stakes are likely to be highest, in other words, when the outcome of a conflict will either severely erode or significantly bolster a multinational's competitive "advantage." This advantage includes technological superiority, control of goods or factor markets, and economies of scale.[4]

Large and complex multinational enterprises, of course, often pursue multiple strategies in different product and geographic divisions. By drawing on past research, however, it seems possible to distinguish among different kinds of strategies and show how the stakes in any particular conflict depend on them.[5] Firms that concentrate on exploiting technological leads, such as IBM, usually consider it essential to maintain an exceptionally strong R&D program, high quality standards, tight control of technological skills, and close supervision of marketing strategy. Other multinationals likewise pursue high technology strategies, but believe themselves to be broad-based enough not to fear an invasion of corporate know-how or quality control. Technological leads by such firms may be exploited in multiple product lines and many markets, although technological preeminence in any one may not be assured. Seeing themselves as comparatively efficient in the development of innovative leads in many areas, these firms do not find the need for tight control of production and marketing as critical as does IBM in conflicts over ownership, patents, quality control, and the like—and the stakes are rarely perceived as a matter of life and death. Thus, companies like Honeywell, Westinghouse, ITT, and L. M. Ericsson were relatively calm when they were indigenized in France, knowing that greener pastures lay right around the corner.

Multinationals in the oil, copper, aluminum, and chemicals industries tend to pursue strategies resting on the advantages of large scale. The success of these capital-intensive firms depends on maintenance of barriers to entry, coordination of decisions at various stages of production, security of raw materials supply, and stability in the demand for their products. These are the "jugular veins" of the natural resource industries, and whenever governments or other opponents take actions that threaten the corporate need for stability, the stakes are likely to be viewed as high.

At the same time, multinationals in the food and pharmaceutical industries rely on strategies based on advanced managerial and marketing skills. Strong trade names are often supported by massive promotional expenditures. Tight control of marketing programs is usually viewed as absolutely essential, and conflicts that threaten them are assigned high stakes. There also are corporate strategies that rest on the multinational's global scanning capability and well-integrated, efficient logistical system. In the automobile and electronics industries, for example, returns are achieved from low-cost production locations and effective global marketing, and tight internal control is needed to tie together this kind of multinational network. Threats to such a network are likely to be viewed as involving high stakes to the firm. Besides strategic factors, elements affecting stakes include the firm's financial condition, the precedents that a particular conflict outcome may establish in the eyes of interested audiences, and accountability to third parties such as joint venture partners and industry associations.

Conversely, perceived stakes may be reduced by a number of factors. One is insurance, which is provided to U.S. companies by the Overseas Private Investment Corporation. Another is the existence of options. A third is the joint ownership of capital-intensive facilities, such as aluminum smelters, copper mines, oil fields, natural gas pipelines, and petrochemical complexes, which tends to create a common cost structure and common exposure to risk for the firms involved. If a jointly owned facility is blocked or expropriated, competitive relationships may remain more or less intact among the rivals; so losing a conflict does not necessarily set one firm back relative to its competitors. In ascertaining its stakes in a conflict outcome, management must also factor in a time element: "the pressure to minimize costs associated with delaying a settlement, e.g., a decision must be reached to cope with immediate threats from the (external) environment, or direct monetary costs are charged for time taken in reaching a decision, or opportunities of superior employment of effort are foregone." [6] As time pressures increase, perceived stakes in obtaining the most desirable outcome may decrease. Increasing urgency increases "decision costs," and to minimize this effect, the firm may soften its demands, reduce its aspirations, or increase its concessions. [7]

When the stakes are perceived to be high, it seems logical that an enterprise will want to be assertive in the pursuit of the desired outcome, and it should be willing to expend considerable time and energy on either competition or collaboration. But when the stakes are low, it may make sense to be unassertive and do nothing (*avoidance*) or simply go along with the other side's position (*accommodation*). With low stakes, major outlays of corporate energy simply may not make sense.

POWER

A multinational's relative power position in a particular conflict does not reside exclusively within the firm itself, but also in the relationship it has with its external environment. This position is a joint function of the firm's characteristics and the characteristics of the situation in which it finds itself, and thus can vary greatly from one conflict to another. [8] A multinational corporation potentially has several bases of power in various conflict situations. The enterprise can exert *informational influence* if it possesses information not previously known to the other party or if it can point out contingencies about which the other has little or no awareness. The firm can utilize *referent influence* if it can emphasize its common interests with the other party and attempt to engender feelings of solidarity. It can exert *legitimate influence* if it can convince the other party that it is justified in making a particular demand on normative grounds: for example, rules, precedents, reciprocity, and fair play. The multinational can use *expert influence* if it is able to convince the other party that it has superior knowledge or ability. It can use *reward influence* if it is able to promise the other party benefits such as prospects of new investment, and the reward clearly depends on a conflict outcome favorable to the enterprise. Finally, it can use *coercive influence* if it is able to deal out negative incentives such as a pullout when the conflict is not favorably resolved. The ingredients of power include size, financial base, potential resources, leadership quality, managerial capacity, prestige, image, reputation, communication and persuasion skills, access to the media, degree of organization, cohesiveness, prior experience in waging conflict, intensity of commitment, degree of trust and legitimacy, knowledge, expertise, risk-taking ability, and available options.

Other important determinants of relative power include the formation of coalitions, which tends to occur frequently in multinational corporate conflict, and the site of the conflict. Waging conflict on one's own territory is a potential source of strength that can increase assertiveness. Because multinationals play most of their games "away" rather than "at home," they must contend with opponents on their own territory, where they are more familiar with the local environment and often enjoy the ability to control or manipulate it.

Multinational corporate power is also strengthened by the existence of *options*. One example is dispersion of production. Enterprises that rely on well-diversified supply sources are less vulnerable to embargoes and nationalizations, and perhaps more resilient in conflicts in general, than firms that rely on more concentrated sources. They also gain strength from market dominance, which can reduce the ability of governments to reach out for alternative sources of technology or capital. After all, a proliferation of local and foreign rivals makes it easier for governments to shop around. Another source of power, in manufacturing industries, derives from breaking down the production process so finely that threats to the firm become meaningless. A government's expropriation of a screwdriver-type assembly operation for electronics components, which puts together imported inputs for export, would yield little. Overall, it seems clear that multinationals attain power through a degree of indispensability, that is, by possessing something unique to offer or withhold when a conflict arises.

If the content of power is complex, it is also the primary determinant of the feasibility of different types of conflict behavior. A clearly superior power position is likely to favor relatively assertive behavior in conflict situations. Such behavior may either take the form of a straightforward *competitive* stance or one of *collaboration,* in which the firm's problem-solving resources imply a position of strength and low risk. But when the multinational's power is very low, it will probably be unable to compel the other side to negotiate, and unassertive behavior (*avoidance* or *accommodation*) may be most appropriate—assuming the option of attempting to increase the firm's relative power is rejected as infeasible or excessively costly.

DETERMINANTS OF COOPERATIVENESS

Outcome stakes and relative power thus may be prime factors in determining a multinational's assertiveness level in a particular conflict. But the multinational also has to decide how cooperative to be. As with assertiveness, there seem to be two critical factors that affect the *desirability* and *feasibility* of cooperative behavior. The former is primarily a function of the "interest interdependence" between the multinational enterprise and the other parties, that is, whether there is a positive or negative correlation between the attainment of the firm's goals and those of the opposition. Feasibility is principally a question of "relationship quality" between the enterprise and the other parties. Divergent interests give rise to competitive or "object-centered" conflict, while poor relations give rise to hostile or "opponent-centered" conflict. [9]

INTEREST INTERDEPENDENCE
Interests among parties in a relationship can be purely convergent (common), purely divergent (different), or both convergent and divergent at the same time. A purely convergent situation has been defined as one in which "the goals are so linked that everybody 'sinks or swims' together, while in the competitive (uncooperative) situation if one swims, the other must sink." [10] Although multinationals occasionally experience conflicts charac-

terized by such extreme divergence or convergence of interest, the most common situations are likely to be those containing a mix of both convergent and divergent goals.

Multinationals affect a wide range of politically sensitive matters in the nations where they operate, including growth, employment, prices, technical change, income distribution, taxation, dependence on external markets, pollution control, balance of payments, national security, competitive position in world markets, and reliance on foreign resources. Actions that are perceived as threatening these interests are likely to represent points of incompatibility. Perhaps the most fundamental source of diverging interests is incompatibility between the global perspective of the multinational enterprise and the national perspective of most of the institutions with which it interacts. In our normal view of the world, macroeconomic policy at the national level sets the conditions in which the microeconomic functions of the firm are carried out; but with multinationals, the global microeconomics of the corporation influences the formation and effectiveness of macroeconomic policy at the national level. As one observer points out: "The most honest corporate manager allocating resources rationally with a transnational perspective is bound to have conflicts of interest with the most reasonable of statesmen whose rationality (and democratic responsibility) is bounded by national frontiers."[11] Multinational managers also worry about the problems that arise from overlapping national jurisdictions, particularly that their affiliates may be used as political tools, conduits, and hostages by competing sovereign states.

RELATIONSHIP QUALITY
Conflicts in multinational corporate operations may occur, even when there is no perceived or actual divergence in goals among the parties, as a result of prior relations and attitudes. The quality of a multinational's relations with an opposing party will help determine the amount of cooperativeness that will emerge. A positive relationship will tend to foster mutual trust, recognition of the legitimacy of the other party's interests, open communications, and an increased willingness to respond helpfully to the other party's needs. A negative relationship, on the other hand, may give rise to suspicion, a low level and quality of communications, increased sensitivity to differences and threats, and a readiness to exploit or respond negatively to the other's demands.

Positive and negative relations and attitudes can emerge in many ways.

Negative relations can result from isolation, stereotypes, failure or disillusionment in prior conflicts, mutual ignorance, awareness of dissimilarity in values, racial differences, distorted perceptions, institutional barriers between the parties, and so on. In many countries, the predominant ideologies and values may reject the multinational enterprise as an institution. An ideological commitment to socialism, and the concepts of capitalist exploitation, imperialism, and class struggle, will naturally place a burden on constructive conflict resolution. So will anti-American, anti-German, or anti-Japanese paranoia. Reprehensible behavior on the part of a few multinationals can also erode the foundation of mutual trust needed for positive relations. Perhaps the foremost sources of negative relations for multinationals are ethnocentrism and nationalism.[12]

Factors that can lead to positive rather than hostile relations between multinationals and their opponents in conflict situations include experiences of successful prior interactions, perceived similarity in beliefs, values, and attitudes, loyalties to a superordinate community and its institutions, mutual allegiances and memberships, cross-cutting identifications, free and continuing exchange of members, recognition of existence and legitimacy, good communications, and concerns of the parties about their ability to work together in the future. A multinational enterprise is likely to exhibit a high degree of cooperativeness (*collaboration* or *accommodation*) when relations are open, friendly, and trusting. Uncooperative behavior (*competition* or *avoidance*) is most likely when hatred, suspicion, distrust, and hostile attitudes prevail.

DIAGNOSING CONFLICT BEHAVIOR

The "motivational structure" of conflict (stakes and interdependence) is probably a more important determinant of conflict behavior than the "capability structure" (power and relationship quality) because capabilities are more readily changeable than basic underlying motives. There are also linkages among the situational variables. Negative interest interdependence and negative relationship quality, for example, may be directly related. Parties who dislike one another are apt to emphasize or develop incompatible goals.[13] Stakes and power may also be linked. As the stakes in a conflict outcome increase, so does the incentive to utilize every source of power that may be available.

The framework presented here suggests that a *competitive* (assertive, uncooperative) response to conflict is likely when a multinational's stakes and power are relatively high, and when interest interdependence and relations are relatively negative. The objective is domination. An *avoidant* (unassertive, uncooperative) mode of handling conflict is likely to be used by a multinational when its stakes and power are relatively low, and when interest interdependence and relations are relatively negative. The objective is withdrawal or neglect. Avoidance can be useful to a multinational firm in many kinds of situations, such as when alternate projects or markets are readily available, when the issues in conflict are trivial and represent only minor annoyances, or when potential disruption and negative publicity seem to outweigh the benefits of conflict resolution.

A *collaborative* (assertive, cooperative) mode of handling conflict is likely to be used by a multinational corporation when its stakes and power are relatively high, and when interest interdependence and relations are relatively positive. Collaboration is effective when both sides want to achieve the same objective but differ over the means; it can serve to enhance commitment by incorporating divergent concerns into a consensus.

An *accommodative* (unassertive, cooperative) mode of handling conflict is likely to be employed by multinationals when stakes and power are relatively low, and when interest interdependence and relations are relatively positive. The objective is appeasement. Accommodation makes sense when issues are more important to others than to the firm itself, when the firm finds itself outmatched and losing the battle, when it finds that it has been wrong, and when organizational energy is needed for other conflicts with higher stakes.

Finally, a *compromising* (moderately assertive and cooperative) mode of handling conflict is likely to be used when the firm's stakes are moderate and the power advantage or disadvantage is slight, and when interest interdependence and relations are mixes of positive and negative elements. The objective is to "split the difference," to share the outcome of the conflict. Compromise is particularly useful when conflicts involve differences in goals, attitudes, and values, and when many issues, accorded different priorities by the two parties, are involved. It makes sense when goals are important, but not worth the effort or potential delays involved with more assertive modes of behavior; it can produce expedient solutions under the pressure of time as well as temporary settlements to complex issues. And it can be a primary backup when collaboration or competition is unsuccessful.

Although one sometimes finds conflict situations that unambiguously call for "pure" competition, avoidance, collaboration, accommodation, or compromise, most conflicts are much more complex and ambiguous. So conflict management will likewise tend to be mixed, both simultaneously and sequentially, and to involve a wide variety of "hybrid" types of behavior, points on the assertiveness-cooperativeness grid that fall elsewhere than the four corners or center.

Two other points need to be noted. First, the likelihood of reaching a satisfactory solution to a conflict can often be increased by separating or "fractionating" the large issues involved into smaller and more workable ones. Many such issues can be so manipulated: hooked together, broken apart, or stated in different language. They can be differentiated according to importance and relatedness, and different conflict management modes applied at the same time: for example, some issues can be avoided, others selected for compromise, and still others subjected to intense competition. Fractionation of issues can help alleviate the negative effects of excessive commitment often associated with attempts to resolve large or all-encompassing conflicts. The parties with whom a multinational is in conflict can also be fractionated, which is often necessary when multinationals find themselves wedged between the hauling and pulling of parties in different countries whose interests point in fundamentally different directions.[14] In many conflicts the enterprise may find it particularly advantageous to use different conflict-handling modes with different parties. The strategy of "divide and conquer" may use mixed modes of conflict behavior to block the formation of powerful opposing alliances, encourage counter-coalitions, or instigate division or contention among weaker parties.

Second, it is clear that most conflicts facing multinationals are dynamic. They usually do not appear suddenly, but usually pass through a series of stages. Conditions related to stakes, power, relationship quality, and interest interdependence can vary from one time period to the next, and so require changing modes of behavior on the part of management. Indeed, the creation of alternatives in situational variables over time can be consciously attempted by the parties in conflict. Values, beliefs, and perceptions can be changed through communication and persuasion. The quality of a relationship can be improved through skillful public relations. The power balance may be shifted by trying to increase the leverage that underlies the firm's position, or coalitions can be formed to offset an initial power disadvantage. Perceptions of the stakes involved in a conflict can be modified by altering variables such as availability of options or decision deadlines. Perceptions of interest interdependence can be changed by developing satisfactory substitutes for the goals in question, by bringing into play third-party intervention, by reformulating the issues involved, or by introducing "superordinate" goals or common threats that outweigh the existing hostility and divergent goals.[15] There may also be changes in circumstances beyond the control of the parties concerned.

This dynamic quality is perhaps best illustrated by the inevitable cycles that appear in the bargaining strength of multinationals and governments of developing countries on the exploitation of natural resources. Often labeled the "obsolescing bargain," original agreements on resources such as oil, bauxite, copper, iron ore, and timber have been shown by various researchers to have a common tendency to become obsolete over time.[16] As existing contractual provisions become increasingly unrealistic, national governments tend to respond by changing external control measures. After the capital has been sunk in and the initial risks have been taken, attitudes often change. The enterprise may now perceive the project as offering more promise than before. The government, with the project now "captured," may come to view the original terms of the agreement as unreasonable. Knowing that the terms needed to retain the enterprise are much less than those needed to attract it in the first place, it presses for renegotiation. As one economist has noted: "lamentations and exhortations are unlikely to change the dynamics of this cycle, which is based on a sharp break from a situation of great uncertainty, asymmetries, and little transnational corporation commitment, to a situation of much more information, symmetry, as well as large transnational corporation investments *in situ.*"[17]

CONFLICT MANAGEMENT AND TECHNOLOGY TRANSFERS

One of the useful features of the kind of model constructed in figure 2.3 is its specific focus on the situational variables affecting conflicts between MNCs and opposing interests; this focus may be especially valuable with respect to technology transfers. IBM differs from Siemens, which in turn differs from Fujitsu in many ways, and so corporate responses to national policies on the terms and conditions of technology transfer will differ as well; the reactions of IBM and Britain's International Computers, Ltd. (ICL) to the Indian Foreign Exchange Regulation Act of 1974 are a case in point. In addition, MNCs do not perceive Brazil as being similar to Pakistan or Ghana as regards their leverage in technology matters. The variables noted by Greer, including market power, business acumen, and technical capability, can all be built into such a generalized conflict management model because they affect each of the four situational variables we have identified as determining MNC conflict behavior.

What this means is that the kinds of structural measures advocated by Greer are more likely to improve terms and conditions for developing countries than are conduct controls. Structural measures, for example, can reduce the "power" available to MNC management in such a way as to limit the degree of assertiveness that seems appropriate and move the management to compromise solutions. Conduct controls tend to be blanket measures and therefore cannot possibly be optimal. One would also suspect that conduct controls at the national level tend to bias outcomes toward *avoidance,* which dumps the baby with the bath water. International conduct controls such as the proposed UNCTAD code move even farther from specific situational factors and may lead to even worse outcomes, except to the extent that they succeed in cutting down MNC leverage by imposing behavioral constraints that reduce the firm's options.

Since we are dealing with a positive-sum game, it is in the interest of the developing countries to move outcomes regarding technology transfers into the *compliance-collaboration-compromise* zone in figure 2.3. Doing so calls for the selective use of carrots and sticks to obtain *collaboration* when an MNC has high stakes and power, and for forcing *compliance* when the firm's stakes and power are low. It also suggests creation of coalitions, promotion of home-country structural policies, and similar measures suggested by Greer to obtain what are essentially *compromise* solutions.

NOTES

1. See Steven P. Magee, "Information and the Multinational Corporation: An Appropriability Theory of Direct Foreign Investment," in J. N. Bhagwati, ed., *Proceedings of a Conference on the New International Economic Order* (Cambridge, Mass.: Massachusetts Institute of Technology Press, 1977), pp. 197–214; and Ingo Walter, "Technology Creation and Technology Transfer by Multinational Firms: Comment," in Robert G. Hawkins, ed., *The Economic Effects of Multinational Corporations* (Greenwich, Conn.: JAI Press, 1979), pp. 178–83.

2. This model is developed fully in Thomas N. Gladwin and Ingo Walter, *Multinationals Under Fire: Lessons in the Management of Conflict* (New York: Wiley, 1980), chapters 2 and 3.

3. In the evolution of conflict-management analysis, most discussions have been in the context of interpersonal or intergroup relations. See, for example, Robert R. Blake and Jane S. Mouton, "The Fifth Achievement," *The Journal of Applied Behavioral Science* (October–December 1970), 6:413–26; Robert R. Blake and Jane S. Mouton, *The Managerial Grid* (Houston: Gulf, 1964); Hans J. Thamhain and David L. Wileman, "Conflict Management in Project Life Cycles," *Sloan Management Review* (Spring 1975), 16:31–50; Kenneth W. Thomas, "Toward Multi-Dimensional Values in Teaching: The Example of Conflict Behaviors," *The Academy of Management Review* (July 1977), 2:484–89; P. R. Lawrence and J. W. Lorsch, *Organization and Environment: Managing Differentiation and Integration* (Boston: Division of Research, Graduate School of Business Administration, Harvard University, 1967).

4. Cf. Charles P. Kindleberger, *American Business Abroad: Six Lectures on Direct Investment* (New Haven: Yale University Press, 1969).

5. See, for example, Raymond Vernon, *Storm Over the Multinationals: The Real Issues* (Cambridge, Mass.: Harvard University Press, 1977); Raymond Vernon and Louis T. Wells, Jr., *Manager in the International Economy,* 3d ed. (Englewood Cliffs, N.J.: Prentice Hall, 1976); John Fayerweather, *International Business Management: A Conceptual Framework* (New York: McGraw-Hill, 1969); and Ashok Kapoor, *Strategy and Negotiation for the International Corporation: Guidelines and Cases* (Cambridge, Mass.: Ballinger, 1976).

6. John Thibaut and Laurens Walker, *Procedural Justice: A Psychological Analysis* (Hillsdale, N.J.: Lawrence Erlbaum, 1975), p. 7.

7. Decision costs are a function, among other things, of the time and effort required by a decision-making or conflict resolution procedure. See J. M. Buchanan and G. Tullock, *The Calculus of Consent* (Ann Arbor: University of Michigan Press, 1962), pp. 342–81. Experimental research on the impact of time limits is reviewed in Jeffrey Z. Rubin and Bert R. Brown, *The Social Psychology of Bargaining and Negotiation* (New York: Academic Press, 1975), pp. 120–24.

8. See Morton Deutsch, *The Resolution of Conflict: Constructive and Destructive Processes* (New Haven: Yale University Press, 1973), pp. 84–85.

9. See Clinton F. Fink, "Some Conceptual Difficulties in the Theory of Social Conflict," *The Journal of Conflict Resolution* (December 1968), 12:448.

10. Deutsch, *Resolution of Conflict,* p. 20.

11. Joseph S. Nye, Jr., "Multinational Corporations in World Politics," *Foreign Affairs* (October 1974), 53:168.

12. For a good framework, see John Fayerweather, "A Conceptual Scheme of the Interaction of the Multinational Firm and Nationalism," *Journal of Business Administration* (Fall 1975), 7:67–89. See also Richard D. Robinson, *International Business Management: A Guide to Decision-Making* (New York: Holt, Rinehart and Winston, 1973), p. 1.

13. Anatol Rapoport, "Game Theory and Intergroup Hostility," in M. Berkowitz and P. G. Bock, eds., *American National Security: A Reader in Theory and Policy* (New York: Free Press, 1965), pp. 368–75.

14. Cf. Alonzo L. McDonald, "The MNC: Monkey in the Middle," *The McKinsey Quarterly* (Spring 1977), 8:15–31.

15. For a discussion of "superordinate" goals, see Muzader Sherif, "Superordinate Goals in the Reduction of Intergroup Conflict," *The American Journal of Sociology* (January 1958), 63:349–56.

16. See David N. Smith and Louis T. Wells, Jr., *Negotiating Third-World Mineral Agreements* (Cambridge, Mass.: Ballinger, 1976); Theodore H. Moran, *Multinational Corporations and the Politics of Dependence* (Princeton: Princeton University Press, 1974); Raymond F. Mikesell, ed., *Foreign Investment in the Petroleum and Mineral Industries: Case Studies in Investor-Host Country Relations* (Baltimore: The Johns Hopkins Press for Resources for the Future, 1971); and Zuhayr Mikdashi, *The International Politics of Natural Resources* (Ithaca: Cornell University Press, 1976).

17. Carlos F. Diaz Alejandro, "International Markets for Exhaustible Resources, Less Developed Countries, and Transnational Corporations," in Hawkins, ed., *Economic Effects*, p. 297.

Commentary

◇

Louis T. Wells, Jr.

The Greer paper is an interesting one. It has a clear subject: how to improve the terms under which developing countries acquire their technologies. And it presents a clear, strong argument that could be summarized as follows. First, in many cases there are few suppliers of a technology. In those cases the bargaining power of a supplier vis-à-vis the host country is greater than it is when there are many suppliers. Moreover, in many cases developing countries offer a small market and have few skills and little information with which to bargain. These disadvantages place them in a weaker bargaining position than that of a large-market country with sophisticated technical skills and a great deal of information.

Greer argues that controls on conduct that reduce the return to a provider of technology are likely to reduce the supply of technology. Under conduct controls, the supply is least likely to be reduced and the terms most likely to be improved for the host country when both the transferor and the recipient are in a strong position (presumably, the controls help resolve the bargain struck in a bilateral monopoly in favor of the recipient) and when both the transferor and the recipient are in weak positions (presumably, this outcome is particularly to be expected if the weakness of the recipient is based primarily on ignorance). Greer concludes that the most effective way to improve the terms for recipients is to change the structure of industries so that there are more (or potentially more) independent suppliers of the technology.

There is indeed considerable evidence—much of it marshaled by the author—to support the claim that a more competitive structure generates better terms for the technology-importing developing countries. An unpublished study by Nathan Fagre and myself confirms the importance of the number of competitors. [1]

In fact, bargaining power does not arise solely out of the possession by several firms of the needed technology. In some cases, the technology may be fairly widely available, but only a few firms can provide access to an export market. This is probably the case for bauxite and, more arguably, for original equipment automobile parts. This additional structural factor, however, could easily be integrated into Greer's analysis.

THE PROPOSALS

The policy proposals that are offered in the Greer paper follow from the analysis. But they leave little room for optimism. At least theoretically, three of the policy proposals could be implemented by the developing countries with little cooperation from the industrialized countries. The fourth is really in the hands of the advanced nations.

Those policies that could be implemented by the recipients of technology are: (1) loosening of patent (and trademark) regulations, (2) economic integration, and (3) encouraging competitive bidding.

Presumably, the purpose of loosening trademark and patent regulations is to enable local firms to copy foreign technologies and thus to provide an alternative to the multinational. In fact, I doubt that patents have generally been the critical barrier to the entry of developing-country firms into a particular industry. Unpatented technology generally presents a formidable barrier to the new entrant from a poor nation. Pharmaceuticals are likely to be the principal exception. If this argument is indeed true, the policy offers only very minor help.

One must also suspect that the chances of help from economic integration are rather limited. As Greer points out, the record of attempts to develop regional markets is dismal in the developing countries. There are, of course, good reasons, but I suspect that optimism about a turn-around in the pertinent factors is unrealistic.

Finally, according to Greer, the developing countries should encourage bidding when they acquire technology. Obviously, bidding is of no help if they are faced with a monopoly supplier. But when there are several suppliers, developing countries have found it difficult to deal with them simultaneously. The problems arise from the lack of available skills and the difficulty of comparing technologies and terms that differ somewhat from supplier to supplier.

The fourth policy suggestion is for more vigorous antitrust action in the advanced countries. Obviously, any steps in this area are out of the hands of the developing countries. Again, I suspect that an observer cannot be very optimistic. Antitrust policies in the advanced countries are not likely to be driven by the needs of the developing countries. In fact, the history of antitrust policy suggests that countries are eager to allow collusive behavior in dealings with foreigners (provisions of the Webb-Pomerene type do not exist only in the legislation of the United States: the French have their "spheres of influence," the Japanese Government has drawn its companies together to do business abroad, and development assistance is still often "tied"). There seems little hope for the abolition of such practices by the governments of the industrialized countries. Moreover, the extension of national antitrust legislation abroad has been meeting with more, not less, resistance from advanced countries. National legislation is increasingly unable to deal with the structural problems that are most likely to reduce the number of suppliers of technology to the developing countries: agreements among companies of different nationalities. But the principal source of potential competition is the rival firms of different nationalities. No one seems willing or able to restrict, say, joint ventures between a U.S. and a Japanese automobile producer to supply technology to a third country.

Greer himself rather summarily dismisses international codes of conduct. The contents of most codes, of course, are more oriented toward changes in conduct than toward changes in structure.

A CASE FOR OPTIMISM

It is easy to arrive at a pessimistic conclusion when one examines the paper's proposals. But there is a more optimistic case to be made.

Even if one accepts the argument that controls on conduct cannot do much to improve the terms for developing countries (I do not accept it, as will be clear later), one can argue that the structure of world industry has been changing, and is likely to continue to change, in ways that favor the recipients of technology.

The principal change is in the number of suppliers of a particular technology. It has not been long since U.S. firms dominated international transfers of technology. Now, a developing country has a choice of U.S., European, Japanese, or even Indian or Korean suppliers of many kinds of know-how. As Greer points out, the latecomers are frequently willing to offer nonconventional terms that are more favorable to the recipients than those of the original firms.

One might worry that the increase in competition is only for the older technologies. But with the higher incomes and the greater size of the European market, European firms have moved much more quickly than might have been expected into the newer technologies. The Japanese have also done so, for somewhat different reasons. By the time a particular technology is required in the developing countries, firms of several nationalities are likely to be in the market.

A second change is the dramatic improvement in the skills and information available in the recipient countries. The skills are higher, and technological information now flows increasingly from developing country to developing country, no longer simply on the north-south routes.

In addition, there is reason to believe that controls aimed at conduct can be more helpful than Greer suggests. After all, the interests of the private firm are not always identical to those of the country. This divergence is particularly likely in the acquisition of technology. Controls on terms ("conduct") can help make the outcome of negotiations between private companies more favorable to national interests.

Consider the simplest case, long recognized by the Japanese. It is to the interest of a private firm, faced with a local competitor having a foreign technology, to purchase similar technology abroad. The interests of the country may be to avoid paying for a technology similar to that already purchased, or at least to avoid the payment of a high price by the second firm.

The more complicated cases arise when even the first firm is willing to pay more for a technology than the technology is worth to the country. Profits to the firm from the know-how may be high, owing, for example, to high tariff protection. In such a case, what the firm is willing to pay for the technology may be much higher than what the country ought to be willing to pay. Restrictions on agreements may be the only feasible way to match the interests of the private buyer and the national economy. In this case, restrictions may indeed reduce the supply of technology, but the reduction is in the national interest. (The best solution would be to eliminate the tariff or other constraint that makes the private interest different from the public interest. In many cases, this action is politically infeasible.)

On exports, again the private and social interests may diverge, especially in a country with an overvalued exchange rate or wage rate. To match the interests, direct controls on terms for the purchase of technology may be the only feasible solution.

Greer himself also pointed out that restrictions on conduct may be helpful when there is a bilateral monopoly involved in the negotiations (the local purchaser can always point out that he simply cannot agree to a set of terms proposed by the supplier) and when both the recipient and the supplier are weak (presumably, because the outcome of the negotiations would be pushed to what it would be if the recipient were aware of the weakness of the supplier's position).

CONCLUSION

The Greer paper offers theoretically attractive policies for affecting the structure of industry so that developing countries can acquire technology on more favorable terms. However, the reader is left with what seem to be overwhelming problems in implementing the policies. On the other hand, Greer does suggest that there are changes occurring in the structure of world industries that will help the developing countries. They give some reason for optimism.

Finally, Greer may overstate the case against the effectiveness of controls on conduct in improving the position of developing countries. The problems he ascribes to each tool are clearly real. But the case can be made that these tools are still an appropriate part of the policy kit of a developing country. Practical solutions will almost certainly require a mix of efforts to influence structure and attempts to control conduct.

NOTE

1. Nathan Fagre and Louis T. Wells, Jr., "Bargaining Power of Multinationals and Host Governments" (Harvard Graduate School of Business Administration, mimeo, 1978).

Discussion

◆

DAVID McQUEEN: I understood Sigmund Timberg to say—and I think Louis Wells seconded the motion a bit here—that the LDCs were really more interested in innovation than in invention, that they don't want or need to be out on the leading edge of technological development, and so forth; they'd go in for more efficient bullock carts in India, construction of VW Beetles in Brazil, and that kind of thing.

It seems to me unlikely that many of these countries will industrialize on traditional, historical patterns, that it will all be a story of our letting them have the dying dogs and the falling portions of our product cycle. If you look at those countries that have gone from LDC status to become—what is it?—NIC, newly industrialized countries, you find leapfrogging, a lot of divergence from traditional industrial patterns. For example, Korea and Formosa are into transistors and all sorts of electronics, and Singapore produces highly advanced cameras.

True, a lot of it is spin-off from Japan and Germany, but it's a pretty close spin-off. It hasn't just been a tale of textiles, boots, shoes, shirts, and all that sort of thing.

I think one may find that in certain of the most promising situations for industrial development in these countries, the relevant and appropriate technology is quite advanced and rather close to the competitively relevant new kind of technology that the transnational corporation has in its portfolio.

SIGMUND TIMBERG: I would like to point out that what has taken place in Korea, Taiwan, Malaysia, and Hong Kong is very largely the result of American enterprises having moved out of this country because of lower wage rates. Because those people have real miniaturization capacities in manufacturing and are willing to work for us, we are getting products of considerable sophistication that come back marked "Korea," "Taiwan," "Hong Kong," and "Malaysia."

JAMES ATWOOD: Does that mean that where the U.S. company takes its technology with it, that's been regarded by the LDCs as basically not part of the transfer of technology debate?

TIMBERG: What I'm saying is that there is a distinct phenomenon that is beginning to be true of a great many multinational corporations, namely, that they're seeking attractive countries where the technology is skilled enough to conduct the operation that they want, and where they also have to pay less.

JOEL DAVIDOW: I have some feeling whenever I hear experts on transfer of technology that antitrust gets lost somewhere here.

The simplest example is when the licensor is requested by the licensee to give the licensee an exclusive, that is, to promise not to license anybody else in that country. And the bargain is eventually for an exclusive the other way: the licensee is not to accept anybody else's technology. If the parties are entirely happy, the antitrust violation may be twice as bad. That is, you may have excluded competitors at both ends of the distribution chain.

The point is that antitrust is always a public standard; it is not a standard that measures whether the bargaining is acceptable to both parties. And as I have said, one of the problems of trying to write a transfer of technology code that's an amalgam of some antitrust concepts and some bargaining concepts is that they really don't come out the same way.

One of the educational functions of the negotiation of a UN code on restrictive business practices is that developing countries must face the fact that there's more to the world than either the interest of their local licensee or even their immediate national interest. For instance, how should an international code deal with the situation where an American licenses a Brazilian with an agreement that the royalty will be favorable if there's an export ban to China? It's acceptable to the United States and the U.S. licensor; it's acceptable to the Brazilian licensee and to the country of Brazil; and it's totally unacceptable to China, which is the victim of the export restraint.

The answer is: either you are interested in some sort of international standard in which the objective is the free movement of goods and the maximum competition, or you're interested in protecting bargains, outcomes, negotiating stages.

Similarly, for a solution, you might look to arbitration, perhaps through the World Bank's International Center for Investment Disputes, treating disputes as another form of investment dispute between the foreign investor and the recipient state. However, when third parties are affected, you have a general principle, which is embodied in U.S. law, that you can't arbitrate antitrust because it involves nonpresent parties' interests.

So I just think that some of the papers are leaving out the real antitrust way of looking at this, which is a very broad world competition point of view, and looking at it quite a bit more narrowly.

DOUGLAS F. GREER: The exclusive dealing arrangement that Joel Davidow hypothetically set out, where the two parties reach an agreement that would injure third parties, does not necessarily call for complete control. That is to say, it doesn't call for a denial of exclusive dealing across the board, per se. There are instances where exclusive dealing can be procompetitive, as in the *White Motors* case.

What is needed is a structural approach so that exclusive dealing is procompetitive. The anticompetitive result of an exclusive dealing arrangement typically stems from market power somewhere, as compared to mere mutual advantage on the part of the contracting parties. Thus, the exclusive dealing example also indicates the heavy-handedness of the conduct approach and the need to consider structural factors.

TIMBERG: Of course, the public interest must be brought into mind; but any notion that the commitments that are being worked out in connection with the transfer of technology amount to optimum U.S. antitrust policy must be rejected. The negotiation of the code involves a trade-off, even among the countries that have competition policies.

JACK BARANSON: I have three points. One is on "unbundling." I think there is a very important economic contribution to unbundling, aside from the pricing issue. The kind of unbundling that uses a technology license to penetrate into the inner logic of a technology and into the industrial management of that technology is a very important factor that contributes to economic development goals. In a country like Brazil, you can see the efforts to penetrate into computer equipment manufacture or into the chemical industry through unbundling; that is how the licensee learns industrial management and penetrates the techniques of inner design engineering and manufacturing.

Secondly, on the structural approach, I would like to mention something that I think is a neglected dimension, namely, the financial mechanisms. For example, the availability of certain kinds of international credits may permit LDC enterprises to bypass the investment mode (such as a foreign multinational using equity as control) or even the licensing mode. They are thus enabled to buy technology on terms and conditions that they feel contribute to their development. Such financial lines of credit, mechanisms that give firms access to funds with which they can buy a technology package outside the licensing or investment mode, are a kind of restructuring that is an important way of improving the bargaining position of the LDC enterprise vis-à-vis the foreign supplier.

My third point concerns the economic justification for the differential treatment of foreign enterprise. The fact is that unless you have a differential policy that screens and preempts the foreign presence of a foreign firm (which, after all, has the preeminent positions in marketing, production, and technology), unless you buffer and favor local industry, it will never get started. The Brazilians now want a computer industry, and they are taking action against IBM, not as far-reaching as in the Indian case, but they've seen to it that IBM was not given permission to introduce a new line of small computers. They want their own industry to develop. And from the developmental point of view, there is a very fundamental reason for differential treatment of the foreigner in order to let your infants be nurtured and developed and given a chance to develop.

ROBERT RADWAY: Jack Baranson just put his finger on something that I've wanted to mention: development and competition are inconsistent in many cases, at least in the beginning.

There is another question I want to raise: who asked the local private sectors in these countries if they wanted the government to interfere on their behalf and protect them and improve their bargaining power vis-à-vis the foreign suppliers of technology?

I have had extensive conversations with representatives of the private sector of several industries in many Latin American countries, and they resent the intervention of their governments. They resent at least some of the policies of control. I'm not saying that these systems should all be thrown out, because I think regulation and control systems seem to have shown a number of benefits. I'm just saying that there must be a significant amount of flexibility built into them.

NATHANIEL LEFF: I think Greer's conceptual formulation of the problem in his paper is very well taken. Specifically, if there are many suppliers of technology on the one side, and if you have well-informed searching buyers of technology on the other side, you don't have an unequal exchange. On the contrary, competition on the supply side will force terms to be competitive, provided again, as Greer pointed out, that purchasers of technology look for bidding, look for alternative sources. In how many industries is that likely? In how many industries are there many suppliers, as contrasted to industries where there is one supplier who can exert monopoly power?

Here we come to empirical judgments. In his paper, Greer mentioned three monopoly-type examples. One is automobiles, one is chemicals, and one is computers. I would question that. If we have half a dozen or ten companies in the world with the technology, we do not have monopoly. That is true of the automobile industry. Jack Baranson's study of the chemical industry in the United States shows that in many of the relevant products—sulfuric acid or fertilizers—there are five, ten, if not more, suppliers of relevant technology.

Computers are usually cited as the great example where there is monopoly, and everyone brings out IBM as that example. We've had observations today that in India and Brazil there are multiple suppliers of relevant computer technology.

Now for the less developed country to make an advantageous deal, to take advantage of the competition among suppliers, you have to have a diligent, well-informed search on its part, which was true in the Brazilian experience with the minicomputers and in the Indian computer industry.

I think that in many industries the presumption of monopoly on the supply side is not empirically valid.

LOUIS T. WELLS, JR.: Why should one protect the interest of the private company that doesn't want protection? The point is that the interest of the private company in a developing country is very often not the interest of the country.

One cannot assume, in most developing countries, that the assumptions of the competitive model that we're willing to live by in an industrialized country apply. We are willing to assume that when it is profitable for the private investor to make an investment, it is profitable for the society. We know that there are some exceptions to that, but it is broadly enough applicable that we're willing to base our decisions on it.

The assumptions simply do not hold in most developing countries. I could go through a whole list of factors that make the assumptions not hold. Consider an industry that has a high rate of tariff protection and only one firm likely to supply the domestic market. The firm is willing to pay a price for technology that is very different from what is in the national interest. The firm doesn't want intervention; but it's in the national interest to intervene. The company's answer is simply irrelevant to the problem.

TIMBERG: I know of almost no situation where know-how of the kind that the developing countries can use is monopolized. It may be oligopolized, but you can have oligopolies like the oil industry where you have sixteen major concerns in the United States.

The real question is: do the developing countries, if they have a proper information base, have sellers' options? And that's where I think empirical evidence—and I might distinguish "empirical" from "statistical" evidence—is necessary.

RICHARD S. NEWFARMER: I would like to pose a question concerning differential treatment of foreign investment vis-à-vis national firms on the issue of transfer of technology. The question relates to the notion of technological independence and what this implies for the long run. Given the fact that developing countries may be condemned to producing, the last leg of the product cycle, can we think of foreign direct investment itself as a structural variable that developing countries might want to begin to look at seriously?

In other words, if foreign direct investment actually divides the innovation and invention function according to an international division of labor that puts innovation and invention primarily in the home country, does this create a structural circumstance that places developing countries in a disadvantageous circumstance, and thus warrants a new set of structural measures, particularly policies that promote domestic business?

That's not to say there is no role for transnationals in this process. Undoubtedly there is, and it can be quite positive. But this may indicate that we should begin to look at other agents and other factors for improving the technological bargaining positions of developing countries.

OSCAR SCHACHTER: Does anybody want to speak on this point?

SAMUEL WEX: When you're working within the multinational framework, can you bring about an innovative capability in the subsidiary so that the subsidiary itself would go from the marketing end all the way backwards to the R&D aspect for particular products?

The General Electric Company in Canada has what is called a "world product mandate" whereby its subsidiaries in certain countries are granted a full innovative capability. From the antitrust field this may be viewed as a product allocation. But I think, going back to the 1974 report of the Group of Eminent Persons, that if there are benefits to the host country from a product or market allocation, one should accept that. The notion of an innovative capability and how we can grasp it is very much discussed in Canada.

WALTER GLASS: When we're talking general state policy, we ought to consider that we are running a $30 billion deficit. And when I talk to my European friends, they point out to me that people who run that kind of deficit in international trade ought not to talk as big as we Americans always seem to do.

I would also point out two other factors that are pertinent to this discussion: one is that research capacity is encouraged where it exists. If it is possible for a multinational company to accommodate itself to local aspirations, it will, of course, do so. I think the problem is in part that in many areas where people would like to establish research or development institutions, the capacity is really not yet there. And when it grows there, I think it will be encouraged.

I would also note that where there are opportunities to invest or to sell technology, the competition is often fierce. I can't speak on a statistical basis, but I have had experience, and what I find is keen competition, either national competition on the Japanese model, or from European competitors. Such competition is often strongly government supported, by means of either credit facilities, counter-trade arrangements, or special credits at specially low rates such as 4 percent loans. It is in that competitive atmosphere that many American multinationals are now operating.

I would like to add that there is increasing competition from the socialist countries for technology sales. They made a major foray into India some years ago, which was not altogether successful. They have sold electrical equipment to Argentina at a 4 percent rate. It's that kind of competition that characterizes the new international marketplace.

VICTOR KRAMER: I'm going to read from Greer: "Recent years have seen substantial progress toward an international code of conduct on the transfer of technology, and we should not divert those efforts in pursuit of structural policies at the international level." Is the thesis that we should pursue them at the domestic level and not pursue them at the international? And if not, what does that sentence mean?

GREER: I'm just very, very pessimistic about structural modification at the international level. So all I'm saying there is that the regulation of conduct should not be diverted to a very frustrating effort at something structural on the international level.

WELLS: I'm very concerned about antitrust at the international level. The structural changes that I described have been taking place in recent years in the international marketplace and are largely the result of the entry of European, Japanese, and, increasingly, LDC firms.

I think business is perfectly capable of reversing that trend, or at least of trying to reverse it. I don't think there's any national antitrust policy capable of dealing with it. Take the example, hypothetically, of a joint venture between General Motors and Toyota in Brazil which enables them both to frustrate Brazilian purchase of technology and to cooperate on some third market. I don't see national antitrust policy as being capable of dealing with that.

M. P. McCARTHY: I would like to ask Louis Wells whether you would limit your antitrust concern to the horizontal variety you just described, or would you also advocate international antitrust-type controls with respect to vertical relationships between, let's say, a multinational and a licensee, or a multinational and purchaser in an LDC? For instance, would you advocate prohibiting a territorial restriction on a licensee of technology?

WELLS: My original statement was aimed at the horizontal, and that's what I feel most strongly about as threatening this trend that I see.

McCARTHY: In other words, competitor with competitor.

WELLS: That's what worries me the most.

McCARTHY: That's what you're concerned about.

WELLS: That's not to say I'm not concerned about the other, but that's what I see as completely uncovered by current institutions.

McCARTHY: I would say that the control of the horizontal would be much easier to accept—

WELLS: No, I think it's very difficult to accept, because I think countries have very different attitudes toward the role of competition; that makes it very difficult for us to agree with the Europeans, much less with the Japanese, on international control of horizontal restrictions.

McCARTHY: I agree with you that they're both difficult, but I think the horizontal may be easier to agree on than the vertical.

DAVIDOW: The horizontal-vertical distinction doesn't hold up very long. If you license somebody's technology, he wasn't a competitor of yours before you did it, but five years later he either is or he's a potential competitor.

The other point that I think is difficult raises the problem of what your philosophy is, that is, how free-market oriented are you? I go back to the *Alkali Export* case of 1948. The charge was that the Americans and the British had divided up Latin America, and that they had an agreement: the British got the northern half of Latin America and the United States the southern half. The argument against this was that this adversely affected American commerce and was illegal. One always wonders: let's say they had simply proved to the court that in the real world the United States would have only gotten 40 percent of Latin America, but by means of the agreement it got 50 percent with less selling effort.

The question is: should you allow the cartel because of the proof that it was a pretty good deal? And the obvious answer of an American is no. The good deal of today becomes the bad deal of tomorrow. The value of allowing world trade to reflect changing competitive and cost advantages is greater than the short-run national advantage of the cartel.

I think this is somewhat the same point that Louis Wells is making, but there's always a little bit of ideology here. You have to be saying that in the long run you favor constant change and reassessment in world trade, and that almost all cartel practices, or even restrictive practices, are trying to hold status quos true for some period of time.

RAYMOND F. MIKESELL: We've been discussing the interests of the private licensor and the private licensee, the MNC, and the host developing country. I just wonder if it would be at all respectable to mention the interests of the government of the parent company, or the interest of the developed country. The United States has been steadily losing its market share in manufactures, particularly in the developing countries, over the last twenty years, and especially over the last ten years. Many people have argued that the loss of this market share has been due, to a large extent, to the establishment of manufacturing affiliates and also to licensing.

Now what might be the interest of a country like the United States in the Code on Restrictive Business Practices? I'm reminded of the fact that one of the arguments given whenever someone has advocated various kinds of restrictions on the movement of technology and capital to developing countries is that this creates additional U.S. exports. It is also argued that by either the licensing arrangement or establishing affiliates, you could tie your exports of components, of related goods, and other things, and you could also prevent the exports to third markets that spoil other markets for the United States. This is pertinent to the interest of a developed country in a code.

BARRY E. HAWK: I was curious about the apparent agreement between Douglas Greer and Louis Wells that a favorable development has been the increase of suppliers of technology to LDCs.

I assume that the increase in suppliers is largely of non-American suppliers. Why is it in the interest of the United States to enforce the U.S. antitrust laws to increase foreign suppliers?

SEYMOUR J. RUBIN: I would like to make a point exactly along that line. Much is said today about the "industrial policy" of developed countries and their need to keep their markets and their industry at home in the interest of maintaining full employment and other national goals.

The question arises as to how sincere these developed countries are with respect to the objectives of the Codes of Conduct on Transfer of Technology and on Restrictive Business Practices.

GREER: Does direct investment abroad constitute a structural variable influencing the performance of U.S. firms in the United States? The answer is yes. The more foreign ties a corporation has, the greater its competitive edge over its domestic rivals. This is shown in the recent book by Bergsten, Horst, and Moran on the multinational corporation and the national interest.

Accordingly, if the aim is to improve the competition of IBM, then divestiture is recommended, namely, IBM–Europe from IBM–U.S. This recommendation has been made on the ground of the U.S. national interest, rather than the interest of the less-developed countries; but it would also help the less-developed countries.

WELLS: I don't think that the reason for the United States to support "international antitrust policy" is because it's in the interests of the LDCs. I think it's in our own interest. Increasingly, industries such as computers and automobiles can hardly be kept competitive inside the domestic market because the economies of scale are simply too great—whether in the production process, in research, or in the marketing process.

We are dependent increasingly on foreign firms for competition in an industry such as computers or automobiles. Such foreign firms compete through imports in the U.S. market. It is necessary to keep that competition and prohibit agreements between American firms and those foreign firms. We have the mechanism that keeps them from entering agreements that very directly affect U.S. markets. We don't have ways to keep them from developing joint ventures in foreign markets that do not directly, but do very indirectly but importantly, affect competition in the United States.

I think there is one element of bargaining power on the part of the multinationals that's been very much underestimated in our discussion. That is, not monopoly control over technology, but monopoly control over access to foreign markets by developing countries. That is still an element that gives a lot of bargaining power to some multinationals when they go to developing countries that are keenly interested in access to an export market.

3

CARTELS AND
CARTEL-LIKE PRACTICES

Economic and Political Characteristics of Cartel and Cartel-like Practices

Robert E. Smith

A cartel, like a labor union, is a political institution with economic consequences. It possesses an internal politics and, increasingly in recent years, exists in an external political environment, especially at the international level. Its economic consequences are a function of the market power it can command. We shall attempt to demonstrate that this market power, in turn, is dependent on the long-run and short-run market power bases available to it and its ability to internalize relevant investment, production, and pricing decisions. The primary purpose of this paper is to make more explicit certain aspects of market power in order to improve our understanding of its nature, determinants, and consequences. Neither the full welfare nor the policy implications have been worked out.

The basic purpose of a cartel is the substitution of an internalized administrativelike decision-making process for aspects of the external market process in the regulation of the allocation and coordination of economic activity. We shall later call this the process of "internalization." This statement, however, leaves unanswered the question as to the metes and bounds of the word *cartel*.

We shall initially adopt the definition of a cartel advanced by Heinrich Kronstein: "In a cartel the members impose parallel restrictions upon their conduct, or have such restrictions imposed upon their conduct, that have the effect of market regulation." [1] Again, following Kronstein, we shall extend the concept of the cartel to include market regulation whether participation by private, public, or some mix of private and public organizations is involved, [2] or whether the organization is formally structured or informal in nature.

Kronstein justified this broader concept on the basis of the development of modern systems of communication and transportation, the establishment of worldwide markets, the increasing horizontal and vertical integration of enterprises, [3] and the more pervasive interpenetration of the private and public sectors. A second, somewhat theoretical, rationale also underlies the adoption of the present definition. Although developed in detail below (see the discussion of figure 3.7), it will be briefly summarized at this point. Industries whose structural characteristics indicate relatively low probabilities of successful cartelization tend to be restricted to the more formal and more direct forms of collusion. Those industries with the most favorable structures have a set of organizational options that range from the formal and the direct to the informal and tacit; in this set the various arrangements are reasonably effective substitutes for one another. If the formal and direct forms are legally vulnerable and if we limit the term *cartel* to such efforts, any analysis of cartels would tend to be limited to those situations in which the expected failure rate would be high. Under these circumstances, it would not be surprising that commentators would tend to view cartelization as ineffective.

In sum, we shall use the word *cartel* to encompass a broad array of techniques to coordinate horizontal interfirm activities. The phrase *cartel-like activities* will additionally cover an assortment of vertical arrangements such as commodity agreements and orderly marketing agreements. These are negotiated arrangements, frequently between buying and selling cartels, in which allocation is effected by internalization efforts.

Cartels and cartel-like arrangements are obviously neutral institutions. They can be used as an instrument by private, public, or some public-private mix of organizations to realize private or public goals. Their scope, just like their membership, can be national or international. Cartels in particular are an amalgam of three elements: goals, coordinating devices, and operational techniques. Each of these elements consists of many diverse particulars.

In general terms, the goal is simply the improved welfare of the group, public or private; more specialized goals (designed to improve that welfare) include price stabilization, income stabilization, improved prices and profits, decrease in import or export competition, creation of barriers to entry or expansion, predation, and maintenance of market share. The coordinating techniques are similarly varied. They include consortium, syndicate, joint venture, merger, licensing contract, cross-licensing, formal agreement, price leadership, mutual forbearance, conscious parallelism, tacit agreement, intercorporate stockholding, and interlocking directorates. The operational techniques include cutbacks, inventories, boycotts, production or export levies, quotas, avoidance of price competition, geographic allocation, investment allocation, bid rigging, supply interruption, embargoes, notification and reporting, price discrimination, limit pricing, pools, loyalty and rebate payments, joint selling agents, and restrictive contract provisions.

Different aspects of these three elements can be combined in many ways to create the great diversity in cartel and cartel-like arrangements that we observe. Although institutions do matter, it is not our present purpose to chronicle or describe, case by case, this diversity. Instead, our purpose is to examine three significant dimensions of cartel and cartel-like arrangements: their ability to exercise market power, their internal politics, and their external politics. In the next section we present a theory of market power with special reference to cartels and cartel-like activities. The second section considers the scope of their internal politics as determined by the structural relationships that characterize the three major cartel and cartel-like arrangements: cartels, commodity agreements, and orderly marketing agreements.

In recent years, the external political relationships characteristic of cartels and related organizations have become of increasing importance. This development has been spearheaded by the less-developed countries (LDCs) in their drive for political and economic independence. In the absence of a legislative body that could impose majority role, a purpose of the LDCs has been to create a political environment, external to and broader than the cartel and cartel-like arrangements themselves, that prompts the negotiation of such organizations and legitimates their existence. This process is best observed in the political maneuvering represented by the drive for the "New International Economic Order." This topic will be treated briefly in the third section. The major emphasis of this paper will be on the first section; consequently, its emphasis is more on understanding the nature of market power than on the development of policy with respect to it.

DETERMINANTS OF MARKET POWER

It is convenient to analyze market power in terms of a constrained set of conduct options. This definition implies that discretion is the essence of power and that discretion, unless absolute, is limited by some constraint system. There is an inverse relationship between the constraint system and the power base; as the effectiveness of the constraint system increases, the effectiveness of the power base decreases. The determinants of each, however, are the same.

If market power is viewed as a constrained set of conduct options, we can identify different types of market power in terms of (1) different subsets of conduct options, (2) different determinants of or different constraint systems associated with each subset, and (3) different policy instruments. *Market power is protean, not monolithic, in form.* Among the more obvious types of market power that can be identified are long-run market power, short-run market power, and rival-oriented market power that is generated primarily by intrafirm internalization.[4] Neither conventional theories of market power nor the law systematically makes these distinctions as to varieties of market power.

The extent to which firms in a given industry possess any of these types of market power will depend, in great measure, on the extent to which their environment provides them with the four basic components of market power: a long-run market power base, a short-run market power base, internalization as a facilitator of market power (e.g., the ability to coordinate interfirm decisions), and internalization as a base for rival-oriented market power. In table 3.1 these four components are summarized and differentiated with respect to five significant characteristics: options, determinants, social problems, policy instruments, and targets. It is suggested that the ability of firms in an industry to exercise effectively any of the three types of market power noted in the paragraph above depends upon their possessing the right combination of the basic components. For example, the exercise of long-run power requires a long-run power base and internalization as a facilitator, and the exercise of short-run market power requires a short-run power base as well as internalization as a facilitator. With respect to each type of market power, each of the relevant components is a necessary but not sufficient condition. These components and their interrelationships are merely summarized in table 3.1; this material

TABLE 3.1
The Four Components of Market Power

	Options	Determinants	Social Problem	Policy Instrument	Target
1. Long-run market power base (LRMP)	1. Price level 2. Profit level 3. Price discrimination	1. Barriers to entry 2. Price elasticity of demand	1. Allocation inefficiency 2. Production inefficiency 3. Equity issues	1. Antitrust law 2. Direct regulation	1. Buyer
2. Short-run market power base (SRMP)	1. Stabilize price/excess capacity 2. Stabilize profit/increased costs 3. Stabilize price/decreased costs	1. Nature of product 2. Break-even point	1. Inflation 2. Allocation inefficiency	1. Antitrust law 2. Direct regulation 3. Incomes policy	1. Buyer

3. Internalization as a facilitator of market power	1. Substitution of internal processes for external market processes	1. Nature of transaction costs
		 2. Benefits
			1. Effectuates
			   a. LRMP
			   b. SRMP
			   c. R-OMP
				1. Antitrust law	1. Buyer
					 2. Rival
					 3. Supplier

4. Internalization as an additional power base: rival-oriented market power (R-OMP)	1. Cross-subsidization
	 2. Reciprocity
	 3. The squeeze
	 4. Tapered integration
	 5. Ties
		1. Form of the firm
		 2. LRMP
			1. No-problem school
			 2. Problem school
			   a. Increase barriers to entry
			   b. Foreclosure
			   c. Predation
				1. Antitrust law	1. Direct effect: rival
					 2. Direct effect: supplier
					 3. Indirect effect: buyer

is further developed below, especially with respect to options and determinants.

Because industries will differ as to the components of market power available to each, we can expect that different industries will possess differing abilities to exercise each type of market power. For example, the determinants of the long-run power base differ from those of the short-run base; consequently, possession of significant long-run market power does not assure significant short-run market power. This combination can have an adverse effect on profit performance and on the incidence of legal problems.

As indicated above, the analysis of two of the bases of market power is divided into the familiar dichotomy of the long-run and short-run time periods of conventional price theory.[5] The long-run time period is sufficiently long to allow a new firm to enter or a firm in an industry to increase its capacity. This lead time can vary across industries from several months to several years. The investment decision is critical here; consequently, the conditions of entry and expansion dominate the analysis of long-run market power.

The short run is the period between the present and the coming of the new capacity on stream. During this period, capacity is given; there is no entry or expansion. However, firms can determine in the short run the rate at which they will utilize their given capacities as they react to changes in demand, costs, or conditions of excess capacity or supply. Decisions with respect to inventories and rates of utilization characterize the exercise of short-run market power.

In short, the concept will be developed that long-run market power determines the persistent price and profit levels that an industry can enjoy and that short-run market power involves the ability to protect (long-run) price and profit levels from the need to make short-run adjustments. Long-run power requires analysis of the more traditional problem of monopoly-like prices and profits, while short-run market power requires analysis of options relative to the short-run adjustment process with respect to changes in demand, costs, and excess capacity or supply conditions. The thrust of this analysis is to integrate a theory of market power by stressing (1) the relationships between the two power bases in generating and protecting price and profit options, and (2) the relationship between the two power bases and the role of the internalization process (i.e., the form of the relationship among firms and the form of the firm itself) in facilitating the realization of these options and in creating additional conduct options. The balance of this section is divided into three major parts: long-run market power, short-run market power, and the several acts of internalization.

THE LONG-RUN MARKET POWER BASE

It is customary to analyze the traditional monopoly problem in terms of a diagram similar to figure 3.1. The restricted monopoly output (Q_b) enables the monopolist to maintain a monopoly price (P_b) persistently above the competitive level (P_c) and to enjoy an average monopoly profit of P_bP_c. If entry and expansion are free of barriers or collusion, entry and expansion will continue—reducing price and profit in the process—until the abnormal profits are eliminated and the long-run competitive solution is reached at P_c and Q_c, where demand (D) intersects the long-run supply curve (LRS). It is in this sense that entry and expansion are the essence of competition. A monopolylike situation, such as that represented by P_b and Q_b, cannot exist in the long run unless barriers exist. And in this sense barriers to entry and expansion are the essence of long-run market power.

Barriers to entry include patents, trademarks, trade secrets, control over scarce resources and other scarce factors, economies of scale relative to the

Figure 3.1 Long-Run Market Power

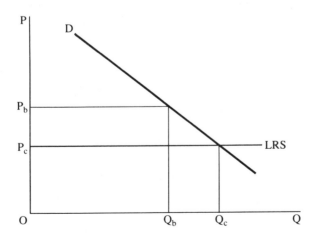

Note: See the accompanying text for an explanation
of the symbols used in the figures in this paper.

size of the market (the so-called percentage effect), and absolute cost advantages. We shall note the role of industrial property and develop the significance of the percentage effect. In addition, we recognize the existence of a lengthy lead time (a lengthy long-run time period) as the equivalent of an effective barrier to entry.

Space limitations constrain the analysis to two general entry conditions: blockaded and restricted. Free entry, the third entry condition, will not be analyzed. Entry will be considered to be blockaded when a potential entrant cannot enter an industry without the prior approval of the entered firm. The most likely examples involve a basic patent or a significant trade secret. Entry will be considered to be restricted when *postentry* profit expectations are insufficient to induce a competitive output. In this case, the effective barrier can consist of scale requirements that are significant relative to the size of the market. Free entry assures the realization of a competitive solution; the treatment of this condition is implicit in figure 3.1.

Blockaded Entry. A firm that enjoys the protection of blockaded entry is in a position to be a pure monopolist. Its management can set a price and limit its expansion without fear of attracting entry. This case is represented by the usual textbook model of monopoly pricing. The monopolist is assumed to be a profit maximizer. This requires that he produce that output at which marginal cost equals marginal revenue, which enables him to charge the monopoly price and to enjoy the related profits. These profits cannot attract entry because the blockaded entry protects the monopolist; he can act independently of potential entrants because they can enter only with his permission. A dominant firm has been born. This profit-maximizing monopolist must be pricing over the elastic portion of the demand curve.[6]

Restricted Entry. In the present context, entry is considered to be restricted when postentry profit expectations are insufficient to induce a competitive output. A full treatment of restricted entry would consist of a simple integer model, a noninteger limit price model, and a noninteger barrier model. Only the first model is considered in this paper. The simple integer model is essentially a restatement of work by Joe S. Bain,[7] Paolo Sylos-Labini,[8] and Franco Modigliani.[9] There is one significant difference:

This version is viewed as *part of a more general theory of market power rather than merely as a model of a strategy of limit pricing.*

We emphasize that the principal focus of the barrier theory of long-run market power presented below is on "the behavioral pattern leading" to a condition of equilibrium rather than on the "condition of equilibrium" itself.[10] In addition, it is suggested that the barrier theory is more a theory of how market power is acquired than an "explanation of how market power will be exercised once obtained."[11] This is the rationale for a concept such as the power base. In short, the barrier theory is more a theory of process than of structure and more a theory of the sources of market power than of the manner of its exercise, given its existence. A major purpose of the analysis is to develop the concept of a barrier price: i.e., of a maximum price or a capped range of price options above the competitive level that the barrier conditions of the long-run market power base allow. These conditions may effectively restrict firms in an industry to operations over the inelastic portion of the industry demand curve. Thus, the firms would have to maximize sales or profits subject to such a constraint.[12] Market power, after all, is a constrained set of conduct options.

The simple integer model establishes a long-run equilibrium price in the case of both perfectly and imperfectly divisible production. Although the model requires a number of restrictive assumptions, it is useful because it indicates a long-run equilibrium price (i.e., a maximum barrier price); because it offers a simplified description of the competitive process that focuses on the central role of entry; and because it also focuses attention upon the basic determinants of the power base of long-run market power in the postulated case of restricted entry.

There are five principal assumptions of the simple integer model. First, we assume that the ratio (Q_c/m) between the competitive output of the industry (Q_c) and the minimum optimal scale (m)[13] is an integer. Second, firms are assumed to enter and operate only at m. These two assumptions simplify the nature of both investment and output decisions. The third assumption is that firms will enter or expand only *one at a time*. This is the queue model of investment and contrasts with other models such as herd reaction and rivalrous investment. Fourth, it is assumed that a potential entrant or expander will distinguish between his preentry price and profit observations and his postentry price and profit expectations. If he anticipates that his entry will reduce price and profit to or below the competitive level, he will not enter although preentry observations were above the competitive levels. There is a positive relationship between the percentage effect and the gap between the preentry observations and postentry expectations. And fifth, we assume that entered firms will react to entry by maintaining output, and thus force the postentry price to fall to the level, given demand, required by the newly enlarged supply. Entered firms will not make way for the new entrant and the entrant knows this prior to entry; this is the so-called Bain-Sylos Postulate.[14]

The last three assumptions enable us to avoid in the long-run model the problem of excess capacity at the equilibrium barrier price and the consequent need to make appropriate short-run adjustments if that price is to be protected. Relaxation of these assumptions can result in entry that expands industry capacity beyond Q_b in figure 3.1, forcing price down to or below the competitive level (P_c). This expanded capacity, that is "excess" with respect to P_b, creates an opportunity or need for a theory of short-run market power in order to protect the price and profit options represented by P_b and Q_b. This theory is developed in the next part of this section.

The barrier model illustrates the process by which an equilibrium barrier price (P_b) and the set of price options (P_bP_c) and associated profit options are determined by the three principal sources of long-run market power when entry is restricted by economies of scale: minimum optimal scale (m), the competitive output (Q_c), and industry price elasticity of demand (E). In addition, we shall define the m/Q_c relationship as the "percentage effect." Following Modigliani,[15] the three determinants of the barrier premium are related so that $B = m/Q_cE$, where B is the barrier premium, expressed here as a percentage markup on costs, and is defined as the persistent monopolylike profit rate that restricted entry conditions allow. By varying each of these three determinants in turn, three subcases of the simple integer model are created. In this model, economies of scale are the effective barrier to entry.

In Case 1 we vary m, holding Q_c and E constant.[16] Given industry demand (D) and the long-run supply curve (LRS) in figure 3.2, the long-run equilibrium solution under competitive conditions would be P_c and Q_c.

We assume two different scales of plant: m is OA in Industry A and OB in Industry B. In Industry A, it is evident that the first five firms will enter because postentry price and profit expectations are greater than their respective competitive levels. For example, the postentry price for the fifth

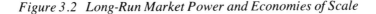

Figure 3.2   Long-Run Market Power and Economies of Scale

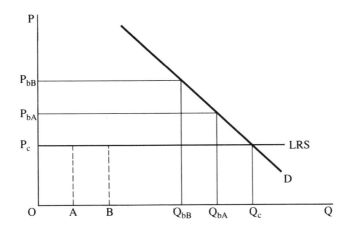

firm is P_{bA} and is greater than P_c. The fifth firm will enter and industry output will expand to Q_{bA}, and will thus validate P_{bA}.

But will the sixth firm enter? Given the Bain-Sylos Postulate, the firm will not enter because the postentry price and profit expectations (P_c) would be insufficient; at the competitive price, profits would be normal and, by definition, inadequate to attract entry. The long-run equilibrium price for Industry A would be P_{bA}. This barrier price would return to the five firms an average barrier premium, measured absolutely, of P_cP_{bA}. Competition, defined as entry, cannot eliminate this barrier premium.

In Industry B, the scale requirements are twice those of Industry A. The first two firms will enter. The third firm will not enter because its entry would push industry output to Q_c and price to P_c. The resulting barrier price (P_{bB}) and barrier premium (P_cP_{bB}) would both be greater than in Industry A. To generalize, there is a positive relationship, given Q_c and E, between m and the barrier premium. This is consistent with the rather common, though somewhat controversial, observation that the more concentrated industries are able to earn greater monopoly-type profits.

The real significance of Case 1, however, is found in three other observations. First, the level of warranted concentration [17] and the magnitude of the barrier premium are simultaneously determined by the three prin-

cipal factors. In this long-run model, therefore, the concentration ratio can
function at best only as a proxy for the long-run market power base; nevertheless, the ratio is important in the process of horizontal interfirm coordination. Second, in Case 1 perfect competition is a limiting case of the
simple integer model. Under perfectly competitive conditions, the percentage effect (m/Q_c) becomes infinitesimally small; entry will consequently
continue until the equilibrium price becomes P_c.

Third, it is important to stress that the effective decision in the establishment of the barrier price need *not* be made by any of the entered firms.
The effective decision can be made by the potential entrant when, confronted by the percentage effect of his entry on his postentry price and
profit expectations, he decides not to enter. In other words, a similarly
effective barrier price can be established either by the limit pricing and
expansion of entered firms or by the entry of new firms. The constraint of
a barrier price is given to the entered firms by the interaction between the
procompetitive process of entry and the existence of barriers to entry. The
firms are constrained as to that portion of the industry demand curve over
which they can operate.

In Case 2 (figure 3.3) we vary market size, holding the other two determinants constant. This case can be viewed as involving either two different industries at one point in time or one industry at two different points
in time. The latter view will be adopted because it represents an opportu-

Figure 3.3 Long-Run Market Power and Growth

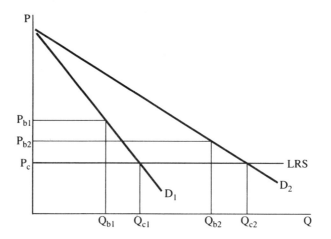

nity to analyze the effect of market growth from D_1 to D_2 on the price-profit performance of an industry. The competitive price for each of the two stages in the product cycle would be P_c.

Following the processes outlined in Case 1, Market 1 will be supplied by two firms. The barrier price will be P_{b1} and the barrier premium will be P_cP_{b1}. Market 2 will be supplied by five firms. The barrier price will be reduced to P_{b2} and the barrier premium to P_cP_{b2}.

Case 2 suggests that the barrier premium is negatively related to the size of the market or, viewed dynamically, growth of a market can be expected to reduce profits. This is, of course, the essence of the product life cycle concept. In short, a firm that would be a persistently abnormal profit center is on an innovational treadmill.

In Case 3 it is again convenient to view the model as involving a single industry faced alternatively with two different markets: D_1 and D_2 in figure 3.4. At any price, however, D_1 is less elastic than D_2. Both m and Q_c are constant.

In both markets five firms will enter. The sixth firm will refuse to enter in each instance because the postentry price would be P_c. The barrier prices and premium, however, will differ: P_{b1} and P_cP_{b1} for D_1 and P_{b2} and P_cP_{b2} for D_2. To generalize, there is a negative relationship between the size of the barrier premium and the price elasticity of demand, given the percentage effect.

Figure 3.4 Long-Run Market Power and Price Elasticity of Demand

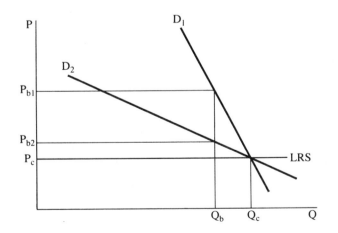

In short, in the case of restricted entry, an industry pricing over the inelastic section of its demand curve will be more profitable, *ceteris paribus*, than an industry pricing over the elastic section of its demand. This creates an apparent anomaly with respect to the exercise of long-run market power: a blockaded profit-maximizing monopolist will operate over the elastic portion of his demand curve, but firms whose power depends on restricted entry will have their profits increase, the more demand is price inelastic. The answer to the anomaly lies partially in the ability of entry, although limited by barriers, to force industry capacity into the inelastic section of industry demand and to prevent firms from raising prices into the elastic portion of industry demand. Under these constraints, profitability increases as price inelasticity of demand increases.

The third case is also helpful in understanding the effectiveness as well as the limitations of interproduct or interindustry competition. The presence of such competition tends to increase the price elasticity of demand for each of the products, although the cross-effects between the two industries need not be symmetrical; A may be a good substitute for B, but B need not necessarily be a good substitute for A. This asymmetry could be important in the definition of a relevant market. If cellophane, for example, is a superior substitute for waxed paper but waxed paper is an inferior substitute for cellophane, cellophane may well be significantly more capable of controlling the pricing of waxed paper than the latter can control the pricing of cellophane. In this sense, it may not be appropriate to include waxed paper in the relevant market that seeks to take account of products that control the pricing of cellophane. Cellophane, on the other hand, would certainly be included in the relevant market that controlled waxed paper.

In short, expansion and entry drive an industry to an eventual barrier price. Industries can differ as to the nature of price-limiting options available to them. Regardless of the option employed or of the use of such an option, the industry will eventually reach a barrier price. The limiting option used can affect the level of the barrier price. Of course, failure effectively to coordinate investment decisions can lead to a price below the maximum barrier level. Once a barrier price has been reached, however, the limiting options become less relevant as strategic variables.

The introduction of international trade [18] into the above theory of restricted entry has rather dramatic effects on predictions of market power.

Assume a domestic industry that is protected only by the percentage effect associated with economies of scale and that is exposed to import competition. When the economies of scale are associated only with production, the associated percentage effect will cease to be a barrier to entry (i.e., to imports) because imports have a minimal percentage effect relative to the importing market. The amount of imports that can be sold can be either quite small or significant; such markets may have no percentage effect.

Import competition is a powerful control when it lacks a significant percentage effect. On the other hand, when the economies of scale are associated primarily with product differentiation and marketing, the situation may well be different. To the extent marketing involves meaningful economies of scale and, therefore, a percentage effect, imports will not be able to avoid the restrictive effects of economies of scale as a barrier to entry (imports). The protection survives.

Exporting creates a different, though related, problem. Assume a domestic industry whose capacity was designed for 50 percent domestic sales and 50 percent exports. In this case, sales into the domestic market by domestic producers are not protected by any percentage effect; there is, in effect, excess capacity relative to the domestic market. Any market power exercised by the industry relative to the domestic market must depend on some type of an understanding among the firms, even assuming that the evident "excess" capacity deters import entry by foreign producers. If imports, however, drive prices to the competitive level in export markets and if antidumping laws tend to equate prices in the exporting country with prices in the importing country, the exporters may then not be able to protect their domestic price. In sum, producers in importing countries may lose the protection or advantage of a percentage effect; and producers in exporting countries may lose the guide of the percentage effect in establishing domestic prices and have to rely on collusion of some type to hold a price. Under these conditions, international trade increases the force of competition (i.e., imports as entry) in domestic markets. This result could be avoided, for example, by an international cartel that allocates markets by regulating the flow of trade between countries.

The situation is quite different, however, when the barrier to entry is industrial property. In the case of patents, imports can be regulated by the patent holder to protect prices in both domestic and export markets. In the case of a trademark, the percentage effect, as noted above, may well remain effective against imports. In these cases, the barriers to entry retain effectiveness,[19] which can be reduced, however, by allowing parallel imports.

In sum, the long-run market power base consists of the institutional blockades to entry in the case of blockaded entry and of both the percentage effect[20] and the price elasticity of demand in the case of restricted entry. In the latter case, the barrier theory predicts that the conditions of entry and expansion will determine where on the industry demand curve and with what price elasticity of demand the industry will operate. In this view, firms cannot always elect to operate in the elastic portion of industry demand or at the point of unit elasticity. Subject to this basic constraint, firms can decide on which price/profit/market-share options to adopt.

Industry output in the model of restricted entry will not exceed the barrier output, and the resulting barrier price will be reached and maintained as long as these three assumptions are observed: (1) the Bain-Sylos Postulate; (2) the supposition that postentry profit expectations will govern the investment decision; and (3) the queue model of investment. If any of these assumptions are relaxed, industrial capacity and output should increase, and thus exceed the barrier output and possibly the competitive output. In the absence of appropriate short-run adjustments, the market price will fall below the barrier price toward or even below the competitive price. If the firms desire to maintain the barrier price, they must be able to stabilize price at that level against the evident excess capacity. This short-run adjustment process involves the exercise of what we shall call short-run market power.

THE SHORT-RUN MARKET POWER BASE

A purpose of the previous analysis of long-run market power was to indicate the upper constraint on the long-run price-profit options of firms in an industry. These options, however, are subject to episodic erosion by changes in demand, capacity/supply, or costs. Such changes require adjustments that depend upon the nature of the short-run adjustment options allowed firms by their industrial environment.

The conduct options that identify short-run market power consist of two stabilization options and one exploitative option. The two stabilization options are (1) the ability to stabilize price or a related variable (e.g., total revenue, income, or export earnings) against excess capacity, supply, or demand, and (2) the ability to stabilize or protect the profit margin against a cost increase.[21] The exploitative option refers to the ability to exploit a relatively long lead time by curtailing supply in order to power a price run-up.

The two principal methods by which management attempts to exercise the stabilization options are inventory regulation and production cutbacks. In other words, those in management can realize these options of short-run market power to the extent that they can effectively coordinate among themselves the decisions to regulate inventories and/or cut back production. Such capabilities—as with long-run market power—are not distributed uniformly across industries. The degree of short-run market power available to an industry depends upon certain characteristics of the product and of the production process as well as upon management's ability to co-ordinate stabilization decisions. This portion of the paper is devoted to an analysis of the appropriate characteristics of the product and of the production process in the determination of a short-run market power base. The next part of this section deals with the internalization process.

Inventory Regulation.   An important, initial characteristic of the production process that affects the short-run market power base is the time interval between inputs and outputs. This distinction is especially important in the analysis of the short-run market power base available to agricultural industries as compared to manufacturing industries. In terms of this time interval, two basic production processes can be identified: a point-input, point-output process and a continuous input, continuous output process.

A point-input, point-output (PIPO) production process involves a significant time interval or lag between the point in time of the inputs and the point in time of the output. This process is typical of agricultural production, in which the lapse between input and output is frequently six months or more and the lapse between two successive outputs may be as much as a year. It is a significant imperfection from the standpoint of the short-run adjustment process, and it has two important consequences. First, it creates a potentially quite inelastic supply function between harvests. Second, PIPO industries are forced to rely primarily on inventory arrangements to exercise their stabilization options because a PIPO process reduces significantly the frequency of, and hence the ability to cut back, production. The use of quotas as a stabilization technique does not exist independently of the ability either to store the product or to effect the limited cutback options available. Quotas are, in effect, a derived instrument whose longer term effectiveness is consequently constrained by the nature of the PIPO process. Quotas cannot by themselves limit production; they provide a target.

To the extent PIPO industries rely on inventory regulation, whatever short-run market power they might possess depends on product characteristics that allow storage at a reasonable cost with respect to both the investment in the inventory and the physical storage. First, a commodity must not be perishable. Second, it should be fungible. If the product is significantly differentiated, there is the additional risk of storing the mix that the buyers desire when the product is sold. It is less risky, for example, to store aluminum ingot than the many different fabricated products. In addition, a high value/low bulk ratio is to be preferred over a low value/high bulk ratio. Finally, inventory regulation is more effective when the short-run demand and supply functions are inelastic with respect to price.

The above discussion has assumed that producers prefer price stability to price instability. Price stability can be preferred in its own right or as the preferred means of achieving stability of total revenue or, in the context of international trade, export earnings. In the latter case, revenue stability can be an intermediate policy goal for producer governments because of its expected beneficial effect on investment and growth, as well as on foreign exchange adjustment costs and costs of capital. Unfortunately, the linkages among price stability, income stability, and growth are characterized by significant uncertainties and possible surprises. Policies designed to stabilize prices (e.g., international commodity agreements) may or may not stabilize income. If income is stabilized, the average of the stabilized income over the cycle may be more or less than the average of the unstabilized prices.[22] In any event, price stabilization schemes have the efficiency disadvantage of generating prices that are not market-clearing prices.

Other policies are designed to stabilize income (export earnings) directly (e.g., the Lomé Convention). These policies do not involve price stabilization; the resulting prices are market-clearing prices. Income stabilization policies utilize lump sum payments. Unfortunately, however, the empirical relationship between revenue stabilization and the realization of investment and growth goals is ambiguous.[23] Nevertheless, LDCs typically act on the presumption that stability of export earnings will improve the chances of realizing investment and growth goals.

With respect to any discussion of the advantages and disadvantages of price stabilization, either as a means of income stabilization or in its own right, there is the general question: Do buyers or sellers benefit from such a policy? Until recently, it was believed, on a priori grounds, that if the price change were due to random fluctuations in supply (typically the agricultural case), producers would benefit from price stabilization; that if the price change were due to random fluctuations in demand (typically the mining case), consumers would benefit; and that, regardless of the source of the change, price stabilization would increase the combined welfare of the producers and consumers. Analysis now challenges the general validity of the first two of these three propositions. As one commentator noted: "One of the major conclusions of the literature is that although price stabilization will always, potentially at least, improve aggregate welfare, the distribution of these welfare gains between various members of society is highly sensitive to the precise specification of the model and the nature of the stochastic disturbances."[24]

Production Cutbacks.   It will be recalled that short-run market power was defined in terms of two stabilization options: stabilization of price against excess capacity, supply, or demand and stabilization of profit margin against a cost increase. The discussion of stabilization by inventory regulation was limited to the first option. Production cutbacks can involve both options.

The ready continuity between inputs and outputs characteristic of continuous input, continuous output (CICO) industries enables managements, when otherwise able, to adjust output rather quickly; consequently, firms in CICO industries are not prevented by the basic nature of the production process itself from achieving stabilization by either inventory regulation or production cutbacks. The determinants of the ability to cut back production are not the same as those for the regulation of inventories. We shall first consider those factors that allow firms to stabilize price against excess capacity and then note characteristics of the second stabilization option.[25]

Under perfectly competitive conditions, firms possess no price stabilization options. The short-run supply curve is derived from the short-run marginal cost curve of the firm and is based on the assumptions of short-run profit maximization and of a perfectly elastic demand curve facing the firm. This short-run supply curve, implying the absence of any price stabilization options, generates the competitive norm of price flexibility in response to changes in either industry demand or costs. This norm is represented by the traditional, upward sloping SRS$_c$ (the short-run supply function of a competitive industry) in figure 3.5.

The ability to stabilize price by cutting back production, given the ability to coordinate these decisions, depends upon the two technical and relatively objective determinants of the break-even point of a representative firm in an industry: the long-run market power base and the flexibility or elasticity of the short-run average total cost curve (SRATC in figure 3.5). Given the SRATC, the break-even point will decrease in percentage terms as the power of the long-run base increases (i.e., as the barrier price, P$_b$, increases). Given P$_b$ and the long-run power base, the break-even point will decrease as the flexibility of SRATC [26] increases (i.e., the intersection of P$_b$ and SRATC moves leftward). The flexibility of SRATC, in turn, increases as fixed costs decrease as a percentage of total costs and as the basic production unit (i.e., the basic production component within a plant) is more addable, adaptable, and interruptible. [27] In this context, firms in an industry possess an increasingly potent short-run market power base as the degree of long-run market power increases; as the addability, adaptability, and interruptibility of the basic production unit increase; and as

Figure 3.5 Short-Run Market Power

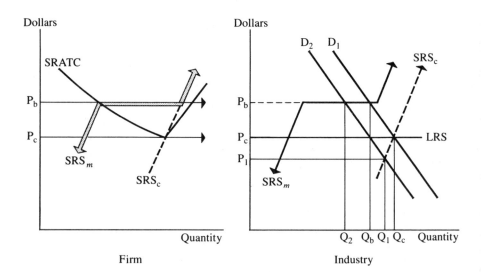

fixed costs become a less significant percent of total costs. This situation is represented by SRS_m (short-run supply function of a firm with a short-run market power base) in figure 3.5. Further explanation, however, is necessary.

SRS_m is the relevant short-run supply function only if it is more profitable to stabilize price at P_b by further decreasing the rate of utilization than it is to allow price to fall and minimize the decline in the rate of utilization. Assume that a recession shifts the industry demand curve from D_1 to D_2 in figure 3.5. In the absence of short-run market power, SRS_c would be the relevant supply function. Price would fall to P_1 and output to Q_1. This performance provides the competitive norm.[28]

If the firms possess a short-run market power base and can effectively coordinate their cutback decisions, they have the option of accepting P_1 or of stabilizing price at P_b by reducing output to Q_2. Presumably their decision will depend upon which option is more profitable.[29] Most generally, the answer will depend upon the relationship between the price elasticity of industry demand and the flexibility of the SRATC. For present purposes, however, we shall consider only the case where P_b is in the inelastic portion of industry demand. Any price reduction would increase total costs because output would be greater than if price were stabilized at the higher P_b. The price reduction into an inelastic portion of demand would decrease total revenue. Consequently, a price reduction, in contrast to price stabilization, would decrease total revenue and increase total costs; price stabilization would be more profitable.[30] In short, pricing over the inelastic portion of the industry demand curve is a sufficient condition, given effective interfirm coordination,[31] for price stabilization to be the profit-maximizing option in comparison to a price cut.[32]

The length of the stabilizing plateau in SRS_m measures the potential of the short-run market power base and increases with the degree of long-run market power possessed, the flexibility of the SRATC, and the importance of variable costs in total costs. It is quite possible that two industries with similar long-run market power bases and concentration ratios could have quite different SRATC flexibilities and fixed/total cost ratios. We should then expect them to have quite different stabilization records. An industry that is severely disadvantaged in its short-run power base might perform very much like a competitive industry in the context of short-run adjustments. However, in its efforts to stabilize regardless of its inadequate power base, the firm might be driven to using the more formal and obvious methods of collusion, and thereby fall afoul of the antitrust laws. While collusion is not an effective substitute for an adequate short-run power base, firms under pressure may be tempted to substitute.

The recent significant increases in the prices of raw materials, especially crude oil as a source of both energy and feedstock, are capable of causing important shifts in the relationship of variable costs to total costs and, consequently, of fixed costs to total costs. These price changes should increase the flexibility of the average total cost curve and lower the break-even point. Given the theory above, this situation should enable some industries, previously unable and not inclined to stabilize price against developing excess capacity by production cutbacks, to cut back production in their efforts to stabilize. With the increased flexibility, they should also have a greater economic incentive to stabilize prices. This projected change appears to have already occurred in the British chemical industry. It was reported that the increase in raw material prices increased the significance of variable costs, which lowered the break-even point from 80 to 85 percent to 60 to 75 percent. As a consequence, "where volume once held the key to profitability, price has now become of paramount importance."[33]

The exercise of the second variant of short-run market power, stabilizing margins against rising costs,[34] would appear to require effective inter-firm coordination as a necessary and sufficient condition, particularly if demand were price inelastic. Firms that possess this type of market power enjoy a pass-through mechanism that enables them to pass through any increase in costs, *with relative speed and certainty,* to the buyer in the form of a higher price for the product. If demand were price elastic, however, the price increase might have enough of an adverse impact on output (and total revenue) to require the simultaneous exercise of the first and second variants of short-run market power.

Thus far, the analysis of this short-run option has involved the adjustment to cost increases and not to an exogenous increase in excess capacity. The development of cost-push inflation can require that a firm be able simultaneously to pass through the cost increases (e.g., wage increases that lag behind previous increases in the cost of living) and to stabilize the *increased* price against the increase in excess capacity that results from deflationary macro-policies. During the "stop" phase of a stop-go policy sequence, firms may be required to exercise simultaneously both short-run options as they attempt to adjust. Generally, if firms in an industry can stabilize price against excess capacity, they can stabilize profit margins against higher costs. The opposite, however, does not hold. Consequently, during stagflation, the ability to stabilize price against excess capacity is essential to protect margins. Without this ability, concentration alone is insufficient to enable firms to protect either price or margins against the consequence of deflationary policies.[35]

Milton Friedman's analysis of the relationship between market power and inflation assumed the existence of only one type of market power— that of the traditional monopolist who is always maximizing his profits. The argument is simple: if those with market power are always and already maximizing their profits, their pricing can contribute to inflation only if and when their market power is increasing. "Insofar as market power has anything to do with possible inflation, what is important is not the *level* of market power, but whether the market power is *growing* or not."[36]

This argument overlooks the significance of the distinction between long-run and short-run market power and, in doing so, overlooks the role of short-run market power with respect to inflation. The possession of such power enables an industry to exploit the associated opportunity to improve its profitability by stabilizing price against developing excess capacity or by increasing price in order to minimize the erosion of profits by rising costs. In the former case, prices that should fall do not fall. In the latter case, prices rise more rapidly and with greater certainty than they would in the absence of short-run market power. In this manner, the exercise of short-run market power can make coping with inflation more complex and costly in terms of unemployment. These costs need not have anything to do with an increase in traditional monopoly power, i.e., with long-run market power. The critical point is not that the long-run market power *base* is or is not cyclically sensitive but that the *use* of the short-run market power base is cyclically sensitive.

On the basis of the distinction between long-run and short-run market power, we can expect the nature and frequency of a cartel's coordination decisions to be cyclically sensitive. On the upswing, especially at the later stages, we would expect investment decisions to be the critical coordination decisions in order to prevent excess capacity. These decisions, however, are difficult to coordinate because of their impact on future market shares. The strength of demand during the upswing should reduce the need to coordinate pricing and production decisions.

The matter is quite different on the downside. During this period the need is to coordinate production and pricing decisions in order to cope with excess capacity and/or rising costs. The urgency to act would be more immediate than in the coordination of investment decisions. In addition, the frequency of action would probably also be greater. Consequently, the nature and frequency of cartel decisions should change over the cycle, reflecting the distinction between long-run and short-run market power. Cartel activity should increase on the downside, representing efforts to make short-run adjustments. As yet, we do not understand the welfare implications of power-oriented short-run adjustments as we do of the use of long-run market power.

INTERNALIZATION AS A STRATEGY OF FIRMS

We shall emphasize that firms will adapt their organizational form—both interfirm and intrafirm dimensions—in order to try to reduce costs or realize benefits that are presented by their environment. This environment includes the available long-run and short-run power bases, the conditions that affect abilities to internalize, and government policies. In short, both the organizational form of the firm and the relationship among firms are strategic or policy variables that managements can utilize to realize their effective goals. Frequently, a change in either the form or the relationship will involve the substitution of an internalized administrative process for the more typical external market process. Recently, economists have given increasing attention to the efforts by which private parties substitute internal organization and administration for external market processes with respect to certain activities. This substitution of internal organization for market exchange we shall call "internalization." [37]

We can identify three functions of the internalization process. First, internalization can be used to reduce transaction costs [38] between buyers and sellers and among sellers (or, in the alternative, among buyers). In this sense, internalization is a benefit to the firms and *can* be a benefit to society. Second, internalization can be used to facilitate implementation of the options created by the long-run and short-run power bases. In this connection, it will be recalled that the power bases were only necessary but not sufficient conditions for the exercise of each type of market power (except in the case of a literally dominant firm); similarly, the ability to internalize effectively was a necessary but not sufficient condition for the exercise of such power. For example, one way that internalization can facilitate the exercise of long-run market power is the internalized coordination of investment decision making by firms in order to avoid excess capacity. And, finally, internalization can involve changes in the form of the firm itself. In this way, the form of the firm can create conduct options—over and above those created by a power base—that enhance its market power.[39]

Two principal functions of the external market process for which internalization can be substituted are allocation and coordination. The usual definition of economics and the bulk of economic analysis, especially that of welfare economics, focus on the allocation process at the expense of the coordination process; consequently, the systematic analysis of the coordination function of the market is underdeveloped.[40] But economists should be concerned with both the allocation and the coordination functions of the market process.

For convenience, a simple distinction will be made between allocation and coordination. The allocation function is defined to involve the relationship among buyers and sellers. The coordination function, on the other hand, is defined to involve the relationship among sellers *or* among buyers. Allocation is a buyer-seller relationship. Coordination is a seller-seller or buyer-buyer relationship. In what follows, we shall consider only the seller-seller relationship.

Welfare economics gives us a rather precise standard for measuring the social desirability of the performance of the allocation process: the well-established standard of allocation efficiency that requires equality between price and marginal cost. This is a consumer-oriented welfare criterion; it considers the welfare of the household from the viewpoint of its role as a consumer and not as a producer or income recipient. Its rationale lies in the efficiency with which it maximizes consumer welfare under the given conditions. This overlooks the possibility that households might and, in fact, frequently do prefer to maximize their welfare as producers. This possibility, however, is suggested by the nature of the coordination process. Although we have no measure similar to the one that we have for allocation by which to gauge the social desirability of the performance of the coordination process,[41] the business and agricultural communities have advanced an amorphous standard for evaluating the coordination function of the market: orderly marketing. The immediate emphasis of this standard is on greater stability and certainty as well as on producer interests.[42]

Interfirm and intrafirm internalization are the two basic forms that internalization can take; they are strategic variables of the firm. Interfirm internalization involves the relationship among otherwise independent firms. It can be designed to substitute for the external market in affecting a variety of allocation or coordination functions. There are two basic dimensions to interfirm internalization: horizontal and vertical. This is the organizational context within which cartel and cartel-like activities play out their effects.

The strategic variable associated with intrafirm internalization is the form of the firm itself; this can be changed by either internal or external growth. The three dimensions of intrafirm internalization are horizontal, vertical, and conglomerate. The main emphasis of this paper will be on horizontal interfirm internalization; it is the basic cartel relationship.

Horizontal Interfirm Internalization.   The horizontal interfirm relationship among sellers can be coordinated either within the external market process or by internalization. Attempts by either private or public bodies to substitute the latter for the former can be expected whenever expected benefits exceed expected costs. This substitution process is the subject matter of this portion of the paper.

Horizontal interfirm internalization provides two principal types of benefits to sellers: the reduction of problems associated with coordination by the external markets (1) of firms that are presumably independent of one another, and (2) of those that are interdependent. These problems essentially involve the costs of disorderly marketing, instability, uncertainty, and discontinuities with respect to both long-run and short-run decisions.

Industries in which firms are truly independent decision units present few, if any, coordination problems. A monopoly and an industry with a literally dominant firm [43] would represent two such industries.

Coordination problems at the industry level, however, can occur in an industry characterized by many small sellers. Such firms are frequently considered to be independent of one another in the sense that each is too small to affect the decisions of others. But this can be the cause of the problem: these individual units are not independent in the sense that their cumulative decisions cannot affect industry capacity and output. G. B. Richardson has analyzed this problem. [44]

Richardson asked this question: Can the *theory* of a competitive market demonstrate that in an external market of many small sellers they will reliably coordinate (i.e., prevent overinvestment) their investment plans? He arrived at a negative answer in this manner. The same entry- or expansion-inducing price signal is given simultaneously to all existing or potential producers. This event, in the absence of some lags or other imperfections, induces entry or expansion by all. Excess capacity results; any contrary price signals come too late. The external market has failed as a coordinator at the industry level. The major problem was found in the nature and timing of the flow of relevant information to potential investors. After exploring alternate institutional arrangements by which to coordinate investment decisions, Richardson concluded that his analysis may have failed:

> The criticism may be made that the analysis . . . fails to indicate unequivocally what particular economic arrangements or systems can be regarded as ideal. The analysis implies that the planned coordination of investment decisions may be necessary in some circumstances and not in others, and that centralization may result in losses as well as in gains. For this I make no apology. We can hope to find which arrangements are optimal only by taking account continuously of different circumstances and by weighing up different requirements, the variety and conflicting nature of which exclude the possibility of a tidy, clear-cut solution. Without some measures of planning and cooperation, whether public or private, harmony between competitive or complementary investment decisions may not be achieved, market uncertainty may not be brought within tolerable limits and the risks of investment may present too great a deterrent to individual firms. Without some degree of competition, on the other hand, it may be difficult for monopolistic exploitation to be checked, for the authority to allocate resources to pass to those most fitted to exercise it, for diversity to be presented and for the springs of individual energy and initiative on which all economic progress must ultimately depend, to be kept unchoked.[45]

This is the problem central to the formation of public policy: When and how should public or private intervention be allowed?

The criterion of interdependence is whether a seller, when it contemplates a decision or action, is conscious of what his rivals might think or do in reaction. In short, interdependence is "rival-consciousness." In such an oligopolistic market, the price is not determined for firms as if by some impersonal market mechanism. Instead, the firms must search out their price from the set of price options that is constrained by the relatively technical and objective considerations noted above. This search involves a trial-and-error process, subject to the ambiguities of conjectural interdependence, as firms learn the range of options that the constraints allow. Failure to reach an effective oligopolistic equilibrium or stability can deny firms the more favorable price and profit options available to them. The existence of a constrained opportunity set does not assure the realization of a favorable option; the set also provides for excessive rivalry and errors in judgment, both of which are capable of driving price down to or below the competitive level.

Both uncertainties and transaction costs are involved in this process by which oligopolistic prices are formed and maintained. Uncertainties refer to a lack of knowledge of the future as well as to the ambiguities of interdependence; both can cause instability of price and market shares which, in turn, can generate customer dissatisfaction and threaten the tenure of management. These uncertainties and instabilities constitute real costs to the participants, taking time and effort as well as creating discomfiture. There is consequently a private premium upon the reduction by internalization of these costs. Internalization involves the coordination, in varying degrees, of certain decisions (e.g., price, output, investment) of the rival sellers by substituting, in effect, internal organization for the rivalry. By decreasing such uncertainties and ambiguities, internalization enables firms to cope more effectively with situations that could otherwise be costly to them. These situations include the fuller and more effective use by firms of their long-run and short-run market power bases, with special reference to excess capacity and supply conditions; the development of countervailing power against their trading partner(s); and the problems associated with infrequent and lumpy sales, as well as with sealed bidding arrangements or other situations in which one of the trading partners is at a significant informational disadvantage. The goal of competition policy, however, should not be to increase the number of available, inadequately regulated options. It should be either to decrease the number of options or to increase the adequacy of their regulations.

The ability to achieve effective horizontal interfirm internalization is not distributed uniformly across industries. There are technical and relatively objective determinants of this ability just as there were such determinants of the long-run and short-run market power bases. Management cannot escape its environment.

The major determinant of the ability to achieve horizontal interfirm internalization is the nature and the extent of the transaction costs in reaching and sustaining the effective level of coordination required. Four basic types of transaction costs are involved: those of (1) searching for relevant information, (2) negotiating the agreement, (3) monitoring, and (4) enforcing the agreement. It is postulated that the ability to internalize becomes more difficult as the conditions characteristic of any industry cause these transaction costs to increase, either in absolute terms or relative to expected benefits (determined primarily by the long-run and short-run market power bases). High transaction costs might make internalization difficult, but expected higher benefits can make the effort worthwhile.

The total transaction costs of horizontal interfirm internalization are influenced by seven characteristics of the group's environment. First, the transaction costs of coordination increase as the number of members increases. Second, such costs increase as the size uniformity among members increases. The presumption is that a 90 percent firm can more effectively dominate a 10 percent firm than one 50 percent firm can dominate another of similar size. The third condition is the degree of cost differences among the firms; the greater the differences, the greater the transaction costs. It is generally thought that the more efficient firms will be more likely to take a longer term view of the industry than will the less efficient. In addition, rapid technological development can be expected to aggravate cost differences.

Fourth, transaction costs increase with the diversity of interests, goals, or values among enterprises and among political and economic systems involved. Fifth, as the complexity and range of issues increase, transaction costs should also increase. Sixth, internalization in connection with fungible goods should involve lower transaction costs than in the case of a heterogeneous product line. And, finally, transaction costs should decrease as the history and complexity of corporate interrelationships, both formal and informal, deepen. In sum, these various conditions will determine the transaction costs and, hence, the ability of firms in an industry to effect horizontal interfirm internalization.

Figure 3.6 summarizes the interrelationships among the long-run and short-run power bases and internalization as a facilitator of horizontal interfirm coordination. The summary indicates (1) that both a long-run power base and the ability to internalize are necessary conditions for the exercise of long-run market power; (2) that both a short-run power base and the ability to internalize are necessary conditions for the exercise of short-run market power; and (3) that, in most cases, the ability to exercise both types of market power is necessary to assure persistent, monopolylike profits.

Fritz Machlup considered the relationship between the degree of ability to internalize and the form or forms that internalization might take.[46] In this analysis he differentiated between the "degree of collusion" and the

Figure 3.6 Relationship Between Long-Run and Short-Run Market Power

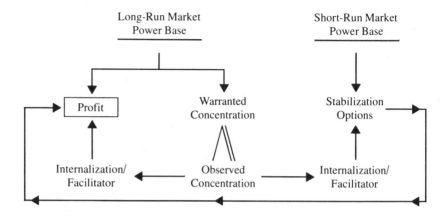

"form of collusion."[47] We interpret the degree of collusion to be the measure of the probable success by which rivals achieve horizontal interfirm internalization[48] and, therefore, to be determined by the transaction costs, noted above, that characterize the environment of different industries. On the vertical axis of figure 3.7, these various sets of transaction costs are ranked in ascending order of their respective probability of successful internalization;[49] industries with the most favorable environments would be at the top.

Machlup saw the forms of collusion as ranging from the formal and direct to the informal and indirect—from written agreements, private or with public sanctions, to informal expressions of opinions about the fairness or ethics of certain practices with an implication of compliance.[50] Accordingly, the forms of internalization are distributed along the horizontal axis of figure 3.7, moving rightward from the more formal and direct arrangements to the more informal and indirect. It is stressed that this is a distribution of sets of accumulated organizational options; movement to the right *retains* all previous options with emphasis on the more formal, structured options and *adds* the more informal, tacit arrangements. This latter ranking suggests that, when in the same set, these options are effective, though not necessarily perfect, substitutes for one another. It may well be that, within the same set, the more formal and direct options are somewhat more efficient than the more informal and indirect arrangements.

There exists a positive relationship (figure 3.7) between the ranked sets of transaction costs and the sets of accumulated options.[51] This relationship suggests the following two propositions: (1) industries with the least favorable environmental conditions (e.g., high transaction costs of agreement) are limited to the most formal and structured organizational options; and (2) industries with more favorable environmental conditions (e.g., low transaction costs) enjoy a full set of similarly effective options that range from the formal to the informal. These two propositions are significant for three reasons.

First and most significant, these two propositions pose an anomaly with respect to the exercise of horizontal interfirm internalization. Those most able to collude effectively can use the more informal and less direct techniques, and thereby avoid detection or escape prosecution when the law does not reach such means. On the other hand, those least able to collude effectively are restricted by transaction costs to the more formal and direct techniques.[52] These tend to be legally more vulnerable. The anomaly lies in the tendency of antitrust measures to concentrate on those industries least able to internalize effectively and to fail to reach those more able to collude successfully.

Figure 3.7   Relationship Between Forms and Degrees of Collusion

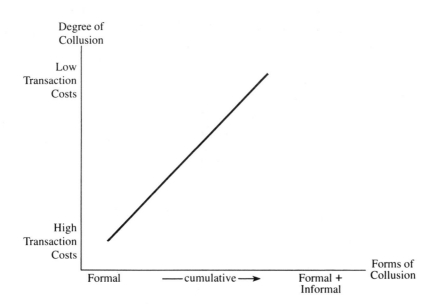

Second and given the above anomaly, any analysis of the enforcement process would tend to be confined to those industries in which the expected failure rate would be high; collusion would appear to be ineffective. In a study of the profitability of colluding and noncolluding firms in the United States, Peter Asch and J. J. Seneca found that collusive firms were consistently less profitable than noncolluders. They offered, in effect, four explanations, one of which is consistent with the analysis given above: "It may be that, within the range of firm and market structures examined, broadly collusive behavior is the rule, . . . but that antitrust prosecution centers largely on the *unsuccessful* manifestations . . . [because of] the possibility that overt agreement, which is clearly more vulnerable to prosecution, is itself a response to conditions that are not conducive to the success of collusion." [53]

Third and as indicated in the introduction, the existence of the positive relationship between ranked sets of transaction costs and accumulated options of the forms of internalization warrants broadening the consideration of cartels to include other less formal and less direct arrangements. Effective policy and, consequently, analysis should take into consideration those less formal substitutes for the more formal means of collusion, especially if it is true that the former can be used with similar effectiveness to that of the latter under certain conditions.

Machlup's analysis reached two other conclusions of interest. The first went to the effectiveness of the more formal options relative to the more informal. He concluded that for "any group of firms it is probably easier to achieve a higher degree of collusion [i.e., greater effectiveness] by a more elaborate form of collusion." [54] Tolerant antitrust policy would therefore tend to breed more formal organizations even in those industries where the more informal arrangements would be similarly effective. The second conclusion consists of two propositions. First, there is a strong tendency for less successful efforts to collude to develop into more successful efforts. [55] There is apparently a learning process involved. Second, there is a greater tendency for more formal arrangements to evolve into less formal arrangements than for the opposite to occur. This tendency occurs because, "if competitors have been cooperating for some time, they may be able to dispense with much of the formality and apparatus previously employed and may maintain the same, or even a higher, degree of collusion with a much lower form of collusion." [56] On the other hand, it may well be more accurate to argue, with Machlup, that successful horizontal interfirm internalization may well result in the evolution of the arrangement from a more formal level to a less formal level but that a failure, contrary to Machlup, would prompt the abandonment of a less structured approach and the adoption of a more structured one. This is certainly what the growers of specialty crops in California did when they abandoned efforts to form private cooperatives to regulate their markets and accepted compulsory cooperatives at the state and national levels.

Surveying the history and evolution of international cartels and the way that their organizational characteristics evolved as economic and political conditions changed, Kronstein identified three "phases" in the development of cartels: the basic regulatory agreement, the planning agreement, and the implementation agreement.

The basic regulatory agreement is the primary understanding—the "preliminary agreement"—that provides the "necessary environment for economic planning."[57] As such, the basic regulatory agreement is a necessary but not sufficient condition for private regulation of the market; the goals and techniques must also be developed in order to cope with particular economic conditions. These ends and means represent the planning agreement which is a horizontal seller-seller relationship. It remains, however, for the cartel to implement its planning agreement with respect to firms operating on different economic levels. This is accomplished by the implementation agreements, a series of vertical arrangements.

Kronstein considered the basic regulatory agreement to be a "new legal concept."[58] It formed the structure of the cartel, identified the members, and was characterized by some minimal degree of organization or institutionalization. This last characteristic could range from a simple understanding that the cartel members would work together (the basic agreement to agree) to the centralizing power of a syndicate. Kronstein noted the impact of the postwar anticartel legislation on the nature of postwar institutionalization of the basic regulatory agreement.

> As a result of post-war anti-cartel legislation, the extensive, powerful cartel administrations—which existed in the international sphere during the pre-war years—did not openly re-appear. Today, the only cartel agencies are those absolutely necessary to enable the cartel members to interfere within the market effectively. These include price agencies, agencies for exchange of information, and agencies for scientific cooperation. The most important agency is the arbitration tribunal, which can be used by the group as a means of conciliation.[59]

A fundamental difference between a basic regulatory agreement and a planning agreement is the relative permanence of the former. It functions as a sort of "social contract." The planning agreement, on the other hand, may change because the relevant situation changes. The "two phases are completely different in character and in substance. It is important to note that the cartel group can remain in existence even if the planning agreement becomes unenforceable owing to changing economic or political conditions. This justifies the distinction made between the two phases."[60]

Kronstein cited the copper industry as an example of the way in which economic changes can effect a change in the nature of the planning agreement, including the means employed. In 1956, copper producers faced an excess supply situation; the planning agreement was to maintain a minimum price and supply restriction was the means. In 1963 and 1964, excess demand was the problem, and the planning agreement was either to equalize distribution of the scarce copper or to practice price discrimination in favor of one group of buyers over another.

The organizations that characterize the planning agreement (and can also frequently be used to institutionalize the basic regulatory agreement) include syndicates, patent-holding groups, price-controlling and price-fixing agencies, technological advisory boards, and trade associations.

The planning agreement has third-party effects because it establishes certain conditions of exchange between buyers and sellers. The implementation agreements are sales contracts encumbered by the aims of the planning agreement. They consist of the conditions and restrictions that, because of the cartel, the coordinated sellers can impose on the buyers. In short, the metes and bounds of the implementation agreements are set by the planning agreement and are the result of its implementation.

Kronstein's insight was in recognizing the nature of the basic regulatory agreement and in exploring, in particular, the relationship between that agreement and the planning agreement. This relationship involves the occurrence of different, successive planning agreements as economic and political conditions change, persistently carried forward by the basic regulatory agreement. The analytical mode provides for quiet moments, failures, the pursuit of different aims, and the adoption of different instruments but all within the same common purpose of the private (or public) regulation of a market. The basic regulatory agreement provides the trend line. In addition, there is the idea of a cumulative capacity to design and implement planning agreements. The idea is an insight into understanding the dynamics of the evolution of cartels and cartel-like activities and may well facilitate analysis of that process.

Vertical Interfirm Internalization. This arrangement between groups of firms internalizes the *allocation* function of the external market; it restructures the allocation process by internalizing to varying degrees the buyer-seller relationship. Vertical interfirm coordination can be classified as either partial or comprehensive efforts relative to the market.

Long-term supply contracts between buyers and sellers are the best example of a partial effort at vertical interfirm coordination. Such contracts can stipulate price and/or quantity or provide for some formula or special negotiation process by which the exchange price is to be periodically determined.[61] The negotiation of these formulas or processes can involve significant transaction costs at both the vertical and the horizontal levels. In fact, such costs might be so large as to render an agreement difficult, if not impossible. At the international level, it is not unusual for government eventually to become involved. The benefits to be offset against these costs include stability of price and security of supply. Other examples of vertical interfirm internalization that are partial with respect to the market include exclusive dealing, full requirements contracts, and ties. Market foreclosure can be a problem associated with vertical interfirm internalization.

Commodity agreements are probably the best example of a comprehensive effort at vertical interfirm internalization. Such agreements involve negotiations between a group of buyers and a group of sellers in an effort to substitute the agreement for aspects of the allocation function of the external market. In this emphasis on bilateral negotiation between buyers and sellers, commodity agreements differ from the unilateral determination of price that is characteristic of cartels. Commodity agreements also differ from cartels in that the former internalize the allocation function of the external market while the latter internalize its coordination function.

Commodity agreements have received much attention in recent years because they are a key part of the drive for a New International Economic Order by the Third World. Since 1970, the United Nations Conference on Trade and Development has been pursuing the establishment of an "Integrated Commodity Programme" in connection with ten "core commodities": cocoa, coffee, cotton, copper, hard fibers, jute, rubber, sugar, tea, and tin.[62] Proposals include the use of buffer stocks in all ten commodities and of supply management techniques in all but cotton and tea.

It is generally conceded that the International Tin Agreement has been the most successful effort among the eighteen major agreements, involving nine commodities, that were organized over the past fifty years.[63] If the tin agreement is to be the measure of success, recent evaluations of its performance do not augur well for the future of other international commodity agreements.

Gordon Smith and George Schink noted that the presence of the U.S. tin stockpile and its use by the General Services Administration reduced the conflict potential implicit in two important issues: the height of the floor in the price band and the size of the buffer stock. "Producers realized that a push for *high* floor prices, after the matter of a producer cartel, would probably have brought the GSA into the market. Consumers, on the other hand, knew that they could rely on GSA sales to mitigate the largest penetrations of the ceiling. Hence, they did not press as much as they otherwise would have for larger, more effective buffer stocks."[64] In short, the GSA stockpile reduced for the International Tin Agreement a major cause of the failure of commodity agreements: the buyer-seller conflict. Smith and Schink suggested that "the *longevity* of the Tin Agreement owes a good deal to its *ineffectiveness*" and concluded that "supporters of commodity agreements can take small encouragement from the experience with tin."[65]

David McNicol examined commodity agreements whose causes of failure were known: one failed because of disputes among sellers over market shares, one because of overshipping, three because of entry, and three because of disputes between exporting and importing countries.[66]

An orderly marketing agreement (OMA) is a negotiated arrangement under which the market of the importing country is divided between domestic and foreign producers. An OMA can be either bilateral or multilateral in nature; the Multi-Fibre Agreement (MFA), which regulates trade in textiles, is an example of the latter. An OMA can be negotiated between private enterprises or governments. If private enterprises are involved, the arrangement is sometimes called a "voluntary export restraint."[67] If governments are involved, the arrangement is called an OMA.

In recent years, OMAs and voluntary restraint arrangements have covered these industries: textiles and garments (the MFA), shoes, specialty steel, carbon steel, ships, television sets, radios, and calculators. The MFA involves some forty-one importing and exporting countries. In other arrangements, the following importing jurisdictions were represented directly or through their enterprises: the United States, the Common Market, and certain individual European countries. The exporters were Japan, the Common Market, Sweden, Canada, South Africa, Spain, South Korea, Taiwan, Italy, and Brazil.[68]

Commodity agreements (CAs) and orderly marketing agreements differ in several significant ways. First, producers in exporting countries provide the drive to develop CAs, but producers in importing countries are the impetus behind OMAs. Both CAs and OMAs, however, usually require some degree of coordination of exports by producers in exporting countries (e.g., Japanese export cartels). Second, CAs are at least theoretically designed to promote producer interests in exporting countries and protect consumers in importing countries; OMAs protect producers in importing countries. Third, at the national level, CAs tend to be involved with international political considerations, while OMAs relate to domestic political considerations. Fourth, CAs do not typically require a division of markets. The purpose of an OMA, on the other hand, is to divide a national importing market between foreign and domestic producers. Because an OMA limits imports into a given market, the amount that would have been imported but for the quota may well spill over into another market, aggravating its internal situation. Finally, CAs should theoretically persist over and through cycles as they alternatively protect producer and consumer interests; OMAs are more popular during a recession or when an industry is in secular decline.

Producers in importing countries want an OMA in order to prevent price wars and protect their collective market share. Importing governments use OMAs because they are not covered by the General Agreement on Tariffs and Trade; the restrictions are agreed to by the exporting government. Producers in exporting countries accept OMAs because they are temporary and therefore preferable to the more permanent restrictions of a tariff, for which an OMA is in part a functional substitute. In addition, an OMA can allow for an annual increase in the quota.

The Lomé Convention is an agreement between the European Economic Community and over fifty developing countries, principally from Africa but also from the Caribbean and Pacific areas; these countries have been dubbed the ACP (Africa, Caribbean, and Pacific). The convention was signed in 1975 and went into force in 1976. It contains provisions covering trade, aid, industrial cooperation, and the stabilization of the export earnings of the ACP countries. This stabilization is accomplished by the Stabex

Fund, which covers a specified list of commodities and minerals. Whenever a country's export proceeds from a covered good fall a specified percentage below a four-year moving average, a lump sum compensatory payment is triggered. Repayment depends upon the classification of the exporting country. Those classified as advantaged are expected to repay; no interest is charged. The less-advantaged group does not have to repay.[69]

The International Monetary Fund (IMF) also offers a program of compensatory payments that differs in significant respects from Stabex. The most significant is that the IMF does not operate on a commodity-by-commodity basis as does Stabex; the IMF operates on the basis of changes in the total balance of payments of a country. Second, the IMF utilizes interest-bearing loans as the means of compensation. Third, the IMF does not discriminate among eligible countries; for example, Australia and Iceland have received payments. Finally, the IMF program is much larger than Stabex in terms of total disbursements.

Direct price stabilization by commodity agreements and compensatory finance can be viewed as either substitutes for each other or complementary. UNCTAD views them as complements and advocates the adoption of both types of programs:

> Such agreements, as envisaged in the UNCTAD Integrated Programme for Commodities, would operate to protect agreed price minima, in real terms, for the principal commodity exports of developing countries. Commodity stabilization operations will need to be supported by a substantial expansion in scope, and improvement in terms, of existing compensatory financing arrangements—which include the Stabex scheme under the Lomé Convention as well as the IMF compensatory financing facility—to offset residual fluctuations in the real export earnings of individual developing countries. Such new, or improved, institutional arrangements would . . . constitute a "safety net" to protect the development effort from the adverse consequences of short-term instability in the developed world.[70]

Such compensatory schemes as Stabex and the IMF program are not potential restrictive government practices as are the direct price schemes that are implemented by means of buffer stocks, production controls, and export quotas. The direct payment policies do not interfere with the market-clearing function of prices. They are a direct transfer mechanism.

Horizontal Intrafirm Internalization.   The strategic variable of the firm associated with interfirm internalization was the relationship among the firms. By contrast, the form of the firm itself is the strategic variable of the firm in the case of intrafirm internalization. That form can be changed by either external or internal growth. The three dimensions of the form of the firm are horizontal, vertical, and conglomerate.

At least three considerations can be identified that encourage horizontal intrafirm internalization.[71] First, there is the desire to rationalize operations, especially with respect to scale economies. The extent of the relationship between size and efficiency, however, is controversial. Second, by expanding the horizontal form of the firm, management can facilitate horizontal *interfirm* internalization. Because horizontal intrafirm internalization is the result of mergers, acquisitions, and internal growth, it substitutes more fully than interfirm internalization for that portion of the relevant market represented by the firm's market share. This more efficient coordination is the result of the more direct lines of communication and control that are internal to the firm. Such firm specific substitution need not be and is usually not as extensive with respect to the relevant market as is that attempted by interfirm internalization (e.g., cartels). Nevertheless, horizontal intrafirm internalization can facilitate coordination within the scope of the market because it reduces the number of firms in the industry or, in the alternate, increases industry concentration; it can also increase the uniformity of firms' interests and costs. These results reduce the transaction costs, as well as increase the possible social costs, associated with horizontal interfirm internalization, which increases the probability of a fuller realization of the options allowed by the long-run and short-run power bases.

A third consideration is the desire to increase the complexity and dimensions of market power by creating new options that are usually targeted more directly on *rivals* than on buyers. To these ends, management can utilize the form of the firm to penetrate or protect markets by the use of cross-subsidization or to stabilize profits by diversification across geographic markets. This is especially true of the multinational corporation as it utilizes its organizational form to take advantage of differences in national markets and policies. It is not suggested that this enhanced market power is necessarily some type of a restrictive business practice. Before such additional options are implemented, their marginal private benefits must exceed their marginal private costs. The key policy question, however, is whether their marginal social costs exceed their marginal social benefits.

Vertical Intrafirm Internalization.   Vertical intrafirm internalization, like its interfirm counterpart, involves internalization of the allocation function. In this case, however, it is done by changing the form of the firm and not the relationships among firms.

Rather obvious private benefits can result from vertical intrafirm internalization. First, such internalization can significantly reduce transaction costs between buyers and sellers.[72] This is especially evident in the case of owners of technology who prefer to transfer the technology to controlled subsidiaries rather than to independent licensees. Second, firms can increase the security of product markets or of supplies by integrating forward or backward. Third, changing the vertical form of a firm as compared to that of rivals or suppliers can create options in addition to those allowed by the long-run and short-run power bases. These options can be targeted upon nonintegrated downstream rivals (as in the case of the profit squeeze) or upon suppliers (as in the case of tapered integration).[73] The fourth benefit includes options to concentrate profits by transfer pricing at one or another level in order to exploit some nonmarket situation, e.g., different taxes on different profitabilities across the several stages of the firm.

The fifth benefit of vertical integration involves a more comprehensive set of price stabilization options than is available to a nonintegrated firm. A firm that is not vertically integrated is limited to the stabilization options of a production cutback or inventory accumulation. A vertically structured firm, on the other hand, can select between these options at each of the vertical stages; it has options as to both technique and stage. This additional option can be used to gain further advantages from the short-run market power base that exists at each of the several stages. The relevant decision trees in figure 3.8 will illustrate; it is developed in terms of two assumptions and four propositions.

First, we assume a decline in the demand for the final product involved (e.g., fabricated aluminum products) and a decision by the firms of the industry to stabilize price. Second, we assume that at the fabrication level the only feasible stabilization technique is the production cutback. This restriction can result from the fact that the mix of fabricated products is very broad; consequently, efforts to accumulate an inventory mix consistent with the mix of future demand is risky. This risk appears all the greater if the upstream output is a uniform, basic product such as aluminum ingot whose accumulation presents no risk of the appropriate mix. For these reasons, we assume that firms have the two stabilization tech-

Figure 3.8 Decision Trees for Vertical Stabilization Options

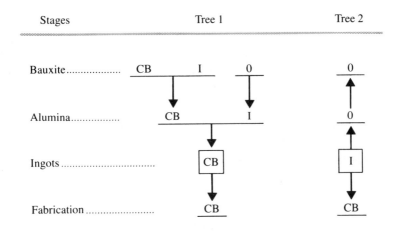

Stages	Tree 1	Tree 2

niques available only at the three stages above the fabrication stage. Management's problem is to select from its options the program that will most efficiently stabilize the fully integrated industry against the recession.

Proposition 1: To cut back production (CB in figure 3.8) at any one stage is to cut back production at all downstream stages and either to cut back production at all upstream stages or to accumulate inventories (I in figure 3.8) at some upstream stage. Decision Tree 1 depicts Proposition 1.

Assume the decision is made to cut back production at the ingot stage. Fabrication must now be cut back, which avoids the need to accumulate an inventory of fabricated products. If downstream production is not cut back, that stage will be starved for upstream supplies. With respect to upstream production, on the other hand, an ingot cutback requires management to decide whether to reduce the output of alumina or to store it. If management elects to cut back, the choice is pushed up again to the bauxite stage. On the other hand, if management decides to store alumina, bauxite production can be maintained at full operation (O in figure 3.8).

Proposition 2: To accumulate inventories at any one stage is to permit full operation at all upstream stages and to require production cutbacks at downstream stages. Decision Tree 2 depicts Proposition 2. In this case, stabilization costs are borne by the last two downstream stages.

Proposition 3: The further downstream that you elect to accumulate inventories, the greater will be the cost of financing that inventory because the accumulated value added will be greater.

Proposition 4: The further downstream that you elect to accumulate inventories, the greater will be the potential accumulated profit because the number of profit centers to be sustained at full operation is greater. Propositions 3 and 4 suggest a trade-off in the determination of the stage at which inventories are to be accumulated: as the placement option moves downstream, both costs and benefits increase. Consequently, in this determination the relative profitability of the four stages is important.

Superior upstream profitability should increase the probability of stabilization by inventory accumulation at some downstream stage—probably at the stage (ingots) for which such accumulation is less costly or risky. Stabilization costs would be imposed on the ingot and fabrication stages. However, these costs would presumably be more than offset by the benefits gained from full operation at the two upstream stages. Tree 2 represents this case. Any attempt to disrupt the vertical integrated structure of the industry would probably force abandonment of Decision Tree 2 and the adoption of Decision Tree 1. And the latter involves an entirely different distribution of costs, and possibly efficiency, of price stabilization policies.

If vertical integration and the suggested stabilization options are characteristic of most firms in an industry (e.g., the global aluminum industry) with the ability to effect horizontal interfirm coordination,[74] we would expect the firms to adopt Decision Tree 2. In the event that any significant vertical disintegration affects the upstream stages, we would, on the other hand, expect the firms to shift to Decision Tree 1. This would shift more of the stabilization costs upstream. To the extent this model is descriptive of the global aluminum industry and to the extent host governments have reduced the profitability of the upstream processes or taken them over, we would expect the global firms to change decision trees; this would shift more of the stabilization costs upstream onto the host governments.

Another characteristic of Decision Tree 2 should be noted. The decision to stabilize by inventory accumulation at an intermediate stage imposes a balance of process on downstream stages. For example, in order to assure disposal of inventories of ingot without production cutbacks at the ingot stage as the recovery begins, fabricating capacity must exceed ingot capacity. Investment in fabricating capacity sufficient to enable it to meet final demand, given stabilization by inventory accumulation, will generate a ratio between fabricating and ingot capacities greater than one.[75] To the extent that this ratio is greater than one, the ensuing peak demand will be met in part out of inventories. One result[76] is that the load factors at the ingot, alumina, and bauxite stages will be increased.[77] An increase in load factor is desirable because it reduces the investment in capacity needed to meet a given demand. Because the ingot, alumina, and bauxite stages are the most capital intensive in the industry, such an increase in load factor is a definite social benefit.

Conglomerate Intrafirm Internalization. Conglomeration increases the size and diversity of the firm. Although such firms remain subject to the limitations of their long-run and short-run market power bases, conglomeration can enhance the welfare of the firm in two ways.[78] First, conglomeration affects the ability and desire of the firm to internalize with respect to its particular markets. This is especially evident in the exercise of mutual forbearance,[79] which increases the probability of effective cartelization. Second, conglomeration offers enriched opportunities to engage in those options that are targeted more on rivals and suppliers than on buyers. As Corwin Edwards summarized it:

> our largest enterprises have become multicorporate, multimarket, vertically integrated, multistate, and even multinational. The options of conduct available to them have become more numerous, more varied, less vulnerable to the curbs of competition in their individual markets, and less vulnerable to the curbs that single governments seek to impose upon them by law. The disparately large and varied resources that these big enterprises possess can be used as sources of one-sided advantage in their dealings with lesser firms that sell them supplies or that buy from them, and in their competition with lesser firms with which they compete. But these resources must be used cautiously in relations with other enterprises that are comparably powerful. The need for caution affects the nature of conduct in the markets when powerful enterprises are dominant.[80]

Conclusion. Internalization was defined as the substitution of internal, administrative decision-making processes for the external market process. Institutionally, internalization, *inter alia,* takes the form of cartels, commodity agreements, orderly marketing agreements, vertical integration, and internal or external growth. This substitution can be realized by changing either the form of the firm itself or the relationships among firms; consequently, the form of the firm and its relationships with other firms are strategic variables of management as it seeks to take advantage of its environment.

Two functions were attributed to the external market: *allocation*, which was defined as a buyer-seller relationship, and *coordination*, a seller-seller (or buyer-buyer) relationship. Given appropriate conditions, management or governments can internalize either function. Welfare economics has developed an accepted definition of optimal allocation results: price equals marginal costs and other related marginal conditions. Key policy questions remain with respect to an optimal coordination performance. What is the socially optimal level of price stability? Is it the maximal tolerable level of price instability? What is the optimal level of certainty? Is it the maximal tolerable level of uncertainty? What is the optimal amount and mix of market information to be available to buyers and sellers? More often than not, these questions appear to be answered within the political process. In this context, Edward Mason's conclusions are relevant: "The issue presented . . . will not . . . be whether to allow or to forbid private international cartel arrangements. The issue . . . involves a choice between authorizing cartel agreements under some type of government supervision or adopting a policy of curbing and limiting cartel arrangements." [81]

INTERNAL POLITICS

Internal politics are the politics of the internalization process, especially those involving interfirm relationships. What can be accomplished is limited by the constraints of the relevant long-run and short-run market power bases. The difficulties encountered will reflect the transaction costs involved as well as the anticipated benefits of the type of internalization desired. The nature and complexity of these politics will be influenced by the structural characteristics of the organizational form that the internalization takes. We shall briefly discuss some of the problems posed by the structural characteristics of commodity agreements, cartels, and orderly marketing agreements.

COMMODITY AGREEMENTS

A commodity agreement is an arrangement between a group of exporters and a group of importers. When governments are involved, this arrangement can involve four sets of relationships: (1) those between producers and their national government; (2) those among exporting governments; (3) those among importing governments; and (4) those between the exporting and importing groups. Efforts to resolve the conflicts potential to these four relationships constitute the internal politics of a commodity agreement. Each of the four relationships will be considered.

Producer-Government Relations.   Both the producers' government and the producers themselves can be organized for domestic purposes. For example, in Ghana the governmental organization is the Cocoa Marketing Board; the producers are represented by the Cocoa Farmers' Committee. Major issues between the growers and their national government involve prices, taxes, and production and export controls. The latter controls can pose allocation problems as well as barriers to entry and expansion.

Major price and tax issues arise when a government elects to use a commodity agreement not so much to protect the growers involved, but more to realize other objectives such as the development of other sectors. The chief executive of the Ghanaian Cocoa Marketing Board has claimed that "development of Ghana's urban sector had been made at the expense of the rural areas, especially the cocoa farmers."[82] The board sets the price received by cocoa farmers. A similar situation exists in Malaysia. A major complaint of Malaysian rubber growers concerns the export levies of their government. They contend that as the "price of rubber goes up, so does the percentage of the export price taken by the duty. . . . Malaysia justifies the tax as necessary for its development."[83] Such price and tax issues present problems not only for the growers but also for consumers; they go directly to the assurance of long-run supplies.

Relations Among Exporting Countries.   Exporting countries can be represented by an international organization. For example, the major rubber-producing countries are organized in the Association of Natural Rubber Producing Countries; they are Indonesia, Malaysia, Singapore, Sri Lanka, Thailand, and India. For cocoa there is the Cocoa Producers' Alliance. Producing countries are also organized into regional organizations. In coffee, for example, there are the Central American Coffee Producers' Federation, an informal "Bogotá Group,"[84] and the Brazilian Coffee Institute.

The existence of such organizations does not assure easy agreement but they can provide an ongoing forum for conflict resolution. For example, in the recent discussions between cocoa-producing and consuming countries, the producing countries disagreed on the floor price; Nigeria, Cameroon, the Ivory Coast, Togo, and Gabon insisted on holding out for a higher floor price. Disagreements among the producing countries as well as between producing and consuming countries terminated the second effort in 1979 to negotiate an international cocoa agreement.

Relations Among Importing Countries.   The number of consuming countries tends to be significantly larger than the number of producing countries that are involved in negotiating a commodity agreement. In addition, the consuming countries are not as formally organized for representation purposes, except in the case of the Common Market. Among the consuming countries, hard-liners and soft-liners emerge during the negotiations. The hard-liners tend to focus on economic issues; the soft-liners place greater emphasis on political considerations. In recent years, the line taken has been influenced by the degree of import dependency that a given importing country experiences; the more dependent the country, the softer the line.

Relations Between Exporting and Importing Countries.   Recent negotiations of international commodity agreements have involved unwieldy numbers: over fifty in the cocoa and rubber negotiations and about thirty in the tin negotiations. These large numbers make conflict resolution difficult.

Another difficulty is the nature of the conflict itself—the basic conflict between buyers and sellers. In particular, the conflict is over the appropriate function of a commodity agreement: Should it function as a price support mechanism or simply as a means to smooth out price fluctuations? Historically, there has been a tendency for producer interests to predominate and for price support to be stressed over price stabilization.[85]

Consuming countries must realize that they are dealing with a potential cartel. There is the possibility that producers will be concerned with protecting the price floor more than the price ceiling and with moving the price band up as the ceiling is penetrated,[86] or that the producers will try to stabilize near the top end of the band by supply restrictions. In the recent rubber negotiations, the United States sought "some clear formulation of supply assurances by producers and repeated its keenness to obtain an appropriate consultative provision regarding Government policies that directly affect natural rubber prices and supplies."[87] The United States failed in this effort, but the producing countries did agree to hold periodic consultations with the consuming countries.[88]

On at least one occasion, producers of a significant substitute product attended negotiations concerning a commodity agreement. When UNC-

TAD convened a preparatory meeting on rubber in January 1977, not only did the Association of Natural Rubber Producing Countries and a representative of the EEC participate, but a representative of the International Institute of Synthetic Rubber Producers also attended.[89] It is interesting to note in this connection that in February 1978, the United States indicated that it was "prepared to participate actively in negotiating a rubber pact on the assumption that it would not cover the synthetic rubber market."[90]

CARTELS

At the international level, there are two basic structural types of cartels: one-tier and two-tier cartels. In a one-tier cartel the members are enterprises, private or public, that operate as independent decision makers except with reference to the cartel. They have internal lines of control over the operating units of the cartel.

A two-tier cartel involves groupings of enterprises. For example, the cartel negotiation might be carried on directly by national or regional groups; this would be the first tier. Negotiations would then have to occur within each of the first-tier groups on any allocation or other decisions that would affect the welfare of the members of the group. This would be the second tier. Each of the two tiers presents its own conflicts to be resolved.

ORDERLY MARKETING AGREEMENTS

An OMA involves three possible bargaining situations or relationships: (1) between the exporting country and its exporting firms; (2) between the importing country and its domestic producers; and (3) between the exporting and importing governments. If the exporting country accepts an export quota of the counterpart country, the former must adopt some mechanism to control exports and allocate them among its exporters. In the case of Japan, this mechanism is frequently an export cartel. In these cases, an export cartel assumes the function of protecting, rather than exploiting, the importing country.

In the importing countries and especially during a recession, protectionism becomes a significant issue. This is the political environment that creates an OMA. Unions, management, and local leaders all bring political pressure to aid local production. In recent years, OMAs or voluntary restraint systems have been a preferred vehicle for protectionism.[91] Presumably, importing states attempt to negotiate an OMA that is consistent with the preferences of their domestic producers.

The exporting and importing countries must then meet to negotiate the division of the importer's market between imports and domestic production. U.S. policy in this area has a peculiar feature; under the Trade Act of 1974, if the Government negotiates an agreement with countries that account for 51 percent or more of the imports involved, it can unilaterally impose quotas on the balance.

EXTERNAL POLITICS

In the period after World War II, the leading market-type economies sought to adopt, in general terms, an international competition policy by liberalizing world trade. The goal was to increase world prosperity through specialization and trade. To this end, governments negotiated a reduction in the use of certain types of restrictive government practices, e.g., tariffs, nontariff barriers, and quotas. The GATT, the EEC, and the European Free Trade Association (EFTA) provided the principal machinery.

It was recognized that the failure to regulate private restrictive business practices could frustrate the efforts to liberalize trade by reducing certain restrictive government practices. As a result, the Treaty of Rome included antimonopoly provisions and the so-called frustration provisions became a part of the GATT and EFTA. The relative success of the EFTA machinery led to the 1973 recommendation of the Organisation for Economic Co-operation and Development.

These efforts constitute the beginning of an international antitrust policy—an interpenetration and use of national jurisdictions or their partial surrender to a central authority—as an integral part of an international competition policy. The reach of these efforts, however, has not been extended to cover restrictive government practices that take the form of cartels or cartel-like activities.

Not all types of restrictive government practices that are capable of disrupting the liberalization of world trade are being reduced by international negotiation and agreement. This is especially true of those restrictive government practices, rationalized in terms of the pursuit of public goals, that take the form of cartel and cartel-like activities. These are on the increase and can be inconsistent with an international competition policy. Several examples can be given. First, there is state participation in or protection of national export cartels or international cartels. Second, commodity agreements and orderly marketing agreements of various types are currently being proposed. Third, state import- and export-trading companies represent potentially restrictive institutions. A fourth type consists of government ownership or subsidization of industry. A significant aspect of this practice is the effect of governmental involvement on the price-cost relationship upon which a policy of liberalized trade is dependent, with special reference to the dumping issue.

Finally, national governments have passed laws that discriminate against foreign enterprises, which adversely affects the flow of trade, technology, or investment. In general, nations that adopt these various restrictive government practices can be expected to seek their exemption from any codes, guides, or other attempts at substantive law that might emerge from international forums. Such exemptions reduce the scope of international competition and antitrust policies.

The penetration of governments into the operations of cartels and cartel-like activities can affect these operations and their outcomes in at least four ways. Government involvement can change the nature of the goals by substituting public for private goals or supplementing the latter. Public goals can be much broader and more general because they presumably represent the welfare of the nation or some other broad constituency; foreign policy and national security can become relevant considerations. Second, government intervention can affect transaction costs involved in the formation and operation of cartels and cartel-like activities. At the national level, governments function most frequently to reduce private transaction costs or, in the extreme, to substitute government authority for private negotiations; this is especially true when private transaction costs are high. On the other hand, governmental involvement may complicate the formation and operation of restrictive institutions at the international level. Such intervention can increase the diversity of interests and decrease constraints on the decision makers; there is no overarching sovereign with power to discipline the recalcitrant.

Third, nations can reduce the legal vulnerability of their sponsored institutions in the jurisdictions of other countries. Finally, government participation can increase the relevant dimensions and sources of power. The economic and military power of the state as well as the power of sovereignty itself can find its way into the balance when governments become involved. In addition, governments are able to trade off a concession in one policy area for a benefit in another area; in this respect, a nation-state is a very diversified organization.[92]

The process by which public goals are pursued by governments through the use of cartel and cartel-like arrangements can best be observed today in the political dialogue and maneuvering over the New International Economic Order (NIEO).

From 1974 to 1976, members of the Organization of Petroleum Exporting Countries (OPEC) and other Third World countries orchestrated a series of political offensives, relying heavily on United Nations organizations. What emerged from this political activity, designed to maintain Third World solidarity and to confront the developed world, was a proposed New International Economic Order and a challenge to the existing "Liberal International Economic Order" (LIEO). The challenge is to the basic institutions of the LIEO: the market, the GATT, the multinational corporation, and the International Monetary Fund, especially to its decision-making process. In short, the NIEO is an attack against the type of international competition policy that is at the heart of the LIEO.

The Third World is concerned because it believes the LIEO institutions function automatically to increase the income gap between the Third World and the developed countries; in this institutional context, the gap is closed only by benevolence and ad hoc adjustments. The purpose of the NIEO is to effect a more automatic and permanent closure of the gap.

The NIEO was set forth in detail at the fourth UNCTAD meeting in Nairobi. Its general function is to effect a significant transfer of income and wealth from the developed countries to the Third World in order to facilitate the development of the latter.[93] The new NIEO features were to include cartels; commodity agreements; development aid; regulation of multinational corporations; preferential, nonreciprocal trade policies; more liberal technology transfers; and external debt relief.

A principal transfer mechanism of the NIEO is the proposed Integrated Commodity Programme (ICP)—a program in which cartel and cartel-like activities are instruments of national and international policy. Within the NIEO they exist as an integral part of the whole; within the LIEO they are at best an exception. The NIEO gives them legitimacy.

The ICP consists of two main parts: a group of international commodity agreements and a "Common Fund." The price objectives of the ICAs are broad enough to include price stabilization within a price band that moves with the long-run competitive price, price indexation, and the raising and maintenance of a price above the competitive level. The ICAs are to achieve their price objective by some negotiated combination of pure buffer stock operations, production controls, and export quotas.

The Fund is to be a permanent bureaucratic organization with two major functions. The first function, the so-called first window, is to provide a line of credit to member ICAs to facilitate financing of buffer stock operations. The other function, the so-called second window, is a direct assistance program under which the Fund would lend money to countries in order to help them find new marketing outlets, raise productivity, and diversify. While demand stimulation and product diversification are at least partial substitutes for other policies designed to stabilize earnings and cope with surpluses, there is a more political reason for the second window: the provision of some benefits for those developing countries that are not significant producers of any of the commodities covered by the ICP.

Although each ICA is to be independent of the Fund, the Fund will be administering a sizable amount of money and will have access to the traditional creditor-debtor power relationship in its dealings with the ICAs and with countries that use the second window. As one observer noted: "The Common Fund would mobilize and focus the economic and political power of the LDCs and, by raising the stakes on specific economic issues, bring pressure on the DCs to take the steps necessary to maintain restrictive arrangements [and stabilize the ICAs]."[94]

In sum, the Fund could become a significant international political institution; consequently, control over its decisions is an important consideration for consuming countries. In negotiations concluded in March 1979, these countries took steps to constrain the impact of the Fund and, more generally, the ICP. They succeeded in (1) establishing the nominal autonomy of the ICAs vis-à-vis the Fund; (2) limiting the financing of any ICA, as opposed to the administrative functions of the Fund, to the producing and consuming countries primarily concerned; (3) assuring that ICAs are financed adequately to protect both the floor and the ceiling of the price band; and (4) assuring for themselves effective participation in the key decisions of the Fund.[95]

OPEC countries provided significant political leadership in designing the New International Economic Order by emphasizing the creation of new cartel-like organizations to offset the costs of OPEC pricing imposed on the non-OPEC South. They tried to appear to be giving with one hand as they took with the other. This political maneuver might be countered by another political/economic maneuver such as expanding or generalizing the Lomé approach to include all the North and non-OPEC South. The aim would be politically to isolate OPEC from the rest of the non-Communist world. In short, one type of cartel-like arrangement (Lomé) could be used to counter both another such arrangement (the ICP) and a cartel (OPEC) in a political context external to such arrangements.

In this political context, in which governments use cartels and cartel-like arrangements to pursue public goals, two other policy recommendations can be suggested. The first deals with OPEC. After the 1973 run-up of oil prices, the OPEC countries sought to maintain the political alignment based on shared Third World values. A major instrument in this plan was the NIEO, especially the ICP. OPEC sought to prevent the formation of a political alignment along economic lines: the division between oil exporters and oil importers. In this political context, the recommendation is to create a shadow OPEC of importing countries which would have two principal functions: (1) the systematic analysis of the past impact of OPEC pricing on selected economic indicators for each importing country, and (2) the prediction of the impact of future price changes by OPEC for each price within the range of probable prices. These analyses would be given worldwide circulation.

These functions of the shadow OPEC would have two expected results. First, in due course the felt impact of OPEC pricing should allow a political wedge to be driven between the oil-exporting and oil-importing countries of the Third World. A more economically oriented, rather than politically oriented, alignment would emerge; the split would be between oil exporters and oil importers rather than between the North and the South. It would be expected that this development would affect politics at the United Nations, presumably by creating a tilt more consistent with the interests of the developed countries. There is some evidence that such a tilt may have been under way in the spring of 1979.[96]

The second expected effect of the shadow OPEC follows from the prediction made just prior to an anticipated price change. If and when OPEC responds to or challenges such a prediction, a dialogue will have been precipitated and eventually a type of negotiation might emerge. In this connection and on at least two occasions, the OPEC countries have shown a concern for their image that raises some hope that this second effect might be realized. In 1975, *Business Week* reported that OPEC had contacts with a delegation of editorial and advertising representatives from the *Readers' Digest* and with a New York advertising agency.[97] And in 1979, the *Wall Street Journal* revealed that at a meeting in Geneva during June 1979, the "oil ministers of the 13 producing countries focused on ways to improve their admittedly tarnished image through creating their own news agency and providing more aid to the developing world."[98]

The second recommendation is concerned more generally with the use of cartel and cartel-like arrangements to realize governmental goals. For several decades, nation-states have used the GATT to negotiate a reduction in certain types of restrictive government practices. It has also been recommended that the GATT procedures be used to negotiate the resolution of some problems created by foreign direct investment and the multinational corporation.[99] It is suggested that the GATT itself or analogous procedures could be used to negotiate some restraint on the use of cartel and cartel-like agreements by nation-states.[100]

CONCLUSION

In general, the purpose of this paper has been to make more explicit certain aspects of market power in order to improve our understanding about its nature, determinants, and consequences. To this end, it was suggested that market power was protean, not monolithic, in form. At least three different types of market power were identified in terms of different options, determinants, and consequences: long-run, short-run, and rival-oriented market power. The existence of such complexity suggests that a similar complexity would be appropriate to the development of policy instruments to cope with the various aspects of market power. In this context, antitrust enforcement would be only one instrument and the courts would be only one forum in efforts to regulate market power. Other instruments (e.g., guidelines and administrative guidance) and other forums (e.g., the executive branches of the U.S. and Japanese Governments and the international political arena) could well be and, to some extent, have been utilized. It would then become necessary to coordinate the several policy instruments, including antitrust measures, in the several forums.

NOTES

1. Heinrich Kronstein, *The Law of International Cartels* (Ithaca, N.Y. and London: Cornell University Press, 1973).

2. "The organizations controlling private market regulation are not only mutually interdependent; they also interact closely with government bodies. . . . the complex interrelationship between governmental and private market regulation is strengthened by the constantly increasing interpenetration of state and private economy. This is one of the most important differences between the present structure of world trade and that prior to World War II. . . ." *Ibid.*, p. 9.

3. *Ibid.*, p. 1.

4. Rival-oriented market power is potentially of antitrust significance because it incorporates many of the issues involved in the controversy raised by the distinction between protecting competition and protecting competitors. This type, however, will not be developed in this paper because of its limited relationship to cartel and cartel-like activities. It is relevant, however, to the extent that interfirm arrangements are necessary to its realization.

5. For a more detailed treatment, see, for example, Campbell R. McConnell, *Economics,* 7th ed. (New York: McGraw-Hill, 1978).

6. This follows because MC is always positive and, if MR must equal MC for profit maximization, then MR will also be positive. And the relationship between MR and price elasticity of demand is such that, if MR is positive, demand must be price elastic.

7. Joe S. Bain, *Barriers to New Competition* (Cambridge, Mass.: Harvard University Press, 1956).

8. Paolo Sylos-Labini, *Oligopoly and Technical Progress,* rev. ed. (Cambridge, Mass.: Harvard University Press, 1969).

9. Franco Modigliani, "New Developments on the Oligopoly Front," *Journal of Political Economy* (June 1958), pp. 215–32.

10. The language is that of Paul J. McNulty. He characterized the view of competition held by classical economists as one of a "market process" and the view held by neoclassicists as one of "market structure." It should be noted, however, that his concern was with the process of price competition rather than with the process of entry. Paul J. McNulty, "Economic Theory and the Meaning of Competition," *Quarterly Journal of Economics* (November 1968), pp. 639–56.

11. This distinction was made by Harold Demsetz, "Contracting Cost and Public Policy," in U.S. Congress, *The Analysis and Evaluation of Public Expenditures: The PPB System,* a compendium of papers submitted to the Subcommittee on Economy in Government of the Joint Economic Committee, 91st Cong., 1st Sess. (Washington, D.C.: Government Printing Office, 1969), 1:167–74.

12. For example, firms would no longer have the option of maximizing sales rather than profits, in the sense that sales maximization requires the option of operating in the vicinity of unit elasticity on the industry demand curve.

13. The minimum optimal scale is that scale of plant (or, more generally, operations) that minimizes the average total cost of production. It is represented by the lowest point on the long-run average cost curve. Total costs can include marketing costs.

14. Other assumptions are (1) that the same long-run average cost function is

available to both entered firms and potential entrants; (2) that neither demand nor costs change; and (3) that entered firms do not intimidate potential entrants other than to the degree implicit in the Bains-Sylos Postulate.

15. Modigliani, "New Developments."

16. To facilitate the use of diagrams, we assume that E varies with each price in a single market but that E is the same for any given price in the two markets.

17. Warranted concentration will be defined as (Q_c/m)-1. It represents the number of equal-sized firms in the industry at P_b. It is expected that observed concentration will exceed warranted concentration.

18. This analysis provides only a partial explanation of price development in international trade. It is limited to the effects of entry, including imports. It does not address itself, for example, to cost differences or cyclical problems.

19. It has been the U.S. experience that industries that make significant use of industrial property are important exporters. If they export and are protected from import competition, such industries should favor liberalized foreign trade. By contrast, industries protected only by economies of scale in production should be more disposed to protection.

20. In a noninteger model, firms can enter at a scale short of m at the cost, however, of higher average costs than those associated with the m scale. In the noninteger model, therefore, the flexibility of the long-run average cost curve supplements m as a determinant of the barrier price and premium: the more flexible the curve, the lower the barrier price and premium.

21. A third short-run stabilization option can be identified: the stabilization of price against an increase in productivity. It is excluded because of low relevance to the issues of this paper. See Robert E. Smith, "A Theory for the Administered Price Phenomenon," *Journal of Economic Issues* (June 1979), pp. 641–42.

22. Jere R. Behrman, *Development, the International Economic Order and Commodity Agreements* (Reading, Mass.: Addison-Wesley, 1978), pp. 30–35.

23. For a brief review of the controversy, see Gordon W. Smith, "Commodity Instability and Market Failure: A Survey of Issues," in Gerard F. Adams and Sonia A. Klein, eds., *Stabilizing World Commodity Markets* (Lexington, Mass.: Lexington Books, 1978), pp. 176–77, and Behrman, *Development,* pp. 114–15.

24. Stephen J. Turnovsky, "The Distribution of Welfare Gains from Price Stabilization: A Survey of Some Theoretical Issues," in Adams and Klein, eds., *Stabilizing,* p. 143.

25. For a more detailed discussion, see Robert E. Smith, "A Theory."

26. When SRATC is flexible, average total cost does not rise significantly as the rate of utilization is decreased. When the SRATC is inflexible, average total cost rises rapidly as the rate of utilization is decreased.

27. Addability refers to the usual number of basic production units found in a facility; an addable unit means a divisible plant. Adaptability refers to the ability to change the rate of output of a single producing unit without significant effect on costs, whether or not the unit is addable. An interruptible unit is one for which

the number of shifts per day or the number of days per week can be changed without significant cost. Convertibility is also a relevant factor.

28. To the extent the minimum point on SRATC approaches full capacity and SRATC rises sharply after that point, the resulting SRS_c will become more inelastic. This suggests that the SRS_c for manufacturing industries can be expected to be quite inelastic, which increases the costs of price instability to the industry.

29. We assume that the fear of entry eliminates an option to increase price. It should be recognized, however, that the exercise of such an option is consistent with the present theory.

30. The social welfare costs of price stabilization depend on the level at which price is stabilized. Stabilization at P_b would be more costly to society and less costly to firms than stabilization at P_c. The statutory requirements to implement a Japanese depression cartel appear to be designed to assure stabilization at or below P_c.

31. A potential price cutter who anticipates that he will not be detected for some time would, in effect, consider the relevant demand function to be quite elastic. Under these circumstances, a price cut would probably be the more profitable option for that firm.

32. As the rate of utilization approaches the break-even point, the probabilities increase that a price reduction will be more profitable than price stabilization. As the firm's demand curve shifts leftward (reflecting a similar shift in the industry's demand curve), demand tends to become more elastic and, as the break-even point is approached, SRATC becomes less flexible. These two developments warrant the expectation that the critical relationship between the price elasticity of demand and the flexibility of SRATC will change so that a price reduction becomes more profitable than price stabilization. It is partially for this reason that SRS_m slopes downward in the vicinity of the break-even point. The upward movement of SRS_m follows the aggregate marginal cost curve of the firms in the industry producing Q_b.

33. *Financial Times* (London), Feb. 20, 1975, p. 17, cols. 3–8.

34. Short-run average total costs can rise because input costs rise for exogenous reasons (e.g., higher wages or fuel costs) or because the rate of utilization is decreasing. Although the analysis applies to both cases, we shall limit the discussion to exogenous cost increases, i.e., to a shift of, rather than a movement along, SRATC.

35. Industries differ as to the conditions that expose them to the need to adjust to reductions in aggregate demand. Industries whose demand is insensitive to changes in aggregate demand will have less need to exercise short-run market power.

36. Milton Friedman, "Comments," in George P. Shultz and Robert Z. Aliber, eds., *Guidelines, Informal Controls, and the Market Place* (Chicago and London: University of Chicago Press, 1966), p. 57.

37. "This substitution of internal organization for market exchange will be referred to as 'internalization.' " Oliver E. Williamson, "The Vertical Integration of Production: Market Failure Considerations," *American Economic Review* (May 1971), p. 112. In a later work, Williamson used the terms "hierarchy" and "inter-

nal organization." For example, a "firm may decide to bypass the market and resort to hierarchical modes of organization. Transactions that might otherwise be handled in the market are thus performed internally, governed by administrative processes, instead." Oliver E. Williamson, *Markets and Hierarchies: Analysis and Antitrust Implications* (New York: Free Press, 1975), p. 9. The substitution of internal organization for external markets has also been analyzed in connection with labor markets and the role of government relative to product markets. For the former, see P. B. Doeringer and M. J. Piore, *Internal Labor Markets and Manpower Analysis* (Lexington, Mass.: D.C. Heath, 1972). For the latter, see Demsetz, "Contracting Cost."

38. This was the function emphasized by Coase in his seminal work on the theory of the firm. Ronald H. Coase, "The Nature of the Firm," *Economica* (N.S., 1937). pp. 386–405. Transaction costs include the costs of gathering the necessary information, of negotiating the exchange, and of monitoring and enforcing the subsequent relationship. The role of transaction costs in determining the ability to internalize is described below.

39. For example, horizontal intrafirm coordination can create the option of geographic, as opposed to interproduct, cross-subsidization. Vertical intrafirm coordination can create options such as tapered integration and the profit squeeze. Conglomerate intrafirm coordination can add reciprocity and cross-subsidization as well as increase the probability of mutual forbearance. This concept was central, though implicit, in Corwin Edwards's theory of conglomerate power. Corwin D. Edwards, "The Changing Dimensions of Business Power," in *Das Unternehmen in der Rechtsordnung, Festgabe für Heinrich Kronstein* (Karlsruhe: C. F. Müller, 1967), p. 260. These types of power options differ from those associated with the two power bases in that they are frequently targeted more on rival sellers than on buyers. They are examples of rival-oriented market power.

40. The conventional analysis of the coordination function is represented by Walras' *tatonnement* process and Edgeworth's recontracting. See Michael Rothschild, "Models of Market Organization with Imperfect Information: A Survey," *Journal of Political Economy* (November/December 1973), pp. 1283–308.

41. The neo-Hayekians define coordination and, consequently, coordination failure differently. Coordination failure exists whenever exchanges that would have occurred, if relevant information had been available to the parties, did not occur because such information was not available. "Successful coordination of these bits of information cannot fail to produce coordinated activity-exchange—benefiting both parties." Israel M. Kirzner, *Competition and Entrepreneurship* (Chicago and London: University of Chicago Press, 1973), p. 217. In sum, the "attainment of equilibrium is a coordination problem." Gerald P. O'Driscoll, Jr., *Economics as a Coordination Problem* (Kansas City, Mo.: Sneed, Andrews and McMeel, 1977), p. 24. This concept of coordination differs significantly from the one proposed in this paper. The problems to which each concept is addressed are also different.

42. Another general distinction can be made between the allocation and coordination functions, a distinction based upon the relationship between each function

and information. In general, allocation *generates* market information. Coordination, on the other hand, *requires, but may not generate,* information.

43. A dominant firm with a competitive fringe may unilaterally coordinate its decisions with those of a small, independent fringe as long as the impact of those decisions on the industry remains small. But if the effect on industry performance increases to some critical threshold, a movement toward interfirm coordination can be expected.

44. G. B. Richardson, *Information and Investment* (London and New York: Oxford University Press, 1960).

45. *Ibid.,* p. 222.

46. Fritz Machlup, *The Economics of Sellers' Competition* (Baltimore: Johns Hopkins Press, 1952), p. 351.

47. *Ibid.,* p. 439.

48. Machlup defined the degree of collusion in terms of the "*Contents* of the expectations which sellers entertain regarding the behavior of their rivals or the *confidence* with which they entertain these expectations." *Ibid.,* p. 440.

49. This assumes given market power bases.

50. Machlup, *Economics,* pp. 440–42.

51. Machlup found no positive correlation between the form and degree of collusion. "Collusion of a relatively high degree may be most informal, based on nothing but tacit understanding. On the other hand, a rather elaborate apparatus is sometimes established to accomplish collusion of a relatively low degree. This lack of positive correlation between form and degree is due chiefly to the presence of other essential variables, especially the number of cooperating firms in the group." *Ibid.,* p. 440. His conclusion resulted from the fact that he did not accumulate the options of form as you move rightward on the horizontal axis.

52. Fraas and Greer concluded in an empirical study of the relationship between market structure and price collusion: "the evidence indicates that as the number of parties increases and/or as the structural conditions become increasingly complex, conspirators must increasingly resort to arrangements of more elaborate design or greater efficiency if they are to achieve their joint profit maximizing objectives . . . formal cartels arise most often where the structural conditions are not particularly favorable to collusion." Arthur G. Fraas and Douglas F. Greer, "Market Structure and Price Collusion: an Empirical Analysis," *The Journal of Industrial Economics* (September 1977), pp. 42–43. It should be noted, however, that firms might consider the benefits of cartelization to be so great (e.g., the costs of not attempting to coordinate might be so great) that they would attempt to cartelize even if the transaction costs were high.

53. Peter Asch and J. J. Seneca, "Is Collusion Profitable?" *The Review of Economics and Statistics* (February 1976), p. 8.

54. Machlup, *Economics,* p. 442.

55. "There is a strong tendency . . . for collusion of low degrees to develop into collusion of higher degrees." *Ibid.,* p.439.

56. *Ibid.,* p. 442; also see p. 439.

57. Kronstein, *Cartels,* pp. 155–56. More generally, see pp. 154–76.
58. *Ibid.,* p. 157 n.6.
59. *Ibid.,* p. 160.
60. *Ibid.,* p. 158.
61. "Perhaps the most widely used approach to commodity control is the long-term contract stipulating price and/or quantity." Alton D. Law, *International Commodity Agreements* (Lexington, Mass.: Lexington Books, 1975), p. 70.
62. There is also a list of secondary commodities to be considered. It has been estimated that by 1982 only three to five international commodity agreements will have joined the Integrated Commodity Programme: tin, cocoa, coffee, sugar, and rubber. *Financial Times* (London), March 21, 1979, p. 14, editorial, and March 22, 1979, p. 18, col. 8.
63. "In the past fifty years, there have been 18 major agreements in nine commodities: bauxite (1), coffee (3), copper (2), cocoa (1), rubber (2), sugar (4), tea (1), tin (1), and wheat (2). Nine of these operated before World War II, principally during the 1930s, and nine have operated since World War II." David L. McNicol, "Political Economy of an Integrated Commodity Program," in Adams and Klein, eds., *Stabilizing,* p. 199.
64. Gordon W. Smith and George R. Schink, "The International Tin Agreement: A Reassessment," Paper no. 69 (Houston: Rice University Program of Development Studies, 1975), p. 10. From 1956 to 1974, the GSA stock was ten to fifteen times the ITA buffer stock authorizations.
65. Smith and Schink, "International Tin," p. 10 and p. 15, respectively.
66. McNicol, "Political Economy," p. 200.
67. According to UNCTAD:

Voluntary export restraints are formal or informal arrangements whereby the producers of an exporting country, usually at the request of the manufacturers in the importing country, agree to limit their exports of a particular product. . . . When export restraints are concluded with the explicit intervention of governments, the consequent arrangements are known as *orderly marketing arrangements.* . . . Recently, a new concept has been gaining ground, that of *organized free trade.* It envisages, under government auspices, global market-sharing arrangements at the sectoral level which would limit imports into individual developed countries of sensitive, highly competitive foreign goods.

UNCTAD, *Monthly Bulletin,* no. 140 (May 1978), p. 3.
68. See "Creeping Cartelization," *Business Week,* May 9, 1977, pp. 64–83.
69. Alexandre Stakovitch, "A European View of Commodity Problems: Stabilization of Prices and Stabilization of Receipts," in Adams and Klein, eds., *Stabilizing,* 235–40.
70. UNCTAD, *Monthly Bulletin,* no. 128 (May 1977), p. 3.
71. Other considerations undoubtedly exist such as the desire to reap promoter's profits and to minimize taxes.
72. Coase wrote the seminal article on the analysis of internalization as a determinant of the form of the firm. "The question always is, will it pay to bring an extra exchange transaction under the organising authority [of the firm]? At the

margin, the costs of organising within the firm will be equal either to the costs of organising in another firm or to the costs involved in leaving the transaction to be 'organised' by the price mechanism. Businessmen will be constantly experimenting, controlling more or less, and, in this way, equilibrium will be maintained." Coase, "Nature," p. 404. In Coase's view, the form of the firm results from the pursuit of organizational efficiency by reducing transaction costs.

73. These rival-oriented conduct options set up a potential conflict between internalization as a source of facilitation, designed to ease rivalry, and internalization as a source of options to be targeted on rivals.

74. For a discussion of the ability of the global aluminum industry effectively to coordinate interfirm relationships, see Zuhayr Mikdashi, "Aluminum," in Raymond Vernon, ed., *Big Business and the State* (Cambridge, Mass.: Harvard University Press, 1974), pp. 170–94.

75. Merton J. Peck, *Competition in the Aluminum Industry* (Cambridge, Mass.: Harvard University Press, 1961), pp. 92–93.

76. Another possible result would be a shortage. For example, at these peak moments, nonintegrated aluminum fabricators have experienced shortages. For this reason, some have integrated backward into ingot production.

77. The load factor is the ratio between average and peak outputs.

78. It is not possible in this article to discuss conglomeration in any detail. For a discussion of "attractive internal efficiency characteristics" of conglomeration, see Williamson, "Vertical Integration," pp. 156–58.

79. For a discussion of mutual forbearance, market allocation, and spheres of influence in the international electrical equipment industry, see Richard S. Newfarmer, *The International Market Power of Transnational Corporations* (Geneva: United Nations, 1978, TD/ST/MD/13).

80. Corwin D. Edwards, "The Veblen-Commons Award," *Journal of Economic Issues* (June 1979), p. 287. He referred (p. 229) to the relationship among large diversified firms as "reciprocal forbearance in competitive trade."

81. Edward S. Mason, *Controlling World Trade* (New York and London: McGraw-Hill, 1948), p. 20.

82. *Financial Times* (London), July 19, 1979, p. 31, col. 6.

83. *Wall Street Journal,* June 29, 1979, p. 26, cols. 2–3. For a discussion of a similar but earlier problem, see P. T. Bauer and B. S. Yamey, *Markets, Market Control and Marketing Reform* (London: Weidenfeld and Nicholson, 1968), pp. 158 ff. In the case of tin, the following counter-argument might be made, within the limits of national policy, in support of increasing the export tax as export prices increase. Assume a high-cost producing country (Bolivia) and a low-cost producing country (Malaysia). If the set price band covers the costs of the former, including incentive to expand, the latter enjoys an economic rent. If it is this rent that the export tax reduces, there should be limited adverse effect on low-cost producers.

84. *Financial Times* (London), July 24, 1979, p. 24, cols. 2–4.

85. See Mohamed Ariff, "International Commodity Control—The Tin Experience," in Lawrence B. Krause and Hugh Patrick, eds., *Mineral Resources in the*

Pacific Area, papers and proceedings of the Ninth Pacific Trade and Development Conference, San Francisco, California, August 22–26, 1977 (Federal Reserve Bank of San Francisco), p. 479; also Law, *Commodity Agreements,* p. 82; also *Financial Times* (London), July 10, 1979, p. 28, cols. 6–8; and the *Wall Street Journal,* July 20, 1979, p. 28, col. 2.

86. "Although the ITA [International Tin Agreement] has consistently failed to defend its ceiling price, floor prices have been penetrated only once (September, 1958)." Smith and Schink, "Tin Agreement," p. 5. Also see Ariff, "Tin Experience," pp. 579 and 584.

87. *Financial Times* (London), March 28, 1979, p. 24, cols. 2–4.

88. *Ibid.,* July 10, 1979, p. 28, cols. 6–8, and July 13, 1979, p. 25, col. 5.

89. UNCTAD, *Monthly Bulletin,* no. 125 (February 1977), p. 2.

90. *Financial Times* (London), March 1, 1978, p. 27, col. 5.

91. Another instrument has been antidumping actions, utilizing duties or the trigger price mechanism. These actions do not take the *form* of a restrictive government practice. Their form is that of an action against international price discrimination; consequently, their form will be considered by some as consistent with competition policy.

92. When New Zealand and Japan reached an impasse in negotiations over dairy products and beef, New Zealand excluded Japan from fishing in the 200-mile maritime economic zone that it had established on April 2, 1978. *Financial Times* (London), April 6, 1978, p. 31, cols. 2–3.

93. Mr. G. Corea, Secretary General of UNCTAD, has "stressed that the Common Fund was not an exercise in aid or assistance from the rich to the poor. It is, on the contrary, predicated on the concept of a cooperative endeavor on the part of the entire international community, which has a common interest in imparting strength and stability to world commodity markets." UNCTAD, *Monthly Bulletin,* no. 147 (December 1978), p. 3.

94. McNicol, "Political Economy," p. 204.

95. *Financial Times* (London), March 22, 1979, p. 18, cols. 3–8.

96. *Ibid.,* Sept. 25, 1979, p. 1, cols. 7–8, and p. 4, col. 8. For a brief discussion of OPEC aid to poor oil-importing countries, see *ibid.,* Oct. 16, 1979, p. 4, col. 5.

97. *Business Week,* March 24, 1975, p. 38.

98. *Wall Street Journal,* June 27, 1979, p. 3, cols. 2–4. See also *Financial Times* (London), Sept. 12, 1979, p. 3, cols. 2–3.

99. Paul Goldberg and Charles Kindleberger, "Toward a GATT for Investment: a Proposal for Supervision of the International Corporation," *Law and Policy in International Business* (Summer 1970).

100. It appears that the United States may have attempted such an approach within the GATT in 1976 when the U.S. representatives proposed negotiations concerning international rules assuring access to raw materials. The proposal was rebuffed by developing countries and some developed countries. *Journal of Commerce,* May 16, 1976, p. 2, col. 4.

International Cartels
and Their Regulation

◇

James A. Rahl

INTRODUCTION

In establishing a Common Market, the members of the European Communities instituted a strict system of cartel control, in part to prevent private agreements from maintaining or erecting trade barriers similar to those being eliminated among the governments.

On the world level, of course, there is no comprehensive legal system to control restrictive practices. But antitrust laws of the United States and other nations, and of the European Communities, have had a major impact on international cartels. Further, important progress is currently being made in the United Nations toward adoption of a set of rules and principles for control of restrictive business practices affecting international trade, especially for the benefit of developing nations. One of the express goals of this project is similar to that of the antitrust rationale of the Common Market. In the language of the Report of the UNCTAD Third Ad Hoc Group of Experts on Restrictive Business Practices,[1] this goal is: "To ensure that restrictive business practices do not impede or negate the realization of benefits that should arise from the liberalization of tariff and non-tariff barriers affecting world trade." Thus, a main objective is to prevent cartels and cartel-like practices from undermining the work of the GATT and other intergovernmental agencies that have made strides toward reducing governmentally created barriers to free trade.

One might state the problem conversely, however, from a different per-

I wish to thank Jeffrey S. Levin, Class of 1979, and David J. Eckert, Class of 1980 of Northwestern University School of Law, for their assistance in research for this paper.

spective on contemporary history. Great progress has been made both in reducing older forms of government-imposed restrictions and in eliminating private cartels. A principal danger today, however, is that both of these advances will be undermined by newer forms of governmental intervention that protect some old kinds of private cartel activity or formulate and carry out on a governmental level restrictive arrangements of a type previously engaged in primarily by private cartels.

Given the problems with which national governments must deal, especially the great majority which lack the unifying pressure of membership in an "economic community," it would not be surprising if counter-pressures to both trade liberalization and anticartel policies were to encourage an increase in some forms of government-implemented restrictive practices.

For example, while the United States is strongly aligned against international restrictive practices, it is also pursuing some restrictive policies with seemingly increasing vigor under the pressure of protectionist influences. At the Paris Conference on International Economic Cooperation in 1977, Secretary of State Cyrus R. Vance, while not renouncing our policy, in former Secretary Henry Kissinger's words, to "condemn" international restrictive business practices,[2] pledged the United States to work toward arranging more international commodity agreements, like those existing for coffee and tin, in order to "stabilize" prices, supplies, and earnings for commodities such as sugar and grains.[3] These cartel-like arrangements are partly the result of pressures from developing countries.

Meanwhile, pressed from within, the United States has also sought to arrange "orderly marketing agreements" with some of its trading partners to restrict imports in such products as steel and color television sets, which are said to be causing domestic injury. These agreements are especially strange in the face of an anticartel policy because they require foreign nations to organize domestic cartel-like arrangements in order to carry out the agreed restrictions on exports to the United States. When more than one foreign nation is involved, the United States must arrange an allocation among the nations and they, in turn, among their exporting firms. A multinational cartel-like program thus may come into being.

Some other nations carry on a great deal of cartel-like activity. Some— especially states that are predominantly raw materials producers—go further, in the manner of the Organization of Petroleum Exporting Countries (OPEC), and form outright intergovernmental cartels. Such arrangements exist, or are being sought today, in many fields in addition to oil, including, e.g., bauxite, bananas, copper, phosphate, iron ore, mercury, and tea.[4]

The problem of government-sponsored restrictions is somewhat humbling. My assignment is to deal with control of restrictive business practices committed by international cartels that are essentially private in nature. Restrictive intergovernmental agreements and arrangements are largely beyond the scope of this paper.[5] But no one should believe that private cartels, though they can be extremely damaging, represent the most serious kind of interference with free trade today. The various governmentally created restraints, including tariffs, quotas, miscellaneous other unilateral trade barriers, commodity agreements, orderly marketing arrangements, antidumping orders, subsidies, national preference requirements in buying, pervasive regulation of some industries, embargoes, and state trading monopolies, surely add up to far more restraint of international competition than do cartels.

Most of these restraints are beyond the reach of restrictive business practice regulation. This paper will discuss some types of government action, however, that aid predominantly private cartel activity, through encouragement, exemption, or compulsion of private cartels. This is an unhappy distinction; the line is far from clear.

"Cartel" will be defined here as an association of competitors jointly restricting competition in markets of more than one nation. This definition is meant to encompass both cartels composed of firms from two or more nations, and cartels formed by firms from one nation to operate in international trade. The focus is mainly on typical horizontal restraints of competition as to prices, production, territory, and customers. Vertical restraints on distribution of the products of a single manufacturer, such as exclusive dealing and territorial restriction of dealers, are not discussed. Mergers, joint ventures, and licensing restrictions also are not covered, although some of these transactions, of course, may involve cartel activities.

Further problems of scope exist even after thus limiting the topic. Representatives of developing nations in UNCTAD meetings sometimes call integrated multinational parent-subsidiary organizations "cartels."[6] This reflects a desire to exercise control of intraenterprise policies considered injurious to host nations of subsidiaries of multinational organizations, such as internal decisions that limit a subsidiary's exports or control its purchasing. This approach to enterprise management abandons competition as the law's guide in favor of balance of trade and other criteria. Its logic does not stop at parent-subsidiary organizations but would include control of trade decisions by divisions and branches, and even by agents or employees in a simple firm.

For these reasons, this approach has been rejected by the Department of Justice and, almost by common consent, by the bar in the United States,[7] though not expressly as yet by the Supreme Court. Common Market law also rejects it if it is shown that the parent-subsidiary organization is an "economic unit" and agreements within it are concerned "merely with the internal allocation of tasks."[8] This is not a cartel because it does not restrain competition, there being no genuine competition within the structure. If the enterprise exercises dominant power or engages in exclusionary anticompetitive conduct toward outsiders, it may be an antitrust problem because real competition is restrained, but not otherwise.

More broadly, the late Heinrich Kronstein, in his book, *The Law of International Cartels,* argued that "modern international cartels cannot be successfully analyzed in terms of traditional antitrust and cartel legislation and literature." To him, present antitrust approaches are pre-World War II oriented and old-fashioned. While he agreed that explicit cartel agreements may still occur, the more serious problem is that "[p]arties so inclined may use agreements not directly concerned with competitive behavior; or covert, non-compulsory agreements may be based on entanglements or friendly relationships between firms. In any case, the effect may be to establish a parallelism fully as regulatory as the old formal cartel."[9]

Kronstein said he was not approaching the matter merely with oligopoly theory. He did place emphasis upon the importance of structural factors but said that he was talking about actual "coordination of the economic behavior of independent partners . . . which results in regulation of one or more markets."[10] This coordination may be of various kinds. His book deals with such examples as joint research and development, licensing arrangements, government-encouraged technological coordination, joint production ventures in raw materials (sometimes with government sponsorship), information-sharing on prices, joint sales agencies, and other arrangements.

To the extent that the practices discussed by Kronstein involve agreements, as most of them do, they are subject to review under traditional antitrust laws if jurisdiction is present. By excluding purely oligopolistic behavior, Kronstein has eliminated the category of multiparty activity with which antitrust has the greatest difficulty. His point then is that a cartel policy must realistically adapt its substantive rules and procedures to informal anticompetitive cooperation as well as to formal cartel compacts. To that, there should be general assent. On the other hand, I could not agree that all of the activities he has described are likely to restrain competition or should be prohibited.

The balance of this paper will review evidence on the incidence of private cartels as a necessary step in appraising the effect of antitrust laws, analyze the coverage of key antitrust laws and of gaps in their scope, discuss various types of government interference with antitrust controls, and suggest some lines of future action.

INCIDENCE OF PRIVATE CARTELS

PREVALENCE OF CARTELS BETWEEN THE WARS

Between the world wars, large-scale cartels of the international variety, many of global dimension, enjoyed a heyday.[11] Available figures are not wholly reliable, but they are fairly indicative of the grip cartels held on world trade. Listing numerous industries in which cartels operated before 1948, Stocking and Watkins concluded that they reached into "practically every branch of the modern economy."[12]

Studies by Corwin Edwards for the Department of Justice during World War II found the existence, as the war started, of 179 international cartels. There were American participants in 109 of them.[13] Fritz Machlup, in a lecture at Columbia University, cited a League of Nations study to the effect that 32 percent of all international trade was under some form of marketing control.[14] Edward S. Mason noted estimates by others that 40 to 50 percent of world trade between 1929 and 1937 was cartelized or "influenced" by cartels. He argued somewhat dubiously that this did not prove that world trade would have been greater absent the cartels. More plausibly, he doubted that cartels were, or in the future would be, as important in restraining trade as tariffs, intergovernmental commodity agreements, and state trading monopolies.[15] But he did not question their prevalence and wrote many pages about policies for controlling them. Raymond Vernon has said that there were major international cartels in practically every processed metal, most important chemicals, key pharmaceuticals, and a variety of other products.[16]

In Europe, cartels were embraced by both free and totalitarian regimes.

Robert Terrill, at the time an economist with the State Department, reported that "[t]here were probably few important commodities in intra-European trade which by the middle 1930's were not subject to regulation as to conditions of competition through the direct or indirect mediation of cartels. . . ."[17] J. D. Gribbin has stated that a recently released British study, made at the end of World War II, estimated that in 1938, from 28 to 34 percent of manufactured exports from the United Kingdom were controlled by cartels and about 40 percent of imports were restricted by them.[18] The relations between cartels and governments—always likely to be greater when cartels are functioning openly—became tighter in some nations. Some provided for "compulsory cartels," which all members of an industry could be made to join.[19] Nazi Germany ultimately went further and made the cartels instruments of total industrial control.[20]

On the eve of World War II, the famous "Düsseldorf" agreement of March 16, 1939 announced a joint declaration of cooperation between the Federation of British Industries and the Reichsgruppe Industrie. Among other things, the two associations of industry stated: "It is essential to replace destructive competition where it may be found with constructive co-operation, designed to foster the expansion of world trade, to the mutual benefit of Great Britain, Germany and all other countries."[21]

Comparison of the European story with concurrent developments in the United States shows that the same tendencies were present here, but also that a strong antitrust law made a big difference. Trade associations grew rapidly in the United States in the 1920s, clearly responding to the same powerful pressures for cartelization found in Europe.[22] With the Sherman Act in force, however, they were generally forced to avoid outright price fixing and other direct restraints of competition and were limited to milder forms of cooperation than were prevalent in Europe and elsewhere.

A notable exception, of course, was the enactment in 1918 of the Webb-Pomerene exemption for American export associations. A Congress that only four years earlier had adopted the Clayton and Federal Trade Commission Acts to strengthen the Sherman Act sought to facilitate anticompetitive conduct by Americans in export commerce, so long as it did not also injure competition or consumers in the home market. This action was partly taken as a defensive maneuver against foreign cartels on both the buying and the selling side of the market, but it was also designed to gain supposed positive trade advantages from elimination of competition.[23] It was apparently not realized at the time that the prohibitions in the Webb-

Pomerene Act against domestic effect from export restraints would render the exemption extremely difficult to use.[24]

With the depression of the 1930s, and the relaxation of antitrust law in the United States in favor of NRA and other cooperative measures, it seemed that America might catch up with Europe in domestic cartelization.[25] Invalidation of NRA and a major change of heart in national policy toward the end of the 1930s, however, produced a reinvigoration of antitrust enforcement that turned back the cartel tide just when it may have been close to engulfing the country.

DECLINE SINCE WORLD WAR II AND REASONS

Since World War II, visible, private, formal, world cartels of the kind that are not supported by governments have rapidly declined in number and are infrequently observed today. Raymond Vernon in 1968 said that global cartels have "passed into history."[26] Douglas Rosenthal, present Chief of the Foreign Commerce Section of the Antitrust Division, stated recently that "the old-fashioned private international cartel . . . is now rarely found."[27] Joel Davidow, Rosenthal's immediate predecessor and now Director of Policy Planning of the Antitrust Division, agrees,[28] as do the substantial number of other expert observers consulted in preparation for this paper.

A few of the old-fashioned cartels do reappear now and then. The famous quinine cartel, for example, surfaced in 1967.[29] The cartel, which controlled world markets for a time, was spectacular partly because of its rarity. At the same time, it reminded us that there could be other world cartels in hiding. Recently, the Commission of the European Communities revealed in a preliminary decision that it is investigating a zinc cartel composed of the largest European, Canadian, and Australian producers.[30]

Other modern examples of private global cartels are difficult to find. The most famous contemporary cartel, the Organization of Petroleum Exporting Countries, is sponsored by governments, and the alleged uranium cartel has received important governmental protection. These government-related cartels will be mentioned later.

The near demise of the private global cartel is a dramatic phenomenon. Before the war, cartels had strong, respectable spokesmen, but they have few vocal apologists today. As Ernest Goldstein has said, "Today, no European government would admit that it favors cartels."[31] Occasionally, a claim is made that special circumstances require deviation from the competitive norm. Developing nations seek special concessions for their raw materials cartels,[32] while sponsoring rules against restrictive practices for the rest of the world. Some Europeans seek special EEC exemption for cooperation in economic "crises" due to oil shortages and textile overcapacity.[33] Some Americans are renewing their periodic contention that antitrust policies hamper U.S. exports, and seek broadened exemption for our variety of export cartels.[34] But these are usually regional or one-nation situations. No one calls for anything like the Düsseldorf agreement's broad endorsement of cartels as a way of life for all industry.

There are several reasons for this change. Corwin Edwards in a study for the State Department in 1964 identified four factors in the weakening of cartels in Europe as he found them then.[35] These were disruptions brought about by the war, a widening of markets and consequent increase in potential competition, new technology and new types of business organization, and changes in legal status and government policy. Raymond Vernon in 1968 attributed the disappearance of global cartels to reduced concentration in sources of raw materials, increased restrictive activity by governments, the rapid growth of U.S. exports and direct foreign investment, changes in communications, the development of integrated parent-subsidiary structures of multinational companies, and U.S. antitrust cases.[36]

A further major factor not mentioned by these writers, which clearly played a significant role, was the odious name international cartels acquired as a result of revelations concerning their part in the temporary success of the totalitarian regimes that launched World War II. In the United States, German cartels were widely believed to have helped the Nazi takeover of German industry,[37] and international cartels were thought to have seriously retarded American and Allied military preparedness.[38] The results were the imposition of anticartel regulations by the Allies upon occupied Germany and Japan, as well as the subsequent adoption of antitrust laws by those countries. The greatly lowered general popularity of cartels made them difficult to defend politically. This facilitated the gradual adoption of some form of antitrust law by most of the developed nations and played a role in the incorporation of antitrust provisions in the treaties establishing the European Communities.[39]

All of these factors have contributed to the decline of the cartels, and it is difficult to determine which among them are the most decisive. The attempt must be made, however, in order to evaluate the past and future role of antitrust law.

Both Edwards and Vernon emphasized several kinds of structural change. One is a reduction of concentration in many markets resulting from increased sources of raw materials, growth of U.S. exports and direct foreign investment, and other factors. Reduced concentration makes cartels more difficult to form and manage. New entrants also may be less cooperative than those accustomed to a cartel way of life.

Empirical research by this writer in Europe in the late 1960s found a strong disinclination on the part of some new American entrants to join local cartels. It was almost impossible to determine, however, whether the underlying factor was a business reason, or the fear of antitrust sanctions at home, or a combination of both. Reliance on reduced concentration as a long-run guarantee against cartelization seems misplaced, even if it has been a major factor. The reduction itself may be temporary; increases in concentration appear to be occurring in some industries in the EEC.[40] Also, only a large increase in the number of firms would be likely to make much difference. Cartels would remain possible even though a few more participants are added. The administrative problems in running a cartel change when the numbers are large, but not when only a minor increase occurs. The biggest hazard of large numbers is discovery and antitrust prosecution.

A second kind of change has been increased technological differentiation in products. A great deal of American export and productive investment abroad since World War II has been in high technology industries, and it does appear that cartels are somewhat less likely in these industries than in fields involving simpler, more homogeneous commodities. But they are still possible and have often existed.

A third kind of change emphasized by writers is an increase in multinational firms with newer, more integrated organizational structures and methods. Certainly, to the extent that a firm perceives that it is more efficient or more powerful than its rivals and has more to gain by acting alone than by combining with competitors, it will avoid cartels if it is legally and politically free to act independently. Some research of mine has tended to verify statements of some multinational company leaders that they believe they have more to gain in markets abroad by not joining a cartel than by doing so. An ideal situation, of course, is when competitors are tied down by a cartel's restrictions and the firm is not, as is still possible in some countries.[41]

I do not have confidence in the proposition sometimes advanced, however, that because of their mode of organization, multinationals have supplanted cartels. Many of the classic prewar cartels were themselves composed of multinationals, and indeed a global cartel, if it exists, is more likely than not to be made up mostly of multinational enterprises. Heinrich Kronstein probably would have agreed, although he would redefine what we mean by "cartel" to include much activity falling outside the usual definition, and outside of antitrust prohibitions as well.[42]

Of the other reasons mentioned above, disruptions brought about by the war have largely disappeared insofar as cartels are concerned. The dramatic impact of rising U.S. exports and direct foreign investment—certainly a disruptive force for established cartels abroad—has eased. Some U.S. firms may be having second thoughts that make joining a cartel seem more desirable, especially in light of recent increases in penetration of U.S. home markets by foreign exporters and direct investors. The political and psychological dislike of cartels because of their association with totalitarian governments and with the war itself may be on the wane, as memories fade or give way to new sets of economic pressures.

Although all of the reasons given above for the rapid decline of private global cartels have doubtless had past effect, antitrust enforcement seems decisive, as explained in the next section of this paper.

Although it has not been possible to assemble data on this, it is clear that cartels continue on a local and regional basis, where no antitrust laws operate vigorously against them. Most of the developed nations have some kind of law regulating restrictive practices, but cartels nevertheless flourish or at least survive in some of these countries.[43] Some of the national laws require registration and official scrutiny of cartel agreements but do not prohibit them unless they are shown to be operating abusively or contrary to the public interest. In somewhat stricter countries, cartels are presumed to be illegal, but means are provided for obtaining exemptions for them on public interest or other grounds. Even the fairly strong West German law and the moderately strong United Kingdom law are of the latter type.

Almost all of the leading developed countries, with varying degrees of leniency, permit export cartels to restrict competition in foreign markets.[44] J. D. Gribbin, working from data in the OECD report in 1974 on export cartels, has estimated that there are about 390 single-nation export cartels and about 80 international cartels with members from more than one nation.[45] In the less-developed countries, there are few significant laws of any kind against restrictive trade practices, and in these countries, local and export cartels may operate fairly freely.

IMPACT AND WEAKNESSES OF PRESENT ANTITRUST LAWS

It is obvious that there is a positive correlation between the presence of a strong, applicable antitrust law and an absence of cartels. This is confirmed by the continued presence of cartels on regional and local levels when effective antitrust laws are absent, as indicated above. It remains to analyze how much of the world's cartel activity is controlled by present-day antitrust law, how this control operates, and what its gaps and weaknesses are.

AN ANTITRUST-CARTEL MAP

The geographic distribution of antitrust control of cartels would appear on a map somewhat as follows. A "global" cartel engaging in the traditional restraints of market allocation or price fixing could probably not operate lawfully today because its scope would cause it to violate in some respect both U.S. and EEC antitrust laws, and probably those of a good many other nations as well.

A regional cartel encompassing either the Western Hemisphere or Western Europe will run afoul of U.S. or EEC law, and probably other laws.

A cartel confined to activity in the following other areas may succeed in avoiding these stronger antitrust laws: Central and South America, Africa, the Middle East, and the Far East. In these areas, it will have to pick its way around a few national antitrust laws, including those of Japan, Australia, New Zealand, India, Pakistan, Israel, and Brazil. These statutes are not as strict as those of the United States and the EEC, but may sometimes prohibit the cartel's operations in the country concerned.

Cartels engaged in trade with the Communist nations generally would not have to fear antitrust laws, except in Hungary and Yugoslavia, provided their actions do not also impinge upon areas with antitrust laws. (It is interesting to note that some Communist nations have taken an active part in the UNCTAD negotiations for a set of international rules and principles on restrictive business practices.)

Local cartels may operate with impunity insofar as antitrust laws are concerned in the great majority of nations—over one hundred countries are without such laws—and with reasonable security in those nations with laws of the milder type. (The same thing can be said of local cartels in the American states, where a minority enforce state antitrust laws and a large majority do not.)

Thus, the antitrust-cartel map will show the developed nation areas to be largely protected against world and regional cartels. The less-developed nation areas have the benefit of the same protection against global cartels, but lack protection against carefully limited regional cartels if the latter can function in their areas without having an impact on other areas covered by antitrust.

Communist nations are in about the same position as the less-developed countries in respect to antitrust protection. They benefit from global protection and are not protected from cartels approaching them on a regional basis.

Almost all nations, developed and less developed, are exposed to the risk of maltreatment at the hands of one another's national, and sometimes international, export cartels, which are almost universally exempted from, or simply not made subject to, antitrust prohibitions. [46]

THE INTERNATIONAL IMPACT OF U.S. AND EEC ANTITRUST LAWS
The international effectiveness against cartels of a given antitrust law is not a function of whether the enforcing agency seeks to be generous by applying its law to help other nations. Its own self-interest will lead a country to oppose a cartel that is restricting supply or raising prices in its domestic or import markets, or restricting its exports.

Whether a pertinent antitrust law can break up an international cartel depends largely on whether the relevant market in which the cartel operates includes one or more major firms that are subject to the law. If it does, and if the law takes that firm out of the cartel, the life of the cartel will probably be short, since the firm will be able to undersell or outbid the cartel. The cartel will then have to disband, or, if possible, confine its activities to a smaller territory. The same principle, of course, will govern cartels whose relevant markets are regional or local.

The importance of the market as determining whether the cartel can survive antitrust prohibitions against a key member underscores the probable futility of a cartel's efforts to avoid the problem by drafting exclusions from the scope of the agreement. Cartel agreements occasionally have expressly provided that they are inapplicable to sales in the EEC and the United States. The first thing one would then look for is a "gentlemen's" agreement, such as was entered into by the members of the quinine cartel,[47] that the cartel controls will apply to the EEC and the United States, though the formal agreement says they will not.

If the parties are indeed free to compete in these two vast markets, then a global cartel has been defeated, and probably at most only a regional cartel in less-developed country markets can be arranged. If such a cartel is economically possible, it still has its perils, particularly under U.S. law. If one of the cartel members is a firm (regardless of its nationality) that exports from the United States to the region being cartelized, its shipments will have to be controlled by the cartel agreement, and under the "foreign commerce" clause, the Sherman Act may apply. If shipments are only from the EEC, however, effect on trade among the member states and on competition within the Common Market would have to be shown, which is more difficult.

Until the antitrust laws effectively came into force in the 1960s, the only decisive weapon against world cartels was the American Sherman Act. In the period between the two wars, a few international cases arose under the Act, but not many. Beginning in about 1940, with the reinvigoration of antitrust enforcement in the United States, however, the Department of Justice carried out what amounted to a war of its own on the cartels.

In his book, *Cartels: Challenge to a Free World,* published in 1946, Wendell Berge, then head of the Antitrust Division, listed about 35 major anticartel cases filed by the Division between 1937 and 1945, mostly involving American defendants.[48] From the various international trade cases listed in *Foreign Commerce and the Antitrust Laws* by Wilbur Fugate, it appears that between 1940 and 1949 inclusive, something like sixty anticartel cases were filed, well over half of which were started during World War II itself.[49]

This American anticartel war tapered off in numbers in the 1950s, because it was largely won by then. The number of cartel cases filed since then has been much less—about twenty between 1950 and 1972, and a handful since. But this is clearly because there have been few cartels to prosecute. The promise of vigorous enforcement has been maintained by the Department.

It thus became clear to American firms, and others as well, that participation in an international cartel, other than an exempt Webb-Pomerene export association, was definitely illegal if it fell within the scope of the American law. Since no worldwide cartel could fail to involve the vast and growing American market, and few could ignore American firms, this meant that practically all such cartels would be out of order. In the quinine cartel, there was no U.S. manufacturing of the product. The participants were all foreign firms, including a subsidiary of an American firm. But the cartel applied to the large American market, seeking to fix prices and establish quotas, as well as to rig bids on the U.S. Government's sale of a large stockpile that loomed strategically over the whole industry supply.

Both the United States and the EEC proceeded vigorously against the members of the quinine cartel, since the markets of both were substantially affected. The EEC has also acted strongly against other horizontal international cartels, including the dyestuffs cartel,[50] and a sugar cartel.[51] The latter two were regional and did not involve the United States.

Since the EEC enforcement program did not come on the scene until after the huge wave of American anticartel prosecutions had had its effect, the European Commission has not had occasion to bring many cases of this kind. There is no basis for thinking that it will not act as strongly against most major cartels as any other antitrust agency when the case is presented. Article 85(1) of the Rome Treaty is very similar to section 1 of the Sherman Act, and, as interpreted by the Commission and the European Court of Justice, its prohibition of market allocation and price fixing is equally unequivocal. While it is true that an exemption may be granted under Article 85(3), two factors strongly militate against exemptions in cases of the kind under consideration here. One is that the exemption must be applied for by notifying the arrangement to the Commission.[52] This has the great disadvantage ultimately of compromising the secrecy usually valued by such cartels, especially in light of the interest in them of the American and other governments. If the parties do not notify until after the Commission has begun an investigation, the Commission is unlikely to receive the application with favor.[53]

The second reason auguring against obtaining an EEC exemption for a major cartel is that most cartels simply could not meet the difficult tests for exemption laid down in Article 85(3). It must be shown that the agreement will contribute to technical or economic progress, that consumers will share in its benefits, that the restrictions are indispensable to obtaining the benefits, and that competition will not be eliminated as to a "substantial part of the products in question." If nothing else stops the cartel, the last requirement is almost certain to do so.

Recently, efforts were made to obtain a change in the exemption requirements to permit special treatment of so-called "crisis" cartels. Such cartels are sometimes allowed in West Germany and some other countries to deal with serious economic emergencies such as overcapacity in textiles, or shortages in oil. The proposal ultimately was defeated in the Commission.[54]

LIMITATIONS ON THE EFFECTIVENESS OF ANTITRUST LAW

Two types of limitation upon the legal force of the antitrust laws as to private cartels must yet be considered: (1) limits on subject matter jurisdiction pertaining to extraterritoriality and related questions; and (2) difficulties of procedure and enforcement in the international setting. It might be sufficient to say that the record of success in antitrust enforcement demonstrates that these limitations are not very serious. Even within the areas of the EEC and the United States, however, problems arise. As for the remainder of the world, questions of subject matter jurisdiction and procedural limitations largely prevent existing antitrust laws from controlling regional (though not global) cartel activity.

Subject Matter Jurisdiction and Extraterritoriality. The extent to which laws such as those of the United States and the EEC may be applied "extraterritorially" is an issue running through the whole problem of cartel control. The argument is often made that application of the Sherman Act to activities of firms carried on outside the boundaries of the United States, especially those of foreign firms, is improper even though effects on American commerce are demonstrated. The argument has been hotly pursued by advocates, jurists, and scholars in an enormous number of books, articles, judicial opinions, and speeches.[55] The present writer has participated in this debate,[56] generally on the side of liberality, though not unbridled license, in the applicability of national antitrust laws to major international restraints of trade. Although it is impossible to describe the debate fully here, its impact on the actual scope and effectiveness of anticartel activity must be appraised. The question has both a substantive and a procedural dimension. Substantively, it is whether an antitrust law, even if its language is explicit, may render conduct illegal that occurs outside the territorial limits of the United States.

The controversy was launched by the *Alcoa* case in 1945, when Judge Learned Hand held that the Sherman Act may make it illegal for a wholly foreign cartel to restrain its members' competition in exports to the United States through acts carried out abroad, if both intent to affect U.S. commerce and actual effect are shown.[57] This so-called "effects" doctrine was endorsed with some rewording by section 18 of the American Law Institute's *Restatement (Second) of Foreign Relations Law of the United States.* The Sherman Act, to my knowledge, has not since been applied to a foreign cartel having no U.S.-affiliated party for activities wholly abroad, and this could be attributable in some degree to the outcry raised against *Alcoa.* The Department of Justice has steadily maintained, however, that the Act does reach such conduct abroad if commerce is restrained. Evidently influenced by the language of the *Restatement,* the recently issued Department of Justice *Antitrust Guide for International Business Operations* puts the rule as follows: "When foreign transactions have a substantial and foreseeable effect on U.S. commerce, they are subject to U.S. law regardless of where they take place" (citing *Alcoa* and other decisions).[58]

The Department recently has made two major concessions as to this doctrine. One is that a principle of comity will be followed to permit modification or withholding of judicial action, though not abdication of jurisdiction, where U.S. interests are in balance outweighed by those of another nation.[59] This principle, found in section 40 of the *Restatement,* recently has been adopted by two courts in private antitrust suits, though neither ultimately held back in its final judgment.[60] The idea is extremely difficult to administer, and it is not clear how it will be used in practice.

Second, the Department of Justice has indicated that it does not intend to apply the law to restraints whose only impact is in foreign markets, even though jurisdiction is present.[61] This policy, as explained by Douglas Rosenthal, is a particularization of the comity principle,[62] in that U.S. interest in foreign markets is considered to be less than that of the foreign state concerned, and the latter can apply its law to the situation if it wishes. The Sherman Act, Department spokesmen say, is not designed to protect foreigners abroad. The Department will not follow this policy if the restraint also has significant effects in the U.S. domestic market, or if it interferes with export opportunities of American firms.[63] It will apply principally to certain restraints of competition carried out in exports from the United States such as price fixing and market allocation, which do not exclude persons from exporting. The theory implies that the Webb-Pomerene exemption for export associations was unnecessary, and Department officials have intimated such a belief.[64]

I have taken an opposite side on this issue, on the ground that the Sherman Act, in the interest of preserving competition in our foreign trade, proscribes restraints of competition in our exports as well as in our imports.[65] This benefits U.S. interests, not merely the interests of foreigners. The Department's policy would substantially limit ability under the Sherman Act to invalidate cartel activity in U.S. export transactions. It would not prevent application of the Act if the restraint were reciprocal to a cartel's restraint of U.S. imports or domestic trade. But it would prevent application to a cartel that only restrains competition in exports, and this could be especially important if the foreign market affected is a less-developed region having no antitrust system of its own. It should be noted that the Department's position is an expression of enforcement policy and is not binding on courts, private parties, or the Federal Trade Commission.[66] In the context of continued arguments about extraterritoriality, however, it may strike a responsive chord with some.

The Commission of the European Communities also has adopted the "effects" doctrine, in the *Dyestuffs* case,[67] and it has adhered to it in subsequent pronouncements.[68] The provisions of the Treaty of Rome do not contain a foreign commerce clause, however, so the issue of the Justice Department's interpretation just discussed does not arise.

Germany also has expressly asserted "effects" jurisdiction in section 98(2) of the German Act Against Restraints of Competition.[69]

The debate over subject matter extraterritoriality has produced many protests to both the United States and the EEC by foreign nations who contend that their sovereignty is invaded by prosecutions to which they object.[70] The protests may have had subtle consequences as to selection of cases for prosecution, consequences that will never be fully known. Outwardly, however, the objections to the "effects" doctrine do not seem to have had much effect on either U.S. or EEC antitrust enforcement, and there is a good reason for this. Both sets of laws are very strong anticartel measures. A strong antitrust policy can no more ignore activity outside the jurisdiction's borders that restrains competition within its area of concern than can criminal law enforcement ignore persons firing shots across the border into the territory. Nations generally recognize the legitimacy of asserting jurisdiction over the latter conduct. The reason some do not recognize it for antitrust law is probably not really so much a reaction to invasion of sovereignty, as often claimed, as it is disapproval of the antitrust policy itself. This attitude, in turn, is recognition of the practical impact that antitrust enforcement is having internationally.

Insofar as classic cartel cases are concerned, the grounds asserted by both the United States and the EEC for taking jurisdiction are usually quite solid. In these cases, almost invariably there has been market allocation, and often price fixing, which excludes or limits competition directly in the internal domestic market of the jurisdiction.[71] Also, almost always there have been one or more participants who are established in the jurisdiction and who are acting in, not merely affecting, the domestic market. There is no extraterritorial objection that can be made to assertion of jurisdiction over the local participants, and all that is left is the argument that foreign participants who participated reciprocally but did not "act" in the territory should not be prosecuted. The cartel will probably be destroyed whether they are sued or not. But standard principles of conspiracy make them equally culpable, and it may seem unjust, as well as less than diligent, not to prosecute them if they can be brought within the jurisdiction.

Problems of International Procedure and Enforcement. Extraterritorial enforcement procedures give rise to more serious practical problems than do substantive matters. As section 7 of the *Restatement* says: "A state having jurisdiction to prescribe a rule of law does not necessarily have jurisdiction to enforce it in all cases." Broadly, these problems are of three types: (1) obtaining personal jurisdiction over foreign parties; (2) carrying out discovery as to parties, witnesses, and documents located abroad; and (3) enforcing orders and judgments abroad.[72]

Great difficulties have been encountered in some of the American cases with respect to these types of problems, and similar problems arise in other jurisdictions also. The inquiry for this paper will be limited to the question of how seriously hampered anticartel enforcement may be.

The answer must be more equivocal than it was on the issue of extraterritorial subject matter jurisdiction. Arguments based on the latter theory are seldom successful in the courts and agencies of the antitrust authority. But in procedural matters, more immediately practical problems are faced, and the effectiveness of the opposition rises, depending upon whether the legal controversy remains exclusively before the antitrust court or agency, or whether its scene shifts in important part to a foreign agency or court.

On questions of personal jurisdiction, if the antitrust court has a party or its agent or alter ego before it, it is able to proceed. Multinational corporations, often claimed to have advantages in being able to maneuver among jurisdictions, have a decided disadvantage in matters of personal jurisdiction. The antitrust court may decide to treat one of the multinational's affiliates in one nation as an agent of the parent or of another affiliate in another nation and thus rein in an organization that might otherwise be untouchable. On the other hand, if no immediate party can be found, the court cannot expect help from other states. There are no extradition procedures for antitrust violations. Some of the foreign defendants in the American prosecution of the quinine cartel have never been effectively served with process.[73]

The most spectacular controversies have occurred with respect to matters of discovery and enforcement of judgments. As to discovery, the multinational corporation again may be at a disadvantage, in that a parent corporation before the court or agency can be ordered to bring records and employees from abroad to provide evidence. Also, a subsidiary can be served with a similar order as agent of the foreign parent, as was done by the EEC Commission in the *Dyestuffs* case.

Two kinds of obstacles may arise, however. Evidence abroad may be in the hands of persons who are not subject to the court's jurisdiction and who will not furnish it voluntarily. In such a case, the only procedure available seems to be issuance of letters rogatory from the antitrust court, seeking the aid of the foreign court to compel production of the evidence. In its private antitrust suit against the alleged uranium cartel, Westinghouse sought evidence from a British corporation and some of its officials through letters rogatory in England. Ultimately, the House of Lords ruled that the evidence should not be furnished, although both the United Kingdom and the United States had signed the Hague Convention on the Taking of Evidence Abroad.[74] The judgments in the House of Lords emphasized the penal nature of the Sherman Act and the fact that the United States was interested in obtaining the evidence from Westinghouse for possible use in criminal proceedings. The Attorney General of the United Kingdom entered an appearance to state the Government's objections to the American efforts. Lord Wilberforce in his judgment symbolized the lack of harmony currently prevailing between the United States and the

United Kingdom over antitrust enforcement,[75] when he said, "It is axiomatic that in antitrust matters the policy of one state may be to defend what it is the policy of another state to attack."[76]

The *Westinghouse* litigation has also dramatized a second obstacle to discovery which may appear in some cases. The Canadian Government had adopted a regulation prohibiting disclosure of any written evidence relating to the matters involved, and the U.S. Court of Appeals for the tenth Circuit held that this regulation was effective to relieve the particular corporation and individual, who were nonparty witnesses, of a contempt of court finding, after a showing that they had sought in good faith to comply with a subpoena.[77] The Ontario Supreme Court had previously refused to order production of the evidence pursuant to letters rogatory.[78]

"Blocking statutes" prohibiting compliance with orders in foreign antitrust cases exist in the Netherlands, the United Kingdom, Ontario, and Quebec, in addition to special blocking provisions like the Canadian uranium regulation.[79]

Such problems of discovery may or may not frustrate the case, of course, depending upon the availability of other evidence. So long as foreign governments refuse to cooperate in antitrust discovery efforts, or actively block discovery and other antitrust orders, a potentially serious gap may be created in present anticartel controls. Multinational corporations and even single-nation firms may be tempted to explore the possibility of obtaining sanctuary for records in jurisdictions that will refuse to honor letters rogatory or will block compliance with antitrust orders.

Other problems occasionally arise in the enforcement of antitrust judgments. In the famous *du Pont-ICI* case, the British courts, by virtue of having control over the subject matter, completely frustrated the American antitrust court's orders with regard to certain nylon patents that had been assigned to the British company by du Pont pursuant to an illegal conspiracy.[80]

The OECD has initiated a study of problems of procedure and enforcement in the international antitrust area.[81]

PROBLEMS OF GOVERNMENTAL ACTION OR INTERFERENCE

At the outset, this paper raised the possibility that the world may be moving backwards somewhat because of increased governmental participation in cartel arrangements, or interference with anticartel controls. The question is not whether antitrust is ahead in the contest with purely private cartels. Surely it is, in the areas it can reach. But it is necessary to ask how serious the problems created by governments are in these areas.

The various kinds of governmental activity with which we are concerned may be grouped into three categories: (1) encouragement, (2) exemption, and (3) positive action or compulsion.

ENCOURAGEMENT

Past American decisions have established that informal governmental acquiescence, approval, encouragement, or even persuasion, whether by the American Government [82] or a foreign government, [83] will not serve as a defense to a charge of violation. This is not to say that this kind of activity may not be influential; such a background may induce prosecutors to exercise discretion not to prosecute.

Also, the result may be different if the "comity" principle endorsed by the Justice Department becomes well established. This principle calls for weighing the interests of the foreign state and the United States. If the foreign state has strongly encouraged the cartel, even though it has not compelled it, this encouragement would rather clearly be a relevant factor to be weighed with other factors, and it could no longer be dismissed out of hand. One might ask, for example, whether the outcome of the *Swiss Watch* case, given the great interest of the Swiss Government in the welfare of the watch industry, might have been different if the judges in *Timberlane* [84] or *Mannington Mills* [85] had decided the case.

In many nations, relations between industry and government are closer than in the United States, and this has substantial practical consequences. Even the European Commission, because of its necessary sensitivity to the powers of the member states, doubtless must listen to a great deal of discussion about national government interests that may be guarded by the activities of cartels. [86] The Commission has a substantial record of staunch enforcement, however, and in its decisions it has not recognized government encouragement as a defense. Even less would it be likely to recognize such a defense in favor of an outside foreign government.

EXEMPTION

By "exemption," reference is made to action of one government in granting lawful status under its own law to a cartel whose activities are subject to challenge under the antitrust law of another jurisdiction. The situation is virtually the same as in the case of encouragement. The fact that one government has not prohibited, or has exempted, the cartel will not normally provide a defense to a charge of antitrust violation under U.S., EEC, or other antitrust laws. Again, however, the exemption may be a factor in applying the comity approach. How much weight it would receive would depend in part upon the reasons for the exemption.

The kind of exemption of greatest importance to international anticartel control would seem to be the exempt status given almost universally to export cartels. The nature and exact requirements of the exemptions vary from jurisdiction to jurisdiction. In the United States, Germany, and the United Kingdom, for example, export cartels are expressly exempted, whereas EEC law simply does not reach them. For our purposes, the result is essentially the same. All of the OECD nations, and probably those of the rest of the world, allow cartels that in many cases would be illegal domestically to operate freely from their territories in sales made to buyers in other nations.[87] Although efficiencies in marketing may sometimes be gained by export cartels, their most popular goals seem to be price fixing and market allocation—the traditional practices of classic cartels. Other goals do exist, however. In Japan, for example, the Government uses export cartels as instruments for managing trade policy, in some instances to encourage exports, and in others to curtail them.[88]

Only fragmentary information exists as to the quantitative importance of these cartels. In the United States, their effect has been small. In 1976, only about 1.5 percent of the nation's exports were "assisted" by associations exempted under the Webb-Pomerene Act.[89] J. D. Gribbin has estimated that as of 1968, export cartels notified under the British law affected between 2 and 5 percent of exports.[90] Germany reports a figure of less than 3 percent for 1965.[91]

Some nations, such as the United Kingdom, do not prohibit exporters from participating in cartels with foreign members, although others, such as the United States, do. In some instances, the exemptions thus may facilitate the formation of international cartels of broader than national dimension. Other adverse consequences include the fact that export cartels sometimes precipitate formation of buying cartels on the other side of the market, and possibly retaliatory selling cartels as well. Still other undesirable results are outlined in the OECD report.[92] Perhaps the most pernicious effect of all is psychological. As long as the strongest nations with the most vigorous antitrust policies allow their exporters to form cartels to restrain competition in other nations, provided they do not injure "the folks at home," there is a major loss of credibility and moral force in the campaign against cartels throughout the world.

There is little doubt that the United States and the EEC could attack each other's export cartels, if they chose. The main legal problems would be with respect to obtaining personal jurisdiction, and while this could be difficult in some cases, it would not be insurmountable in all cases. Yet one almost never hears of such a case being brought, and it is apparent why. A sort of stand-off exists in the world, with no one in a very good position to throw the first stone. As Donald I. Baker, then head of the Antitrust Division, candidly stated in a letter to Senator Edward M. Kennedy in 1977, in response to the latter's questions about enforcement policies on behalf of a subcommittee of the Senate Judiciary Committee: "we have generally followed for some years a policy against suing members of a foreign export association for conduct which the U.S. would permit under the Webb-Pomerene Act."[93]

The report of the U.S. National Commission for the Review of Antitrust Laws and Procedures concluded that the Webb-Pomerene exemption is "overbroad" in allowing associations to restrain competition irrespective of a showing of need and without regard to industry structure or the antitrust and trade policies of foreign governments.[94] Accordingly, it recommended a legislative reexamination of the exemption.

On occasion, others have recommended an effort to obtain piecemeal reduction of the problem by negotiation of reciprocal agreements to rescind the exemption for cartels operating against parties to the agreement. Perhaps a simpler approach would be to announce a policy of attacking the cartels, in the expectation that retaliatory actions would cause a general collapse. The Justice Department would perhaps not be in the best position to do this, however, because of the view stated in the *Guide* that the Sherman Act does not apply, irrespective of whether there is an express exemption, to restraints whose effects are purely in foreign markets.[95]

Thus, the policy expressed in the letter to Senator Kennedy would still have force: it would be inappropriate to attack other people's cartels while we allow them. To fill this gap, legislation might become necessary to make it clear that the Sherman Act *does* apply to export restraints with impacts only on foreign markets. Such a measure, in turn, would further heat the controversy about extraterritoriality. All in all, it would seem better for the Justice Department simply to change its interpretation of the Sherman

Act as it now stands, assuming—as seems reasonable—that the Department's historic opposition to international cartels is unabated.

GOVERNMENT ACTIVITY

Two general types of governmental activity in cartel affairs may prevent effective antitrust action. One type, illustrated by OPEC, is outright participation by a government in a cartel, either through its own ministries or agencies, or through business entities owned and controlled by it. The other is governmental action or compulsion that requires cartel activity on the part of private persons.

Government Cartels. Direct participation by a government in a cartel is not necessarily beyond the reach of antitrust laws. American case law, applying a "restrictive theory" of immunity of sovereign states, has established a rule that if the government is engaging in "commercial activity," it loses immunity and may be sued. This test was embodied in the U.S. Foreign Sovereign Immunities Act of 1976.[96]

The question of what constitutes "commercial activity" is as difficult to administer as the governmental-proprietary distinction in tort law concerning municipal governments. Yet if any liability is to be recognized for foreign governments, some such standard will have to be used. Sigmund Timberg, in a thorough analysis of the problem,[97] has recommended that the issue turn on the nature of the activity involved, rather than the alleged purpose (governmental vs. commercial) of the activity. This test would probably avoid immunity in cartel cases, which involve activities that by nature are commercial, e.g., selling, as distinguished from the many other activities of a government.

If the immunity question is answered so as to establish antitrust liability, the problem may only have begun. Perhaps, as sometimes occurs, the foreign government consents to be sued, or acquiesces in the litigation. This may be necessary for it to be allowed to do business in the antitrust nation, as with various commercial enterprises owned wholly or partly by governments and selling a variety of products in the American market. The European Commission recently exercised control over two state trading enterprises in the German Democratic Republic as to licensing practices in the Common Market.

But if the foreign government-owned operation does not consent to be sued, purely practical considerations will prevail. In the recent suit against

OPEC by the International Association of Machinists and Aerospace Workers, the plaintiffs contended that the OPEC cartel members (all of whom are governments) are engaged in the commercial activity of selling oil. The defendants declined to appear, but the trial judge dismissed the suit anyway, ruling, *inter alia,* that the activity is "sovereign," not commercial.[98] He also held that foreign governments are not "persons" who can be sued under the Sherman Act, that subject matter jurisdiction is lacking because U.S. Energy Department "pass-through regulations" prevented "direct" effect on U.S. oil prices, and that plaintiffs were not "direct purchasers," as required by the *Illinois Brick* decision for private antitrust damage suits.

Had the judge ruled otherwise, the question arises as to how a judgment against OPEC could be enforced. At this level, one is confronted not by mere procedural difficulties, but by serious problems of international relations, whose breakdown can cause all kinds of difficulty, even war.

For largely practical reasons, then, antitrust laws can sometimes be effective against government cartels, and often cannot be.

Government Action or Compulsion.   Private persons who are required by a foreign government to engage in activities that are challenged under another jurisdiction's antitrust law are likely to raise a defense of "act of state," or of "foreign sovereign compulsion." These two doctrines are similar to concepts of "state action," recognized since *Parker v. Brown* as a limitation upon applicability of the Sherman Act to activities directed by an American state.[99] The complexities and troubles of the latter doctrine are emerging in the foreign field as well, further complicated by the confusing terminology.

"Act of state" originated, not as an antitrust defense, but in other types of cases, in which American courts said that they would not adjudicate the leoality of a foreign state's actions in its own territory. As applied in antitrust cases, the doctrine has taken on the meaning that if the restrictive practice or action complained of in the antitrust case was caused by the action of a foreign state in its territory, the defendant may not be held responsible. It has recently been held that this doctrine will not be applied if the act of state was one in which the state itself was not, as a matter of policy, interested in the outcome[100] (an approach which Eleanor Fox has pointed out is like that taken by the Supreme Court in denying the "state action" defense in *Cantor v. Detroit Edison Co.*).[101]

The "foreign sovereign compulsion" defense, as Sigmund Timberg has said, is very similar to "act of state," as the latter has developed in antitrust cases.[102] The only difference, it would seem, is that in "act of state" the restrictive action is by the state itself, whereas in a "compulsion" case, the private defendant is required by the state to commit the restrictive act. The distinction seems a very formal one.

Certain limitations on these twin doctrines are emerging in American law. The action of the foreign sovereign, it is said, must be a matter of significant governmental policy, not a mere ministerial act. In *Mannington Mills,*[103] the court went so far as to call issuance of a patent "ministerial," and thus not an act of state in this sense. Similarly, in *Timberlane,*[104] a decree of a foreign court issuing an attachment of plaintiff's property at the request of defendant was held not an act of state. The Department of Justice, in the *Guide,* has added that the foreign government's action must not be illegal under its own laws,[105] which seems to be a departure from the original basis for the act of state doctrine.

The *Guide* also states that the foreign government's command must not seek to compel conduct in the United States that would be unlawful,[106] as distinguished from conduct in the foreign state. On its face, this latter qualification seems a practical necessity. But under the "effects" doctrine of subject matter jurisdiction accepted by the United States, an act committed in a foreign state having effects in the United States is as unlawful under U.S. law as an act committed inside the United States. The distinction made by the *Guide* thus draws a line by way of compromise, and not as a matter of jurisdictional principle.

The blocking statutes referred to earlier, which prohibit compliance in a foreign state with antitrust laws and orders of the antitrust state, are really a form of foreign sovereign compulsion, negative in character. As such, they are difficult to combat, even given the qualifications mentioned above. They clearly express a governmental policy, are presumably quite lawful in the foreign state, and seek to compel conduct there, not in the antitrust state. Understandably, these statutes are giving the United States and private plaintiffs considerable difficulty. Since they operate most frequently at the critical level of efforts to obtain evidence located in the relevant countries, they pose a serious problem for antitrust enforcement. So far, they exist in only a handful of states. If more nations adopt them— a step that would seem contrary to the whole spirit of United Nations and OECD efforts to control restrictive practices—a serious setback could occur.

It is interesting to note that the European Commission has taken a strong position against allowing a firm to refuse to furnish information demanded by it on the ground that the secrecy laws of a third country, Switzerland, would subject the firm and its officers to fines and imprisonment. [107] The firm was a Dutch company operating in the Common Market, and the information, according to the Commission, was available in the Common Market, but had also been furnished to a "combine" established in Switzerland. The Commission may have doubted that Swiss law would apply, but said that even if it did apply, this would not warrant disobedience of the Commission's order.

PRINCIPAL CONCLUSIONS AND RECOMMENDATIONS

The most important conclusion to be derived from this study is that antitrust laws are determinative of whether private international cartels will flourish or be reduced to a minor role. Changes in economic conditions have not rendered cartels obsolete; they continue to exist where antitrust controls are weak or absent. On the level of world markets and of markets in the developed countries of the free world, major international cartels are rare today primarily because of the impact of U.S. antitrust law, and more recently also of EEC law. It would be a serious mistake to fail to maintain these laws in full force and to extend their force in the cartel area.

The developing nations benefit from present controls of global cartels along with the developed nations. They are without much protection, however, from regional and local cartels operating outside the reach of present antitrust laws. These nations can and probably should adopt antitrust laws of their own, but they also need the protection of laws of greater scope. Ongoing efforts in the United Nations to provide more international protection against restrictive business practices are thus of great importance.

This study highlights the effectiveness which national antitrust laws can have on a global and regional basis, when applied vigorously, in protecting the interests of the nation enforcing its laws. Because of the fragility of cartels and their vulnerability to prohibitions against any one of their key members in the relevant market, national or community antitrust law could provide protection in all areas if a strong antitrust policy were established in one nation in each significant relevant market area. A true "international antitrust law" would be a great improvement, but strategically placed national or community laws could accomplish much that a world law would provide.

There are, however, substantial limitations and problems that curtail the effectiveness of present laws. The largest danger lies in what appears to be a trend toward more activity by governments through government cartels and governmental action in aid of private cartels. No easy solution appears for government cartels. Even if they do not enjoy sovereign immunity, which is debatable, it is not clear how one nation can issue orders to another through antitrust law without the other's cooperation. This problem must be approached in some way at the international level, such as through bilateral negotiations, United Nations codes, and OECD recommendations.

Since problems of national sovereignty quickly arise, cooperative efforts may not suffice. In his *Memoirs,* Jean Monnet states his conviction that lasting progress against problems of sovereignty cannot be made by reliance upon promises of cooperation.[108] Nations must be made somehow to agree to give up some of their authority in the area of concern to a larger "community." This is being accomplished in Europe, with antitrust law as a major part of the evolving new arrangement. Other parts of the world are perhaps not ready for anything so comprehensive as the European Communities. But might they not at least consider a limited community approach to selected problems, one of which would be restrictive trade practices? It would be a big step forward.

The problem of government compulsion or acts of state is almost, but not quite, as intractable. Private persons, rather than governments themselves, are the ones carrying out cartel activity in most of these cases. The comity approach presently endorsed by the United States as a general stance in cases of antitrust conflict with other nations represents a generous attitude in the abstract. It may have to be abandoned, however, if other nations conclude that antitrust authorities such as the United States will give immunity to those who act under compulsion or refuse to act because of blocking legislation. One can imagine that some firms seeking security from American antitrust law internationally may even now be searching for ways to obtain this kind of help. Comity is a weak gesture if it is unrequited, and the EEC may be right in taking what appears to be a less compromising stand.

Apart from government interferences, problems of both substantive and procedural extraterritoriality limit antitrust effectiveness. Some kind of territorial concept, even as widened by an effects doctrine, will inevitably confine the scope of any national antitrust law. The effort of some nations to force strict territoriality, absent an effects doctrine, upon U.S., EEC, and other strong antitrust laws, however, is unfortunate, but it is destined to be relatively ineffectual if not coupled with such things as blocking legislation.

The Antitrust Division's self-limitation against applying the Sherman Act to restraints whose effects are felt in foreign markets, despite subject matter jurisdiction under the "foreign commerce clause," reduces somewhat the ability to cope with the export facet of international cartels. It also would greatly hamper the ability of the United States to rid itself of the effects of the Webb-Pomerene exemption for U.S. export cartels. For if that law were repealed, the privilege of restraining competition in foreign trade that it now gives would still be present under the Antitrust Division's interpretation of the Sherman Act. This interpretation should be reexamined. Not only does it tie the hands of the United States in eliminating its own export cartels, but it reduces its credibility generally in the anticartel field.

NOTES

1. United Nations Conference on Trade and Development (UNCTAD), Report of the Third Ad Hoc Group of Experts on Restrictive Business Practices on its Sixth Session (Geneva: United Nations, 1979, TD/B/C.1/AC.6/20), p. 4.

2. Address by Secretary of State Henry Kissinger, "Global Consensus and Economic Development," read before Seventh Special Session of the United Nations General Assembly by Ambassador Daniel Patrick Moynihan, Sept. 1, 1975, *Department of State Bulletin* (1975), 66(1891):433.

3. Address by Secretary of State Cyrus R. Vance before Conference on International Economic Cooperation, Paris, May 30, 1977, *Department of State Bulletin* (1977), 68(1982):645.

4. Costello, "International Cartels," *Editorial Research Reports* (Nov. 8, 1974), p. 848. See also Dempsey, "Economic Aggression and Self-Defense in International Law: The Arab Oil Weapon and Alternative American Responses Thereto," *Case Western Reserve Journal of International Law* (1977), 9:320; C. Fred Bergsten, "Resource Scarcity: Cartelization and Contrived Shortages," *American University Law Review* (Summer 1975), 24(4–5):1129–31. For broad analysis and review of this whole area, see Oscar Schachter, *Sharing the World's Resources* (New York: Columbia University Press, 1977), pt. III.

5. The agreed text of the draft of the UNCTAD rules and principles on restric-

tive business practices at present does not explicitly reach sovereign acts of state, and both Group B (non-Communist developed nations) and the Group of 77 (developing nations) favor express statements that the rules do not apply to intergovernmental agreements. UNCTAD, Report of Third Ad Hoc Group of Experts.

6. Joel Davidow, "The United States, Developing Countries and the Issue of Intra-Enterprise Agreements," *Georgia Journal of International and Comparative Law* (1977), 7(2):511–12.

7. Antitrust Division, U.S. Department of Justice, *Antitrust Guide for International Operations* (Washington, D.C.: Government Printing Office, 1977), p. 12; Letter of Assistant Attorney General R. W. McLaren, Feb. 27, 1971, ATRR no. 516, D–1.

8. Centrafarm B.V. v. Sterling Drug, Inc., EC Ct. of Justice, Oct. 31, 1974, Comm. Mkt. Rep. (CCH) ¶8246; Christiani & Nielsen N.V., EC Comm., June 18, 1969, Comm. Mkt. Rep. (CCH) ¶9308.

9. Heinrich Kronstein, *The Law of International Cartels* (Ithaca, N.Y.: Cornell University Press, 1973), p. 39.

10. *Ibid.*, p. 41.

11. Evidence on cartels during this period is documented in the following sources: Corwin D. Edwards, *Economic and Political Aspects of International Cartels*, U.S. Congress, Senate, A Study for the Committee on Military Affairs, 78th Cong., 2d Sess. (Washington, D.C.: Government Printing Office, 1944), based on files of the Antitrust Division; Wendell Berge, *Cartels: Challenge to a Free World* (Washington, D.C.: Public Affairs, 1946), detailing many cartels and listing anti-cartel cases filed by the Justice Department between 1937 and 1945; Report of Commissioner, *Combines Investigation Act, Canada and International Cartels* (1945), describing cartels in about twenty-five industries which affected Canadian imports, restricted Canadian manufacturers to the home market, or involved Canadian exporters; *A Cartel Policy for the United Nations* (New York: Columbia University Press, 1945), papers by Corwin D. Edwards, Theodore J. Kreps, Ben W. Lewis, Fritz Machlup, and Robert Terrill; Ervin Hexner, *International Cartels* (Chapel Hill: University of North Carolina Press, 1946); Philip C. Newman, *Cartel and Combine* (Ridgewood, N.J.: Foreign Studies Institute, 1964); George W. Stocking and Myron Watkins, *Cartels in Action* (New York: Twentieth Century Fund, 1946); George W. Stocking and Myron Watkins, *Cartels or Competition?* (New York: Twentieth Century Fund, 1948); L. Seraphin, "International Cartels and the Impact of American Antitrust Law," unpub. study in Northwestern U. Law Library, made under the Senior Research Program, 1968, finding 97 cartels operating at some time between 1940 and 1967.

12. Stocking and Watkins, *Cartels or Competition?*, p. 92.

13. Corwin D. Edwards, "International Cartels as Obstacles to International Trade" (AER Supp., March 1944), referred to in J. D. Gribbin, rev. of OECD, *Export Cartels*, Report of the Committee of Experts on Restrictive Business Practices, 1974, *Antitrust Bulletin* (Summer 1976), 21(2):341.

14. Machlup, *A Cartel Policy*, p. 11.

15. Edward S. Mason, *Controlling World Trade* (New York and London: McGraw-Hill, 1946) p. 26 et seq.

16. Raymond Vernon, "Antitrust and International Business," *Harvard Business Review* (Sept.–Oct. 1968), 46:81.

17. Robert Terrill, *A Cartel Policy*, p. 55.

18. Gribbin, rev. of *Export Cartels*, p. 342.

19. Article 6(1) of the Dutch Economic Competition Act still permits the Government to make a cartel compulsory; Thomas Silbiger, "The Netherlands," in Harlan M. Blake, gen. ed., *Business Regulation in the Common Market Nations* (New York: McGraw-Hill, 1969), 1:299, 384. For Germany, see Friedrich Juenger, Kurt Markert, Manfred Pfeifer, and Rainer Steckhan, *West Germany, ibid.* (1969), 3:94.

20. Juenger, Markert, et al., *West Germany*, pp. 94–95.

21. Hexner, *International Cartels*, p. 402; Stocking and Watkins, *Cartels or Competition?*, p. 62.

22. David Lynch, *The Concentration of Economic Power* (New York: Columbia University Press, 1946), p. 95. And on p. 100: "the trade association is the American counterpart of the German cartel." See also Stocking and Watkins, *Cartels or Competition?*, p. 44.

23. Federal Trade Commission (FTC), *Economic Report on Webb-Pomerene Associations: A 50-Year Review,* Staff Report to the Federal Trade Commission (Washington, D.C.: Government Printing Office, 1967), pp. 3–7; FTC, *Webb-Pomerene Associations: Ten Years Later,* Staff Analysis (mimeo, 1978), p. 13.

24. FTC, *Economic Report*, pp. 16–21.

25. Lynch, *Concentration of Economic Power.*

26. Raymond Vernon, *Storm Over the Multinationals* (Cambridge, Mass.: Harvard University Press, 1977), p. 75.

27. Remarks of Douglas Rosenthal, "An Overview of the *Guide* and Its Objectives," in J. Griffin, ed., *Perspectives on the Extraterritorial Application of U.S. Antitrust and Other Laws* (Chicago: American Bar Association, 1979), p. 89.

28. See Davidow, "The United States," p. 512.

29. U.S. Congress, Senate, *Prices of Quinine and Quinidine,* pt. 2, Hearings Before the Subcommittee on Antitrust and Monopoly of the Committee on the Judiciary, 90th Cong., 1st Sess. (Washington, D.C.: Government Printing Office, 1967). For U.S. proceedings, see case 2023, Trade Reg. (CCH) ¶45,068. For EEC proceedings, see Boehringer Mannheim GmbH v. Commission, EC Ct. of Justice, July 15, 1970, Comm. Mkt. Rep. (CCH) ¶8085.

30. Commission Decision, July 6, 1979, on investigation into AM & S Europe Ltd., Comm. Mkt. Rep. (CCH) ¶10,153. For a report of a lead and zinc cartel said to be operating within a UN study committee in the early 1960s, see Corwin D. Edwards, *Cartelization in Western Europe,* U.S. State Dep't Policy Research Study (Washington, D.C.: Government Printing Office, 1964), p. 28.

31. U.S. Congress, Senate, *International Aspects of Antitrust Laws,* Hearings Before the Subcommittee on Antitrust and Monopoly of the Committee on the Judi-

ciary, 93d Cong., 1st and 2d Sess. (Washington, D.C.: Government Printing Office, 1974), p. 31.

32. Davidow, "The United States," p. 508. See Stanley D. Metzger, "Cartels, Combines, Commodity Agreements," *Texas International Law Journal* (Summer 1976), 11(3):535–48; Charles N. Brower, "Charter of Economic Rights and Duties of States and the American Constitutional Tradition: A Bicentennial Perspective on the 'New Economic Order,' " *International Lawyer* (Fall 1976), 10(4):703–4; G. W. Haight, "The New International Economic Order and the Charter of Economic Rights and Duties of States," *International Lawyer* (Fall 1975), 9(4):592–97.

33. A proposal for a new regulation to exempt so-called "crisis" cartels was dropped after discussion by the Commission, July 26, 1978, Comm. Mkt. Rep. (CCH) ¶ 10,068.

34. See statements by Senators Mathias and Javits in connection with introducing a bill (S. 1010) to establish a national commission to study international application of antitrust law, *Cong. Rec.* (April 25, 1979), 125:S4705 et seq.

35. Edwards, *Cartelization*, p. 1.

36. Vernon, "Antitrust," p. 80.

37. See E. Hexner, *International Cartels;* Juenger, Markert, et al., *West Germany.*

38. See Edwards, *Economic and Political Aspects,* p. 53.

39. Jean Monnet, *Memoirs,* trans. Richard Mayne (New York: Doubleday, 1978), pp. 292–317. Monnet recounts how Secretary of State Acheson first feared that the Schuman plan for the Coal and Steel Community was just another vast European cartel idea, until it was further explained to him; *ibid.,* p. 301.

40. Recent Commission studies of concentration in the Common Market conclude that while integration of the Common Market has reduced the number of national monopoly positions, oligopoly has increased; EC Commission, *Eighth Report on Competition Policy* (Brussels and Luxembourg: European Communities, 1979), p. 238.

41. Statement of E. Ernest Goldstein in Hearings on *International Aspects of Antitrust Laws;* see colloquy with the author in U.S. Congress, Senate, *International Aspects of Antitrust,* Hearings Before the Subcommittee on Antitrust and Monopoly of the Committee on the Judiciary, 89th Cong., 2d Sess. (Washington, D.C.: Government Printing Office, 1966), p. 370.

42. Kronstein, *Law of International Cartels.*

43. Over one hundred nations have no antitrust law. Twenty-one of the 24 OECD member nations have some sort of law regulating restrictive business practices, and about a dozen developing Third World nations also have such a law, along with Yugoslavia; Joel Davidow, "International Antitrust Codes of Conduct: A Progress Report," address to Fordham Corporate Law Institute, New York, Nov. 14–15, 1978, p. 4.

Most of the laws do not prohibit cartels outright. See Corwin D. Edwards, *Trade Regulation Overseas: The National Laws* (Dobbs Ferry, N.Y.: Oceana, 1966) and

Control of Cartels and Monopolies: An International Comparison (Dobbs Ferry, N.Y.: Oceana 1967); OECD, *Comparative Summary of Legislations on Restrictive Business Practices* (Paris: OECD, 1978); Collin R. Greenhill, "UNCTAD: Control of Restrictive Business Practices," *Journal of World Trade Law* (1978), 12(1):68–73.

44. OECD, *Export Cartels,* Report of the Committee of Experts on Restrictive Business Practices (Paris: OECD, 1974).

45. Gribbin, rev. of *Export Cartels,* p. 346; see note 13 above.

46. See OECD, *Export Cartels,* and Dudley H. Chapman, "Exports and Antitrust: Must Competition Stop at the Water's Edge?" *Vanderbilt Journal of Transnational Law* (Spring 1973), 6(2):399–445.

47. See note 29 above.

48. Berge, *Cartels: Challenge,* p. 250.

49. Wilbur L. Fugate, *Foreign Commerce and the Antitrust Laws,* 2d ed. (Boston: Little Brown, 1973), p. 507 et seq.

50. In the *Dyestuffs* case, price fixing in the Common Market was found and fines were levied against ten firms from France, Germany, Great Britain, Italy, and Switzerland; *see* Francolor v. Commission, EC Ct. of Justice, July 14, 1972, Comm. Mkt Rep. (CCH) ¶8166.

51. In the sugar case, sixteen Common Market firms were found to have engaged in unlawful market sharing, and fines totaling 9 million u.a. (about U.S. $12 million) were assessed. On appeal, several firms were dismissed and fines as to others were reduced to a total of 1,590,000 u.a.; *see* Suiker Unie UA v. Commission, EC Ct. of Justice, Dec. 16, 1975, Comm. Mkt. Rep. (CCH) ¶8334; also EC Commission, *Fifth Report on Competition Policy* (Brussels and Luxembourg: European Communities, 1976), p. 26.

52. EC Council Reg. no. 17, Art. 4, para. 1.

53. In denying an Article 85(3) exemption, the Commission has on occasion made mention of the fact that the notification was not made until after a proceeding had begun; *see* Commission decision in Bronbemaling V., July 25, 1975, Comm. Mkt. Rep. (CCH) ¶9776.

54. Comm. Mkt. Rep. (CCH) ¶10,068.

55. Many of the writings up to 1970 are listed in James A. Rahl, ed., *Common Market and American Antitrust: Overlap and Conflict* (New York: McGraw-Hill, 1970), p. 54 n.13. For recent discussion, see Griffin, ed., *Perspectives on Extraterritorial Application.* See also the treatise by Barry E. Hawk, *United States, Common Market and International Antitrust: A Comparative Guide* (New York: Harcourt, Brace, Jovanovich, 1979), p. 19 et seq.

56. *Common Market and American Antitrust,* chs. 2 and 4; "American Antitrust and Foreign Operations: What is Covered?" *Cornell International Law Journal* (Dec. 1974), 8(1):1–15; and "Rejoinder," *ibid.,* pp. 42–44; "Foreign Commerce Jurisdiction of the American Antitrust Laws," *Antitrust Law Journal*(1974), 43(3):521; "Antitrust and International Transactions—Recent Developments," *ibid.* (1978), 46(3):965.

57. United States v. Aluminum Co., 148 F.2d 416, 444 (2d Cir. 1945).

58. Department of Justice, *Antitrust Guide,* p. 6.

59. Remarks of Assistant Attorney General John Shenefield, "The Perspective of the Department of Justice," in Griffin, ed., *Perspectives on Extraterritorial Application,* pp. 12–25. Calling the comity approach a "jurisdictional rule of reason" which is "long overdue," Shenefield emphasized that "Judge Choy did not require the courts to balance the interests of the U.S. parties against those of the other nations involved. What he required was that the interests of the United States in prosecuting the violation be measured both quantitatively and qualitatively against the potential damage to U.S. foreign relations generally that might result" (p. 23). See also remarks of Douglas E. Rosenthal, Chief of the Foreign Commerce Section of the Antitrust Division, in *ibid.,* p. 87.

60. Timberlane Lumber Co. v. Bank of America, 549 F.2d 597 (9th Cir. 1976); Mannington Mills, Inc. v. Congoleum Corp., 595 F.2d 1287 (3d Cir. 1979). Both cases were private suits, and accordingly the interests of the United States at best were only indirectly represented. The defendants were all private parties, largely with American ownership or connections, and it is difficult to see how under these circumstances the court could be adequately informed so as to weigh the interests of the two nations involved. In both cases, after adopting the comity principle, the courts ultimately held for the American plaintiffs, anyway.

61. Department of Justice, *Antitrust Guide,* p. 7; Douglas E. Rosenthal, "Subject Matter Jurisdiction in United States Export Trade," remarks at 71st annual meeting of American Society of International Law, San Francisco, Apr. 23, 1977, p. 3 et seq. (partially reprinted in ASIL, *Proceedings* (1977), p. 214).

62. Remarks in Griffin, ed., *Perspectives on Extraterritorial Application,* p. 146. It appears that reliance on the comity principle assumes subject matter jurisdiction, whereas Mr. Rosenthal has argued previously, p. 8 of his remarks before the ASIL annual meeting, that restraints whose only impact is in a foreign market (by hypothesis, and ignoring that they occur in U.S. foreign trade) are outside the scope of the Act.

63. Department of Justice, *Antitrust Guide,* pp. 4–6.

64. *Ibid.,* p. 4; Rosenthal, remarks before the ASIL annual meeting, p. 10.

65. See note 56 above.

66. See Rahl, "Antitrust and International Transactions," pp. 966–67.

67. EC Commission Decision in Dyestuffs case, July 24, 1969, Comm. Mkt. Rep. (CCH) ¶9314, p. 8693; *aff'd,* EC Ct. of Justice, July 14, 1972, Comm. Mkt. Rep. (CCH) ¶8166.

68. EC Commission, *Sixth Report on Competition Policy* (Brussels and Luxembourg: European Communities, 1977), p. 31; Avis relatif à l'importation de produits japonais dans la Communauté tombant sous l'application du traité de Rome, 15 J.O. (no. C 111) 13 (1972) (notice that voluntary limitation by Japanese of imports into the EEC would fall within Rome Treaty because of effect on competition in Common Market).

69. West German Act Against Restraints of Competition, of July 27, 1957, as amended, §98(2): "This Act shall apply to all restraints of competition which have

effect in the area in which this Act applies, even if they result from acts done outside such area." Section 4 of the Austrian Act of Nov. 22, 1972 contains a similar provision.

70. Protests are collected in International Law Association (ILA), *Report of the Fifty-first Conference* (London: ILA, 1965), pp. 564–92. See also note 75 below.

71. Rahl, ed., *Common Market and American Antitrust,* pp. 67–68, 101.

72. *Ibid.,* ch. 3; A. Paul Victor and Robert K. Hood, "Personal Jurisdiction, Venue and Service of Process in Antitrust Cases Involving International Trade: Amenability of Alien Corporations to Suit," *Antitrust Law Journal* (Winter 1978), 46(4):1063; James H. Carter, "Obtaining Foreign Discovery and Evidence for Use in Litigation in the United States," *International Lawyer* (Winter 1979), 13(1):5; James A. Rahl, "Enforcement and Discovery Conflicts: A View from the United States," in *Proceedings of Fifth Annual Fordham Corporate Law Institute on International Antitrust,* Nov. 15, 1978 (New York: Harcourt, Brace, Jovanovich, 1979), pp. 343–57.

73. *See* United States v. N.V. Nederlandsche Combinatie Voor Chemische Industrie, [1977–1] Trade Cases ¶61,345 (S.D.N.Y. 1977), refusing Government motion to dismiss as to remaining defendants, some of whom had not been served.

74. Rio Tinto Zinc Corp. v. Westinghouse Electric Corp., Dec. 1, 1977, [1978] 1 All E.R. 434 (H.L.); Robert H. Merhige, Jr., "The Westinghouse Uranium Case: Problems Encountered in Seeking Foreign Discovery and Evidence," *International Lawyer* (Winter 1979), 13(1):19 (article by the U.S. judge in the case); Samuel C. Silkin, "The Perspective of the Attorney General of England and Wales," remarks in Griffin, ed., *Perspectives on Extraterritorial Application,* p. 28 (address by the British Attorney General who appeared in the case).

75. At this writing, the British Government has introduced a bill in Parliament to provide authority to prohibit furnishing of documents for use in U.S. antitrust cases, and to permit British companies to recover in British courts any punitive damages obtained against them by Americans in American antitrust suits; *Wall Street Journal,* Nov. 1, 1979. In general, see David Lord Hacking, "The Increasing Extraterritorial Impact of U.S. Laws: A Cause for Concern Amongst Friends of America," *Northwestern Journal of International Law and Business* (Spring 1979), 1(1):1–10.

76. Rio Tinto Zinc Corp. v. Westinghouse Electric Corp., [1978] 1 All E. R. at 448.

77. *In re* Westinghouse Electric Corp. Uranium Contracts Litigation, 563 F.2d 992 (10th Cir. 1977).

78. *Re* Westinghouse Electric Corp. and Duquesne Light Co. et al., 16 Ont. R.2d 273 (1977).

79. See Hacking, "Increasing Extraterritorial Impact," p. 8 n.30.

80. British Nylon Spinners, Ltd. v. Imperial Chem. Indus. Ltd., [1953] Ch. 19, [1952] 2 All E.R. 780 (C.A.); [1955] Ch. 37, [1954] 3 All E.R. 88 (Ch.).

81. The OECD Council Recommendation of July 20, 1978 recommends that member nations develop rules to facilitate obtaining information outside their na-

tional territory, and also recommends greater international cooperation in this area. Working parties have been set up to study the problem. See EC Commission, *Eighth Competition Report*, pp. 51–52, summarizing this.

82. United States v. Socony-Vacuum Oil Co., 310 U.S. 150, 206, 228 (1940).

83. United States v. The Watchmakers of Switzerland Information Center, Inc. (S.D.N.Y. 1962), [1963] Trade Cases ¶70,600, at 77,457.

84. Timberlane Lumber Co. v. Bank of America, 549 F.2d 597 (9th Cir. 1976), adopting a comity test for exercise of jurisdiction.

85. Mannington Mills, Inc. v. Congoleum Corp., 595 F.2d 1287 (3d Cir. 1979).

86. In the sugar cartel case, Comm. Mkt. Rep. (CCH) ¶8334, the Court of Justice dismissed the Italian firm because of tight controls exercised over it by the Italian Government. Later, the Commission initiated proceedings against the Italian Government under Article 169 of the Rome Treaty because of these controls; EC Commission, *Fifth Competition Report*, p. 26.

87. OECD, *Export Cartels*, pp. 7–8, 22.

88. *Ibid.*, p. 49.

89. FTC, *Webb-Pomerene Associations: Ten Years Later*, p. 15.

90. Gribbin, rev. of *Export Cartels*, p. 347.

91. *Ibid.*

92. OECD, *Export Cartels*, p. 51.

93. Letter of Assistant Attorney General Donald I. Baker to Senator Edward M. Kennedy, Feb. 16, 1977, p. 5 (on file at the Department of Justice).

94. National Commission for the Review of Antitrust Laws and Procedures, *Report to the President and the Attorney General* (Washington, D.C.: Government Printing Office, 1979), pp. 302–4. A number of the members favored outright repeal of the exemption, but a majority did not support this position. A Business Advisory Panel indicated that the exemption is important to some industries and advised against repeal; *Report*, 2:292–99. Both the commission and the panel believed that the act, if retained, should cover services as well as goods (currently, it is limited to the latter).

95. See note 61 above and accompanying text.

96. Foreign Sovereign Immunities Act of 1976, 28 U.S.C. §1605(a).

97. Sigmund Timberg, "Sovereign Immunity and Act of State Defenses: Transnational Boycotts and Economic Coercion," *Texas Law Review* (1976), 55(1):1–37; the author also has published a later version under this title in the *Swiss Review of International Antitrust Law*, no. 6 (1979), p. 1.

98. Since the above text was written, the opinion of U.S. District Judge Hauk has been reported, International Ass'n of Machinists v. OPEC, 477 F.Supp. 553 (C.D. Cal. 1979). Neither OPEC nor any of the thirteen member nations who had been served appeared. Two organizations appeared *amici curiae* in support of dismissal, and the court appointed two expert economists to testify. The court concluded that OPEC itself could not legally be served under existing law and dismissed it. The court held for the member nation defendants on the following

grounds: (1) plaintiff was only an "indirect purchaser" under the *Illinois Brick* rule and could not sue for damages, although injunctive relief might be obtained; (2) subject matter jurisdiction was lacking, however, because the defendants' price fixing on oil sales is governmental control over a principal natural resource of the country and does not constitute "commercial activity" within the meaning of the Sovereign Immunities Act; (3) a foreign sovereign cannot be made a defendant in a Sherman Act suit anyway, even though the Supreme Court has held in *Pfizer Inc. v. India* (434 U.S. 308 (1978)), that it may sue as a plaintiff; and (4) plaintiff failed to show that defendants' price hikes were the proximate cause of the general rise in prices, or the specific cause of higher prices of gasoline purchased by it. The court went on to find that the general rise in prices was due to reduced refining capacity in the United States and inept federal and state regulation. Accordingly, the court declined to enter a default judgment and held that defendants had not waived sovereign immunity by failure to appear.

For analysis generally, see Mark R. Joelson and Joseph P. Griffin, "The Legal Status of Nation-State Cartels Under U.S. Antitrust and Public International Law," *International Lawyer* (Fall 1975), 9(4):617–45; Covey T. Oliver, "State Export Cartels and International Justice," *Northwestern University Law Review* (May–June 1977), 72(2):181–97.

99. Parker v. Brown, 317 U.S. 341 (1943); for discussion of this and later cases involving state action, see Ronald E. Kennedy, "Of Lawyers, Lightbulbs and Raisins: An Analysis of the State Action Doctrine under the Antitrust Laws," *Northwestern University Law Review* (March 1979), 74(1):31.

100. See the Timberlane Lumber, 549 F.2d 597 (9th Cir. 1976), and Mannington Mills cases, 595 F.2d 1287 (3d Cir. 1979).

101. Remarks of Eleanor M. Fox, "Roundtable on Sovereign Compulsion Defense in Antitrust Litigation: New Life for the Act of State Doctrine?" in American Society of International Law, *Proceedings* (1978), pp. 97, 98; also see *ibid.* for remarks of Mark R. Joelson, Richard Schwartz, John S. Williams, and Douglas E. Rosenthal. Reference in the text is to Cantor v. Detroit Edison Co., 428 U.S. 579 (1976).

102. Timberg, "Sovereign Immunity and Act of State Defenses," 1979 version, p. 20.

103. 595 F.2d 1287 (3d Cir. 1979).

104. 549 F.2d 597 (9th Cir. 1976).

105. Actually, the *Guide* states on p. 52 that while "legality under foreign law may not be controlling for U.S. antitrust purposes, it is an issue which bears on the good faith of the defendants." It also says that illegality reduces the "command" to what amounts to "informal encouragement." If so, it would no longer be a defense.

106. *Ibid.*, pp. 50–52.

107. EC Commission Decision *re* CSV, June 25, 1976, Comm. Mkt. Rep. (CCH) ¶9859.

108. Monnet, *Memoirs*, p. 294 et seq.

Commentary

◆

David G. Gill

The theme of this conference is the international regulation of restrictive business practices. James Rahl has discussed the various national (U.S.) and supranational European Community efforts toward this end. I will begin this commentary by drawing a conclusion from his paper which he demonstrates but does not fully accept: that, by and large, the sum of the various parts of governmental regulation of cartels and restrictive business practices works rather well and that in consequence no major changes in the current regime of regulation are indicated or justified. Rahl would accept the first half of that statement but resists accepting the second half, instead calling for some expansion of, for example, U.S. regulation of restrictive business practices and/or cartels which affect only foreigners.

For reasons I shall develop later, I disagree with Rahl as to the need for or propriety of increased extraterritorial extension of national or supranational laws. Although Rahl asks whether the less-developed nations "lack protection against carefully limited regional cartels if the latter can function in their areas without having an impact on other areas covered by antitrust" (p. 251), neither he nor anyone else writing about the subject has come up with convincing case histories or evidence that such "carefully limited" cartels exist in great numbers or pose any significant threat that is not already largely met by existing antitrust statutes. Indeed, both Rahl and Robert E. Smith acknowledge that great progress has been made in eliminating private cartels and that a principal danger today is that such advances will be undermined by cartel-like activity by governments or government-owned or directed companies.

One of the principal obstacles today to an international consensus on how to regulate international restrictive business practices is the inability to achieve agreement on our objectives. Some representatives of the Third

World and the Eastern European countries have seized upon the so-called restrictive business practices issue as a tactical weapon in their attempted march to the "New International Economic Order." These groups still brandish the old arguments against private cartels and the restrictive practices of private business while defending the rights of their governments to engage in anticompetitive restrictive economic policies and other actions as a means of preventing competition from private international business. We will be interested in the comments of Joel Davidow and Timothy Atkeson tomorrow on whether the proposed UNCTAD code to control restrictive business practices is indeed a code to aid or restrict competition.

A second principal conclusion which I derive from Rahl's paper is that he is inclined to challenge the accepted jurisdictional and pragmatic bases for U.S. antitrust policy, particularly with respect to extraterritorial regulation and the current interpretation of the "act of state" and "foreign sovereign compulsion" defenses. You will recall that application of the U.S. antitrust laws requires the showing of effects upon U.S. domestic or foreign commerce. Although some initially tried to limit the legislative jurisdiction of the Sherman Act to acts committed within the United States, this interpretation has long since been abandoned by all ranges of opinion. The ongoing debate has not been on the propriety of the standard but rather on the wisdom of its application in particular instances.

There now appears to be a general consensus in favor of a "balance of interests" approach to international antitrust regulation. As enunciated in *Timberlane* and *Mannington Mills,* the accepted approach now seems to be a determination by the court (and, one would hope, after a similar decision by the Antitrust Division) that "the interests of, and links to, the United States—including the magnitude of the effect on American foreign commerce—are sufficiently strong, vis-à-vis those of other nations, to justify an assertion of extraterritorial authority."[1] In answering that question, the following "elements" are to be weighed:

1. the degree of conflict with foreign law or policy;
2. the nationality or allegiance of the parties and the locations or principal places of business of corporations;
3. the extent to which enforcement by either state can be expected to achieve compliance;
4. the relative significance of effects on the United States as compared with those elsewhere;

5. the extent to which there is explicit purpose to harm or affect commerce;
6. the foreseeability of such effect; and
7. the relative importance to the violations charged of conduct within the United States as compared with conduct abroad.

Obviously, this approach relies heavily on the conflicts-of-law approach of the *Restatement (Second) of Foreign Relations Law* set forth in sections 18 and 40; the latter section states the principles of forbearance to which courts should look in tempering their exercises of jurisdiction in cases where two or more states have jurisdiction. In assessing the degree of conflict which exists with foreign law or policy, it is necessary to consider the type, goals, and implementation of the particular foreign policy or policies with which a conflict is perceived.

Unfortunately, the Justice Department has sometimes chosen to give a narrower reading to section 40 in antitrust situations. Assistant Attorney General John Shenefield in his 1978 speech to the American Bar Association proclaimed that the Antitrust Division endorsed the restatement of this rule by Judge Choy in *Timberlane.* In so doing, Shenefield emphasized that, in the Division's view, the courts are not required to balance the interest of the U.S. parties against those of the other nations involved but only "that the interest of the U.S. in prosecuting the violators be measured both quantitatively and qualitatively against the potential damage to foreign relations generally that might result." In my view, this reading does not adequately weigh the interests of the other nations involved since it weighs only the respective U.S. interests, in enforcement and in avoiding foreign relations "embarrassments."

When antitrust issues are involved, broader and more sophisticated questions of national economic policy arise than are involved in, say, drug control enforcement or measures to counter smuggling. It is now conventional wisdom to note that many other countries have antitrust statutes and policies. To recognize the existence of such statutes or policies is a far cry from concluding that they will reach similar or even noncontradictory results in an international dispute. The respective statutes and policies differ widely in both their provisions and their implementation. I have already noted the wide divergence in ideologies involved in the discussions of the proposed UNCTAD Code on Restrictive Business Practices. Rahl has quoted Lord Wilberforce's language in the judgments in the House of Lords involving Westinghouse's private antitrust suit against the alleged uranium cartel, particularly Lord Wilberforce's reminder that "it is axiomatic that in antitrust matters the policy of one state may be to defend what it is the policy of another state to attack."

Rahl goes on to discuss the act of state and foreign sovereign compulsion defenses and endorses the territorial approach to these defenses. You will recall that the act of state doctrine requires U.S. courts to refrain from examining the validity of acts of foreign states within their jurisdiction. Foreign sovereign compulsion is a special case of the application of the act of state doctrine. Briefly stated, the doctrine immunizes, under U.S. antitrust laws, otherwise unlawful actions or agreements pursuant to requirement of law of the foreign nation or nations within which the transactions take place. The desire to avoid embarrassment of the executive branch in the conduct of foreign relations and the doctrine of comity, as well as the lack of legal standards for testing the validity of the foreign sovereign's acts, all support the doctrines. I would suggest a further consideration for the application of the doctrines, that of "fairness."

In the *Bechtel* case, the Government initially indicated that it would challenge agreements by American companies, in response to foreign governmental decree, allegedly to take actions (i.e., boycott enforcement) which had a direct anticompetitive effect within the United States. In its motion to enter a final judgment in the *Bechtel* case, the Antitrust Division's papers emphasized that the act of state and foreign government compulsion defenses are essentially territorial in their nature and may not excuse actions taking place within the foreign jurisdiction which have effects on United States commerce.[2]

Barry Hawk, in his address to the American Bar Association in August 1978, criticized the proposed territorial limitation on the act of state and foreign government compulsion defenses. He noted that the major policy consideration which underlies the sovereign compulsion and act of state defenses is that of fairness, fairness to a defendant caught between conflicting demands from two or more sovereigns. In the event of such a conflict, fairness requires rejection of any "absolute mechanical territorial limitation on the defense" and suggests the propriety of the balancing-of-interests approach suggested in *Timberlane*.

I can only applaud Hawk's insight. I would also urge two further considerations.

First, the foreign sovereign compulsion defense should protect persons complying with the compulsions of foreign country law with respect to exports from, imports into, and activity within that country. Such actions are clearly within the jurisdiction of the foreign sovereign, and firms engaging in such business have no choice but to obey. Refusal by private parties to comply with such practices compelled by foreign nations would put an end not only to any competition but to the very commerce itself.

Second, the antitrust laws only apply to agreements which cause restraints of trade; agreements in compliance with foreign law or with a unilateral selection by a foreign sovereign are not the cause of such restraints. It is the act of the foreign sovereign which causes whatever restraint or competitive injury there may be. (I will note parenthetically that the Second Circuit opinion in *Hunt* provides support for this second argument. [3])

My final comment is to call your attention again to the time-tested practical reasons for observing the jurisdictional restraints imposed by both international law and comity in our country's attempts to regulate international transactions. I agree with Rahl's observation that leaders of multinational companies believe that they "have more to gain in markets abroad by not joining a cartel than by doing so," but the plain fact is that the doctrine of business competition is not accepted everywhere abroad as the Holy Grail of economic and political policy. Those governments which do not flatly oppose business competition are inclined to rank it somewhere beneath their perceived interests of national security and economic survival in the pantheon of national policy. They are profoundly disturbed when, with well-meaning but frequently simple-minded missionary zeal, we presume to lecture them on how their economies should be managed.

My statement may strike some of you as timeworn, but its relevance continues to be assured by such actions as S. 1246, the bill recently introduced by Senator Edward M. Kennedy and supported, with amendments, by the administration. S. 1246 as amended would outlaw certain foreign acquisitions by foreign corporations, even though neither party to the acquisition is involved in United States commerce and even though the acquisition has no effects on competition in the United States. In testifying against the bill last month, Monroe Leigh made this cogent comparison, with which I shall close:

> Would the United States be willing to accept as consistent with international law the passage of a statute by the British Parliament which forbade Standard Oil Company of Ohio, which happens to be controlled by British Petroleum Corporation, from making acquisitions in the United States in excess of a

stated value determined by Parliament? Suppose the British, for reasons of national policy, invoked such a law to prevent Standard Oil of Ohio from participating in the Alaska Pipeline because the British Government would rather see Sohio resources devoted to the North Sea. Or suppose the British statute required the Ohio company to divest itself of other properties owned by it in the United States. Would the United States accept such an extraterritorial projection of British Law? That is the reciprocal question which this Committee must ask itself.

NOTES

1. Timberlane Lumber Co. v. Bank of America, 549 F.2d 597, 613 (9th Cir. 1977); Mannington Mills, Inc. v. Congoleum Corp., [1979–1] Trade Cases ¶62,547 (3d Cir. 1979).

2. U.S. v. Bechtel Corp., Civ. No. C–76–99 (GBH) (N.D. Cal.), Department of Justice Response to Comments Received Regarding Proposed Final Judgment, *Federal Register* (March 28, 1978), 43:12,953.

3. Hunt v. Mobil Oil Corp., 410 F.Supp. 10 (S.D.N.Y. 1976), 550 F.2d 68 (2d Cir. 1976), *cert. denied,* 432 U.S. 904 (1977).

Commentary

⬥

G. C. Hufbauer

I am reminded of Harry G. Johnson's 1951 critique of James C. Meade's monumental book, *Trade and Welfare*.[1] Johnson, then young and unknown, criticized Meade for constructing an elaborate taxonomy of international economic theory without paying much attention to the contents of his conceptual boxes. Johnson argued that taxonomy was a fine pedagogical beginning, but to qualify as useful economics it should either point to verifiable forecasts or better policies.

Johnson, it should be noted, went on to illuminate the skies of international economics. Meade, undaunted by Johnson's criticism, shared the 1978 Nobel Prize in economics with Bertil Ohlin.

My major complaint with Robert E. Smith's paper is that it, too, is largely taxonomic, and does not go much beyond the first step of putting economic phenomena into boxes. The paper catalogs the determinants of long-run and short-run market power, and begins to discuss the implications of these determinants for the effectiveness of cartel behavior. A portion of the paper sketches the implications of "internalization," both as a facilitator of market power and as a determinant of what the author terms "additional power bases." The paper concludes with thoughts on the "New International Economic Order," a subject too murky for comment here.

Overall, the paper offers a reasonably comprehensive review of economic theories of market power. Once developed, the paper could serve as a useful text. I have some problems, however, with its present form.

The paper is simply too long, and despite its length it seems to have no central theme. The patient reader may hope that major policy implications or conclusions will emerge from the elaborate taxonomy. But the numerous hints of policy-relevant implications are seldom developed in an explicit fashion. Let me give three examples.

1. *Per se rules.* Smith throws out a challenging proposition: "broadly collusive behavior [in a wide range of industries] is largely the rule, . . . but . . . antitrust prosecution centers largely on the *unsuccessful* manifestations . . . [because of] the possibility that overt agreement, which is clearly more vulnerable to prosecution, is itself a response to conditions that are not conducive to the success of collusion" (p. 210). This passage seems to suggest the need for per se rules with respect to size or other industry characteristics, but Smith does not articulate possible rules or explore their implications.

2. *Impact of oil prices.* Equally desirable would have been greater discussion of the predictive capabilities of the theories discussed by Smith. In this regard, my attention was caught by a paragraph on page 200. In this paragraph, Smith indicates that recent oil price increases have significantly altered the cost structures of industries which intensively use energy and petrochemical feedstocks, and predicts that these price increases may change the pricing behavior of firms. Specifically, rising oil prices should cause the ratio of variable to fixed costs of firms to rise; consequently, their break-even volumes would decline. The suggestion is that, faced with relatively higher variable costs and reduced break-even points, the firms will pay less attention to full utilization of capacity and more attention to maintenance of price levels. Maintenance of prices, in the short run at least, can be assured if demand curves are relatively inelastic and firms are able to coordinate their actions with one another. This is an interesting hypothesis. More insights of this sort would improve the paper.

3. *Internalization.* Smith defines "internalization" to mean efforts by producers to "adapt their organizational form—both interfirm and intrafirm dimensions—in order to try to reduce costs or realize benefits that are presented by their environment" (p. 202). In short, external workings of the marketplace are replaced by internal administrative mechanisms. Smith suggests that internalization can result in real cost savings, notably, lower transaction costs as between buyers and sellers. He further suggests that internalization is a necessary (but not sufficient) condition for the exercise of both short-run and long-run market power. Finally, he suggests that internalization can create options for the firm which go beyond the traditional notions of market power. "Internalization" clearly can impose costs on society but, at the same time, can offer the benefits of coordination. Are there ways that the policy maker can weigh the costs against the

benefits? In other words, do prescriptive rules emerge? Again, Smith could take the analysis further than he does.

NOTE

1. Harry G. Johnson, "The Taxonomic Approach to Economic Policy," *Economic Journal* (December 1951), 61(244).

Discussion

◇

G. C. Hufbauer: Although the problem of the international cartel today is a small one, nevertheless the question arises: How are we to deal with it? Dealing with it is greatly complicated by the fact that governments in Europe, and Japan, take a more relaxed view than we do of cartel activity. The faith in free competition as an ordering mechanism is in a long-term decline, to my regret. In particular, the Darwinian aspects of the competitive model are no longer favored. Bankruptcy is not in vogue.

Since this is the temper of the times, I think it suggests some practical consequences. One that should be considered, at least in the realm of international commerce, is decriminalization of antitrust remedies. Each nation's criminal code is its most basic expression of right and wrong, and international problems are certain to follow when we label criminally wrong those policies that other nations label right and proper.

So I turn to the suggestion that economic sanctions may be preferable to criminal penalties. There are various kinds of economic sanctions, including certain kinds of trade actions, that we could take in response to foreign cartels. If we took this approach, we could shift the larger part of the burden of proof to the defendant, with much advantage. And I think economic sanctions could be more easily digested by our colleagues in Europe and Japan than our present criminal penalties, which at least lurk in the background if they are not actually brought into play.

Joel Davidow: Let me address the matter of decriminalization. I think there are a number of difficulties with it. First, there is no question that criminal penalties are the most effective deterrents. The fear of criminal conviction is simply stronger than the fear of having to pay some money. And the stronger the deterrent we use, the more likely we're going to be able to hold down cartelization.

A related point is that because of the conflicts between antitrust policy and mercantilist (or cartelizing) forces there is always an enormous amount of political pressure on our government's international antitrust policy. One of the few bulwarks against political pressure is the idea that in a criminal case diplomacy is inappropriate, that one shouldn't interfere with federal grand juries in criminal cases. Decriminalization would suggest it was just a matter of regulatory policy, and would serve as an open invitation to the procartel, or promercantile, forces to bring pressure on the policy.

Every European antitrust official I have talked to, and other foreign officials—with very rare exceptions—envies the independence that the Justice Department has in the United States. Where competition policy is largely economic, it is subordinated to other policies.

DUDLEY H. CHAPMAN: I want to applaud Gary Hufbauer's thought about decriminalization. The shipping case is one of the best illustrations of the inappropriateness of criminal penalties. Congress years ago conceded that the shipping market is not competitive; it's cartelized. Every other country in the world endorses the cartel approach to shipping. We also carved out an exception to our antitrust laws for shipping, but we then said, in effect: "We don't trust these foreign cartels so we will give supervisory power to the Federal Maritime Commission." Now that agency, like most, takes a long time to act, which causes great problems for the United States shipping industry. Moreover, the industry now lives under two inconsistent regimes: one understands and agrees that the industry is cartelized, and the other says there must be competition.

Shipping is just one example. There are other industries (steel, forest products, cement) that are prosecuted so often for attempting to fix prices they should open a charge account with the Department of Justice. It isn't because they're stupid, or greedy, or evil. It's because businessmen in those industries believe with a conviction bordering on religious fervor that it's not possible to do business responsibly in those industries without some kind of collaboration with competitors.

This brings me to another of Joel Davidow's points. No doubt it is true that the criminal sanction gives protection and freedom to antitrust enforcement. But that raises a basic question. On the very day that the Nixon White House released the white paper on the *ITT* cases, the *Wall Street Journal* carried an item that a steel merger that had been disapproved by the German Cartel Office was being appealed to the Ministry of Economics. Under the German law, it is possible to treat these issues as ques tions of simple economic policy. If the head of the government wants to overrule policy decisions made by the antitrust authorities, it can be done legally, formally, out in the open—and it's honest.

In the United States, if government officials want to make an exception to the antitrust laws, they have to do it through an interpretation of those laws. Then the President is able to overrule the antitrust authorities. Maybe the German system is better.

DANIEL J. PLAINE: I take it that James Rahl has written off antitrust as a weapon against government-sponsored cartels in the international arena, and I'm not sure why. Antitrust has been effective in the past with regard to international cartels that involved serious government support, and in some cases partial or total government ownership of some of the partici- pants.

JAMES A. RAHL: I did not mean to indicate that I had given up with regard to government-sponsored cartels. I do pretty much give up with respect to intergovernmental agreements. That is, where two or more governments agree to restrain competition with respect to something they're either sell- ing or buying, through a commodity agreement, through an orderly mar- keting arrangement, or in some other way. And I would put a producer cartel of governments in that same category.

I just don't think antitrust is equipped to prosecute governments, unless they have consented to be prosecuted. Now sometimes they do. For ex- ample, the Soviet Trading Agency, AMTORG, consents to be sued as a condition of its doing business in this country. But I don't understand how you can prosecute England and France if they agree on something we don't like. They don't have to pay any attention to us. However, we can prose- cute private people if they are participating in cartel activity, even though it's at the urging of a foreign government. The foreign government may sometimes intercede to stop the prosecution and its right to do so must then be resolved. Sometimes we lose; sometimes we win.

SIGMUND TIMBERG: I join those who think that the decriminalization of the Sherman Act would be desirable. It injects a moral and nontechnical element that shouldn't be there into a problem of serious public policy.

As for deterrence, I think of the *Uranium* case. That was as clear an example of a cartel as I have ever found, and the criminal sanction imposed was a $40,000 fine against Gulf. If it's a cartel, what kind of deterrence is that? At the same time, I do feel that treble damage penalties are a very strong deterrent. And I think the threat of an injunction that could change the pattern of an industry would be a strong deterrent.

We have strong antitrust sanctions, particularly in the international arena. We do not need something that arouses people's indignation unnecessarily. I don't think we need the criminal sanction.

JAMES R. ATWOOD: Without taking a position on the issue, because I'm pulled both ways, I would like to point out one serious problem with criminalization. The problem comes out of one of the advantages that Joel Davidow alluded to, namely, the insulation of the Justice Department in enforcing the law. I don't object to the insulation in general, but there is a problem with the cloak of secrecy that surrounds grand jury proceedings. In the shipping case, for example, foreign governments were very interested and wanted information. But they were not able to get the full facts on which the Justice Department was proceeding because of grand jury secrecy. I was involved in those discussions, and it was very frustrating for the foreign governments not to be told why the Justice Department was doing what it was doing.

To its credit, the Justice Department did tell the foreign governments everything it could, consistent with the requirements of grand jury secrecy. But that fell far short of the full facts. If the people in the Justice Department could have revealed all the facts on which they were proceeding, I think it would have dissipated much of the indignation of the foreign governments.

RICHARD S. NEWFARMER: The easiest way to recommend a "do nothing" policy on international cartels is to downplay their importance by coming up with statistics showing that they occupy only a certain percentage of international trade. I have two responses to that:

First, in some industries and in some countries, cartels are extremely important. That is why we see the developing countries, particularly in the UNCTAD negotiations, singling out export cartels for international policy action. In the electrical industry, after subtracting intrafirm trade, aid that is tied to producers in one particular home country, and technical contracts that tie trade between producers, I would estimate that about 40 to 60 percent of what's left is cartelized today. That amounts to nearly $2 billion in sales, which is a substantial amount. And it is primarily sales from developed countries, particularly Western Europe and Japan, to developing countries.

I estimate that price markups are on the order of 15 to 25 percent. If this is so (and the data are good because they come from the companies themselves), it means that well over $100 million annually goes to cartels in the electrical industry from the pockets of developing countries.

A second response to the argument that export cartels are not important is that we do not have enough information to judge. If we look at countries that require export registration—the Federal Republic of Germany, the Netherlands, the United Kingdom, even the United States—we often find that registration is not complete. For example, it may not cover product lines, or there may have been certain periods when registration was halted.

We should be very careful not to assume that we know more than we do.

4

MERGERS, ACQUISITIONS, AND JOINT VENTURES

Merger Control in Western Europe: National and International Aspects

Kurt Markert

The purpose of this paper is to provide a survey of the present state of merger control law and its application under European Common Market law and in the three major Western European countries with special legislation on the subject, France, the Federal Republic of Germany, and the United Kingdom. This will be done within the context of a discussion of the international aspects of restrictive business practices in general and their regulation. The survey will include a brief description of the current statutory framework, some indication of the law's practical impact, and an examination of the extent to which the laws considered are applicable, and are in fact applied, to international mergers.[1]

In dealing with mergers, the paper will also cover joint ventures to the extent that they are organized as separate enterprises jointly owned and controlled by two or more parent companies (*Gemeinschaftsunternehmen, filiales communes*). This discussion will include the question whether and to what extent the agreements normally involved in setting up such joint ventures are considered not only under merger control law, but also under the provisions dealing with restrictive interfirm agreements (cartels).

Two of the laws under consideration, those of West Germany and the EEC, apply market domination as the main standard in defining the effects of mergers to be dealt with by merger control law. At the same time, market domination, as an aspect of "abuse," is applied in these legal systems to controlling the conduct of "market-dominating" enterprises. This paper will cover market domination only to the extent that it is used as a merger control standard; questions of conduct control are outside its scope. [2]

Finally, the paper will consider what international policies are desirable and realistically feasible in the field of merger control. As will be seen, within the law of restrictive business practices, merger control probably presents the greatest difficulties for possible intergovernmental harmonization of policy and international action.

ANALYSIS OF STATUTORY LAW

There are special statutory provisions on merger control in the three countries covered by this paper. As regards the European Common Market, statutory merger control law exists only for coal and steel products within the definitions of the European Coal and Steel Community (ECSC) Treaty of April 18, 1951. [3] Mergers involving other products or services are at present only subject to the general rules on competition of Articles 85 and 86 of the European Economic Community Treaty of March 25, 1957, [4] which deal with interfirm restrictive agreements and abuses by market-dominating enterprises, but a special regulation to control mergers as well is currently under consideration in the Council of Ministers.

FEDERAL REPUBLIC OF GERMANY

German merger control law is contained in sections 23 to 24b of the Act Against Restraints of Competition. [5] One of the main features of this law is a mandatory notification system. Large mergers, defined as mergers in which at least two participating firms [6] have annual sales of 1 billion marks (DM) or more, have to be notified in advance and may not be consummated before clearance has been given or before the one-month or four-months' intervention period has elapsed. [7] Other mergers involving either an aggregate market share of the participating firms of 20 percent or more of any market, or at least 500 million DM annual sales, [8] or 10,000 employees need only be notified after consummation of the merger, [9] but may be notified in advance on a voluntary basis. While consummated mergers may be prohibited within a year of the submission of a complete notification, the shorter prohibition periods of one or four months also apply in the case of voluntary advance notifications.

The merger definitions under section 23, paragraph 2 of the Restraints of Competition Act cover:

1. the acquisition of the assets of another enterprise wholly, or a substantial part thereof,[10] by means of amalgamation or in any other way;

2. the acquisition of shares of another enterprise—including newly established joint subsidiaries—if the acquired shares alone, or together with other shares already possessed by the acquiring enterprise or its affiliates, represent either 25 percent[11] or 50 percent of the voting capital of the other enterprise or a majority participation;[12]

3. *"Konzern"* agreements between enterprises establishing joint direction, agreements under which one enterprise assumes the obligation to operate its business for the account of another enterprise or to transfer its profits wholly or in part to the other enterprise, and agreements to lease the whole or a substantial part of another enterprise;

4. interlocking directorates;[13]

5. any other relationship between or among enterprises enabling one or several enterprises together to exercise directly or indirectly a dominating influence over another enterprise.

Under the West German law, mergers are subject to control only if:

1. the participating firms have aggregate annual sales of 500 million DM or more;[14]

2. the merger does not merely involve the joining of a firm with annual sales of less than 50 million DM with another firm;[15] or

3. The merger has anticompetitive effects in the entire domestic market or a substantial part of it.[16]

The Federal Cartel Office is required to prohibit any proposed or consummated merger subject to merger control if it finds that the merger may be expected to create or strengthen a dominant position in any market, unless the participating enterprises prove that the merger will also result in improvements in the competitive conditions and that such improvements will outweigh the detrimental effects of the market domination.[17] A market-dominating position is defined in the Restraints of Competition law as the situation in a particular market of either a single firm that has no competitor, is not exposed to substantial competition, or has a paramount market position in relation to its competitors; or of two or more firms if no substantial competition exists between them and together they meet the requirements of a single market-dominating firm (market-dominating oligopoly).[18] Market domination is rebuttably presumed if a single firm with annual sales not exceeding 250 million DM has a market share of one-third or more, or if two or three firms together have a market share of 50 percent or more, or four or five firms have a market share of two-thirds or more.[19]

The requirement, "improvements in the competitive conditions," is not defined in the statute. There is general agreement, however, that this term refers only to market structures more favorable to competition. Moreover, for the defense to be applicable in a particular case, the merger must be the only means of bringing about such an improvement. The participating firms have the full burden of proof that the alleged improvements result from the merger and could otherwise not be achieved to the same degree and within the same time period.[20]

If the Federal Cartel Office has prohibited a merger under section 24, paragraph 1 of the act, the participating firms may apply to the Minister for Economic Affairs for an exemption based on the public interest. The Minister has the power to grant such exemptions if the restraint of competition resulting from the merger is outweighed by its overall economic advantages, or if the merger is justified by an overriding public interest.[21] In this connection, the ability of the participating firms to compete in foreign markets may also be considered. Before making his decision, the Minister may ask the Monopolies Commission for an advisory opinion but is not required by law to do so.[22]

A decision of the Federal Cartel Office to prohibit a merger is subject to full judicial review, including the findings of fact.[23] It is doubtful whether third parties have a right to appeal a decision of the Federal Cartel Office not to prohibit a merger under section 24, paragraph 1.[24] It is clear, however, that the provision does not give the right to a private antitrust action against the merging firms.

The decision of the Minister for Economic Affairs to refuse the exemption or only to grant it subject to certain restrictions or requirements is also open to court review, but the appeals court has limited review power.[25] The decision to grant an exemption is not open to appeal by the Federal Cartel Office.[26]

EUROPEAN ECONOMIC COMMUNITIES

The merger law of the European Economic Communities includes three different parts: (1) Article 66 of the Coal and Steel Community Treaty, which deals with mergers involving firms engaged in activities relating to coal and steel products, as defined in the treaty; (2) Articles 85 and 86 of the European Economic Community Treaty, which, in relation to all other products or services, deal with restrictive interfirm agreements and abuses by market-dominating firms; and (3) the proposed draft of an EEC regulation on merger control.[27]

ECSC Treaty. Article 66 of the ECSC Treaty provides for a system of mandatory prior authorization of "concentrations" involving at least one firm engaged in the production or distribution of coal or steel within the meaning of the treaty, unless the merging firms do not meet certain minimum production requirements.[28] The term "concentration" is identical with "control of an enterprise" and includes acquisitions of shares and assets and contractual arrangements.[29] In ECSC practice Article 66 also is applied in cases of control of a joint subsidiary.[30]

Authorization of mergers subject to advance clearance shall be granted if the merger will not give the participating firms the power "to determine prices, to control or restrict production or distribution or to prevent the maintenance of effective competition in a substantial part of the market," or "to evade the rules of competition as they result from the execution of this Treaty, in particular by establishing an artificial privileged position involving a substantial access to supplies or markets."[31] In authorizing mergers, the Commission must further take into account the "size of enterprises of the same kind existing in the Community, as far as it finds this justified to avoid or correct the disadvantages resulting from inequality in the conditions of competition."

There is no ex post facto control of mergers not falling under the prior authorization requirements. Decisions of the EC Commission to authorize a merger, to refuse authorization, or to grant it subject to certain restrictions may be reviewed by the European Court of Justice.[32]

Article 85 of the EEC Treaty. In EC Commission practice, "concentration" agreements are not treated as restrictive agreements (cartels), falling under the general prohibition of Article 85, paragraph 1 of the EEC Treaty.[33] The criterion for distinguishing concentration agreements from cartel agreements is whether the agreement brings about a permanent structural change in the enterprises involved that results in their ceasing to be actual or potential competitors.[34] Thus, Article 85 has been applied to agreements on jointly owned subsidiaries when the Commission has concluded that the parent companies have continued to be potential competitors in the markets of the joint venture.[35] Since the Commission is stretching the concept of potential competition relatively far, joint venture agreements between actual or potential competitors will normally be covered by Article 85(1).[36] So far, however, the Commission has been relatively lenient in applying the exemption clause of Article 85(3), so that very few joint ventures have definitely been banned.[37]

Article 86 of the EEC Treaty.   Pursuant to the *Continental Can* judgment of the Court of Justice, a merger made by a market-dominating firm constitutes an abuse prohibited by Article 86 if, as a result of the merger, the dominating firm strengthens its position "to the point where the degree of domination thus achieved hamper[s] competition to an appreciable extent, i.e. would leave only enterprises depending, in their action, on the dominant enterprise."[38] This rule, however, can only apply if the acquiring firm already had a dominant position before the merger and if competitive conditions in the dominated market are further deteriorated by the merger. As there are no subsequent decisions applying the rule of the *Continental Can* case, it is difficult to specify the exact degree of such deterioration necessary to constitute an abuse. But the fact that since 1973 no further cases have been decided by the Commission is a rather strong indication that the requirements for prohibiting a merger under Article 86 are relatively strict and can hardly ever be met.

Draft Council Regulation of 1973.   In 1973 the EC Commission submitted to the Council of Ministers for adoption a draft regulation designed to set up a special system of merger control in the EEC.[39] The draft combines elements of ECSC and German merger law. It empowers the Commission to prohibit mergers of firms with combined assets of 200 million units of account or more, or a 25 percent or more market share in any member country, if the merger in question creates or strengthens the position of the parties "to hinder effective competition in the common market or a substantial part thereof."[40] However, an exemption to an anticompetitive merger may be granted if the merger is "indispensable to the attainment of an objective which is given priority treatment in the common interest of the Community."[41]

The definitions of a merger in the draft are identical with those of ECSC merger law.[42] The draft further provides for compulsory advance notification of large mergers involving combined annual sales of 1 billion units of account or more, unless the sales of the acquired firm are below 30 million units of account.[43] Other mergers may also be notified in advance on a voluntary basis. The Commission must decide whether to commence proceedings against a particular merger within three months after a "complete" notification is made.[44] If proceedings are duly commenced, the Commission can prohibit the merger only within the following nine months.[45] In cases of mandatory advance notification, the merger may not be put into effect until three months after notification or the Commission has issued a statement that it will not commence proceedings.[46]

The Commission's draft is still under consideration by a special working party of the Council of Ministers. As there are still basic differences among member governments as to concentration policy in general, and merger regulation in particular, it is unlikely that the draft will be adopted in the foreseeable future.[47]

UNITED KINGDOM
Special provisions on merger control are contained in sections 57 and 77 of the Fair Trading Act 1973,[48] applying both to mergers in general and, with somewhat different criteria, to newspaper mergers.[49] General merger control is applicable to any merger in which the value of the assets taken over exceeds £5 million, or the result of the merger is to create or intensify a "monopoly," defined as a situation in which at least one-quarter of goods or services of any description supplied in the United Kingdom are supplied by the merging firms.[50] Under these conditions, the competent Secretary of State can refer proposed or consummated mergers to the Monopolies and Mergers Commission, an independent advisory body, to examine whether the merger in question in fact falls under the control criteria and whether it operates, or may be expected to operate, against the public interest.[51]

A merger is generally defined as "the fact that two or more enterprises, of which one at least was carried on in the United Kingdom or by or under the control of a body corporate or incorporated in the United Kingdom, have ceased to be distinct enterprises."[52] This condition is met when two or more enterprises are brought under common ownership or control or when there is an arrangement or transaction by which one or more of the enterprises involved ceases to function in order to prevent competition.[53] The criteria cover acquisitions of majority and substantial minority shareholdings, acquisitions of plants, and arrangements that one participating firm will cease to operate in consideration of receiving certain benefits from the other firm.[54]

The decision whether to refer a merger to the Monopolies and Mergers Commission is a matter of discretion of the competent Secretary of State. The Director General of the Office of Fair Trading, as competent antitrust authority, can only make nonbinding recommendations as to whether or not a reference to the Commission should be made.[55] The Director General is advised by a "Mergers Panel," a standing interdepartmental committee, which includes as members representatives of other governmental departments. None of these considerations—those of the Mergers Panel, the Director General, or the Secretary of State—are made public.

As to the standard for determining whether a merger operates, or may be expected to operate, against the public interest, the Fair Trading Act 1973 merely lists a number of criteria to be taken into account by the Monopolies and Mergers Commission: namely,

the desirability
(a) of maintaining and promoting effective competition between persons supplying goods and services in the United Kingdom;
(b) of promoting the interests of consumers, purchasers and other users of goods and services in the United Kingdom in respect of the prices charged for them and in respect of their quality and the variety of goods and services supplied;
Zc) of promoting, through competition, the reduction of costs and the development and use of new techniques and new products, and of facilitating the entry of new competitors into existing markets;
(d) of maintaining and promoting the balanced distribution of industry and employment in the United Kingdom; and
(e) of maintaining and promoting competitive activity in markets outside the United Kingdom on the part of producers of goods, and of suppliers of goods and services, in the United Kingdom.[56]

The Fair Trading Act 1973, however, establishes no priorities, and there is no presumption against mergers that have significant anticompetitive effects.[57]

If the Monopolies and Mergers Commission finds that the merger operates or will operate against the public interest, the Secretary of State may issue an order prohibiting the merger or requiring its dissolution.[58] This power, however, is normally applied only after the firms concerned have refused to make satisfactory voluntary undertakings.[59] The decision by the

Secretary of State to seek undertakings or to issue a prohibition or dissolution order is again a matter of his discretion. Only if the Commission has not given an adverse report is the Secretary of State bound by the Commission's findings.

Theoretically, the orders of Secretaries of State may be appealed to the ordinary courts, but the courts will normally not review the merits of the case. [60]

FRANCE

Merger control was introduced in France by Act No. 77–806 of July 19, 1977, on the Control of Economic Concentration and Prevention of Unlawful Cartels and Abuses of Dominant Positions. [61] This law confers discretionary reference and prohibition powers on the competent minister similar to those in the UK law. The Minister may refer certain mergers to the Competition Commission [62] and, upon an unfavorable report by the Commission, order the prohibition or dissolution of the merger in question. [63]

Mergers ("concentrations") to which the law applies are defined as "the result of any legal act or transaction, whatever the form adopted, involving transfer of ownership or tenure of all or part of the assets, rights and obligations of an enterprise or having the object or effect of enabling one enterprise or a group of enterprises to exercise an influence, directly or indirectly, on one or more enterprises which is of such a nature as to direct or even orientate the management or working of the latter." [64] Application of the law further requires that the merger be of such a nature as to prevent adequate competition on the market. [65]

To meet the latter requirement, two additional conditions must be fulfilled: either the participating firms together must have a share of at least 40 percent "of domestic consumption in the case of similar or substitutable goods, products or services," or at least two participating firms must each have 25 percent "of domestic consumption in the case of different and nonsubstitutable goods, products or services." [66] Domestic consumption is defined as "the total amount of sales of goods and services in France during the calendar year preceding the legal act or transaction." [67] In consequence, mergers are subject to control only if in the case of horizontal mergers the merging firms have an aggregate domestic market share of 40 percent or more, or, in the case of vertical and conglomerate mergers, at least two participating firms have individual domestic market shares of 25 percent or more on different markets.

The mandate of the Competition Commission is to determine whether the merger "makes a sufficient contribution to economic and social progress to compensate for the restraints on competition which it implies." [68] In making this determination, the Commission also has to take into account the international competitiveness of the enterprises concerned. If the Commission finds that the merger is anticompetitive and that this effect is not outweighed by a "sufficient contribution to economic and social progress," the Minister for Economic Affairs, as a matter of discretion, may prohibit the merger, order its dissolution, or take "any other measure to ensure or reestablish adequate competition." [69] If the Commission finds that on balance the merger has no adverse effects, no measures may be taken. [70]

There is no mandatory system of notification of proposed or consummated mergers, but notification may be made on a voluntary basis (in cases of consummated mergers, within three months after consummation). If the merger is duly notified, reference to the Competition Commission may only be made within three months of the date of notification, [71] and no measures may be taken later than eight months after receipt of the notification. [72] This provision is undoubtedly a strong incentive in favor of notification. A ministerial decision against a merger is open to appeal to the administrative courts by the merging parties.

SUMMARY

The foregoing description of the statutory merger provisions in the four legal systems covered by this paper shows substantial differences among them. These differences begin with the law's degree of specificity on such technical questions as the definition of mergers. While all four systems appear to cover the main forms of merger activity, including acquisition of shares and assets of other enterprises, the precise scope of what falls under such general terms as "control" or "concentration" is mostly left to be clarified by law enforcement. Thus, as regards minority shareholdings, only German law specifically provides that the acquisition of 25 percent or more of the voting capital of another enterprise constitutes a merger, irrespective of whether the acquiring firm gains a controlling influence in the other firm. Likewise, only German law has a statutory provision that acquisitions of shares in connection with the establishment of jointly owned subsidiaries also fall within the scope of the statutory definition of a merger.[73]

There is furthermore no uniform picture as regards notification and advance clearance procedures. While such procedures are a dominant feature in the continental European systems, not even voluntary notifications are provided for in United Kingdom law. The difference in practice, however, is less substantial, as the British authorities have developed an informal advance clearance procedure that is apparently used in most cases.[74]

The main differences relate to the standards used to distinguish between "good" and "bad" mergers, and the nature of the decisions to prohibit "bad" mergers. Although a final evaluation of this matter can only be made on the basis of a thorough analysis of enforcement in the systems covered here, it is apparent from the statutory provisions themselves that several pertinent questions are not uniformly answered. For example, should mergers be controlled primarily because of their possible anticompetitive effects? What is the extent of such effects that makes it necessary to prohibit a particular merger? Can such effects be offset by other policy considerations, and, if so, under what circumstances? Obviously, these divergences reflect basic differences of policy on business concentration which cannot be discussed here in greater detail.

These differences also have relevance to a procedural question: whether the decision to select particular mergers for closer examination and to prohibit them if sufficient adverse effects have been found is primarily seen as the application by law enforcement agencies of objective legal standards open to review by independent courts, or as a matter of the competent minister's political discretion with no, or only very limited, judicial review. In this respect, the more "political" systems of France and the United Kingdom may be distinguished from the more "legal" systems of the European Communities and the Federal Republic of Germany. That this distinction only expresses tendencies, however, can be seen from the facts that the decisions in the European Communities are made by the Commission itself, i.e., the top political body of the Communities' executive branch, and that German law provides exemption powers in the public interest for the Economics Minister. Therefore, it may be said that in none of the European systems is merger control regarded merely as a matter of ordinary antitrust law enforcement, such as the prosecution of illegal cartel agreements or the administration of cartel exemption clauses. Examination of the statutory law makes apparent, although in varying degree, the "political" character of all merger control systems in Western Europe. The particular consequences of this feature on questions of international policy will be discussed at the end of this paper.

THE OPERATION OF MERGER CONTROL LAW

The description of statutory merger law in the preceding section is not a sufficient basis for an assessment of the practical impact of the various systems under consideration. Because statutory law is formulated in many respects in relatively vague, general terms which are open to narrow or wide construction, it is only by analyzing law enforcement that the real meaning of these terms can be ascertained. But the respective enforcement authorities for the most part have wide discretionary powers, and it is not always possible to determine what use is actually made of these powers. To provide at least some basis for an appraisal of the operation of the laws in question and their practical impact, the present chapter gives some indication as to major enforcement developments and plans to amend the law in the light of experience under the current law. Because the author has limited expertise as regards the application of merger control law outside Germany, but also because few cases have so far arisen under some of the other laws, the following survey will essentially cover German law only.

FEDERAL REPUBLIC OF GERMANY

In 1978, 558 notifications of consummated mergers falling under the criteria of section 23(1) of the Restraints of Competition Act were made (including a major number of cases that had previously been notified as proposed mergers and were consummated after clearance).[75] The number of advance notifications in 1978 was 109 (63 mandatory, 46 optional).[76] Of the 558 notified consummated mergers, 266 did not reach the minimum requirements of section 24(8) for qualifying as mergers subject to control (58 because the aggregate annual sales were below 500 million DM, 206 because the merger merely involved the acquisition of a firm with less than 50 million DM annual sales, and 2 because the anticompetitive effects were limited to an area not constituting a substantial part of the Federal Republic or to markets with less than 10 million DM annual sales).[77] Of the 322 merger cases that did qualify for merger control (226 cases of consummated mergers and 96 cases of advance notification),[78] 247 were given clearance (including 85 cases of advance notification, of which 63 were cleared within the first month after notification), 11 were prohibited, and the rest were still under examination at the time of reporting.

Twenty-three prohibition orders have been issued since merger control began in 1973.[79] In seven of these cases the orders became final, in four the Economics Minister granted a public interest exemption,[80] in two the orders were rescinded by the Federal Cartel Office or finally reversed by the courts, and in ten appeal proceedings before the appellate courts were pending. In several cases clearance was given only after the participating firms had given assurances that they would divest themselves of certain assets or subsidiaries, or that they would take other structural measures to remove the grounds for prohibiting the merger.[81] In twenty-three cases since 1973, advance notifications were rescinded by the notifying firms, partly as a result of objections to the merger raised by the Federal Cartel Office.[82] There is no statistical record of deleted merger plans in cases only informally brought to the attention of the Federal Cartel Office.[83]

In applying the definitions of market domination under section 22 to merger cases, the emphasis is clearly on the structural criteria: the paramount market position in relation to competitors and the presumptions about market share. The market conduct test (no exposure to "substantial" competition) practically plays no role in findings that a single firm, as the result of a merger, has acquired a dominant position or has strengthened a previously existing dominant position. This primarily structural approach was strongly supported by the Supreme Court holding that a firm may have a paramount market position in relation to its competitors even though it is exposed to substantial competition, "as long as it possesses a predominant scope of action in its competitive behavior."[84] Only in cases where a single firm is not dominant individually but as part of a dominant oligopoly is it necessary to rely on the conduct test of not being exposed to substantial competition, because the group of oligopolists as a whole may be treated as a single entity in relation to outsiders only if there is, for factual reasons, no substantial competition among the group members.[85]

As a result of this structural approach, the present state of law enforcement as regards horizontal mergers in the single-firm context is relatively clear. The Federal Cartel Office will normally prohibit any merger of firms in any market with annual sales exceeding 10 million DM if the merger will make those firms the leading supplier with a substantial market share (20 percent or more) and, taking into account all the criteria listed in section 22, paragraph 1(2) of the Restraints of Competition Act, they will obtain a substantially stronger market position than any of the other suppliers. Thus, in the *Thyssen/Hüller* merger case the Berlin Court of Appeals upheld the Federal Cartel Office's prohibition order, based on the findings that the merging firms had shares in the two relevant markets of 21 and 26 percent, as compared to 11 and 13 percent of the next largest suppliers, and that Thyssen, the acquiring firm with total annual sales of about 21 billion DM, was financially much stronger and had better market access facilities than the main other suppliers, which were small or medium-sized firms.[86] Particularly where one of the firms involved already enjoyed a strong market position before the merger, even relatively small increases of market shares are sufficient to find that the merger has resulted in creating or strengthening a paramount market position for one of the merging firms.[87]

On the other hand, horizontal mergers not involving market domination by a single firm are much more difficult to prejudge. Although the Federal Cartel Office has issued several prohibition orders based on the finding that the merger in question resulted in creating or strengthening a market-dominating oligopoly,[88] none of these cases has confronted the courts with the issue that must be proven in a merger case: that two or more firms are not exposed to substantial competition in relation to each other, for factual reasons, and thus qualify under the market-dominating requirements for oligopolies. The position taken by the Federal Cartel Office in the *Haindl/Holzmann* case that the fact that the firms fall under the market share presumptions establishes a strong *prima facie* case[89] is open to doubt; therefore, in its bill to amend the law,[90] the Government proposed a special oligopoly clause for merger cases. Under this clause, if the two or three leading firms in a market have an aggregate share of 50 percent or more, they would be irrebuttably presumed to constitute a market-dominating oligopoly, unless together they do not hold a paramount market position in relation to their competitors. The clause, however, would not apply to markets with less than 100 million DM annual sales, to firms with less than 500 million DM annual sales, and to mergers in which the firms' combined market share does not exceed 15 percent. In effect, therefore, only larger firms in close oligopolies involving important markets would be covered by the new clause.[91]

Still less case law exists with regard to vertical and conglomerate mergers. As to vertical mergers, if a strong, dominant supplier of a product acquires its main buyer, which has a substantial share of the buyers' market (over 20 percent), the acquisition will be regarded as strengthening the supplying firm's dominant position.[92] There are no cases yet of prohibition solely on the ground that a vertical merger created a market-dominating position that had not existed before.

As to conglomerate mergers, in principle the courts have accepted entrenchment and restriction of potential competition as a basis for finding that a merger strengthens existing dominant positions. In the case of the proposed merger between Sachs AG, the leading German supplier of automobile clutches with a market share of about 70 percent, and the British firm Guest, Keen and Nettlefolds (GKN), the Supreme Court upheld the Federal Cartel Office's prohibition order on the ground that Sachs, as part of a much more widely diversified and financially powerful firm such as GKN, would have a greater potential to deter actual or potential competitors from engaging in active competition in the market for clutches, or from considering entry into it, and would thus perceptibly strengthen its already strong dominant position.[93] The Supreme Court, however, limited its entrenchment rule to mergers of firms operating in "proximate markets within each others' competitive spheres." Thus, it is uncertain whether this rule also reaches conglomerate mergers of firms not operating in closely related markets.[94]

In applying current law to vertical and conglomerate mergers, the Federal Cartel Office faces great difficulties in identifying particular markets in which the merger in question creates or strengthens a dominant position. As a result, the Federal Cartel Office has suggested that merger control law be "untied" entirely from the market domination standard of section 22 and that it be given the power to intervene against any merger that is likely substantially to deteriorate the conditions for competition, either in particular markets or generally.[95] The Government in its 1978 bill,[96] however, merely proposed the following three rebuttable presumptions for the creation or strengthening of a market-dominating position by a merger: (1) if a firm with annual sales of at least two billion DM merges with another enterprise operating in a market in which small and medium-sized enterprises have a combined share of at least two-thirds, and the enterprises participating in the merger have a combined share of at least 5 percent; (2) if a firm with annual sales of at least two billion DM merges with another enterprise that dominates a market involving annual sales of at least 100 million DM; and (3) if the enterprises participating in the merger have annual sales of at least 10 billion DM and at least two of them each have annual sales of at least one billion DM. The latter presumption does not apply if two or more firms merely set up a jointly owned company in a market that has annual sales not exceeding 500 million DM. The presumptions would thus cover cases of entry by large firms into "small-business markets" by the acquisition of leading firms, combinations of large firms and dominant positions, and the formation of "superconcentration mergers."

In spite of criticism that a mere presumptive approach that does not shift the burden of proof and limit the rebuttal to specific narrow defenses [97] is likely to be ineffective, the Government's bill was approved by the *Bundestag* with only very slight modifications. Thus, the absolute size requirement for the presumption of "superconcentration" mergers in clause (3) was raised to 12 billion DM, and the minimum sales requirement in cases of joint ventures to 750 million DM. Also, the minimum firm size in clause (2) was raised to 150 million DM. It remains to be seen whether the new presumptions will be construed by the courts in such a manner that at least some of the difficulties in showing domination of particular markets can be overcome.

Joint ventures were involved in a number of cases in which the Federal Cartel Office vetoed mergers by formal decision [98] or informally. [99] This type of merger may strengthen a dominant market position of the parent companies if the joint venture supplies a substitute product [100] or an important product used by the parent companies for their own production. [101] The only prohibition order against a joint venture on the ground that the joint venture itself would acquire a dominant position in the market in which it operated [102] was subsequently rescinded because the Federal Cartel Office no longer regards merger law as applicable to joint selling agencies that fall under the provisions for exempted cartels. [103]

The general question as to what extent jointly owned subsidiary arrangements, including ancillary agreements between the parent companies, are covered by the prohibition on cartels of section 1 of the Restraints of Competition Act is not yet settled. [104] Under the administrative guidelines the Federal Cartel Office published in its *Annual Report 1978*, [105] a distinction is made between "cooperative" joint ventures, which fall under both cartel and merger law (except joint selling companies, which are merely covered by cartel law) and "purely concentrative" joint ventures, which fall, in principle, only under merger law. A purely concentrative joint venture is defined as a functioning enterprise that performs the essential operations of an enterprise and renders market-related services rather than acting exclusively or predominantly for the parent companies at a preceding or subsequent stage of the product's economy. Furthermore, the parent companies must no longer be active in the product market of the joint venture. In such cases the Federal Cartel Office does not consider section 1 applicable to the agreement between the parent companies to set up the joint venture; to agreements of the parent companies not to compete, provided that in terms of product, territory, and time the agreement does not go beyond the object of the joint venture; and to any other ancillary agreement necessary to the functioning of the joint venture. In principle, the same rule is applied to other joint ventures if they differ from purely concentrative joint ventures only by acting partly or wholly for the parent companies at a preceding stage of production. The reason for not applying section 1 to most aspects of concentrative joint ventures is that these aspects are necessary, or at least typical, elements of concentration ("partial merger"), and as such are considered under merger law.[106]

As regards the application of the improvements in competitive conditions defense, the Federal Supreme Court held that the enterprises invoking the defense must show not only that such improvements may reasonably be expected to result from the merger, but also that they could not otherwise be achieved to the same degree and within the same time.[107] A major merger case "saved" by the "improvements" defense was the merger between Karstadt and Neckermann.[108] Karstadt is the largest department store firm in Germany. Neckermann before the merger was the third largest mail order retail company and also the second largest operator of packaged travel tours. The Federal Cartel Office took the position that Karstadt, together with the three other major department store firms, had to be regarded as a market-dominating oligopoly that was likely to be strengthened by the acquisition of a major mail order retail firm. However, it accepted that Neckermann was in such critical financial condition that, but for the merger with Karstadt, bankruptcy would have been unavoidable, and that consequently the market structure in mail order retailing and packaged travel tours would have deteriorated considerably, particularly that of the latter sector where the largest firm, Touristik Union International (TUI), already had a dominant position. Clearance for the merger was therefore given, after Karstadt promised to divest itself of its 12.5 percent interest in TUI.[109]

In the four cases since 1973 where a ministerial exemption was granted, two exemptions were given mainly on grounds of energy policy,[110] one on grounds of regional employment policy,[111] and one in the interest of preserving technology.[112] In the merger case *VAW/Kaiser Aluminium,* an exemption was applied for and refused.[113] In the *Sachs/GKN* case the application was withdrawn after the Minister indicated that he would refuse to grant an exemption.

EUROPEAN ECONOMIC COMMUNITIES

ECSC Treaty. In 1977 fifteen, and in 1978 nine cases of mergers falling under the prior authorization criteria were decided by the EC Commission, which granted authorization in them all.[114] The major cases during this period were several restructuring measures in the French and Belgian steel industry[115] and the acquisitions by the Luxembourg steel firm Arbed of the German steel firm Neunkircher Eisenwerke AG and of a 25.09 percent interest in the Belgian steel firm Rodange-Athus.[116]

The application of Article 66 to mergers of coal-mining firms was strongly influenced by the growing role of other forms of energy after the 1950s. Thus, while a single joint selling organization of the Ruhr coal-mining companies was refused authorization in 1960,[117] a merger of practically the same companies, creating the Ruhrkohle AG, was authorized in 1969.[118]

As for steel, the EC Commission dealt with the structure of that industry in its memorandum of 1970 on competition policy.[119] The Commission pointed out that an oligopoly of about ten large firms whose individual production did not exceed about 13 percent of the crude steel in the Community would be consistent with the maintenance of effective competition within the Common Market. Thus, the Commission authorized a number of mergers that either involved large steel-producing firms[120] or resulted in substantial market shares for the merging firms.[121] Undoubtedly, the economic difficulties of the European steel industry, which in 1978 caused the Commission to declare a state of "manifest crisis" within the meaning of Article 61(c) of the ECSC Treaty,[122] have strongly influenced the Commission's enforcement policy with respect to the merger control provisions of Article 66.

EEC Treaty. As pointed out earlier, Article 85 of the EEC Treaty is generally not applied by the EC Commission to mergers, with the exception of "cooperative" joint ventures.[123] As regards the application of Article 86 to mergers, no further decision has been made since the *Continental Can* case.[124] In the course of several authorization proceedings under Article 66 of the ECSC Treaty, the Commission has also examined whether the merger violated Article 86.[125] In 1978 the Commission dealt with three cases of complaints made against particular mergers for allegedly violating Article 86.[126] But to date, in none of these cases has the Commission found that Article 86 was violated.

UNITED KINGDOM

During the period from 1965 to 1977, 1273 proposed mergers that met the statutory reference requirements were considered by the Mergers Panel.[127] By March 3, 1978, forty-three cases had been referred to the Monopolies and Mergers Commission.[128] In fifteen of these cases the merger was abandoned without a report by the Commission, in thirteen the Commission found that the merger was against the public interest, in fourteen no such violation was found, and one report was still outstanding.[129] The competent Secretary of State has apparently accepted the adverse findings of the Monopolies and Mergers Commission in all cases.

The pragmatic case-by-case approach based on a broad public interest standard makes it extremely difficult to assess the practical scope of merger law in the United Kingdom.[130] The case selection policy of the competent Secretary of State and the reports of the Monopolies and Merger Commission will not be analyzed here. Instead, the following conclusions from the "Green Paper" of 1978 on the operation of the present system and on future policy are cited:

> 5.18. Instead of so drastic a change, we consider that the evidence and the UK's situation call for a shift from the present policy which tends to operate in favour of mergers to an essentially neutral approach that would have due regard to the danger of abuse of market power resulting from reduced competition and to the possible dangers of further increases in aggregate concentration, but would also recognise the economic benefits that may accrue from improved industrial structure. The general legislative and institutional framework of merger control would remain, and in particular the scope of the control would be the same except for the suggested increase in the size of assets criterion from £5 million to £8 million to take account of the fall in asset values (see paragraph 4.20.). However, in assessing merger proposals within the scope of the control greater emphasis would be put on competition. The first test would be whether a significant reduction of competition was foreseen; if it was, we should look critically at the prospects of benefits accruing to the

economy and weigh up the balance of advantage. A critical assessment would similarly be made of cases where there would be a significant accretion of economic power through further acquisitions by large companies. Special factors affecting the overall public interest would also be taken into account; in particular, mergers encouraged or supported by the Government with a view to strengthening particular sectors of manufacturing industry would not be hindered.

5.19. A number of steps would be needed in order to bring about this shift of policy; to be effective all these steps should be made at the same time. First, we suggest that there should be a clear Government statement about the new policy; this would warn those preparing merger proposals of the new hurdles they would have to surmount and also serve as guidance to those implementing the policy. It should stress the greater emphasis that would be put on competition, leading to critical assessment of the balance of advantage, as explained in the previous paragraph. It should also reassure industry that the Government recognised the importance of restructuring in some sectors.

5.20. Secondly, the Mergers Panel should be provided with clear non-statutory guidelines (at present no such guidelines exist). The DGFT [Director General of the Office of Fair Trading] would in turn provide further guidance to industry on the revised Mergers Panel procedure, beyond that contained in the OFT's recently issued guidance booklet on the merger control procedures. It should be made clear in this further guidance that the DGFT would still reserve the right to recommend the reference of mergers which fall outside the guidelines if he considered there were implications that justified investigation by the MMC. The Mergers Panel's guidelines would lay down that the assessment of all merger proposals falling within the scope of the 1973 Act should be essentially a two stage process:

(i) in stage 1, the Mergers Panel Secretariat would carry out a quick assessment of the possible effects of the merger on competition either through the creation of an increased market share (horizontal mergers) or through the undue concentration of economic power (vertical and conglomerate mergers). Mergers that did not have a significant effect on competition would generally be cleared on a circulated paper basis (subject to any other special consideration affecting the public interest). The guidelines for judging a significant effect on competition or economic power might be:

(a) horizontal mergers: any merger which increased the combined companies' share of the UK market for a particular product or service to 25 per cent or more; except where:

(i) the size of the UK market concerned was less than £4 million; or

(ii) the value of the gross assets of the acquired company was less than £1 million;

(b) vertical mergers: any merger where either the acquiring or the acquired company has a 25 per cent or greater share of the UK market for a particular product or service, and the merger involved the acquiring company taking over a significant supplier or customer;

(c) conglomerate mergers: any merger where

(aa) the acquired company had at least a 25 per cent share of the UK market for a particular product or service, except where the size of the UK market concerned was less than £4 million; or

(bb) the worldwide turnover of the combined companies was £350 million or more, of which a significant proportion arose in the UK, and where the gross value of the assets to be transferred was £16 million or more (ie twice the level of the minimum assets criterion in section 64(1) of the Act after the proposed increase to £8 million).

(ii) in stage 2, those mergers that were judged likely to have a significant effect on competition would be reserved for further detailed consideration and discussion in the Mergers Panel. Firms would be expected to provide convincing evidence of offsetting benefits, and the probability of their achievement, if reference to the MMC was to be avoided, and this would be the opportunity for sponsor Departments to explain the case for proposals being supported in accordance with the industrial strategy. The Panel would consider whether the benefits expected, in terms of increased efficiency, export potential etc, would offset the detriments from the potential effects on competition; and would also take into account other possible detriments, such as collapse of the firm being acquired or loss of jobs in rescue cases, which might arise from abandonment of the merger or from the delays inherent in a reference to the MMC.

5.21. Thirdly, the Fair Trading Act 1973 should be amended so as to alter the way in which the MMC report on merger investigations:

(i) Sections 69 and 72: The MMC should be required to report first whether the merger might be expected to prevent, restrict or distort competition significantly; or to have other adverse effects on the public interest; if so, to assess the benefits to be expected from the merger and the likelihood of their being achieved; finally to balance the benefits and detriments and recommend what action should be taken. Such action might include allowing the merger provided that certain conditions were met.

(ii) Section 84: The matters relevant to the public interest listed in this section of the 1973 Act (see Annex F) should be supplemented so as to require the MMC, at least in merger references, to take into account further considerations on the following lines:

(a) the desirability of minimising the detriments of reduced competition and increased concentration; and

(b) the desirability of restructuring to improve the international competitiveness of British industry.

We have not been able in the time available to review the matters listed in this section as a whole, and some other revisions might be needed following these additions. We recommend that this question should be further examined.[131]

According to the EC Commission's *Eighth Report on Competition Policy,* several merger notifications had been made to the competent Ministry by the end of 1978, but in none of these cases was the merger considered to be preventing adequate competition. Therefore, no reference was made to the Competition Commission as to application of the "compensation" clause.[132] A number of other cases not notified were still under consideration by the Economics Ministry. In 1979 the Competition Commission gave approval under the compensation clause to a joint venture for the production of small steel tubes established by Société Vallourec and Société Tubes de la Providence, and the Economics Minister decided that the merger might be effected subject to certain conditions.[133]

APPLICATION TO INTERNATIONAL MERGERS[134]

The merger laws covered by this paper use different legal techniques to determine their international territorial scope. In all the systems except those of France and Germany, the statutory merger law provisions themselves contain territorial clauses. Thus, Article 66(1) of the ECSC Treaty applies only to mergers "within the territories mentioned in the first paragraph of Article 79," i.e., the territory of the Community. Article 66(1) furthermore requires that "at least one enterprise [be] subject to the application of Article 80," i.e., "engaged in production in the field of coal and steel within the territories mentioned in the first paragraph of Article 79."[135] Similarly, Article 1(1) of the EC Commission's draft on merger regulation requires that at least one of the merging parties be "established in the common market" and that the anticompetitive effects of the merger take place "in the common market or a substantial part thereof." Although Articles 85 and 86 of the EEC Treaty do not provide that at least one participating firm must be engaged in domestic production or distribution or "established within the common market," the restraint on competition or the abuse must take place within the Common Market.

In the United Kingdom the application of merger law requires that two or more enterprises, "of which one at least was carried on in the United Kingdom or by or under the control of a body corporate incorporated in the

United Kingdom," have ceased to be distinct from one another.[136] Furthermore, section 84(1) of the Fair Trading Act 1973, which specifies the standards to be applied by the Monopolies and Mergers Commission in considering whether a merger is operating, or may be expected to operate, against the public interest, refers to the "desirability of maintaining and promoting effective competition between persons supplying goods and services in the United Kingdom."

The French act, No. 77–806 of July 19, 1977, does not expressly define its territorial scope. However, in order to be covered by it, the act requires that the merger must "prevent adequate competition in the market," specifically, that the parties must have certain shares of the domestic market. Consequently, the law indirectly provides that only domestic anticompetitive effects of the merger are relevant. On the other hand, it expressly provides that, in applying the compensation clause of section 4(8), the international competitiveness of the merging firms shall be taken into account. There is no requirement, as in the United Kingdom, that at least one participating firm must be operating on domestic territory or be controlled by a domestic firm.

German law is the only system covered by this paper with a special statutory rule that generally defines the territorial scope of domestic antitrust law. Section 98(2) of the Restraints of Competition Act provides that this law "shall apply to all restraints of competition which have effect in the area in which the Act applies, even if they result from acts done outside such area." The term "restraints of competition" refers to all types of restrictive business practices covered by the act, including mergers.[137] In addition, sentence 4 of section 23, paragraph 3 provides that if two or more firms merge, this action shall also be deemed a merger of the enterprises controlled by them. The main purpose of this clause is to facilitate the application of domestic merger law to cases of mergers by foreign companies having subsidiaries in Germany, which the merger of the parent companies has brought under common control.[138] Finally, the Economics Minister, in deciding upon applications for a public policy exemption, shall also take into account the competitiveness of the merging firms in foreign markets.[139]

It appears that all the laws discussed in this paper reach international mergers in the form of a foreign firm's taking control, either directly or through a domestic subsidiary, of a domestic firm if such a merger has the same adverse domestic effects as a purely national merger.[140] There is no general requirement that the acquiring foreign firm must be present in the domestic market before the merger, but in almost all cases of this type such presence in fact existed. The most restrictive attitude on this question is apparently taken by French law in requiring that in cases of vertical and conglomerate mergers both the acquiring and the acquired firm must have a domestic market share of 25 percent or more.

In principle, the same rules apply to the reverse situation of international mergers in the form of a domestic firm's acquiring a foreign firm, although this principle at present is much less supported by case law.[141] The main reason for this scarcity of case law is that in view of the absence of mandatory notification in most systems and their relatively strict requirements for prohibiting a merger, only in extremely rare cases will the acquisition of a foreign firm with no substantial domestic operations before the merger be prohibited. Such a case may arise under German law if, for example, a domestic firm with a strong dominant position in a domestic market acquires a foreign firm that either has a significant share in the same market or is the main potential competitor.[142]

Finally, as regards the third type of international merger cases, mergers of foreign firms that affect domestic territory, the case law is still the least developed. Some laws do not expressly require that, to make domestic merger law applicable, at least one participating firm must have domestic operations (e.g., producing or distributing subsidiaries or branch offices) but regard domestic anticompetitive effects as sufficient.[143] Nevertheless, at the least for practical reasons, it seems very unlikely that a merger of foreign firms not having domestic subsidiaries will be attacked.

Even if at least two of the merging firms have domestic subsidiaries and this domestic presence is regarded as sufficient (as in the German law under section 23, paragraph 3, sentence 4), action against the merger under domestic merger law is unlikely where it is obvious that no adequate remedy is available. This would be the case if two foreign competing manufacturers merge, and each of them has a domestic distributing subsidiary. Divestiture of these subsidiaries is normally not feasible and could also not prevent the anticompetitive effects of the merger.

Special problems in international merger cases are raised by the mandatory premerger notification systems of Germany and (though with only minor relevance to such cases) the ECSC. Since the obligation to notify cannot depend on whether the merger in question meets the requirements of a prohibition order—this determination, of course, can only be made on the basis of a full investigation after notification—substantially more cases of international mergers are covered by the notification requirements than are seriously considered for prohibition.

For this reason, the German Federal Supreme Court has accepted that the domestic effects requirement of section 98(2), in cases of ex post facto notification of international mergers under section 23(1) of the German law, should be given a broad interpretation.[144] In the *Bayer/Allied Chemical* case, the court regarded the following as sufficient domestic effect: a domestic firm that was the fourth largest seller in the relevant domestic market with about a 4 percent share acquired a manufacturing division of a foreign company with domestic sales (imports) of 343,000 DM in 1976 (0.14 percent market share) and 700,000 DM in 1977 (0.23 percent market share). In the court's view, a merger of two firms competing in the relevant domestic market, at least one of which was a significant supplier, had a perceptible adverse effect on the structure of that market.

As the Supreme Court also pointed to the purely informational function of section 23(1), i.e., to inform the Federal Cartel Office about concentration developments irrespective of whether merger control law applies in the particular case, it is still an open question whether the Court's ruling in the *Bayer/Allied Chemical* case applies to the mandatory premerger notification system under section 24a(1). The only purpose of premerger notification is to facilitate merger control. Moreover, mandatory premerger notification directly restricts the freedom of action of the merging firms by prohibiting the consummation of the merger before certain time periods have elapsed or express clearance has been given. It may therefore be questioned whether international law and rules of comity permit the imposition of such waiting periods on mergers between foreign enterprises merely because the merger may have "perceptible" domestic anticompetitive effects.[145]

This question may also be raised in regard to the Federal Cartel Office's guidelines on the applicability to international mergers of the domestic effects clause of section 98(2) of the Restraints of Competition Act.[146] These guidelines deal with both ex post facto notification under section 23(1) and the mandatory premerger notification requirement under section 24a(1). They distinguish between mergers "realized" domestically and mergers "realized" abroad. The first category, involving the acquisition of shares or assets of enterprises established and operating in Germany (including domestic joint ventures) or the establishment of a controlling influence over such enterprises, is regarded as having domestic effects per se. This category also includes cases covered by sentence 4 of section 23(3).

The second category, which involves the acquisition of shares or assets of enterprises established and operating abroad or the establishment of a controlling influence over such enterprises, is generally considered as having domestic effects "if the merger influences the structural conditions for domestic competition and if at least one domestic enterprise (including subsidiaries and other affiliated enterprises) is participating." In elaborating on this general principle, a further distinction is made in the guidelines between all mergers except joint ventures and joint ventures in particular. Cases of the first kind are considered as having domestic effects per se if both firms were doing business in Germany before the merger, either directly or via subsidiaries, branch offices, or importers. If only one participating firm meets the latter requirement, the merger may have domestic effects if future supplies by another participating firm are likely or if the domestically active participant, as a result of the merger, perceptibly increases its technological potential.

As to joint ventures established abroad, the guidelines indicate that the existence of domestic effects depends primarily on the product and the geographical market in which the joint venture operates.[147] Such a joint venture may also have domestic effects, if (1) a participating foreign enterprise has already been operating in the field of business of the joint venture in domestic territory or if it is reasonably likely that without the merger it will start doing business in that territory, or (2) the domestic enterprise participating in the joint venture acquires such extensive production capacities that its domestic supply capacity is perceptibly changed.

INTERNATIONAL POLICY ASPECTS

The foregoing analysis of merger control law and its application to national and international mergers in three major Western European countries and the European Common Market is only a limited basis for a discussion of the problems of international policies in this area. But even without considering the other merger control systems in the world, particularly that of the United States, the oldest and most stringent in scope, and the reasons why a number of other countries have no merger control at all, this analysis demonstrates two points with special relevance to discovering to what extent international policies in the field of merger control are feasible.

First, there are substantial international differences both in overall political attitudes towards mergers and business concentration in general and in opinion about standards and procedures to be used to control merger activities. Second, more than any other aspect of policy on private restrictive business practices, merger control policy is linked with other governmental policies, particularly those on industry, employment, and foreign trade.

Obviously, the facts that there is much less international agreement about when mergers should be regarded as adverse and what should be done about it, and that merger policy is more closely intertwined with national policy in general, increase the difficulties to be overcome in any international scheme to harmonize national antitrust policies and agree on international action. That it is difficult is reflected by the various attempts made within international organizations, such as the OECD and UNCTAD, and in bilateral negotiations between governments, where merger control has always played a minor role.[148] Even within the supranational context of the European Economic Community, agreement on an international system of merger control is not in sight.

On the other hand, the need for stricter national laws and policies against anticompetitive mergers is increasingly being recognized, as is illustrated by the recent adoption of merger control legislation in France and the current discussion in Germany and the United Kingdom about amending their laws on the subject. Stricter national merger control systems, designed to preserve competitive market structures with at least a minimum of independent sellers, benefit not only domestic competitors and customers but also customers in foreign markets, including developing countries. Of course, independent national sellers may still restrict competition in foreign markets by joining export cartels and similar concerted practices, but national or international action against such practices is more feasible than attempting to deal with the adverse effects of sellers' monopolies or the domination of markets resulting from business concentration outside national boundaries.

In view of the growing international operations and foreign investments of business enterprises, stricter national merger controls, particularly in those countries with wide coverage of international mergers, will increase the need for intergovernmental cooperation. There are several specific reasons for such cooperation: first, the prohibition of mergers with major foreign aspects may interfere with important interests of the governments of those countries. Second, at times it may be more feasible to prevent domestic anticompetitive effects of international mergers by applying the law of another country where the merger also has substantial domestic effects. Finally, a full appraisal of the domestic effects of an international merger may require information on its foreign aspects that only the respective foreign governments can make available. The 1967 OECD Council Recommendation Concerning Co-operation between Member Countries on Restrictive Business Practices Affecting International Trade [149] provides an international mechanism for notifications, consultations, and exchanges of information among governments, and use of these procedures has been made in a large number of cases. [150] There are also bilateral procedures, such as under the 1976 Agreement between the Government of the United States of America and the Government of the Federal Republic of Germany Relating to Mutual Cooperation Regarding Restrictive Business Practices. [151]

The procurement of information on foreign aspects of mergers and business concentration in order to provide a better basis for assessing the full impact of international mergers in the application of national merger control law could also be facilitated if an international documentation center were established to collect all publicly available relevant information on enterprises operating on an international scale and to make it available to governmental agencies and any other interested person or institution.

NOTES

1. The term is used here in its broadest sense. It covers any merger that does not merely involve a purely national transaction, as seen from the country whose merger law is applied (e.g., the acquisition of shares of a company by another company, both of which are chartered under domestic law and have a domestic situs); that includes no affiliated foreign firms; and that has no substantial impact on trade with other countries.

2. For a recent survey of the application of German law concerning abuses by market-dominating enterprises, see Kurt Markert, "The Control of Abuses by Market-Dominating Enterprises under German Antitrust Law," *Cornell International Law Journal* (Summer 1978), 11:275–301. Since the preparation of this article, three cases have been decided by the Berlin Court of Appeals. *See* judgments of April 14, 1978, WuW/E OLG 1983, "Rama" (loyalty rebates as part of a temporary sales promotion action by the leading margarine manufacturer not seen as sufficiently adverse to competitors to warrant a temporary restraining order); of Aug. 24, 1978, WuW/E OLG 2053, "Valium" (partial affirmation of the Federal Cartel Office's order after the Supreme Court's remand for a second trial); and of May

30, 1979, WuW/E OLG 2153, "Sonntag Aktuell I" (reversal of the Federal Cartel Office's temporary restraining order against a market-dominating group of newspaper-publishing companies for allegedly harming competition by tying the distribution of a jointly produced special Sunday newspaper to the purchase of any of their daily papers). As to EEC law (Article 86 of the EEC Treaty), see particularly European Court of Justice, judgments of Feb. 14, 1978, [1978] E.C.R. 207 (United Brands Company), and of Feb. 13, 1979, [1979] E.C.R. 461 (Hoffman-La Roche). British law on abuses by market-dominating firms ("monopolies") is analyzed in *A Review of Monopolies and Mergers Policy* (London: Her Majesty's Stationery Office, 1978, Cmnd. 7198), hereinafter cited as Green Paper.

3. English text in *United Nations Treaty Series* 261:142, and *American Journal of International Law* (Supp. 1952), 46:107.

4. English text in *United Nations Treaty Series* 298:11, and *American Journal of International Law* (October 1957), 51:865–954.

5. Gesetz gegen Wettbewerbsbeschränkungen of July 27, 1957, [1957] Bundesgesetzblatt (BGBl) I 1081, as republished April 4, 1974, [1974] BGBl I 869, amended by law of June 28, 1976, [1976] BGBl I 917, and by law of April 26, 1980, [1980] BGBl I 458 (hereinafter cited as GWB). An English translation of the GWB is published in Organisation for Economic Co-operation and Development (OECD), *Guide to Legislation on Restrictive Business Practices* (Paris: OECD, regularly updated looseleaf), vol. 2, pt. D, §1.0, and in *World Law of Competition,* Julian O. von Kalinowski, ed., vol. B5, *Federal Republic of Germany,* App. I (New York: Mathew Bender, 1979).

6. This definition excludes firms that are "participants" only as affiliates of the direct participants.

7. GWB §24a(1). The amendment of April 26, 1980 provides that compulsory notification shall also apply if one participating firm has annual sales of 2 billion DM or more.

8. In the case of banks, the sales figures are to be replaced by one-tenth of their total assets, and in the case of insurance companies, by their premium income. Only three-fourths of the trading activities of firms are counted. Newspaper enterprises are subject to special rules; see Hermann H. Hollmann, "Antitrust Law and the Protection of Freedom of the Press," *Antitrust Bulletin* (Spring 1979), 24:149–68.

9. GWB §23(1). Notification must be made "without unnecessary delay" after the merger has been consummated. The persons under obligation to notify and the requirements of a "complete" notification are specified in GWB §23(4) and (5).

10. The term *substantial part* includes any part of an enterprise that can be distinguished from the rest of the assets by its "organizational independence, geographical separation or specific production or distribution purposes." *See* Federal Supreme Court, judgment of Nov. 20, 1975, WuW/E BGH 1377, "Zementmahlanlage." In practice, any separable division of a firm is a substantial part, irrespective of its size in relation to the total assets of the firm. *See also* Federal Supreme Court, judgment of March 13, 1979, WuW/E BGH 1570, "Pfaff/IWKA."

11. The amendment of April 26, 1980 provides that a merger also be considered

to exist if shares of less than 25% are acquired, "insofar as the accquiring firm obtains, by means of an agreement, by-laws, articles of association, or a resolution, the legal position held in a joint stock company by a shareholder owning more than 25% of the voting capital."

12. This term covers a majority of the voting capital or a majority of the voting rights. See Stock Corporation Act §16(1), Sept. 6, 1965 as amended. In the case of acquisition of shares of 25% or more of a jointly owned company, the law presumes a merger between the parent companies in relation to the markets in which the joint venture operates; GWB §23(2), no. 2, 3d sentence.

13. GWB §23(2), no. 4. The law requires that at least half of the same persons be represented in the management, supervisory board, or any other managing body of the enterprises involved.

14. GWB §24(8). As a result of the 500 million DM sales requirement, a merger may be subject to ex post facto notification under the market share clause of GWB §23(1), no. 1, but not subject to merger control.

15. The amendment of April 26, 1980 provides that this clause is applicable only if the acquiring firm has annual sales of less than 1 billion DM. If it has sales exceeding that amount, the merger is to be subject to merger control if the acquired firm has annual sales of 2 million DM or more.

16. This clause was deleted by the amendment of April 26, 1980.

17. GWB §24(1). However, under rules of administrative practice developed by the Federal Cartel Office and approved by the Berlin Court of Appeals (*see* judgment of Oct. 6, 1976, WuW/E OLG 1758, "Weichschaum"), the Federal Cartel Office may abstain from prohibiting a merger meeting the requirements of GWB §24(1) if the participating firms give binding assurances that they will take, within a specified period, structural measures, such as divestiture of subsidiaries or assets, that either exclude the market-dominating effect of the merger or bring about sufficient improvements in the competitive conditions. See Alexander R. Riesenkampff and David J. G. Gerber, "German Merger Control: The Role of Company Assurances," *Antitrust Bulletin* (Winter 1977), 22:889–912.

18. GWB §22(1) and (2). For a detailed analysis of the application of GWB §22's definitions of market domination in cases of control of abuses, see Markert, "Control of Abuses," pp. 283–88.

19. The nature of these presumptions is still controversial, particularly whether they are mere administrative guidelines for closer investigation or amount to a shifting of the burden of proof to the firms involved. The Federal Supreme Court decided in a merger case that the Federal Cartel Office must consider any substantiated evidence offered by firms falling under the presumptions indicating that they do not meet the definitions of market domination. *See* judgment of Feb. 21, 1978, WuW/E BGH 1501, "GKN/Sachs."

20. *See* Federal Supreme Court, judgment of Dec. 12, 1978, WuW/E BGH 1533, "Erdgas Schwaben." The "improvements" clause may also be applied in cases of failing companies. *See, e.g.,* Federal Cartel Office (FCO), *Annual Report 1976* (Berlin, 1977), pp. 79–81 (Karstadt-Neckermann case). Statutory law does not contain a special clause on failing companies nor has there been development of a

doctrine on failing companies comparable to that in U.S. antitrust practice. See Kurt Markert, "Auch bei Sanierungsfusionen entscheidet die Wettbewerbsprüfung," *Blick durch die Wirtschaft,* no. 103 (May 5, 1977), p. 4.

21. GWB §24(3).

22. To date, with one exception, the Minister has always asked for such an opinion. Under the amendment of April 26, 1980, a prior opinion by the Monopolies Commission was made compulsory.

23. GWB §§69(1) and 70(2) to (4).

24. *See* Federal Supreme Court, judgment of Oct. 31, 1978, WuW/E BGH 1547, "Weichschaum," granting the right of appeal against the decision of the Federal Cartel Office not to prohibit a merger to a participant in a consummated merger in view of his special property interest only. Even if third parties had the right to appeal, no further action against the merger could be taken after expiration of the intervention periods of one month, four months, or one year after notification.

25. *See, e.g.,* Berlin Court of Appeals, judgment of Feb. 7, 1978, WuW/E OLG 1937, "Thyssen-Hüller."

26. Whether third parties admitted to the proceedings because the decision significantly affects their interests within the meaning of GWB §51(2), no. 4, have a right of appeal is still an open question.

27. See notes 3 and 4 above and Proposal for a Regulation (EEC) of the Council on the Control of Concentration between Undertakings, Doc. COM (73) 1200 (final), 16 O.J. Eur. Comm. (no. C 92) (1973).

28. *See* decision no. 25/67 of June 22, 1967, 10 O.J. Eur. Comm. (no. 154) (1967), as amended by decision of Oct. 20, 1978, 21 O.J. Eur. Comm. (no. L 300) 21 (1978), OECD *Guide,* vol. 6, E.C.S.C., §1.2.4. For example, the minimum aggregate production requirement for crude steel is 5 million tons a year.

29. *See* decision no. 24–54 of May 6, 1954, OECD *Guide,* vol. 6, E.C.S.C., §1.2.1.

30. *See, e.g.,* decisions of April 25, 1962, and Jan. 22, 1964, *ibid.,* §3.0, cases no. 10 (SIDMAR) and no. 15 (SOMOSID).

31. ECSC Treaty, Art. 66, §2.

32. *Ibid.,* Art. 33.

33. *See, e.g.,* decision of Dec. 20, 1974, 17 O.J. Eur. Comm. (no. L 38) 14 (SVH/Chevron). The reasons for the Commission's position are generally stated in its memorandum, Concentration of Enterprises in the Common Market, Doc. SEC (65) 3500 (Dec. 1, 1965), Comm. Mkt. Rep. (CCH), no. 26 (1966). For a critical review of the Commission's position, see Kurt Markert, "Antitrust Aspects of Mergers in the EEC," *Texas International Law Forum* (Spring 1969), 5:46–54.

34. *See* the Commission's decision of Dec. 20, 1974.

35. *See, e.g.,* decisions of July 25, 1977, 20 O.J. Eur. Comm. (no. L 215) 11 (1977) (de Laval/Stork) and of Nov. 23, 1977, 20 O.J. Eur. Comm. (no. L 327) 26 (1977) (GEC/Weir).

36. See generally Lennart R. Ritter and Colin O. Overbury, "An Attempt at a

Practical Approach to Joint Ventures under EEC Rules on Competition," *Common Market Law Review* (1977), 14:602–37.

37. An example of a prohibition order against a joint venture is the decision of Oct. 20, 1978, 21 O.J. Eur. Comm. (no. L 322) 26 (1978) (ICI/Wasagchemie). The Commission seems to be hesitant, however, about applying its policy to the great number of joint ventures already in existence.

38. Judgment of Feb. 21, 1973, case 6/72, [1973] E.C.R. 215, [1971–1973 Transfer Binder] Comm. Mkt. Rep. (CCH) ¶8171.

39. See note 27 above. For a critical analysis of the Commission's draft, see Kurt Markert, "EEC Competition Policy in Relation to Mergers," *Antitrust Bulletin* (Spring 1975), 20:107–41.

40. EEC Draft Merger Regulation, Art. 1(1).

41. *Ibid.*, Art. 1(3).

42. *Ibid.*, Art. 2.

43. *Ibid.*, Art. 4(1).

44. *Ibid.*, Art. 6(2).

45. *Ibid.*, Art. 17(1).

46. *Ibid.*, Art. 7(1). After the decision to commence proceedings, the merger may be put into effect, but the Commission has the power to issue standstill orders; see Art. 7(2).

47. In its *Competition Report 1978,* the Commission again expressed concern that no progress on its proposal had been made. See EC Commission, *Eighth Report on Competition Policy* (Brussels and Luxembourg: European Communities, 1979), p. 20, para. 4.

48. Published in OECD *Guide,* vol. 3, pt. Gb, §1.6 (the act will hereinafter be cited as FTA).

49. FTA secs. 57 to 62. Newspaper mergers are not further discussed in this paper.

50. *Ibid.*, sec. 64.

51. *Ibid.*, sec. 72(2).

52. *Ibid.*, sec. 64(1).

53. *Ibid.*, sec. 65(1).

54. See Office of Fair Trading, *Mergers: A guide to the procedures under the Fair Trading Act 1973* (London: Her Majesty's Stationery Office, 1978), p. 3.

55. *Ibid.*, p. 9.

56. FTA sec. 84(1).

57. See Green Paper, p. 26, which even speaks of a bias of the present legislation in favor of mergers.

58. FTA sec. 73(2).

59. See Green Paper, p. 25.

60. An appeal against an order made by the competent Secretaries of State under the monopolies and mergers legislation has to date apparently only been made in the *Hoffmann-La Roche* case. As a result of a subsequent out-of-court settlement, however, the issue of the reviewing power of the courts in such cases was not

finally settled. See Office of Fair Trading, *Annual Report 1975,* p. 80. On other aspects of the case, see Laurens H. Rhinelander, "The Roche Case: One Giant Step For Antitrust," *Virginia Journal of International Law* (Fall 1974), 15:1–38.

61. Loi relative au controle de la concentration économique et de la répression des ententes illicites et des abus des positions dominantes, *Journal Officiel* (July 20, 1977), p. 3833. An English text is published in OECD *Guide,* vol. 3, pt. F, §1.5. The English text of the bill is published in *Antitrust Bulletin* (Spring 1977), 22:169–87. See also Dominique B. Brault, "Current Developments in Competition Policies," *ibid.,* pp. 157–68.

62. Act of July 19, 1977, sec. 6(1).

63. *Ibid.,* sec. 8(1).

64. *Ibid.,* sec. 4(1).

65. *Ibid.,* sec. 4(2).

66. *Ibid.,* sec. 4(3) to (5).

67. *Ibid.,* sec. 4(7).

68. *Ibid.,* sec. 4(8).

69. *Ibid.,* sec. 8(1).

70. Under sec. 8(1), the measures taken by the Minister must be "within the limits of the opinion of the Competition Commission."

71. Act of July 19, 1977, sec. 6(2).

72. *Ibid.,* sec. 8(3).

73. GWB §23(2), no. 2, 3d sentence.

74. See Green Paper, p. 27.

75. FCO, *Annual Report 1978* (Berlin, 1979), table 2, p. 115. The notification requirement for consummated mergers is also applicable where the merger proposal was previously notified under the premerger notification procedure, if the merger is consummated after clearance. See GWB §24a(3). For an analysis of German merger law, see also Rolf Belke and W. David Braun, "German Merger Control: A European Approach to Anticompetitive Takeovers," *Northwestern Journal of International Law and Business* (Autumn 1979), 1:369–449.

76. FCO, *Annual Report 1978,* table 2, p. 115.

77. *Ibid.*

78. *Ibid.* In 8 out of 109 cases of advance notification, the merger plan was dropped afterward; in 4 cases merger control was not applicable because of GWB §24(8); and in 1 case of an optional advance notification, the merger was consummated before clearance.

79. A complete list of all cases appears in FCO, *Annual Report 1978,* table 2a, p. 116.

80. *See* decisions of Feb. 1, 1974, WuW/E BWM 147, "Veba/Gelsenberg"; of Oct. 17, 1976, WuW/E BWM 155, "Babcock/Artos"; of Aug. 1, 1977, WuW/E BWM 159, "Thyssen/Hüller"; and of March 3, 1979, WuW/E BWM 165, "Veba/BP." *See also* decision of June 25, 1975, WuW/E BWM 149, refusing to grant an exemption in the *VAW/Kaiser Aluminium* case.

81. *See, e.g.,* FCO, *Annual Report 1975* (Berlin, 1976), p. 37 (Siemens-Osram) and p. 40 (Bayer-Metzeler); and *Annual Report 1977* (Berlin, 1978), p. 52 (Krupp-Iran).

82. FCO, *Annual Report 1978*, table 2, p. 115.

83. Unofficial estimates by the Federal Cartel Office speak of about thirty such cases.

84. Judgment of Dec. 16, 1976, WuW/E BGH 1445, 1449, "Valium." That the term *scope of action* is not merely another conduct test comparable to the test of not being exposed to substantial competition is made clear by the Supreme Court judgments of Feb. 21, 1978, WuW/E BGH 1501 (GKN/Sachs), and of Dec. 12, 1978, WuW/E BGH 1533, "Erdgas Schwaben." *But see also* judgment of Dec. 2, 1980, WuW/E BGH 1749, "Klöckner-Becorit."

85. See GWB §22(2).

86. *See* judgment of Feb. 7, 1978, WuW/E OLG 1921, "Thyssen-Hüller." The Economics Minister in this case granted an exemption under GWB §24(3) for a 45% shareholding, so that Thyssen is required to divest the remaining 55%; see note 80 above. For further examples of prohibition orders against horizontal mergers of firms not yet dominant before the merger, see Federal Cartel Office decisions of March 25, 1976, WuW/E BKartA 1653, "Babcock-Artos" (aggregate market share approximately 60%), and of Dec. 15, 1978, [1979] AG 111, "Klöckner/Becorit" (aggregate market share approximately 50%). *See,* however, Berlin Court of Appeals, judgment of May 18, 1979, WuW/E OLG 2120, "Mannesmann-Brueninghaus," reversing a Federal Cartel Office order on the ground that a market share of 21.9% was not enough to constitute a paramount market position in relation to competitors, where the two largest competitors each had shares of 11% and were similar to Mannesmann in size. The Federal Cartel Office has appealed to the Supreme Court.

87. *See, e.g.,* Berlin Court of Appeals, judgment of March 15, 1978, WuW/E OLG 1998, "Klöckner/Hansa Zement" (increase by 4.3%) (*affirmed* by Federal Supreme Court, judgment of Oct. 23, 1979, WuW/E BGH 1700); FCO decision of March 31, 1978, WuW/E BKartA 1747, "Anzag-Holdermann."

88. *See* decisions of Jan. 7, 1974, WuW/E BKartA 1457, "Veba/Gelsenberg"; of Feb. 4, 1974, WuW/E BKartA 1475, "Haindl/Holzmann"; of May 29, 1974, WuW/E BKartA 1517, "Bitumen-Verkaufsgesellschaft"; of Dec. 23, 1974, WuW/E BKartA 1571, "Kaiser/VAW"; of May 24, 1978, WuW/E BKartA 1753, "Makadam"; and of March 30, 1979, WuW/E BKartA 1799, "Metallgesellschaft/Tonolli."

89. Decision of Feb. 4, 1974, WuW/E BKartA 1475.

90. Bill of May 17, 1978, Art. 1, no. 4 (§23a(2)).

91. In the amendment of April 26, 1980 (see note 5 above), the oligopoly clause proposed in the Government's bill was modified in several respects. The presumption under the modified text is only a rebuttable one; it can be rebutted if the affected firms "prove that the conditions for competition are such that it can be expected that there will be substantial competition between them." On the other hand, the modified clause also applies to oligopolies where the leading four or five

firms have a market share of two-thirds. Finally, the restriction of the clause to large markets with 500 million DM was deleted. The minimum firm size needed to make the clause applicable was changed to 150 million DM.

92. *See, e.g.,* FCO, *Annual Report 1975,* p. 40 (Bayer/Metzeler). Bayer, the dominant supplier of foam raw materials and polyurethane textile coating materials, acquired the Metzeler group, the leading producer of polyurethane foam and polyurethane artificial leather. The case was settled after Bayer had given assurances that it would divest itself of Metzeler Schaum GmbH, the relevant firm of the Metzeler group, before the end of 1979. *See also* Berlin Court of Appeals, judgment of March 15, 1979, WuW/E OLG 2113, upholding the Federal Cartel Office's prohibition order in the *RWE/Steag* case, *inter alia,* on the ground that RWE, as a market-dominating supplier of electricity, strengthened its position by acquiring a minority shareholding in Steag, a major electricity-generating firm.

93. Judgment of Feb. 21, 1978, WuW/E BGH 1501. Although GKN manufactured automobile clutches in the United Kingdom, the case was not tried as a potential competition case. Potential competition was also an issue in the *RWE/Steag* case. For a similar case, see the Federal Cartel Office's decision of Nov. 18, 1974, WuW/E BKartA 1561, "Hahn/Johnson & Johnson," *rev'd on procedural grounds,* Berlin Court of Appeals, judgment of Feb. 16, 1976, WuW/E OLG 1712.

94. For comments on the *Sachs* case, see Karlheinz Moosecker in *Gewerblicher Rechtsschutz und Urheberrecht* (Sept. 1978), 80:517–26; Ernst Steindorff in *Zeitschrift für Unternehmens- und Gesellschaftsrecht* (1977), 7:778; Kurt Markert in *Der Betriebs-Berater* (May 1978), 33:678–81; and Christian Hootz in *ibid.* (June 1978), 33:826–27.

95. See FCO, *Annual Report 1977,* p. 20.

96. Bill of May 17, 1978, Art. 1, no. 4 (§23(1)).

97. See Kurt Markert, "Zusätzliche Eingreifkriterien sollen die Fusionskontrolle verbessern," *Blick durch die Wirtschaft,* no. 125 (May 31, 1979), p. 4.

98. *See, e.g.,* decision of March 9, 1976, WuW/E BKartA 1647, "Erdgas Schwaben," concerning a joint venture set up by two electricity companies for the distribution of natural gas. The Supreme Court, by judgment of December 12, 1978, WuW/E BGH 1533, affirmed the finding that the merger strengthened the dominant position of the parent companies regarding electricity by restraining competition between electricity and natural gas, but remanded the case to the Court of Appeals for a new trial on the question whether the merger improved the conditions for competition by increasing competition with fuel oil.

99. *See, e.g.,* FCO, *Annual Report 1978,* p. 54 (Daimler-Benz/Iveco: plan to establish a jointly owned subsidiary by the two leading manufacturers of trucks for the development, production, and sale of automatic gears dropped after FCO raised objections), and *1977,* p. 57 (Bosch/Pierburg: jointly owned subsidiary of the leading manufacturers of electrical appliances for automobiles and of carburetors to develop an electronically controlled carburetor cleared only after the joint venture was limited to the probable development time). *See also* FCO, *Annual Report 1978,*

p. 52 (BMW/Steyr-Daimler-Puch: joint venture of two smaller manufacturers of motor vehicles for the development and production of diesel engines cleared).

100. *See* the *Erdgas Schwaben* (WuW/E BKartA 1647) and *Bosch/Pierburg* (FCO, *Annual Report 1977*, p. 57) cases.

101. *See* the *Daimler-Benz/Iveco* case (FCO, *Annual Report 1978*, p. 54).

102. *See* decision of May 29, 1974, WuW/E BKartA 1517, involving a joint selling company to be established by several oil companies for the distribution of liquid-asphalt products.

103. *See* decision of June 27, 1975, [1975] BB 1314, "Bitumen-Verkaufsgesell-schaft." The application of the parent companies for a cartel exemption was rescinded in 1978; see FCO, *Annual Report 1978*, p. 47.

104. For elaborate discussions of this problem, see Ulrich Huber and Bodo Börner, "Gemeinschaftsunternehmen im deutschen und europäischen Wettbewerbs-recht," Forschungsinstitut für Wirtschaftsverfassung und Wettwerb, Heft no. 80 (Cologne, 1978); Ernst-Joachim Mestmäcker, "Gemeinschaftsunternehmen im deutschen und europäischen Konzern- und Kartellrecht," in Mestmäcker, *Recht und ökonomisches Gesetz* (Baden-Baden, 1978), p. 342.

105. FCO, *Annual Report 1978*, pp. 23–24.

106. This position corresponds to ECSC practice; see note 30 above and accompanying text.

107. Judgment of Dec. 12, 1978, WuW/E BGH 1533, "Erdgas Schwaben" (joint venture for the distribution of natural gas to households as a competitive alternative to fuel oil; the case is currently pending on remand to the Berlin Court of Appeals).

108. *See* FCO, *Annual Report 1976*, pp. 79–81.

109. The interest was meanwhile sold to Horten AG, another department store firm. For other failing company cases "saved" by application of the "improvements" defense, see FCO, *Annual Report 1975*, p. 42 (WAZ/NRZ); *1976*, p. 44 (Bente-ler/Niederrheinstahl); and *1978*, p. 50 (ARBED/Neunkircher Eisenwerk). *But see also* Berlin Court of Appeals, judgment of Feb. 7, 1977, WuW/E OLG 1921, "Thyssen/Hüller," refusing to apply the defense in a case of acquisition of a leading firm.

110. The *Veba/Gelsenberg* and *Veba/BP* cases, cited in note 80 above.

111. The *Babcock/Artos* case, cited in note 80 above.

112. The *Thyssen/Hüller* case, cited in note 80 above. In this case the exemption was restricted to a 45% shareholding. The appeal by Thyssen against this restriction was rejected. *See* Berlin Court of Appeals, judgment of Feb. 7, 1977, WuW/E 1937, "Thyssen/Hüller."

113. See note 80 above.

114. See EC Commission, *Seventh Report on Competition Policy* (Brussels and Luxembourg: European Communities, 1978), p. 290, and *Eighth Competition Report*, p. 266. In some cases authorization was only given subject to certain restrictions.

115. See EC Commission, *Seventh Competition Report*, p. 140.

116. See EC Commission, *Eighth Competition Report*, p. 112.

117. *See* High Authority, decision no. 16–60 of June 22, 1960, OECD *Guide,* vol. 6, E.C.S.C., §3.0, case no. 6; and European Court of Justice, judgment of May 18, 1962, [1962] E.C.R. 183.

118. EC Commission, decision of Nov. 27, 1969, OECD *Guide,* vol. 6, E.C.S.C., §3.0, case no. 32.

119. 13 O.J. Eur. Comm. (no. C 12) 5 (1970). See also EC Commission, *Third Report on Competition Policy* (Brussels and Luxembourg: European Communities, 1974), p. 64, para. 70, outlining the situation after the accession of the United Kingdom to the Common Steel Market.

120. *See, e.g.,* decision of Jan. 21, 1970, OECD *Guide,* vol. 6, E.C.S.C., §3.0, case no. 33 (Thyssen/Mannesmann); of Dec. 20, 1973, 17 O.J. Eur. Comm. (no. L 84) 36 (1974) (Thyssen/Rheinstahl); of Nov. 20, 1974, 18 O.J. Eur. Comm. (no. L 49) 1 (1975) (Thyssen/Solmer); and of Dec. 5, 1974, OECD *Guide,* vol. 6, E.C.S.C., §3.0, case no. 43 (British Steel Corporation/Johnson & Forth Brown Ltd.).

121. EC Commission, *Seventh Competition Report,* p. 140.

122. See EC Commission, *Eleventh Report on the Activities of the European Communities* (Brussels and Luxembourg: European Communities, 1978), p. 94, paras. 148–52.

123. See text accompanying notes 35 and 36 above. See also on the application of Article 85 to "concern" agreements: EC Commission, *Seventh Competition Report,* p. 34, paras. 29–32.

124. See note 38 above.

125. See, e.g., EC Commission, *Third Competition Report,* p. 68, para. 75 (Thyssen/Rheinstahl): and *Sixth Report on Competition Policy* (Brussels and Luxembourg: European Communities, 1977), p. 107, para. 182 (GKN/Sachs).

126. See EC Commission, *Eighth Competition Report,* pp. 116–18, including the case of the acquisition by Peugeot-Citroen of the European automobile activities of Chrysler Corporation.

127. See Green Paper, p. 108 (App., table 3).

128. *Ibid.,* p. 111 (App., table 7).

129. *Ibid.* In the latter case (*Redfearn National Glass Ltd.*) the Commission later found that the merger was against the public interest.

130. For an analysis of cases, see Valentine Korah, *Competition Law of Britain and the Common Market* (London: Elek, 1975); J. D. Gribbin, "Recent Antitrust Developments in the United Kingdom," *Antitrust Bulletin* (Summer 1975), 20:377.

131. Green Paper, pp. 35–38. In the Government's bill of July 12, 1979, to amend the existing legislation on restrictive business practices (Competition Act 1979), no changes in merger control law were proposed.

132. EC Commission, *Eighth Competition Report,* p. 70, para. 62.

133. See *Bulletin Officiel des Services des Prix* (May 19, 1979), 39:139. According to the Commission's findings, the merger results in joint control of 80% of French production capacity. The beneficial effects of the merger were seen by the Commission in the amelioration of the ability of the participating firms to rationalize and specialize production and to increase exports. A second case, involving the

takeover of the French television rental firm Locatel by the British firm Thorn Electrical Industries, is at present still pending before the Commission.

134. As to the meaning of the term *international merger,* see note 1 above.

135. In cases covered by Articles 65 and 66, the treaty also applies to "any enterprise or organisation regularly engaged in distribution other than sale to domestic consumers or to craft industries."

136. FTA sec. 64(1).

137. *See* Federal Supreme Court, judgment of May 29, 1979, WuW/E BGH 1613 (Bayer/Allied Chemical).

138. See Explanatory Memorandum to the Government Bill for a Second Amendment of the GWB, Bundestag Doc. VI/2520 (1971), p. 27.

139. GWB §24(3).

140. *See, e.g.,* as to German law, *Sachs/GKN* case (note 93); as to ECSC law, *Texaco/Deutsche Erdöl AG* case (OECD *Guide,* vol. 6, E.C.S.C. §3.0, case no. 25); as to EEC law, *Continental Can Co.* case (note 38); as to British law, *Dentists Supply Co. of New York/Amalgamated Dental Ltd.* and *FMC Corp./Alginate Industries Ltd.* cases (note 127); and as to French law, *Vallourec/Tubes de la Providence* case (note 133).

141. See, e.g., FCO, *Annual Report 1978,* p. 61, reporting that eight cases in which German firms acquired shares or assets of U.S. firms were investigated for anticompetitive effects on the German market. No case of this type has been prohibited as yet.

142. As to precedents established in national merger cases of this type, see those mentioned in notes 87 and 93. Meanwhile, a first international case of this type has been decided. *See* FCO decision of Sept. 23, 1980, WuW/E BKartA 1837, "Bayer-Firestone"; *rev'd* by Berlin Court of Appeals, judgment of Nov. 26, 1980, to be published in *Recht der Internationalen Wirtschaft* (June 1981), vol. 27. On this case, see also Carsten T. Ebenroth and Karlheinz Autenrieth, "Die Fusionskontrolle beim Zusammehschluss ausländischer Unterhehmen unter direkter Beteiligung eines inländischen Unternehmens, "*Der Betriebs-Berater* (1981), 36:16–24.

143. See particularly GWB §98(2) in German antitrust law.

144. Judgment of May 29, 1979, WuW/E BGH 1613 (acquisition of the organic pigments division of Allied Chemical Corp. by Harmon Colors Corp., a subsidiary of Rhinechem Corp. controlled by Bayer/Germany). *See also* Berlin Court of Appeals, judgment of April 5, 1978, WuW/E OLG 1993, "Bayer/Allied Chemical."

145. For a critical view, see Karl Matthias Meessen, "Zusammenschlusskontrolle in auslandsbezogenen Sachverhalten," *Zeitschrift für das gesamte Handels- und Wirtschaftsrecht* (1979), 143:273–87.

146. FCO, *Annual Report 1975,* p. 45. English text in appendix to this paper.

147. See GWB §23(2), no. 2, 3d sentence, providing that the parent companies of a joint venture are regarded to have merged in the markets in which the joint venture is operating.

148. See, e.g., OECD Guidelines for Multinational Enterprises ("Competition Guidelines"), annex to OECD Declaration on International Investment and Multinational Enterprises of June 21, 1976. On mergers, the guidelines in paragraph

1 merely provide that "Enterprises should . . . refrain from actions which would adversely affect competition in the relevant market by abusing a dominant position of power, by means of, for example, (a) anti-competitive acquisitions." For a discussion of the guidelines in general and in regard to merger control, see Barry E. Hawk, "The OECD Guidelines for Multinational Enterprises: Competition," *Fordham Law Review* (Nov. 1977), 46:241–76; Joel Davidow, "Some Reflections on the OECD Competition Guidelines," *Antitrust Bulletin* (Summer 1977), 22:441–58. See also OECD, *Mergers and Competition Policy* (Paris: OECD, 1974), which is limited on the question of future action by OECD member countries to suggesting to those that have not yet done so "to consider the adoption of an effective system of merger control," and to drawing attention to OECD consultation and conciliation procedures. The UNCTAD Secretariat's first draft of a "Model Law or Laws on Restrictive Business Practices to Assist Developing Countries in Devising Appropriate Legislation," Doc. TD/B/C.2/AC.6/16 of June 1, 1978, contains detailed proposals on premerger notification and on merger control, but the prospects for adopting those proposals are apparently dim. See also UNCTAD Secretariat, "Considerations for the Drafting of a Model Law or Laws on Restrictive Business Practices to Assist Developing Countries in Devising Appropriate Legislation," reprinted in *Antitrust Bulletin* (Winter 1977), 22:831–55.

149. OECD Doc. C (67) 53 (final), reprinted in *Antitrust Bulletin* (Summer 1968), 13:370–72.

150. According to an OECD report, 29 notifications concerning mergers and acquisitions were made during the period 1967–1975. See OECD, Report on the Operation of the 1967 Council Recommendation Concerning Co-operation between Member Countries on Restrictive Business Practices Affecting International Trade during the Period 1967–1975, reprinted in *Antitrust Bulletin* (Summer 1977), 22:459–85.

151. *U.S. Treaties and other International Agreements* 37:1956, *Treaties and Other International Acts* no. 8291, [1978] 5 Trade Reg. Rep. (CCH) ¶50,283.

Appendix

◇

FEDERAL CARTEL OFFICE GUIDELINES ON DOMESTIC EFFECTS WITHIN THE MEANING OF SECTION 98(2) OF THE ACT AGAINST RESTRAINTS OF COMPETITION IN THE CASE OF MERGERS*

For an interpretation of the term "domestic effect" within the meaning of Section 98(2), the protective purpose of the relevant provision of the Act to be applied in each case must be considered (Federal Supreme Court decision of July 12, 1973, WuW/E "Ölfeldrohre").

The purpose of Sections 23 et seq. is to cover concentration because it may impair competition. The term "restraints of competition" in Section 98(2) sums up restraints of competition regulated in the relevant provisions of the Act. With regard to Sections 23 et seq., the restraint of competition within the meaning of Section 98(2) is the merger process as such. It is irrelevant whether the intensity of domestic competition is actually reduced by a merger.

A. Domestic effects within the meaning of Section 98(2) are, therefore, present *whenever* a merger is completed *within the Federal Republic* (e.g., acquisition of the assets or the shares of a domestic enterprise, formation of a joint venture within the Federal Republic—even where the acquirers or the founders are foreign enterprises). As regards the domestic subsidiaries of the participating enterprises, a merger effected abroad is held to be a merger completed in the Federal Republic (Section 23(3), sentence 4 of the ARC).

B. *Mergers completed abroad* have domestic effects if the merger affects the structural conditions for domestic competition and if the domes-

---

*The German text is published in Federal Cartel Office, *Annual Report 1975*, p. 45. The above text is an unofficial translation by the Federal Cartel Office.

tic enterprise (including subsidiaries and other affiliated companies) is a party to the merger.

1. As regards mergers effected abroad *between two directly participating enterprises only* (all merger situations except for the formation of joint ventures—e.g., acquisition of the assets or the shares of a foreign enterprise by a domestic enterprise):

   a) there are domestic effects, if both enterprises were already operating in the Federal Republic before the merger either directly or through subsidiaries, branches or importers;

   b) there may be domestic effects, if only one of the enterprises was operating in the Federal Republic before the merger but if, for instance,

      aa) after the merger a foreign party to the merger is likely to deliver goods to the Federal Republic owing to production links with the domestic party (preceding or subsequent production stages) or to links relating to the range of products. Whether such future deliveries to the Federal Republic are likely usually depends on whether goods of the same or a similar kind are already covered by trade between the countries involved and whether there are no technical and administrative trade barriers to such deliveries;

      bb) the know-how of a domestic enterprise is perceptibly enhanced or industrial property rights accrue to it as a result of the merger.

2. As regards the *formation of joint ventures* abroad, the domestic effect primarily depends on the product and geographical markets in which the joint venture operates. The question of when a joint venture's activities have domestic effects is determined on the principles set out under B.1.; in this connection the production links and/or links affecting the range of products have to be judged by the relationship between the joint venture and the domestic party.

   Furthermore, the formation of a joint venture abroad may also have domestic effects, if

   a) a foreign enterprise participating in the joint venture was already operating in the joint venture's field of activity within the Federal Republic before the merger or if it can be reasonably expected to enter the domestic market without the merger (cf. B.1. aa);

   b. the domestic party to the joint venture thereby obtains additional production capacity which perceptibly alters its capacity available for domestic supply (substitution of domestic production destined for exportation by production abroad). In general, for a change in capacity to be perceptible, a prerequisite is that the domestic party enjoyed a strong market position before the merger.

Commentary

Mark R. Joelson

This note has been prepared as a brief summary of the United States antitrust law relating to mergers and acquisitions. It is intended to be read in connection with the paper of Kurt Markert entitled "Merger Control in Western Europe: National and International Aspects."

THE STATUTORY FRAMEWORK AND ENFORCEMENT

The statute primarily applicable to the antitrust aspects of mergers and acquisitions is section 7 of the Clayton Act. It provides:

> No person engaged in commerce or in any activity affecting commerce shall acquire, directly or indirectly, the whole or any part of the stock or other share capital and no person subject to the jurisdiction of the Federal Trade Commission shall acquire the whole or any part of the assets of another person engaged also in commerce or in any activity affecting commerce, where in any line of commerce or in any activity affecting commerce in any section of the country, the effect of such acquisition may be substantially to lessen competition, or to tend to create a monopoly.[1]

The Federal Trade Commission and the Justice Department have concurrent jurisdiction to enforce section 7. Under the statute, it need not be shown that the acquiring firm had a market-dominating position before the merger or even that the merger actually substantially lessens competition or creates a monopoly at the time of challenge. Since the law is an "incipiency" statute, it is sufficient for the Government (or, in some cases, a private plaintiff) to establish that there is a "reasonable probability" that the merger may produce such anticompetitive effects in the future.[2] The remedy normally sought is an injunction of the merger or, if it has already taken place, a divestiture that will restore the competitive situation.

Mergers or acquisitions may also be challenged by the Federal Trade Commission under an incipiency test pursuant to section 5 of the Federal Trade Commission Act,[3] which declares unlawful "[u]nfair methods of competition in or affecting commerce." Moreover, mergers or acquisitions may be challenged under sections 1 and 2 of the Sherman Act,[4] but, since the standards are more stringent than those of the Clayton Act, little use is made of the Sherman Act in this connection.[5]

In order to avoid duplication of effort, the Federal Trade Commission and the Justice Department participate in a joint clearance program on matters under their joint jurisdiction, including mergers. Which agency is to pursue a particular proceeding turns on such factors as past experience in an industry, present manpower, and remedies available to each agency.[6] Since 1968, the Department of Justice has had publicly available, as a statement of enforcement policy, guidelines outlining the Department's standards for determining whether it will oppose corporate acquisitions or mergers.[7]

APPLICATION OF THE LAW

For application of section 7, an anticipated lessening of competition must be established in the context of a relevant product market (the line of commerce) and a relevant geographic market ("any section of the country"). "The outer boundaries of a product market are determined by the reasonable interchangeability of use or the cross-elasticity of demand between the product itself and substitutes for it. However, within this broad market, well-defined submarkets may exist which, in themselves, constitute product markets for antitrust purposes."[8] Indicia of a product submarket include industry or public recognition of the submarket as a separate economic entity, the product's peculiar characteristics and uses, unique production facilities, distinct customers, distinct prices, sensitivity to price changes, and specialized vendors.[9]

As to the relevant geographic area, "Congress prescribed a pragmatic, factual approach . . . and not a formal, legalistic one. The geographic market selected must, therefore, both 'correspond to the commercial realities' of the industry and be economically significant. Thus, although the geographic market in some instances may encompass the entire Nation, under other circumstances it may be as small as a single metropolitan area."[10] Economic factors that tend to confine the relevant area may include significant transportation costs, lack of distribution facilities, customer inconvenience, or established consumer preferences.[11]

HORIZONTAL MERGERS

A horizontal merger is one between two actual competitors in the same product and geographic markets or submarkets. The emphasis, in appraising such mergers, is on the size of the market shares held by the merging firms and on the level of concentration of the market. In *United States v. Philadelphia National Bank,* the Supreme Court stated that "a merger which produces a firm controlling an undue percentage share of the relevant market, and results in a significant increase in the concentration of firms in that market, is so inherently likely to lessen competition substantially that it must be enjoined in the absence of evidence clearly showing that the merger is not likely to have such anticompetitive effects."[12]

Where a market shows a trend toward concentration, a combination of relatively small market shares may be held unlawful. For example, in *United States v. Von's Grocery Co.,* a merger involving market shares of 4.7 percent and 4.2 percent, for the third and sixth largest firms in the market, was struck down.[13] Likewise, the Department of Justice Merger Guidelines state that, in a market in which the shares of the four largest firms amount to approximately 75 percent or more, the Department will ordinarily challenge mergers between firms accounting for, approximately, the following percentages of the market:[14]

Acquiring Firm	Acquired Firm
4%	4% or more
10%	2% or more
15% or more	1% or more

Other measures of anticompetitive effect include the triggering of additional mergers, erection of barriers to entry, and acquisition by a substantial firm of one that possesses an unusual competitive advantage. On the other hand, as the Merger Guidelines indicate, a merger the Government would otherwise challenge "will ordinarily not be challenged if (i) the resources of one of the merging firms are so depleted and its prospects for rehabilitation so remote that the firm faces the clear probability of a business failure, and (ii) good faith efforts by the failing firm have failed to elicit a reasonable offer of acquisition more consistent with the purposes of Section 7 by a firm which intends to keep the failing firm in the market." [15]

VERTICAL MERGERS

Vertical mergers are those in which the participating companies are positioned so as to be in a supplier-customer relationship. "The primary vice of a vertical merger or other arrangement tying a customer to a supplier is that, by foreclosing the competitors of either party from a segment of the market otherwise open to them, the arrangement may act as a 'clog on competition' . . . which 'deprive[s] . . . rivals of a fair opportunity to compete.' " [16] Vertical integration may raise barriers to entry in either the supplying or the purchasing market, as well as disadvantage existing competitors. The effect of such foreclosure is measured in terms of the market share of sales of the supplying firm and the market share of purchases of the buying firm. Other pertinent factors may include the trend towards integration or concentration in the relevant market, the financial resources of the merging parties, and the purpose of the acquisition. [17]

CONGLOMERATE MERGERS

Conceptually, conglomerate mergers may be one of three basic types: (1) *market-extension,* where two firms sell the same product, but in different geographic markets; (2) *product-extension,* where the product lines of the acquired firm àre complementary to the business of the acquiring firm; and (3) *"pure" conglomerate,* where the two firms' businesses have no such economic relationship.

The elimination of potential competition is a particular concern with respect to market-extension or product-extension mergers. As the Merger Guidelines enunciate, "potential competition (*i.e.,* the threat of entry, either through internal expansion or through acquisition and expansion of a small firm, by firms not already or only marginally in the market) may often be the most significant competitive limitation on the exercise of market power by leading firms, as well as the most likely source of additional actual competition. . . ." [18] Applying a "perceived potential entrant" theory, the Supreme Court has held that, where the firms in a concentrated market perceive a firm outside the market as likely to enter and moderate their conduct accordingly, the firm may not acquire a leading firm in the market. [19] While the Supreme Court has reserved the question of the applicability of section 7 to "actual potential entrants," the Federal Trade

Commission has taken the position that the statute bars a company from acquiring a leading firm in a concentrated market when the acquiring company would otherwise be likely to enter the market *de novo* or by acquisition of a smaller firm.[20]

A conglomerate merger that will enable the resulting firm to use purchasing power to induce suppliers to buy from it can be struck down under section 7. "Reciprocity" has been described as "one of the congeries of anti-competitive practices at which the antitrust laws are aimed."[21]

A theory of "entrenchment" has also been articulated in the conglomerate context. The reasoning is that, if the acquiring firm has great financial resources (a "deep pocket"), it may use those resources so as to give the acquired company a significant advantage over existing competitors, as well as to raise barriers to new entry.[22] However, the likelihood of specific, anticompetitive advantages must be established; it is not enough simply to show that the acquiring firm has a deep pocket.[23]

APPLICABILITY OF ANTIMERGER LAW TO JOINT VENTURES

In *United States v. Penn-Olin Chem Co.*,[24] the U.S. Supreme Court held that section 7 of the Clayton Act applies to joint ventures. The Court reasoned that the formation of a new corporate offspring by two separate corporate parents and the acquisition of the offspring's stock by each of the parents was an "acquisition" within the meaning of section 7. The Court also reasoned that "[o]verall, the same considerations apply to joint ventures as to mergers," with section 7 not requiring proof of actual restraint but merely a showing of a tendency toward monopoly or the reasonable likelihood of a substantial lessening of competition in the relevant market.[25] Section 5 of the Federal Trade Commission Act is also potentially applicable to joint ventures.

In the *Penn-Olin* decision, Mr. Justice Clark listed some fifteen factors which are to be taken into account in assessing the lawfulness of a joint venture. These include, *inter alia*, the number and power of the competitors in the relevant market; the competition existing between the joint venturers; the reasons and necessities for the venture's existence; an appraisal of what the competition in the relevant market would have been if one of the joint venturers had entered it alone instead of through the joint venture; the effect, in the event of this occurrence, of the other joint venturer's potential competition; and such other factors as might indicate potential risk to competition in the relevant market.[26]

PREMERGER NOTIFICATION

Prior to the passage of Title II of the Hart-Scott-Rodino Antitrust Improvements Act of 1976,[27] the Federal Trade Commission maintained a premerger notification requirement in cases where the merger resulted in combined sales or assets for the merged company in excess of $250 million. Under the new statute, and rules promulgated thereunder, which went into effect on September 5, 1978, acquisitions of assets or voting securities of specified size or larger involving "persons" of specified size or larger must be reported to the Antitrust Division of the Department of Justice and to the Federal Trade Commission.

The "size-of-person" test essentially provides that the act reaches transactions where one of the parties to the transaction has sales or assets of $100 million or more and the other has sales or assets of $10 million or more. The "size-of-transaction" test provides that the act applies to transactions between two persons meeting the size-of-person test if, as a result of the transaction, the acquiring person will hold at least 15 percent of either the assets or the voting securities of the acquired person or more than $15 million worth of the assets or voting securities of the acquired person.

The reporting process requires the submission of detailed information and documentary material concerning the proposed transaction. Of particular importance is the requirement that, following submittal of the reports, the parties must wait a prescribed period of time before the transaction may legally be consummated. A violation of the statutory requirements may bring penalties of up to $10,000 per day for violations. This new law has given the Government important new procedural powers, enabling it to preclude "midnight mergers." The reporting and waiting requirements give the enforcement agencies sufficient information and an opportunity to determine in advance whether to seek to enjoin a proposed transaction.

Although the statute does not mention joint ventures, the Federal Trade Commission believes that it was intended to reach them when an acquisition of voting securities occurs.[28]

INTERNATIONAL APPLICATION

The more important merger cases having international implications have been brought under section 7 of the Clayton Act. As the Department of Justice's *Antitrust Guide for International Operations* points out, section 7 can be applied where an American firm seeks to buy a foreign company that already competes directly in the U.S. market; it can also be applied where the American firm is acquiring a foreign firm that is a major potential entrant in a U.S. market. "Here the inquiry will be whether (1) the U.S. market (or relevant local market) is highly concentrated; (2) the foreign firm is by virtue of its capability of entering the market one of a relatively small group of potential entrants; (3) the foreign firm has the incentives to enter the U.S. market; and (4) the foreign firm has the capability of entering the market or threatening to enter." [29] The same type of reasoning can be applied where in form the foreign firm is acquiring the American firm. [30] The *Guide's* of discussion is, however, somewhat obsolete because of the 1980 amendments to section 7 which substituted "persons" for "corporations" and further extended the statute to cover merger or joint venture activity "affecting commerce."

In a situation in which the merger is of two foreign corporations, the theoretical and economic analysis is the same. However, in this context, problems of extraterritoriality, comity, and other jurisdictional aspects may well be severe, often sufficiently so to prompt an enforcement decision not to attack the transaction. In one case, however, where two large Swiss chemical companies agreed to merge their worldwide operations, including their respective U.S. subsidiaries, the Justice Department brought suit under section 7 and obtained a consent settlement with respect to the activities of the U.S. subsidiaries. [31]

Multinational joint ventures also can be attacked under section 7 or section 5 where they pose the requisite threat to U.S. commerce and otherwise meet the jurisdictional standards. [32]

CONCLUSIONS

Control of mergers is, relatively speaking, quite stringent in the United States. While it has occasionally been suggested that the Government's decision not to attack a particular transaction was inspired by political, rather than legal, considerations, this situation is the exception rather than the rule. A trend in court decisions in favor of the defendants in conglomerate merger cases has spurred the administration and some legislators to propose new legislation that, in effect, would put the burden of justifying the merger on the parties in the case of large consolidations. One proposal, for example, would bar certain sizable combinations in terms of assets or sales unless the parties could show that the preponderant effect of the acquisition would be substantially to increase competition. At the time of this writing, however, the passage of such legislation is not imminent.

NOTES

1. 15 U.S.C. §18.
2. FTC v. Procter & Gamble Co., 386 U.S. 568, 577 (1967); United States v. Phillips Petroleum Co., 367 F.Supp. 1226 (C.D. Cal. 1973), *aff'd mem.*, 418 U.S. 906 (1974).
3. 15 U.S.C. §45.
4. 15 U.S.C. §§1–2.
5. *See, e.g.,* United States v. First National Bank & Trust Co. of Lexington, 376 U.S. 665 (1964); United States v. Columbia Steel Co., 334 U.S. 495 (1948).
6. American Bar Association, *Antitrust Law Developments* (Chicago: The Bar Association, 1975), pp. 231–32.
7. Department of Justice, Merger Guidelines, 1 Trade Reg. Rep. (CCH) ¶4, 510.
8. Brown Shoe Co. v. United States, 370 U.S. 294, 325 (1962).
9. 370 U.S. at 325–26.
10. 370 U.S. at 336–37.
11. Merger Guidelines, 1 Trade Reg. Rep. (CCH), p. 6883.
12. United States v. Philadelphia National Bank, 374 U.S. 321, 363 (1963).
13. 384 U.S. 270 (1966).
14. Merger Guidelines, 1 Trade Reg. Rep. (CCH), p. 6884.
15. *Ibid. See also* Citizens Publishing Co. v. United States, 394 U.S. 131 (1969); International Shoe Co. v. FTC, 280 U.S. 291 (1930).
16. Brown Shoe Co. v. United States, 370 U.S. 294, 323–24 (1962).
17. Merger Guidelines, 1 Trade Reg. Rep. (CCH), p. 6887.
18. *Ibid.*
19. United States v. Marine Bancorporation, 418 U.S. 602 (1974); United States v. Falstaff Brewing Corp., 410 U.S. 526 (1973).
20. United States v. Marine Bancorporation, 418 U.S. 602 (1974); United States v. Falstaff Brewing Corp., 410 U.S. 526 (1973); British Oxygen Co., 86 F.T.C. 1241 (1975), *rev'd*, 557 F.2d 24 (2d Cir. 1977); Budd Co., 86 F.T.C. 518 (1975).

21. FTC v. Consolidated Foods Corp., 380 U.S. 592, 594–95 (1965); Allis-Chalmers Mfg. Co. v. White Consolidated Indus, Inc., 414 F.2d 506 (3d Cir.), *cert. denied,* 396 U.S. 1009 (1969).

22. FTC v. Procter & Gamble Co., 386 U.S. 568 (1967); Reynolds Metal Co. v. FTC, 309 F.2d 223 (D.C. Cir. 1962).

23. Missouri Portland Cement v. Cargill, Inc., 448 F.2d 851 (2d Cir.), *cert. denied,* 419 U.S. 883 (1974); FTC v. Atlantic Richfield Co., 549 F.2d 289 (4th Cir. 1977).

24. 378 U.S. 158 (1964).

25. 378 U.S. at 170–71.

26. 378 U.S. at 177.

27. 15 U.S.C. §18A.

28. *Federal Register* (1978), 43:33,486.

29. Antitrust Division, U.S. Department of Justice, *Antitrust Guide for International Operations* (Washington, D.C.: Government Printing Office, 1977), p. 16. *See* United States v. Jos. Schlitz Brewing Co., 253 F.Supp. 129 (N.D. Cal. 1966), *aff'd per curiam,* 385 U.S. 37 (1966), *rehearing denied,* 385 U.S. 1021 (1967).

30. British Oxygen Co., 86 F.T.C. 1241 (1975), *rev'd,* 557 F.2d 24 (2d Cir. 1977).

31. United States v. CIBA Corp. (S.D.N.Y. 1970), 5 Trade Reg. Rep. ¶45,070.

32. See Mark R. Joelson and Joseph P. Griffin, "Multinational Joint Ventures and the U.S. Antitrust Laws," *Virginia Journal of International Law* (Fall 1974), 15:487–538; see also Department of Justice, *Antitrust Guide,* pp. 19–32.

Commentary

❖

W. F. Mueller

We are indebted to Kurt Markert for his rich, succinct, and insightful review of European merger law. He covers the laws pertaining to merger in the Federal Republic of Germany, France, the United Kingdom, the European Coal and Steel Community (ECSC), and the European Economic Community (EEC). These laws have some common themes as well as diverse ones, and differ substantially from U.S. merger law and its enforcement.

The EEC antitrust law is embodied in Articles 85 and 86 of the EEC Treaty. In the *Continental Can* case, Article 86 was interpreted as prohibiting mergers that enhance appreciably the domination of an already dominant firm. The potential scope of the law is unclear, however, since no cases have been decided since 1973.

Article 66 of the ECSC Treaty requires premerger clearance of "concentration." The criterion is whether the merger confers the power "to determine price, to control or restrict production or distribution or to prevent the maintenance of effective competition in a substantial part of the market. . . ." In authorizing mergers, the Commission must also consider the size of competing enterprises. In 1977 and 1978, the twenty-four cases examined by the EC Commission were authorized. A change in the policy of the Community seems to be reflected in its approval in 1969 of a merger of practically the same coal companies that were prohibited in 1960 from forming a single joint selling organization. Markert explains this change as recognition of the growing importance of other forms of energy since the 1950s.

The United Kingdom's merger law, included in the Fair Trading Act of 1973, covers mergers of firms exceeding £5 million that create or intensify a "monopoly," defined as a situation where the combined companies hold a market share of 25 percent or more. In evaluating mergers the Monopolies Commission is to use five criteria. Though generally quite broad, most of the criteria are susceptible to interpretation as being concerned with maintaining or promoting competition. Up to March 3, 1978, the commission found thirteen mergers contrary to the public interest and fourteen mergers legal.

In 1977, France enacted its first law covering mergers, the Act to Control Economic Concentration and Prevent Unlawful Cartels and Abuses of Dominant Positions. The law covers anticompetitive horizontal mergers where the combined market share is at least 40 percent of domestic consumption and vertical and conglomerate mergers where each firm has a market share of 25 percent of some product. For such a merger the French Competition Commission must determine whether it "makes a sufficient contribution to economic and social progress to compensate for the restraint on competition which it implies." By the end of 1978, no mergers had been considered a threat to competition, though several were still being reviewed.

The Federal Republic of Germany has the most comprehensive merger law and enforcement effort in Europe. The law is embodied in sections 23 to 24b of the Act Against Restraints of Competition. The act requires premerger notification and clearance of large mergers [1] and prohibits mergers that may result in a dominant market position. Market domination is rebuttably presumed to exist if a single firm with sales of 250 million DM has a market share of 33 percent or more, if two or three firms have a combined share of 50 percent, and if four or five firms have a market share of 67 percent. Mergers creating dominant firms may be justified by a showing that they will improve competitive conditions, and that such improvement exceeds the adverse effects of market domination.

The German merger enforcement effort is quite extensive, at least by European standards. In 1978 the Federal Cartel Office received 558 notifications of consummated mergers; 332 of these qualified for control under the Restraints of Competition Act. Of these, 247 were cleared, 11 prohibited, and the rest are still under examination. Since the beginning of the merger control act of 1973, there have been twenty-three prohibition orders. In seven of these the order became final, in four the Economics Minister granted a public interest exemption, in two cases the orders were rescinded or reversed by the courts, and ten cases are still pending. In twenty-three cases advance notifications were rescinded, partly because of objections raised by the Cartel Office.

Structural as opposed to conduct criteria have been emphasized in defining market domination. The Supreme Court's application of structural criteria has established quite clear standards for horizontal mergers: any merger is in peril when the merging firms acquire a 20 percent market share or more in a market with sales exceeding 10 million DM. Conglomerate mergers have been found illegal on grounds of entrenchment and reduction in potential competition. The entrenchment theory, to date, has been limited to firms operating in "proximate" markets.

I have summarized the nature of these European laws and their enforcement as introduction to an examination of differences among these laws and U.S. merger law.

A common thread running through all these laws is a concern with the criteria for market dominance, as opposed to the American notion of incipient monopoly. In this respect the laws more closely approximate the standards of section 2 of the Sherman Act than section 7 of the Clayton Act. They also differ importantly from U.S. law in that most contain a presumption of illegality if the merger results in an industry structure meeting some fairly objective standard of dominance.

Another contrast with U.S. law is that most of the European laws have explicit public interest defenses for a merger. The most recent law, that of France, illustrates the interaction of the presumptive illegality approach coupled with a public interest defense. After identifying dominant firm mergers, the law requires that the French Competition Commission make an explicit finding as to whether a merger "makes a sufficient contribution to economic and social progress to compensate for the restraint on competition which it implies." Such a law gives great discretion to the enforcement officials and courts, much like that enjoyed by U.S. banking agencies in deciding whether mergers are in the public interest.

Such discretion becomes especially important in the context of the European enforcement scheme, which contemplates considerably more political involvement in the process than does the U.S. system. As I interpret Markert's discussion of these matters, all of the European laws involve a degree of "political" involvement in the initiation of investigations and/or final determination of legality. This is accomplished through the political discretion granted appropriate ministers with no or little opportunity to review their decisions. In the United Kingdom the competent Secretary of

State refers mergers to the Monopolies and Mergers Commission; and if the latter finds a merger contrary to the public interest, the Secretary of State "may" fashion an appropriate remedy. The French system is quite similar to that of the United Kingdom. While the EEC and ECSC laws provide for judicial procedures, the final decisions are made by the top political body of the Communities. Even German merger law gives the Economics Minister discretion to permit an otherwise illegal merger on public interest grounds, discretion that he has exercised.

This political character of the laws differs markedly from the U.S. enforcement scheme. Although the Attorney General may overrule the Antitrust Division on public interest grounds, section 7 provides no explicit public interest standard for such action.

The peculiarly political character of European merger law has important ramifications for efforts to harmonize national antitrust policies in the merger area. Although there also are formidable obstacles to the harmonization of antitrust laws in other areas, Markert believes the problem is magnified because "merger control policy is more than any of the other parts of policy on private restrictive business practices linked with other government policies, particularly industrial policy, employment policy, and foreign trade policy." Though the U.S. law differs in this respect, I believe Markert's pessimism regarding the prospect for international harmonization applies in the United States as well as Europe. Politicians generally are not enthusiastic about interfering with private industrial restructuring even when it involves purely domestic firms and markets. They are even more reluctant to intervene when American firms go abroad; they are especially impressed by arguments that public restraints may interfere with American firms' ability to compete abroad.

The main hope for more effective control over mergers threatening the economic and political effectiveness of the Western market economies lies in strengthening existing national laws. Apparently, serious discussions on this subject are occurring in the United Kingdom, France, and Germany, as well as some discussion in the United States.

I turn now to a few comments contrasting the apparent scope and impact of European and U.S. enforcement efforts. Direct comparisons are not possible because the European enforcement effort has not been quantified to the same extent as that in the United States. But as I understand Markert, European enforcement effort to date may be summarized as follows:

1. Relatively few mergers have been challenged.
2. Enforcement has involved almost entirely horizontal mergers.
3. Challenged mergers have nearly always involved firms with substantial market shares.

The small volume of cases partly reflects the relative newness of the European laws. The most ambitious European enforcement effort is that of Germany, which has prohibited twenty-three mergers since the enactment of its 1973 act.[2] In contrast, since enactment of the Celler-Kefauver Act of 1950, U.S. antitrust agencies have brought about 450 cases challenging about 1,500 mergers.[3] This represents an enormous enforcement effort by antitrust litigation standards. Nearly each of the 150 or so largest U.S. industrial corporations (those with assets over $1 billion) had at least one complaint challenging one or more of its acquisitions.

Although more vertical (thirty-four) and conglomerate (thirty-eight) acquisitions have been challenged in the United States than in Europe, the majority (68 percent) of all challenges were horizontal and geographic market extensions, nor has this changed as conglomerate merger activity accelerated in recent years. During 1978 and the first nine months of 1979, 91 percent (thirty-one of thirty-four) of the Federal Trade Commission and Justice Department complaints challenged horizontal mergers. Clearly, the merger law has left virtually untouched conglomerate mergers (defined as those between firms that have neither vertical nor horizontal market relationships) in the United States as well as in Europe.

Although both American and European laws have aimed primarily at horizontal mergers, there is a large difference in the standards used in judging the probable competitive effects of such mergers. Whereas the European laws use market dominance as their touchstone, American law emphasizes incipient monopoly. This is not merely a matter of semantics. The authors of the 1950 Celler-Kefauver amendment to section 7 made it manifestly clear that Sherman Act standards were not to be used in judging mergers under section 7. The antitrust agencies and the Supreme Court have generally been faithful to this intent, despite a growing clamor among some that this has resulted in overzealous enforcement. *Vons, Brown Shoe,* and most other section 7 decisions of the Supreme Court involved mergers that likely would not have violated the European merger laws.

This difference reflects a fundamental divergence in public policy. European laws seem bent on preventing merger-created monopoly, whereas

American law is aimed at maintaining loose oligopoly and creating opportunities for eroding hard-core oligopolistic industries.

The American law on horizontal merger has been quite successful in preventing a worsening of the oligopoly problem. The agencies' attack on horizontal mergers has been enormous: about 30 percent by number and 55 percent by assets of all large (assets over $10 million) acquired manufacturing firms involved in horizontal mergers were challenged. Based on an analysis of the effects of enforcement in particular industries and an examination of overall trends in market concentration, I believe this enforcement effort has promoted much more competitive horizontal market structures than otherwise would have developed.[4]

Neither American nor European laws have influenced significantly the growing "super" or "aggregate" industrial concentration resulting from the huge conglomerate merger waves of the 1960s and 1970s. Although American law clearly covers potentially anticompetitive conglomerate mergers, its outer boundaries have not been fully explored. Several conglomerate merger theories—potential competition, entrenchment, cross-subsidization, and reciprocity—received high court approval in the 1960s. The late Assistant Attorney General, Richard W. McLaren, briefly pursued an aggressive policy designed to obtain expeditious Supreme Court review of conglomerate mergers, issuing in 1969 complaints challenging five big conglomerate mergers. These cases were based in part on the broad theory of merger-induced increases in aggregate concentration as well as on more conventional theories of potential competition, entrenchment, and reciprocity. This brief interlude foundered, as Henry C. Simons might have put it, "on the orderly process of democratic corruption." The three *International Telephone and Telegraph* cases—which McLaren had intended to culminate in important Supreme Court precedents—ended in an unfortunate consent settlement negotiated under a cloud of political intrigue.[5] The most unfortunate result of these decrees was to deprive the Warren Court of the opportunity of ruling on McLaren's broad conglomerate theories.

The emergence of the Burger Court's "new antitrust majority" in 1973 and 1974 does not augur well for the future of merger enforcement. But despite the Court's apparent hostility to an activist interpretation of the Celler-Kefauver Act, it is premature to infer that the Court will reverse existing precedents. After all, the Chief Justice authored the *Reynolds Metal* "deep pocket" theory when he was a member of the D.C. Court of

Appeals. The antitrust agencies therefore have a mandate to apply the existing law to conglomerate mergers until it is clarified by the Supreme Court.

But the hour is late. The glacial pace of evolving conglomerate merger law argues persuasively that the existing law will not become a vital tool in slowing the current upward trend in industrial centralization. Only a new law with presumptive standards of illegality of large conglomerate mergers is likely to have a timely impact on conglomerate merger-induced centralization of economic power.

In conclusion, there is much to be learned from the European merger law and its enforcement procedures. Students of American merger law should especially examine the public interest defenses commonly found in European law. American "antitrusters" often are intolerant of such defenses, arguing that competition is the only appropriate standard. This is nonsense. Matters relating to a merger's impact on communities, employment, and trade may well transcend in importance the purely competitive effects of a merger. It would be well that American antitrust experts learn from European experience more about procedures used in weighing these matters. Such defenses become particularly relevant in legislation that declares certain types of large conglomerate mergers presumptively illegal.

As food for thought, I'll throw out the question of whether there exists today the distinction between the philosophy underlying European and American antitrust laws as alleged by the *Economist* in 1962, when it chastised UK policy for its excessive commitment to "empiricism." It said that the Government's "entranced indecision" arose partly from

> the mistaken assumption—which economists are guilty of encouraging—that political objections to monopoly can be altogether based on evidential grounds, economic or technical. The United States—which is often accused in Europe of having an exaggerated animus against monopoly, because it has a policy that quite often works—seldom falls into this trap. Its legal prejudice, *per se,* against anything calculated to restrain competition, is avowedly based, in the last resort, on social and even moral grounds; the economic efficiency that it believes competition generally promotes is the secondary justification, not the first. Primarily, American attitudes towards monopoly (public as well as private) are based upon a distrust of concentrations of economic power, irresponsible in that they are not finally accountable to the public. This does not make American antitrust legislation emotional and ineffective: it makes it at times even embarrassingly effective. [6]

My own view is that, for good or ill, European and U.S. merger policies differ less today than they did in 1962, as each has moved perceptively toward the other.

NOTES

1. Clearance must be received before consummation of mergers where at least two participating firms have annual sales of 1 billion DM. Mergers involving an aggregate market share of 20 percent or more in any market with annual sales of at least 500 million DM or 10,000 employees need only notify after consummation.

2. In seven of these cases the orders became final, in four the Economics Minister granted a public interest exemption, in two cases the orders were rescinded or reversed, and ten cases are still pending. These twenty-three actions compare with eighty-six merger complaints issued by the U.S. antitrust agencies during the years from 1973 to 1978.

3. These and other statistics are taken from W. F. Mueller, *The Celler-Kefauver Act: The First 27 Years,* a study prepared in 1978 for the use of the Subcommittee on Monopolies and Commercial Law of the Committee on the Judiciary, House of Representatives, 95th Cong., 2d Sess. (Washington, D.C.: Government Printing Office, 1980). Some statistics are updated. Of the 364 nonbanking cases brought during the years from 1951 to 1977, 44 were dismissed and 28 were pending at the end of 1977. The remainder were settled with consent agreements or were found illegal. *Ibid.*, p. 119.

4. *Ibid.*, pp. 22–69, 70–74.

5. W. F. Mueller, "The ITT Settlement: A Deal with Justice?" *Industrial Organization Review* (1974), 1:67–86.

6. "No Policy for Mergers," *The Economist,* February 3, 1962, pp. 393–94.

Discussion

◆

MICHAEL D. BLECHMAN: As I see it, the German law at present falls somewhat short of the American law in terms of its effectiveness in combating certain kinds of mergers because of no incipiency doctrine, and so on. A new law is under contemplation which I hear is expected to pass, and that law would go beyond some of the presumptions in the American jurisprudence. In particular, it would do so with respect to the rebuttable presumptions (which Kurt Markert mentions at page 307 of his paper) that a merger is going to be presumed to create or strengthen a market-dominating position in three different kinds of circumstances.

One is where a very large company with two billion DM of turnover, I believe, is going to acquire a business in a market characterized by small or medium-sized businesses. That would institutionalize or codify the "deep pocket" theory, which I think has some echoes in American law in the *Reynolds* case, and in the court of appeals decision in *Brunswick,* but, as Mark Joelson said, isn't the American law generally now.

And the second and third presumptions, particularly the third one, would create a presumption of illegality where the turnover of the two firms, or several firms involved, is very large—10 billion DM with two of them tapping for 2 billion DM.

My question is: is the Federal Cartel Office sponsoring or in favor of the new German legislation? And if it is, why? Why is there the feeling that it's necessary or desirable to go beyond the American jurisprudence and attack mergers on the basis of very strong presumptions in the deep pocket area, or strictly on the basis of turnover?

KURT MARKERT: As I said in my paper, which was finalized two months ago, it was very uncertain whether the new legislation now in Parliament would be passed. And this statement still holds true today. The difficult aspect of this is that the Government at present only has a majority in one of the two houses of Parliament. In order to get some legislation of this sort enacted, the Government will have to get the approval of the opposition party, which is more business-minded than the two coalition parties supporting the Government.

For that reason, I personally have great doubts that, for example, this size presumption, the 10 billion DM aggregated annual sales, will be accepted. I just can't see that the opposition will go along with that, being business-minded as it is. And also, I am not at all sure—on the contrary, I'm relatively pessimistic—that the opposition will go along with that incipiency clause, which I didn't cover in my paper, but which since then has been introduced as an alternative. There are no great hopes that radical improvement in the substantive merger law will be achieved in the very near future.

However, may I just add one remark? There is also one clause in the bill extending the compulsory premerger clearance procedure. Under the bill, this procedure also applies if there is only one large firm involved, with 2 billion DM annual sales. Now I have told you before what the impact of that procedure will be, and I foresee as a result of that clause in the bill that the merger law in the future will be much more stringent than it is now.

JAMES A. RAHL: Thinking of this in international terms rather than comparative terms for a moment, I would be interested to know if any panelist could give us more insight into what the nature of the international problem is. What is the quantity of international mergers occurring?

MARKERT: If you understand the term "international merger" in a very wide sense, I would guess from what I see as cases notified to the Cartel Office that about half of the mergers, or even more, have some international aspect. For example, multinational companies may be involved, or the merger may involve the setting up of a joint venture of two German companies somewhere abroad, or an American company may take over a German company, or vice versa.

Now whether this, taken together, amounts to an increase in overall concentration worldwide is very difficult to say. In particular, it is very difficult to say whether, in terms of the competitive alternatives developing countries have for certain products, the mergers we see nowadays are a serious problem. We just know too little about international concentration, just as we know too little about export cartels. In that respect I see a need for international activities, and I hope the Documentation Center at the United Nations is in a position to engage in that.

DAVID N. GOLDSWEIG: I would like to ask Kurt Markert to speak for a moment to the political considerations involved in the evaluation of acquisitions in Germany, and in the EEC generally. In particular, I wonder whether an acquisition in Germany or the EEC by an American firm of an indigenous company would have stricter standards applied to it than a similar acquisition by a European-based company, one based in Germany or elsewhere in the EEC.

MARKERT: The standards for distinguishing between "good" and "bad" mergers differ to a great extent within the Common Market. German companies in their own country can do much less in terms of more concentration than French industry can. Even with the new French merger law, 80 percent market share was accepted in one case. For us, this is absolute sacrilege.

And, of course, we have seen the allowance of a number of superconcentration mergers in the British economy, for example in the electrical industry, in spite of their merger laws. Our position has always been that if in Germany, by having strict national merger laws, we make national firms competition-minded in their home market, they will be better off on an international level.

TIMOTHY ATKESON: In the draft text of the UNCTAD Code on Restrictive Business Practices, there appears the following provision:

> Enterprises either should or shall refrain from the following acts of behavior in a relevant market when, through an abuse or an acquisition and abuse of dominant position of market power, they limit access to markets or otherwise unduly restrain competition having or being likely to have adverse effects on international trade, particularly that of developing countries, and on the economic development of these countries: . . . mergers, takeovers, joint ventures, or other acquisitions of control whether of a horizontal, vertical, or a conglomerate nature.

I wonder if you have any comment on that.

MARK JOELSON: I am aware of that text, but I have doubts that an agreement of this sort can really set forth a meaningful standard that will be applied in the different countries in the same way. I think we need some agreed national standards before we can attain an international standard that is meaningful.

ROBERT J. RADWAY: In the developing countries there is a clear trend toward, and a clear preference for, attracting foreign capital and technology in the form of a joint venture. This may lead to increased competition or it may not.

MARKERT: Well, I certainly would not consider joint ventures of several enterprises from an industrialized country, or several industrialized countries entering markets in developing countries in which they otherwise could not enter, as per se bad. It might be the only way to provide competitive alternatives in these countries, and certainly we would never consider bringing an action against such a joint venture for the reason that it would be very difficult to establish domestic effect (which is, of course, the necessary requirement for bringing an action in Germany).

WALTER CHUDSON: The term *joint ventures* has been used frequently, and I'm a little puzzled about the definition with regard to joint ventures between a parent firm and another firm in a developing country, which, of course, is the normal thing to think about under the name *joint venture*. I wonder, for instance, have you had any cases involving a German firm in a joint venture, let's say, with an Indonesian or Brazilian firm that required prior approval?

MARKERT: I think I already gave the answer. I just cannot see that in such a case you have the necessary domestic anticompetitive effect to prohibit such a merger.

SIGMUND TIMBERG: I would ask where the dividing line is between the kind of price discrimination that is the essence of competition (the reason why all the antitrust lawyers condemn Robinson-Patman), and the predatory pricing and price discrimination that is a determinant of monopoly power.

WILLARD F. MUELLER: I think the test should be in terms of what actually has happened or is likely to happen in price discrimination within a particular industrial structure. We must look at the disparity of power, and then at what the likely effects are.

THEODORE L. BANKS: To follow up on an earlier question, I would give the example of France, where they evaluate mergers solely on the identity of the acquiring party and without regard to any effect of competition. I wonder if any of the panel will comment on why they feel that this type of "public interest" standard should be used, say, in a country like France, where they allow local concentration with the acquisition by French firms, but not if a German or American firm wants to acquire a French firm. Should this standard be applied to developing countries or developed countries?

JOELSON: I would like to just reaffirm, as I said, that I have problems with the public interest standard. In theory, it should bring out the best in people, but it seems to bring out the worst.

BARRY E. HAWK: In examining the antitrust validity of a particular domestic merger, or in formulating legislation covering domestic mergers, how much consideration should be given to the international implications, and what are those implications? Should we be expanding the definition of "market" to consider impact of domestic merger on foreign markets?

JOELSON: It seems to me that section 7 of the Clayton Act, at least, is flexible enough, and it should be understood to take account of international reality.

M. P. McCARTHY: I have a question for Kurt Markert which refers back to one of his answers to a previous question. One of the areas of great confusion is, what is the objective to be served by prohibiting large conglomerate mergers? I understand Markert to say that one of the reasons behind the proposed German legislation against large mergers is the presumption that concentration achieved by the large conglomerate merger will lead inevitably to predatory pricing.

MARKERT: No, that was not what I intended to say. When I spoke of predatory pricing, I didn't mean the superconcentration cases; I meant the case where there is a single large firm in a market of basically small and medium-sized firms. That's where the entrenchment, the deep pocket problem, comes up.

When it comes to superconcentration, two large firms going together, I think there are other problems involved. We have the general feeling that these "elephants' marriages" cannot be reasonably evaluated by looking at the effect of such mergers on particular markets. If we let those giants or elephants grow further because we are not able to find sufficient competitive effects on certain markets, we as a society, as a state, are just faced with such conglomerations of power that we can't do anything about them anymore.

So I think, at this point, antitrust must reach other dimensions of social policy. In effect, antitrust was always a device to control social power that got too big.

5

INTERNATIONAL CODES OF CONDUCT AND CONVENTIONS

The Seeking of a World Competition Code: Quixotic Quest?

<·>

Joel Davidow

There is an American tradition, personified by idealists such as Jefferson and Wilson, of believing that the United States has developed new and better freedoms that can be extended to the whole world. Seekers after this goal have tended to die with their dreams unfulfilled, if not totally frustrated.

Such a death occurred in 1979, when Corwin Edwards succumbed to a stroke at age 73. Edwards devoted his career to supporting and spreading antitrust doctrine. He was policy planning director for Thurman Arnold in the Justice Department's Antitrust Division, and then chief economist of the Federal Trade Commission. In numerous books and articles, he explained and advocated competition policy of the American style, i.e., grounded in the economic case for free markets but also motivated by a political suspicion of unchecked private economic power.[1]

Shortly before the defeat of Germany, President Roosevelt personally embraced the anticartel philosophy of Edwards and the Antitrust Division, and expressly linked this policy to the embryonic United Nations. Roosevelt wrote:

> During the past half century the United States has developed a tradition in opposition to private monopolies. The Sherman and Clayton Acts have become as much a part of the American way of life as the Due Process clause of the

Mr. Davidow has been a member of the U.S. delegations to the OECD, and to the UNCTAD negotiations on restrictive business practices and transfer of technology. The views expressed in this paper are personal, however, and do not represent those of any government agency.

Constitution. By protecting the consumer against monopoly these statutes guarantee him the benefits of competition.

. . . .

Unfortunately, a number of foreign countries, particularly in continental Europe, do not possess such a tradition against cartels. On the contrary, cartels have received encouragement from these governments. Especially is this true with respect to Germany. Moreover, cartels were utilized by the Nazis as governmental instrumentalities to achieve political ends. . . . Defeat of the Nazi armies will have to be followed by the eradication of these weapons of economic warfare. But more than elimination of the political activities of German cartels will be required. Cartel practices which restrict the free flow of goods in foreign commerce will have to be curbed. With international trade involved, this end can be achieved only through collaborative action by the United Nations.[2]

After World War II, Edwards went to Japan to work on the de-cartelization of that country and the development of an antitrust law there.[3]

Also just after the war, the United States and Great Britain jointly proposed creation of an international trade organization. In 1948, Edwards was a key part of the U.S. delegation when fifty-three nations met in Havana and drafted the charter of such an organization. Article V of the ITO Charter condemned a list of restrictive business practices, defined as:

(1) Fixing of prices, or of terms or conditions to be observed in the purchase, sale, or lease of any product;

(2) Exclusion of enterprises from, or allocation or division of, any territorial market or field of business activity, or allocation of customers, or fixing of sale or purchasing quotas;

(3) Discrimination against particular enterprises;

(4) Production limitations or quotas;

(5) Prevention of development or application of technology or invention, whether patented or not, or withholding of same with the result of monopolizing an industrial or commercial field;

(6) Illegal extension of rights under patents, trademarks, or copyrights; and

(7) Any similar practices which the Organization may declare, by a majority of two-thirds of the Members present and voting, to be restrictive business practices.[4]

The ITO Charter was submitted at one session of the U.S. Congress, which adjourned without voting on the measure. It was never resubmitted, the State Department apparently having concluded that it would not be ratified. Some opponents of the Havana Charter were not averse to its provisions on restrictive business practices (RBPs) but were critical of its support for international commodity agreements and hostile to its declarations on foreign investment and full employment. The representative of the National Association of Manufacturers (NAM) said of the charter's provisions: "they contain a mild—a very mild—indictment of private cartels, while opening the gates widely to intergovernmental ones."[5]

There were those, like Edwards and Sigmund Timberg of the Antitrust Division, who therefore rationalized that the ITO Charter was rejected in the United States because of its controversial provisions favoring commodity stabilization agreements and worldwide full employment, rather than because of its RBP provisions, and that therefore a separate international antitrust agreement would still have a chance for U.S. support.[6]

In 1952, Edwards headed the American delegation to a UN ad hoc committee under the Economic and Social Council (ECOSOC) which, on the motion of the United States, was delegated to draft restrictive business practice rules and an implementing procedure. Timberg acted as secretary to the group. The committee's report surveyed the existing state of antitrust or anticartel law in the ten or so nations which provided information on that subject. It concluded that there were great disparities in the treatment of cartels and restrictive business practices, but that there had been substantial progress toward the development of new and stronger legislation in this area as compared to the period prior to World War II. The committee's final recommendation was extremely similar to that contained in the Havana Charter. In essence, the proposal was that the same list of restrictive practices be promulgated, and that a UN body with an executive board be available to arrange consultation between states affected by such practices or for investigation of complaints presented by member states, to be followed by findings and possible requests that members take remedial measures in accordance with their own laws and procedures. Practices required by national law would not be subject to investigation.[7]

In the following year, substantial opposition developed to the recommendations of the UN committee. The report was condemned by the International Chamber of Commerce and the National Association of Manufacturers.[8]

In March 1955, the U.S. representative to the United Nations withdrew American support for the concept of an international body for the control of restrictive business practices. He stressed that the substantial differences that then existed between national laws and policies in regard to competition would make it very difficult for a multinational body to determine which business practices are harmful and which are not, and would also make it unlikely that recommendations of the UN commission could be or would be effectively carried out in all countries. In closing, the U.S. delegate stated:

> The elimination of harmful restraints on international trade and the furthering of the development of free competitive enterprise continue to be basic objectives of this country's economic policy. In the present circumstances, however, the endeavor to effectuate a plan of international co-operation along the lines envisaged by the current proposals might well prejudice rather than promote the attainment of these objectives.
>
> It is therefore the opinion of the United States Government that present emphasis should be given not to international organizational machinery but rather to the more fundamental need of further developing effective national programmes to deal with restrictive business practices, and of achieving a greater degree of comparability in the policies and practices of all nations in their approach to the subject. [9]

In the years following the abandonment of the ECOSOC antitrust proposal, the United States did help achieve substantial progress in strengthening national antitrust laws and beginning antitrust cooperation within groups smaller than the United Nations. With American assistance and encouragement, the European Coal and Steel Community in 1951 and then the European Common Market in 1957 adopted treaties and regulations aimed at preventing restrictive business practices. [10]

Recalling these events in a book written in 1967, Edwards concluded that while there was an excellent case for regional control of restrictive business practices, a global agreement was impractical because many states used restraints of trade as a weapon against other countries and rejected private enterprise as the optimum form for economic activity. He stressed that "[d]evelopment of a common policy towards cartels and monopolies is possible, if at all, only within a free trade area or in a setting in which public and private restrictions are reduced to a roughly comparable extent." [11] Noting also the wide differences among nations concerning regulatory methods and concepts of due process, he concluded:

> In the light of the difficulties which have been summarized above, international collaboration to control restrictive business practices cannot be global. It cannot succeed if it includes countries that are widely divergent in their legal and political systems or in the place that they give to private enterprise. It cannot succeed if it undertakes a program that is markedly inconsistent with the commercial policies of the participating states. It cannot succeed if the participating states do not have a substantial degree of common experience

as to the nature of the business enterprises and of business practices. If it includes any substantial number of states that are without experience in domestic control of restrictive business practices, it must be seriously handicapped. Comprehensive collaboration, such as was contemplated by those who drafted the ITO charter and the ad hoc committee's report, is not now practicable.[12]

Thus, Edwards's reflection in retirement was that he had been wrong in 1948 and 1953 in believing that a global code for the control of RBPs was feasible or politically acceptable. Nor did he believe that the conditions of 1967 were significantly more favorable.

Despite Edwards's pessimism, the issue of international antitrust principles refused to die. It was revived in the 1970s in connection with increasing political controversy about investment and marketing practices of multinational corporations. Also, the issue was pushed by a group that had played no significant role in the debates of the 1940s, the developing countries.

ANTITRUST DEVELOPMENTS AT UNCTAD

Although no "International Trade Organization" was created in Geneva following the failure of the Havana Charter, in 1964 a United Nations Conference on Trade and Development (UNCTAD) was established in that city. This organization achieved a membership as large or larger than that of the UN General Assembly. Its mission, however, was solely to focus on furthering the trade and development of the "southern" nations of the world, who negotiated as a bloc called the "Group of 77," while the West was styled as "Group B" and the East as "Group D."

At its third planning conference in 1972, UNCTAD took up the topic of controlling "restrictive business practices adversely affecting the trade and development of developing countries."[13] Further work followed in 1974 and 1975 on codes of conduct.

Developing countries' pressure for international RBP rules was undoubtedly the primary factor in rejuvenating UN activity in this field, but the peculiarity of the South's approach often threatened to stalemate the negotiations it demanded. The southern states made their understandable interest in securing development, control of foreign investment, and legitimization of national measures the preoccupation of the United Nations and of their versions of these codes of conduct, initially to the almost complete exclusion of the concepts of free competition, free trade, and international law. Restoring these fundamentals became the key task of the North.

The Group of 77 countries stressed in the earliest drafts of their codes that international RBP rules should not impede but endorse southern cartels "in defense of" their primary commodities. Their national enterprises were to be accorded special and preferential treatment so they could achieve countervailing power against firms from developed countries. Codes should be legally binding, but developing countries' national officials should be free to exempt RBPs for national policy reasons. Besides their specific points, there was a basic difference in approach: Western nations were prepared to condemn, and to seek limited forms of international cooperative action against, those traditional restrictive business practices which would likely injure international trade and development, particularly that of developing countries. The Group of 77 countries sought international endorsement of the concept that all corporate conduct that was injurious to, or not positively helpful for, their development should be branded as restrictive and altered to their specification.

A central feature of the new approach of the 1970s was the effort to link the issue of restrictive business practices to disputes concerning activities of multinational corporations. Obviously, those restrictive business practices that occur in international trade and investment are committed by businesses engaged in such commerce. Such firms, unless they deal solely in exports, are by definition "multinational" or "transnational" companies. But the most relevant questions are whether major transnational enterprises have accounted for a substantial or increasing number of offenses in recent years, or more than firms that only export, or than the local firms with which they compete abroad. The considered judgment of Western enforcement officials is that the answer to all these questions is in the negative. In the late 1930s, it was estimated that 30 or 40 percent of world trade in manufactures was controlled by cartels.[14] Many of these cartels were highly organized, operated with impunity, and could have their agreements enforced in the courts of hospitable countries like the United Kingdom and Germany.[15] In the quarter century after the end of World War II, civil and criminal prosecutions by U.S. antitrust agencies, the spread of antitrust laws to almost all OECD countries, and million-dollar-plus fines by an aggressive EEC competition directorate caused traditional cartel practices to become rare, episodic and usually ineffective unless backed by home governments.

In a perceptive article on multinational enterprises, Detlev Vagts of Harvard Law School argued in 1970 that while MNEs may occasion antitrust problems because of their mergers, joint mergers, and dominance of small markets, their primary clashes with host states will more likely stem from five major types of issues that are not really antitrust problems:

1. Management strategies that are inconsistent with national development goals,
2. Transfer pricing causing customs and tax disputes,
3. Exclusive use, or non-use or non-transferral, of patents and know-how,
4. Repatriation of earnings,
5. Termination of investments. [16]

It has been the intermixture of these issues with conventional antitrust questions that delayed and complicated UNCTAD RBP and transfer of technology negotiations.

In 1974, the United Nations recruited a group of "Eminent Persons" to report on problems caused by MNEs. In the section of their report dealing with competition questions, the Eminent Persons recommended that transnational enterprises should be required to report restrictions on their export and purchasing policies to host governments, that governments should agree to prohibit the market allocation of exports by multinational corporations (except when such allocations secure other benefits for the countries concerned), that preparatory work in appropriate UN bodies should be undertaken for the adoption of an international antitrust agreement, and that pending such an agreement, home countries should show restraint in applying their antitrust policies if other governments were affected. [17] The most controversial of the recommendations was the one that appears to condemn market allocation. This recommendation was obviously not unanimous even within the group, particularly in regard to market allocations within a single MNE, or ones based on patent rights and technology licensing. Notwithstanding this recommendation, and despite their strong pro-developing country emphasis, the Eminent Persons warned: "Most countries should be careful not to discourage the transfer of technology by rejecting a measure of control over its use which may be inseparably linked to its wider advantages. Such advantages usually accompany wholly-owned or majority-controlled affiliates rather than minority-owned ventures." [18]

Some of the free economy Eminent Persons explained their views at length. Ryutaro Komiya, Professor of Economics at Tokyo University, observed that

> one cannot ask a majority-owned subsidiary of a multinational corporation to compete with its parent or with other majority-owned subsidiaries of the group. The branch offices of a bank cannot be required to compete with each other or with the head office, whether in one country or internationally. There is no country whose antitrust laws require that the parent and its majority-owned subsidiaries compete with each other.
>
> . . . [A] third type of market allocation arrangement, namely territory arrangements accompanying patent and know-how licensing, is very different from other restrictive practices, since it is based upon the proprietary right to patents and know-how. The main difficulty here is that a prospective licensor is often unwilling to let a prospective licensee use the technology and wants simply to export products from the home country, unless he is somehow protected at least to some extent from competition with the licensee. Thus, total prohibition of territorial restriction accompanying patent and know-how licensing will certainly retard, rather than promote, the transfer of technology, and will not be beneficial to the developing countries. Moreover, exclusive licensing arrangements are generally not illegal in most countries.[19]

Another group member, Hans Schaffner, former President of Switzerland, pointed out that "it would be completely unrealistic in many other cases to expect or demand that intense competition should be fostered between a parent and its offshoots abroad. This is particularly clear where the latter depend to a large extent on a continuous flow of sophisticated technology service from their parent."[20]

In 1977, the OECD published the results of a three-year study of multinational enterprises by its experts on restrictive business practices.[21] The report concluded that MNEs can produce substantial beneficial effects on national and international competition, as by entering concentrated markets dominated by local firms. It was acknowledged that MNEs are often large, and often compete in major oligopolistic markets, so that their restrictive business practices, when they do occur, will often be of great significance. The report goes on to emphasize that

> large national enterprises may present many problems similar to those just discussed. Restrictive practices of multinational enterprises do not differ in terms of competition theory or in terms of the substantive antitrust rules of Member countries. It does not therefore seem necessary or appropriate to seek to create different substantive antitrust laws for national and multinational enterprises. Such different substantive antitrust rules could have the effect of handicapping some competitors as against others.

In considering whether there were any antitrust problems peculiar to MNEs, the OECD experts concluded that the most significant of these were procedural problems in obtaining information or relief abroad, and problems of conflict of national policies and jurisdiction.[22]

In regard to the issue of market allocation within a multinational enterprise, the experts concluded as follows:

> Competition laws and policies in the OECD Member nations generally provide that intra-enterprise practices such as allocation of functions among branches or subsidiaries of a single enterprise are not considered in themselves as an unreasonable restraint of trade. Holding such practices unlawful would be likely to discourage internal growth and decrease efficiency. It might also force upon competition authorities the impracticable task of seeking to create and maintain competition within a single enterprise on an ongoing basis. In no case have arrangements within the same legal entity, such as between branches or operating divisions of the same company, been held to be unlawful. Even in cases involving separate legal entities under common control, findings of illegality have been rare and have been based upon exhaustive factual analysis of the particular cases.

In light of this analysis, they recommended no change at this time in relation to the treatment of intracorporate arrangements.[23]

In 1974, a group of RBP experts invited by UNCTAD, mainly from academia, met and formulated an initial report on restrictive practices, including tentative RBP rules for enterprises.[24] This report was not endorsed by the Trade and Development Board of UNCTAD, except for the experts' call for further meetings, this time among experts representing governments. Accordingly, UNCTAD authorized a second, and then a third, ad hoc group of experts, designated by governments. Their mandate included (1) the identification of restrictive business practices likely to injure international trade, particularly the trade and development of developing countries; (2) the formulation of principles and rules to deal with such practices; (3) the development of systems for information exchange and collection; and (4) the formulation of a model antitrust law for developing countries. The ad hoc groups of experts each met about six times over a two-year period, until all parts of the mandate except negotiation of principles and rules were largely accomplished.[25]

Also in the early 1970s, developing countries began to press UNCTAD to work on a "Code of Conduct for the Transfer of Technology" which would, *inter alia,* condemn RBPs imposed by licensors. Serious negotiation began during 1975.

During 1976, the Western countries, plus Japan, partly because of a desire to stay ahead of the UN and UNCTAD work on MNE issues, promulgated their own thirty-nine-point code of conduct for multinational enterprises under the auspices of the OECD. The OECD code includes four competition principles. These reflect a more conservative approach than that of the ITO and ECOSOC codes. Monopolization is condemned only when a dominant position in a relevant market is abused by means of specific conduct such as certain acquisitions, refusals to deal, predatory practices, price discrimination, and patent abuse. Participating in a cartel is to be avoided, but only when the cartel is not permitted by "applicable" law. Multinational corporations, it is stated, should permit their purchasers, distributors, and licensees to buy, sell, and export freely, but may restrict such freedom when doing so is justified by trade conditions, the need for specialization, or sound commercial practice. The guidelines, reflecting enforcement officials' recognition of the importance of procedural and information problems in regulating the competitive conduct of multinational enterprises, contain a final principle stressing the duty of MNEs to consult and cooperate with authorities of directly affected countries in regard to competition investigations, and to furnish requested information if the adequate safeguards for its confidentiality are provided by the requesting government. [26]

At UNCTAD in Geneva between 1976 and 1980, during many weeks of difficult negotiating sessions each year, and after two diplomatic-level conferences, agreement was reached on principles and rules for the control of restrictive business practices. About 70 percent agreement was reached on the restrictive licensing chapter of a code of conduct for the international transfer of technology. [27] Transfer of technology, which was more closely associated with developing country demands for a "New International Economic Order" than were RBPs, was initially pursued with great political vigor at the United Nations and reached the diplomatic conference stage earlier, in 1977, as opposed to 1979 for RBPs. On the other hand, for a number of important reasons transfer of technology RBP rules are more difficult to negotiate than traditional anticartel RBP rules, which caused the diplomatic-level conferences on this subject in 1977 and 1978 to be partially stalemated, and the 1980 fourth transfer of technology conference to fail while the RBP conference was succeeding.

The highly politicized nature of the transfer of technology issue led the

Group of 77 to put forward an ambitious and confrontational text, combined with a demand that the code be legally binding, and to be largely unwilling to compromise issues unacceptable to the West.[28] Second, developed countries, which had traditionally encouraged innovation and its disclosure and transfer by granting important exclusive rights to inventors through national patent systems, legal protection of trade secrets and know-how, and international protection under the Paris Convention, have accepted, within a narrow range of debate, the legal principle that industrial property rights are a proper exception to antitrust laws, entitling a licensor to set price, quantity, field of use, and territorial and other conditions consistent with the scope and duration of the relevant rights but not to go beyond or abuse those rights.[29] Developing countries, whose inventors secured only a tiny percentage of all protected inventions, even within their own countries, were largely unwilling to accept the concept that owners of technology should be granted any rights to restrict transfer but instead insisted that they should be required to license or sell the technology to developing country recipients on a "no strings attached" basis.[30]

The success of the conference on an RBP Code partially results from the fact that transnational enterprises, under the threat of harsh sanctions from at least U.S., German, and Common Market antitrust laws, appear to have substantially abandoned many traditional cartel practices, except for those allowed or encouraged by governments, such as export associations.[31] On the other hand, UN studies indicate that restrictions in technology transfer agreements, such as export prohibitions designed to protect home or third markets, remain in relatively common use.[32] In fact, developing country regulations limiting repatriation of profits have actually encouraged tying clauses or other restrictions designed to extract money from the country. Thus, while for developed countries to agree to rules against traditional cartel practices would usually involve only symbolic concessions or hypothetical difficulties (except for the issues of export cartels and intraenterprise restrictions), weakening the restrictive rights of licensors might well involve the surrender of real advantages currently being exercised. Accordingly, Western delegates, representing the patent bar as well as the antitrust bar of their countries, insisted in the negotiation that each rule explicate in detail when a restriction would be justified, as well as when it would not.

A final irony of the transfer of technology negotiation has been that some Group of 77 nations, particularly of Latin America, who desired the code in order to universalize their stringent national laws, came to realize that lengthy bargaining with developed country experts was resulting in an exception-ridden document that would tend more to undermine their harsh rules than to endorse them. Thus, a resolution of the UNCTAD conference in May 1979 stated that the third transfer of technology conference, in November, would be the "concluding" conference, to signal that the Group of 77 preferred breaking off the negotiations to having the West gradually eat away at the international level the gains developing countries had achieved nationally and regionally through weakening the regime of supplier hegemony in technology transfer.[33] This threat was not carried out after the third conference, and a fourth conference was adjourned after it reached an impasse.

The two UNCTAD codes were and are being negotiated on a global basis, among nations with vastly different economic systems and degrees of experience with and attitudes toward the control of RBPs, and without any guarantee that a code's adoption will coincide with a global free trade system or a rule against state-organized cartels. Edwards's prediction of 1967 was that global rules lacking the prerequisites just discussed would not succeed. Success, however, has many meanings, particularly in the ephemeral realms of international politics and "soft" international law. By the end of 1980 UNCTAD's global antitrust principles were endorsed by the UN General Assembly, based on the success of the 1980 RBP conference. These principles are more comprehensive, more detailed, and more balanced between obligations of governments and enterprises than were the drafts of 1948 and 1953. But it is doubtful that they would have been ratified by all major states if put in treaty form. Nor does it seem probable that the codes by themselves, or by means of the forms of implementation that will be acceptable to most nations, will substantially reduce the prevalence of RBPs. The most important questions are whether principles negotiated to be acceptable in the political context of the late 1970s, particularly its emphasis on rapid development and achievement of a New International Economic Order, can retain enough clarity of meaning and philosophy to provide a basis on which the United Nations of the 1990s can build a system to protect competition at least comparable to the GATT in acceptance, neutrality, and effectiveness, and can be developed into a system that has some working effectiveness.

TEXTS AND ISSUES

Much of the remainder of this paper will attempt to deal with these questions by examining the texts negotiated or still at issue in terms of substance as well as problems of implementation and effectiveness.

SCOPE OF APPLICATION

Defining the scope of application for an international code of conduct on RBPs was a task greatly complicated by political considerations. The West has generally pressed for broad coverage imposing like rules on both state-controlled and private enterprises, and on both transnational enterprises (TNEs) and the local enterprises with which they compete. Socialist states initially insisted that abuses stem only from private TNEs and sought to narrow the scope of application accordingly. Developing countries tended to favor "universal" application to foreign enterprises of East and West, and favored exceptions based on their national laws, or on special preference principles, which would favor or exempt their enterprises or allow their officials to permit RBPs when doing so would secure some development goal.

In the RBP code, it is stated expressly that the rules are universally applicable to all types of enterprises engaged in commerce, including those owned or controlled by states.[34] The principles and rules apply to all acts and practices having the requisite effects, regardless of whether such practices involve enterprises in one or more countries.

For purposes of the UNCTAD RBP rules, "restrictive business practices" are defined as acts or agreements that through an abuse of a dominant position of market power, "limit access to markets or otherwise unduly restrain competition, having or being likely to have adverse effects on international trade, particularly that of developing countries, and on the economic development of those countries."

The definition reflects compromise achieved by ambiguity which is potentially controversial. The stress on effect on trade and development, especially of developing countries, suggests that adverse effect on developing countries is a test in determining whether conduct is a restrictive business practice. However, the better reading appears to be that the definition does not define any offense, since those are defined in a later section. In the definition, there is no word *"or"* preceding the reference to having an adverse effect on trade and development. Thus, the definition must be read to state that an offense exists when a practice abuses a dominant position by limiting access to markets or unduly restraining competition, *and* such practice has an adverse effect on trade or development. The text exempts from the principles and rules all enterprise conduct which is directly caused by intergovernmental agreements.

The scope of application of the Transfer of Technology Code is not yet fully agreed. All groups concur that the code is "universally" applicable to all states and to all transactions in which a supplying party, private or state owned, transfers technology internationally to an acquiring party. Developing and socialist states would also apply the code to similar transactions within a state between the subsidiary of a foreign firm and a local recipient. Developed countries, objecting that such a rule would subject subsidiaries to more stringent rules than their local rivals, would leave the regulation of all intrastate transactions to local law. A suggested compromise would apply the code to those intrastate trnasactions in which the subsidiary acts as an intermediary in transferring technology developed abroad.[35]

In regard to exceptions, a text proposed by the Group of 77 and partially supported by Group D would exempt those practices that competent national authorities of the technology-acquiring country decide to be in its public interest. Group B has so far argued that such an exception is unnecessary.

GENERAL PRINCIPLES AND OBJECTIVES

There are five agreed objectives of the restrictive business practice rules. These include ensuring that RBPs do not interfere with trade liberalization, encouraging efficiency through the creation and protection of competition, promoting consumer interests, eliminating disadvantages that may result from the RBPs of transnational corporations and other enterprises, and providing rules that can be emulated at national and regional levels.

A subsequent section sets forth general principles that are agreed upon. These call for action at national, regional, and international levels to eliminate restrictive business practices, collaboration between governments at bilateral and multilateral levels for this purpose, creation of international mechanisms to facilitate exchange and dissemination of information among governments in regard to RBPs, and the creation of means to facilitate the holding of multinational consultations relating to RBPs and their control. The principle is also agreed that the provisions of the rules should not be construed to justify conduct by enterprises that is unlawful under applicable national legislation.

Two of the most controversial issues in the negotiations on the RBP Code concerned exceptions for conduct approved by developed country governments and special treatment for conduct important to the trade and development of developing countries. The South opposed the former principle and the North the latter one. Compromise was achieved by accepting both concepts, but in less absolute terms than desired by their proponents. Principle C–6 urges that "due account" be taken of the extent to which conduct has been accepted or required under applicable legislation or regulation, bearing in mind the desirability that such laws and regulations should be clearly defined and public and the need to achieve the most comprehensive possible application of the principles and rules. Similarly, states, particularly of developed countries, are instructed by principle C–7 to "take account" in their control of restrictive practices of the needs of developing countries to promote the establishment of domestic industries and encourage economic development through regional arrangements among themselves.

Both principles enbody the concept of "comity" in international antitrust enforcement, an idea that has been approved by U.S. courts in a number of recent rulings on antitrust jurisdiction over foreign events.[36]

In the Transfer of Technology Code, there is an agreed section on special treatment for developing countries, but it deals with governmental assistance to developing countries and in no way suggests that their enterprises may commit offenses condemned by the RBP chapter of the code. The only reference there to private transfers is the principle that developed countries should "facilitate access, to the extent practicable, to technologies whose transfer is subject to private decisions."

PRINCIPLES FOR GOVERNMENTS

A major innovation in the modern UN codes is that they contain principles for governments as well as for enterprises. Both the ITO and ECOSOC rules consisted simply of lists of restrictive practices from which enterprises should refrain. The only principle for governments was that they should enact legislation that would cause the elimination of such practices. Yet the experience in the ensuing decades was that far more international problems arose from attempts at state enforcement of antitrust laws against foreigners or foreign transactions than from the issue of prevention of international antitrust violations. The extraterritorial application of U.S. antitrust law occasioned a whole series of significant diplomatic problems and even engendered blocking legislation by a number of other nations.[37] Similarly, when the Common Market Commission attempted to apply its antitrust law to activities outside the territory of the member states, or to gather information from neighboring countries, diplomatic problems and efforts at thwarting jurisdiction were quickly encountered.[38] It is instructive that when the OECD considered the international application of antitrust law, its first major agreement, reached in 1967, concerned itself primarily with the duty of one state to notify another of antitrust actions that might affect the important interests of the other.

In both the UNCTAD RBP principles and rules and the Transfer of Technology Code, the idea of setting forth principles for governments as well as for enterprises was quickly introduced and accepted by all groups, and has remained an integral part of the texts.

Section E of the UNCTAD RBP principles sets out in substantial detail principles and rules that states should follow at the national, regional, and subregional level. A clause urges states to adopt and improve legislation for the control of restrictive business practices. The next one suggests they should base their legislation on the principle of eliminating behavior or acts that abuse dominant positions, limit access to markets, or otherwise unduly restrain competition, and that have adverse effects on trade or development.

The key provision is the third, which instructs that when states do control restrictive business practices, they should ensure treatment of enterprises that is fair, equitable, and in accordance with established procedures of law, and that laws and regulations should be readily and publicly available. Group B insisted on additional language in the provision that national RBP laws should be not only fair and equitable, but also "nondiscriminatory." The Group of 77 eventually accepted this concept by adding language that enterprises should all be treated "on the same basis."

Paragraph E(4) commits states to seek appropriate measures to prevent the use of restrictive practices within their competence when it comes to their attention that such practices adversely affect international trade and development. Under paragraph 5, when states obtain information from enterprises that contains legitimate business secrets, they are obliged to accord such information reasonable safeguards normally applicable in this field.

There was a proposed paragraph 6, supported only by Group B, which, like the OECD recommendation of 1967, would have committed states contemplating enforcement action that would affect important interests of other states to notify those states of such action, preferably sufficiently in advance to facilitate consultation. The Group of 77 countries opposed on the grounds that they did not want to encourage diplomatic protests against their RBP cases. The clause was dropped as part of an overall compromise.

Paragraph 7 was a particularly important and controversial text. It dictated that states should take measures to prevent their legislation or administrative procedures from "fostering" the participation of enterprises in cartels when such participation would cause a dominant position of market power likely to have adverse affects on international trade or development. There were two disagreements over the wording of this provision. The Group of 77 would have preferred that the provision be directed particularly at developed countries, but this was not accepted by Group B. Group B, on the other hand, would have limited the provision to condemning participation of enterprises in "international" cartels, which arguably would have made the provision inapplicable to export arrangements involving companies selling out of a single nation.[39] Both the Group of 77 and Group D insisted that the provision should condemn national export cartels. The clause was ultimately dropped because no consensus was reached on it. The primary argument for reaching agreement to prevent export cartels was that the alternative is export warfare. This argument has some basis in recent events, though some export cartels are used to reduce trade surpluses and thus prevent trade wars. Also, it was difficult to devise a neutral principle concerning what should be condemned and what allowed. An unqualified condemnation of export cartels would have ignored the reality that many of them lack market power and are designed merely to achieve minor economies of scale in selling abroad. Moreover, such a condemnation would not have prevented other practices, such as merger of exporting firms or government-controlled export, that eliminate export competition even more effectively than does an export association.

The principles for enterprises also provide that states should institute notification procedures for obtaining such information from enterprises as is necessary for the control of restrictive business practices.

Provision 8 commits states with greater expertise in the control of restrictive business practices, on request, to share their experience with, or otherwise provide technical assistance to, other states wishing to develop such systems. Lastly in this section, a ninth provision urges states, on request or at their own initiative, to supply publicly available information, and possibly other information, necessary for its control of restrictive business practices to a requesting, interested state.

In the Transfer of Technology Code, the issue of rules for states had an opposite genesis. The Group of 77 wished to have a document proclaiming the unfettered right of recipient states to screen technology transfers. Developed states agreed to recognize the right of states to adopt measures concerning the "evaluation, negotiation and registration" of agreements, but in addition demanded text declaring that national regulation must be consistent with "international law." Thus, they indirectly raised the controversial issues of whether national regulation of technology transfer contracts could be deemed an expropriation of rights, and whether such a taking would necessitate prompt, adequate, and effective compensation.[40]

Though not conceding the appropriateness of an international law standard, the developing nations eventually agreed that national regulations "should be applied equitably, in accordance with established procedures of law." Group B has pressed for guarantees also of "fundamental fairness" and enforcement that is "without discrimination." The socialist countries, Group D, joined in the demand for a nondiscrimination standard.

The chapter affirms the right of a nation to govern the "terms and conditions and the duration of transfer of technology transactions," but counterbalances this right with the admonition that regulation should "promote a favorable and beneficial atmosphere for the international transfer of technology . . . under mutually agreed, fair and reasonable terms and conditions" which "take into account differing factors . . . such as local conditions."[41]

Lastly, strenuous negotiation produced a closing paragraph that, though somewhat tautological and obscure, attempts to balance respect for industrial property protection with development objectives: "Each country adopting legislation on the protection of industrial property should have regard to its national needs of economic and social development, and should ensure an effective protection of industrial property rights granted under its national law and other related rights recognized by its national law."

PRINCIPLES AND RULES FOR ENTERPRISES

Section D of the UNCTAD RBP principles and rules sets forth principles and rules for enterprises, including transnational corporations. It is provided, first, that enterprises should conform to the RBP laws of the countries in which they operate and be subject to the RBP laws and agencies there. Concern was expressed by business groups that this provision might imply a very broad theory of enterprise unity under which a host country would be presumed always to have antitrust jurisdiction over a foreign parent owing to the operations there of its subsidiary. Both the intent and the better reading of the language are that it is neutral on this complex issue. The definition of enterprise includes parents, subsidiaries, and the entity as a whole, but since they all cannot possibly be relevant in each instance, the only reasonable construction is that "enterprise" refers to the relevant parts of the whole, depending on standards such as which parts are operating in a country or are actually involved in the RBP in question.[42]

A second provision states that enterprises should cooperate with competent authorities in the countries in which they operate, and in particular should provide information such as details of restrictive arrangements required for RBP control. Information is to be provided even if it is located in foreign countries, unless such production is prevented by the applicable law or established public policy of the country where it is located.

Provision 3 deals with restrictive business practices of a cartel nature, and, after much hard negotiation on the parent-subsidiary issue, finally reads as follows:

3. Enterprises, except when dealing with each other in the context of an economic entity wherein they are under common control, including through ownership, or otherwise not able to act independently of each other, engaged on the market in rival or potentially rival activities, should refrain from practices such as the following when, through formal, informal, written or unwritten agreements or arrangements, they limit access to markets or otherwise unduly restrain competition, having or being likely to have adverse effects on international trade, particularly that of developing countries, and on the economic development of these countries:

   (a) agreements fixing prices including as to exports and imports;
   (b) collusive tendering;
   (c) market or customer allocation arrangements;
   (d) allocation by quota as to sales and production;
   (e) collective action to enforce arrangements—e.g., by concerted refusals to deal;
   (f) concerted refusal of supplies to potential importers;
   (g) collective denial of access to an arrangement, or association, which is crucial to competition.

This text is somewhat less clear than it appears to be. A "price-fixing" arrangement might set a maximum rather than a minimum price,[43] might merely fix prices overnight,[44] or might fix a price as a standard, e.g., medical fees for insurance compensation, with all sellers knowing they are free to charge a higher or lower price.[45] The legality of such practices would involve fine points of law and policy, with results varying from country to country. Moreover, in most countries workers, through unions, are free to fix the price they will demand for their labor; farmers are free, through cooperatives, to fix the prices for their crops going to market; and certain regulated industries, such as shipping conferences, are free to fix prices, possibly subject to public filing and review. In most countries, because of an inward theory of jurisdiction and a mercantilist trade policy, exporters are free to fix prices for products that will be sold only in other countries. It is often not forbidden for firms to form a joint venture to mine or manufacture a product, with the designated manager of the joint venture being allowed to fix the price of the product to be sold on behalf of the partners in the venture. Lastly, almost any form of price fixing might be ordered by, or authorized by, national law or a national official.

Thus, a UN code banning even well-known, relatively clear offenses like price fixing is nowhere near as certain a guide as it might seem. To a considerable extent, the sections of the document dealing with objectives, definitions, scope of application, exceptions, and general principles could clarify some of the ambiguities. Nevertheless, in most legal systems, rulings or guidelines issued by enforcing authorities, combined with decisions by a tribunal, would be needed to resolve subtle or unanticipated cases. Relying on voluntary compliance, or on separate interpretations by each UN member nation, will probably not produce uniform conduct or interpretations in regard to many of the most important behavioral questions, though particularly heinous forms of price fixing, such as secret bid rigging, will almost certainly be nearly universally condemned in theory and practice.

The other major horizontal cartel practices—market allocation, customer allocation, boycotts, etc.—raise essentially the same issues as those just discussed in relation to price fixing. The prohibitory rule is easy to draft, and securing agreement on it is not politically difficult, but major issues of interpretation and application remain.

The issue of how to deal with single-firm conduct, or with restrictive vertical agreements imposed by a stronger firm on a weaker one, is complicated by differing views—sometimes even within a single legal system—about what are the proper purposes of antitrust measures. The primary objective of all, or at least most, antitrust laws is to preserve the competitive process by deterring private restraints on it. A secondary, more political objective is to prevent the concentration of economic power. Third, there is a desire to control unfair methods of competition, though these may purposely be left to private tort law rather than be made part of public law. It is usually not an objective of RBP law to ensure that strong firms treat weak firms fairly in a commercial sense. But that issue has clouded the treatment of abuse of a dominant position, particularly in the context of technology transfer.

In the UNCTAD RBP negotiations, it was decided, as in the OECD guidelines, to deal with issues of single-firm conduct under the concept of "abuse of a dominant position of market power in a relevant market." The *Alcoa* case's concept of "monopolization" as primarily a structural offense requiring structural relief has not always found favor even in the United States, where recent decisions have moved quite close to an abuse standard. [46]

Eight types of conduct were listed as being potentially abusive when employed to limit access to markets or unduly restrain competition:

4. Enterprises should refrain from the following acts or behaviour in a relevant market when, through an abuse or acquisition and abuse of a dominant position of market power, they limit access to markets or otherwise unduly restrain competition, having or being likely to have adverse effects on international trade, particularly that of developing countries, and on the economic development of these countries:

    (a) predatory behaviour towards competitors, such as using below cost pricing to eliminate competitors;
    (b) discriminatory (i.e. unjustifiably differentiated) pricing or terms or conditions in the supply or purchase of goods or services, including by means of the use of pricing policies in transactions between affiliated enterprises which overcharge or undercharge for goods or services purchased or supplied as compared with prices for similar or comparable transactions outside the affiliated enterprises;
    (c) mergers, takeovers, joint ventures or other acquisitions of control, whether of a horizontal, vertical or a conglomerate nature;
    (d) fixing the prices at which goods exported can be resold in importing countries;
    (e) restrictions on the importation of goods which have been legitimately marked abroad with a trademark identical or similar to the trademark

protected as to identical or similar goods in the importing country where the trademarks in question are of the same origin, i.e., belong to the same owner or are used by enterprises between which there is economic, organizational, managerial or legal interdependence and where the purpose of such restrictions is to maintain artificially high prices;

(f) when not for ensuring the achievement of legitimate business purposes, such as quality, safety, adequate distribution or service:

   (i) partial or complete refusals to deal on the enterprise's customary commercial terms;

   (ii) making the supply of particular goods or services dependent upon the acceptance of restrictions on the distribution or manufacture of competing or other goods;

   (iii) imposing restrictions concerning where, or to whom, or in what form or quantities goods supplied or other goods may be re-sold or exported;

   (iv) making the supply of particular goods or services dependent upon the purchase of other goods or services from the supplier or his designee.

It was also agreed to include a note stating that whether a particular practice was abusive should be examined in terms of its purpose and effects in the actual situation, with reference also to the economic relationship of the firms involved, to any special conditions or economic circumstances in the relevant market, to whether the practice is of a type usually treated as acceptable under national and regional RBP laws, and to whether its effects are consistent with the purposes and objectives of the principles and rules.

Developing and socialist countries would have included excessive pricing as an abuse. Certain Group B nations, however, particularly the United States, Canada, and Australia, have always reasoned that a firm illegally monopolizes a market only when it engages in exclusionary conduct. High prices invite entry and thus are the opposite of exclusionary.[47] On the other hand, the RBP laws of at least West Germany, the United Kingdom, and the EEC are applicable to instances of excessive pricing.[48] The compromise was to tie the issue of excessive pricing to the discriminatory pricing offense, since even in the United States a seller can violate the Robinson-Patman anti-price discrimination act by charging a higher price to a disfavored consumer as well as by charging a lower price to a favored one.

The definition of "dominant position of market power" referred to enterprises that not only alone, but also when "acting with a few others," are in a position to control a relevant market. This reference would normally apply to concerted domination of a market. Even if it were interpreted to apply to parallel conduct amounting to "shared" or "joint" monopolization of a market, it would still be entirely consistent with existing Common Market and West German law regarding dominant positions,[49] but might involve a more controversial point under laws such as the American or Canadian antitrust statutes.[50] Nevertheless, the effect of the provision is essentially conservative, since nothing in the principles and rules defines being a member of a "shared monopoly" as an offense in itself. The effect of the substantive provisions, when combined with the definition, is to create a rule that offenses like price discrimination and tying arrangements are objectionable only when engaged in by one or a few of the leading firms dominating an industry. In a number of Group B jurisdictions, such as the United States and the EEC, these practices could be illegal even when engaged in by a nondominant firm.[51]

That provision D(4) (iv) focuses on trademark-related antitrust abuses in the UNCTAD RBP exercise, rather than in the Transfer of Technology Code, results partially from a formal Group B position, namely, that "naked" trademark licenses should not be deemed transfers of technology but should be covered instead by general RBP rules. In fact, there are precedents in the OECD countries condemning efforts by dominant firms to use licensed or assigned trademarks to prevent the importation of genuine parallel imports legitimately bearing the same mark where the purpose is to avoid competition, rather than to protect buyers from confusion or disappointment.[52] Curiously, the trademark area is one of the few in which under Western law the imposition of the restriction on an affiliated firm tends to make the practice more objectionable rather than less.[53]

The Group of 77 would have attacked the use of marketing strategies to hinder imports or exports by related enterprises as the high point of their effort to introduce investment and development issues regarding multinational enterprises into the RBP rules. Group B has rejected such a rule not only on this basis, but also because it could be so vague as to cast doubt on the legitimacy of countless management decisions by multinationals. Moreover, Group B contended that provisions (v) (a) and (v) (c) in paragraph 4, dealing with unreasonable refusals to deal and restrictions on sale or resale, provide adequate rules against any such practice by a multinational enterprise that would have the effect of entrenching a dominant firm, or injuring a competitor, in an unjustifiable manner. Western experts were prepared to tie the issue of parent-subsidiary export restraints to the doctrine of abuse of a dominant position of market power, but not to treat such restrictions as cartels. A practical example is the U.S. Justice Department's suit against the Everest and Jennings wheelchair company, a firm with about 70 percent of the U.S. market, which prevented its English affiliate from selling its lower priced chairs to American buyers. The complaint charged Everest and Jennings not with a conspiracy in violation of section 1 of the Sherman Act, but with monopolization and attempted monopolization in violation of section 2. The case was settled on the basis of "affirmative" relief, not only removing all restrictions on exports of foreign wheelchairs from E&J affiliates to the United States, but obligating the parent company to reward managers of its affiliates for making such exports.[54] Nevertheless, even this case falls far short of the rule suggested by the developing countries. The ruling applied to a multinational enterprise with a dominant market position that was preventing export to the market in which it was dominant, not to every multinational enterprise preventing exports to any market. Also, the *E&J* case challenged a refusal to sell for export to America a product that already was for sale and for which the buyer was prepared to pay the customary price, when the refusal was solely for the purpose of protecting the higher price structure of the parent in the United States. The Group of 77's attack on marketing strategies preventing or hindering exports is potentially applicable to much more defensible business conduct by MNEs. It now appears that UN delegates can reconcile the two positions into a sensible RBP rule, perhaps by reserving the broader investment issues for inclusion in the general code of conduct for TNEs being negotiated by the United Nations in New York.[55]

One of the more disputed antitrust offenses was the abuse of transfer pricing by overcharging or underpaying subsidiaries. Western opposition was based partially on a matter of principle. Group B delegates contended that transfer pricing is more properly treated as a tax or investment question than an antitrust issue. Transfer pricing is assigned a separate chapter in a general code of conduct for TNEs.

It is likely that, in the context of taxation, the United States and other developed countries would support the principle that parent-subsidiary transactions should be made on an arm's-length basis, compared to equivalent transactions.[56] But this does not conclusively settle whether or under what circumstances transfer pricing should be treated as an antitrust offense. Group B was prepared to support a text based on the OECD competition guideline, which condemns discriminatory pricing, including transfer pricing among affiliated firms, that is used as a means of adversely affecting competition outside those firms. Clearly, if a transfer price is to a wholly owned subsidiary and does not alter resale prices, there appears to be no competition issue at all. The colorful phrasing of this point is that the antitrust laws are indifferent to corporate self-abuse.[57]

As has been noted earlier, negotiation of the substantive rules concerning restrictive technology transfer practices has been a slower, more difficult, and more painstaking process than was negotiation of substantive rules in the RBP code. The developing countries sought in their original draft to outlaw or make unenforceable a list of forty practices encompassing virtually every form of control a licensor could seek in regard to a licensee.

The developed countries were initially prepared to condemn only eight licensing restrictions, and even most of those only when "unreasonable" in the circumstances. Gradually, the chapter narrowed to twenty practices, fourteen accepted in principle by all groups and six more pressed for by the developing countries or socialist states. Only four practices were in fully agreed text, with five more all agreed except for the modifier "unreasonably" insisted upon by Group B.

The conflict over the extent to which RBP prohibitions should be applied to parent-subsidiary restrictions, eventually settled conservatively in the UNCTAD RBP rules, remains in the introduction (*chapeau*) to the RBP chapter in the Transfer of Technology Code. The Group B text states that restrictions "for the purpose of rationalization or reasonable allocation of functions between parent and subsidiary" should "normally" not be considered contrary to the chapter unless amounting to an abuse of a dominant position of market power within the relevant market. The Group of 77 text states that the rules are applicable to parent-subsidiary relations, but that "such practices may be considered as not contrary . . . when they are otherwise acceptable and which [*sic*] do not adversely affect the transfer of technology."

It is essentially agreed that a licensor should not impose obligations extending beyond the life of the industrial property rights, should not seek to prevent the licensee from challenging the validity of a patent, should not prevent research or development into new products or processes, should not require the licensee to grant back exclusive sales or representation rights except where the licensee is acting as a manufacturing sub-contractor, and should refrain from entering into patent pools that unduly restrain competition. Most of these rules have analogues in U.S. and Common Market law.[58]

Other rules demanded by the developing countries, such as prohibitions against restrictions on the use of local personnel or restrictions on adaptation of the technology to local conditions, do not commonly arise as RBP issues in developed countries, but text was found that compromises what seem to be more investment or commercial than competition issues. The transformation of these provisions by negotiation from the simple prohibitions demanded by the Group of 77 to complex, carefully balanced rules is exemplary of the hard bargaining involved in drafting this code. The negotiated texts read as follows:

Restrictions on Use of Personnel
[Unreasonably]** # requiring the acquiring party to use personnel designated by the supplying party, except to the extent necessary to ensure the efficient transmission phase for the transfer of technology and putting it to use or thereafter continuing such requirement beyond the time when adequately trained local personnel are available or have been trained; or prejudicing the use of personnel of the technology acquiring country.

Restrictions on Adaptations
Restrictions which [unreasonably]** prevent the acquiring party from adapting the imported technology to local conditions or introducing innovations in it, or which oblige the acquiring party to introduce unwanted or unnecessary design or specification changes, if the acquiring party makes adaptations on his own responsibility and without using the technology supplying party's name, trade or service marks or trade names, and except to the extent that this adaptation unsuitably affects those products, or the process for their manufacture, to be supplied to the supplying party, his designates, or his other licensees, or to be used as a component or spare part in a product to be supplied to his customers.

Undoubtedly, the most important and hotly contested issue in the RBP chapter of the Transfer of Technology Code has been how permissive to be in regard to export restrictions imposed by a technology supplier. Such restrictions restrain international trade and may hinder the development of the recipient state. On the other hand, they often reflect the basically national and territorial nature of industrial property rights. Moreover, they

#Two asterisks following bracketed words denote text proposed by Group B.

frequently are the *sine qua non* for licensing and transferring valuable know-how to a developing country where lower labor or raw material costs might otherwise permit successful invasion of the technology supplier's home market or other markets where it has granted or retained exclusive rights.

The United States has usually applied its antitrust laws to export restrictions only in the context of *cross-licenses* between powerful companies who are using the restrictions to divide up world markets.[59] Even when the restrictions are based on pure know-how licenses, the relevant test is whether the licenses were necessary for the development of competitive products, and whether the restrictions are of reasonable scope and duration.[60] Common Market rulings are hard on export restrictions within that market, but not outside of it.[61]

In the context of the technology code negotiations, the debate over export restrictions has tended to center on when they are acceptable, rather than when they are not. Group B would have been content with a rule stating that export restrictions are bad when they are of unreasonable scope in terms of the products and countries they seek to cover, or when their duration exceeds that of the technology rights being transferred. Pressed to state when export bans are permissible, Group B took the position that they are justified when they prevent export to countries where the technology is legally protected, where the know-how is still secret, or where others have been licensed. Group D, which is relatively conservative on certain industrial property questions, supported the first and third justifications, but would not agree that know-how licensing justified export restraint. The Group of 77 has reluctantly indicated that it might acknowledge a supplier's right contractually to ban export to a country where the goods could in any event be excluded as infringing rights there, or to countries where others have been licensed for production. The insistence on licensing for production is consistent with a long-standing developing country position that technology rights should not be internationally protected when they are used to protect a market whose technology is not being exploited.[62] Group B has recognized this position in negotiations over revision of the Paris Convention for the protection of industrial property rights by agreeing to the validity of "march-in" compulsory licensing rights after three years or so of nonuse; but the issue is more complex in regard to know-how that is being constantly licensed or transferred for various purposes.[63] Moreover, Group B has been unwilling to accept the principle that it is impermissible to license "exclusives" for a group of countries except when production is contemplated in every one of them.

An important and largely agreed provision prohibits conditioning the transfer of a particular technology on the acceptance by the recipient of additional technology, goods, or services that he does not want, unless such tying is required to maintain quality where the supplier's name is used or to fulfill the specific obligations of a guarantee (it is noted here that the supplier should specify ingredients rather than tying, if feasible). Developing countries were so anxious to cause the "unbundling" of technology they purchase that they secured agreement that "avoiding undue or unnecessary packaging" of technology is a stated objective of the Code of Conduct.[64] There is a long history of Western antitrust cases condemning tying clauses in technology licenses, so agreement that there would be a provision on this topic was easy to obtain, though difficult negotiations accompanied the formulation of the exceptions to the rule.

Other carefully worded agreed texts define when a supplier may or may not restrict the right of the recipient to deal in competing products or technologies or to publicize the products resulting from the transferred technology in his own way.

A provision condemning supplier regulation of prices to be charged by a technology recipient remains bracketed because of insistence by the United States and a few other Group B countries that this practice is sometimes justifiable, particularly when there is only one licensee who is not in competition with the supplier.[65]

Agreement on a fourteenth provision is blocked by a small but significant difference in conception between the Group of 77 and Group B about the nature of know-how licensing. The developing countries have pressed for a rule condemning all restrictions or obligations that continue after the conclusion of a technology transfer arrangement, while the West would allow restrictions based on know-how that is still secret. The Group of 77 position would mean that if a firm licenses know-how for five years, it may not thereafter seek to prevent the licensee from continuing to make products based on that technology, or otherwise using or disclosing it. The conceptual argument is that you can sell knowledge but not lease it, since it cannot be erased from people's minds. Group B espouses the more conventional view that what happens to the know-how or use of it after the arrangement is a matter of commercial bargain. If the know-how has remained secret at the end of the contract, it should not be illegal for the licensor to have contracted for its return and its nonuse and nondisclosure. Interestingly, a U.S. Court of Appeals upheld approximately the Group of 77 theory in a two to one decision, but was promptly reversed by a unanimous Supreme Court, which held that the unfortunate licensee could be held to its bargain even when the know-how had become public and was being used by others who paid no royalty.[66] However, it should be noted that the American case involved only an obligation to pay royalties, not a ban on use which might have been found more anticompetitive. Also, the developing countries stress that Western cases are based on the assumption of fair bargains among equals, while the purpose of the Code of Conduct is to redress a perceived inequality of bargaining power resulting in one-sided agreements.

Provisions 15 through 20 would prohibit limitations on volume or field of use, abusive use of quality controls, required use of trademarks, required payment in equity shares, insistence on arrangements of unlimited duration, and limitations on use of technology "already imported." Not one of the provisions would clearly be illegal under most Western RBP laws, though certain of the practices could be considered objectionable if employed to achieve market division or significant restraint of competition.[67] The twentieth practice, moreover, is so purely development oriented that no acceptance of it seems possible. Western suppliers of technology do not seem likely to accept the principle that if they have licensed technology to a recipient in a particular country, they thereafter may not prevent the recipient from disseminating it to others and may not charge new royalties to later licensees.

LEGAL NATURE AND IMPLEMENTATION

Difficult issues in the UNCTAD negotiations on both the RBP and the Transfer of Technology Codes have concerned the legal nature and implementation of the rules being formulated. The position of Group B on their legal nature has been long-standing, clear, and adamant: The agreed rules or principles should be viewed as guidelines to be accepted on a voluntary basis by agreeing states and recommended by them to their enterprises. In the spring 1976 meeting of the UNCTAD RBP experts, the developed country experts offered the following text:

[P]rinciples for governments should be voluntary because of the greatly varying states of development among members of the United Nations and the divergencies in approaches to restrictive business practices, a field in which many member countries had no legislation or little experience. . . . [P]rinciples for enterprises should also be voluntary, since, in the foreseeable future, national or regional law, as perhaps guided by model laws, would be the most appropriate instrument for the enforcement of binding rules on enterprises. . . . There exists no worldwide international machinery for the enforcement and interpretation of any conceivable worldwide restrictive business practice rules, and little likelihood, given the wide divergence in national objectives, attitudes and experience in this field, that countries would be prepared to create and accept binding international enforcement and adjudication. . . . [A]ny attempt to enforce general principles for enterprises separately in each nation would lead to wide variations in interpretation, procedures and sanctions . . . this would be unfair and inequitable, would create an unstable and unpredictable atmosphere in which enterprises would be forced to operate, and could exacerbate conflicts among nations. On the other hand, voluntary principles could help to harmonize international opinion about restrictive business practices, shape the general behaviour of most enterprises, and facilitate international co-operation.

In drafting the codes, Group B was prepared only to agree to "encourage" its enterprises to "follow" the rules, rather than to "ensure" that they "conform" to the rules, as the Group of 77 would have preferred.[68]

The Group of 77, stressing that multinational enterprises in particular should not feel free to disregard these new international norms, for some time insisted that the words "shall refrain" rather than "should refrain" precede the listing of offenses to be avoided. Also, they initially insisted that the Transfer of Technology Code expressly obligate states to agree to an "internationally legally binding Code of Conduct on the transfer of technology."[69]

Nevertheless, the developing country position has been far less clear or consistent on this issue than appears on the surface of the texts. In the transfer of technology negotiations, when it became certain that the West would not agree to a binding code, the Group of 77 agreed to create a review committee that would reexamine the code and its legal nature after five years. But the Group of 77 would not publicly acknowledge that acceptance of this alternative signaled abandonment of its original position. In the UNCTAD RBP negotiations, the Group of 77 never expressly came out in support of a legally binding set of rules, probably because of the extreme sensitivity of OPEC nations and some other developing countries that the rules might boomerang against the practices of their national enterprises.

Moreover, the developing countries made it obvious that they do not favor international adjudication of rights and wrongs in RBP matters, particularly if the issue is the fairness of national treatment of a foreign enterprise.[70] Thus, the binding nature of the rules for enterprises was to be achieved essentially by national action in furtherance of the international agreement. For developed countries this would necessitate an extreme form of extraterritorial application of their antitrust or RBP laws. For instance, if an American firm licenses technology to Brazil with a clause restricting exports to China that is arguably violative of the RBP chapter of the Code of Conduct, Brazil can invalidate the restriction under its national law even without a binding international code. If Brazil for some reason wants the United States to invalidate the restriction, U.S. courts would face innumerable problems of jurisdiction and evidence. Nor would it be clear that Brazil would accept the result if U.S. courts found the restrictions reasonable and not violative of the code. If China wishes to have either Brazil or the United States invalidate the restriction, and both refuse to do so, it is totally unclear how such a dispute could be resolved absent an international tribunal.

Western countries are fully aware of, and reconciled to, the fact that even voluntary international guidelines can be promptly enacted as binding national law by any country wishing to do so, or adopted as a sort of investment pledge an enterprise must adhere to as a condition of doing business in a country. Developing countries have so far shown little inclination to make an antitrust code binding, as in the European Common Market, by means of an international commission armed with subpoenas and sanctions and an international court endowed with exclusive jurisdiction. Rather, they seem to favor the approach espoused by the United States in UN bribery code negotiations, namely, urging that signatories should bind themselves to amend national law to achieve comformity with the standards of the code. Such an approach in the antitrust or transfer of technology context could have the ironic and unworkable effect of obligating TNE home bases like the United States and the EEC to seek to engage in enforcement of antitrust laws on an even more extraterritorial basis than that which has previously caused substantial diplomatic controversy.

But the reality was that the West, the Communist nations, and the more conservative or nationalistic of the developing countries were unwilling to accede to a binding antitrust or technology code in the foreseeable future. Thus, after agreement by all groups that neither code would be binding at present, the remaining issues centered on the delineation of implementation, review, and consultation procedures that were consistent with the nonbinding nature of the rules.

In both UNCTAD negotiations, the developed country position in regard to implementation was to favor approximately the same approach as in the OECD, though with somewhat greater hesitation about agreeing to even as extensive a review process as was acceptable in the friendlier and more reliable confines of the OECD. The 1976 OECD declaration provides for a limited form of follow-up and implementation. It was agreed there that the Investment Committee of the OECD should examine and review "issues" arising under the guidelines. Such review was not to involve judging the practices of a single enterprise in a particular situation, though enterprises would be permitted to participate in a review when their information would be pertinent. Lastly, it was provided that the operation of the guidelines would be reviewed in general terms after three years (in 1979) in order to determine whether they should be altered or supplemented. Since 1976, the guidelines have been promulgated and endorsed, have been cited in a number of diplomatic negotiations and a few legal briefs, and have been used by the Investment Committee in the review of at least one controversy concerning the behavior of a multinational enterprise in which they appear to have caused an alteration in corporate behavior (in a labor relations matter.)[71] They were thoroughly reviewed in 1979, but only one small change was made.

The most substantial implementation provision of the UNCTAD RBP rules is a procedure for consultation at the request of a state, particularly a developing country, when it believes that bilateral diplomacy is appropriate in regard to an issue concerning control of restrictive business practices. States agree to give full consideration to such requests and, upon agreement as to subject matter and procedure, to consult in good faith. It is then stated that if the states involved so agree, a report on the matter should be made available to interested states or international organizations. The Group of 77 also would have provided that, with the permission of the involved states, any unresolved matter arising out of a consultation on restrictive business practices should be brought to the Trade and Development Board of UNCTAD in order that it might consider what further action might be taken to resolve the issue. Group B successfully opposed any such "conciliation" procedure.

An additional section provides that states should implement the agreed provisions by means of appropriate national legislation and regulation. A second provision in the section commits states to the creation of a permanent group of experts within a committee of UNCTAD to monitor implementation and to make proposals for possible improvements in the principles and rules.

In the negotiations on the Transfer of Technology Code, it is agreed in regard to implementation that states that have accepted the code should "take appropriate steps at the national level to meet their commitment to the Code." In addition, it is agreed that a committee of UNCTAD should provide a forum for exchange of views among states on matters related to the code, particularly on its application and experience gained in its operation. The committee is authorized to undertake studies and research for the purpose of furthering the aim of the code, to invite and consider studies from other parts of the UN system, to collect and disseminate information relating to the code, to make appropriate recommendations, and to organize symposiums and workshops about the application of the provisions of the code. Group B has so far rejected an additional provision that would empower the committee to provide a forum and procedure for negotiations and consultations between states concerning the interpretation or application of the code.

It is agreed that the committee shall review the implementation and application of the code five years after its adoption and make a decision whether to recommend an additional UN conference to revise all or part of the code for its improvement or further development.

Past experience suggests that consultation procedures will more likely be used to complain about antitrust investigations or prosecutions than to seek relief against an RBP. A study by the OECD in 1977 shows that the first paragraph of its 1967 resolution, calling for notification of enforcement proceedings, and usually in fact resulting in consultations about those proceedings, has been employed more than 150 times, by a large number of nations. [72] The second paragraph of the 1967 resolution, dealing with enforcement cooperation, has been used far less frequently. The 1973 resolution, dealing directly with the elimination of international restrictive business practices, has never been used; nor has the 1960 GATT consultation procedure on RBPs. [73] Thus, it appears that national law, not international cooperation or conciliation, remains the major method for eliminating those restrictive business practices that nations are willing to prevent or punish, while the only popular topic for consultation is conflict of jurisdiction and of national interests involved when one state attempts to investigate, prevent, or punish an alleged restrictive business practice involving nationals of another state.

Why is it that consultation is seldom used to attack RBPs? First of all, the adversely affected state is seldom totally dependent on aid from the home state of the TNE. It may have laws to control RBPs, or it can enact them. It may also control mergers, licensing, or pricing by means of investment or technology transfer screening laws. It may well be able to rely on an "effects" doctrine or on the presence of a branch to establish jurisdiction.[74] Second, most restrictive arrangements are discovered after they end, or cease upon being discovered. Consultation is not particularly helpful in obtaining punishment for past violations, or damages to compensate customers or other victims. Lastly, many modern states do not accept the premise that they are responsible for the behavior of "their" enterprises abroad. Moreover, they would likely be reluctant to seek to restrain conduct occurring outside their territory and probably not violative of their law, or as to which facts are unknown or in dispute.

On the other hand, in light of agreement on the creation of committees empowered to gather information concerning experience under the codes as well as to discuss "issues" arising under them, it seems likely that indirect pressures for avoidance of certain RBPs or of certain governmental encouragement of them will result from such multilateral consultations. The latter would probably be workable if carried out with UNCTAD's emphasis on consensus rather than on voting by nation. This approach, although slow and tending toward generalities, avoids embarrassing the leading home countries of TNEs by means of lopsided majority votes, and forcing them into defensive postures.

CONCLUSION

The subject of international antitrust codes is full of paradoxes. As has been discussed earlier here, in 1967 Corwin Edwards wrote that global approaches to control of RBPs could not succeed for many reasons, mostly related to differences in national laws, in degree of development, and in attitudes toward the free market system. Yet, in 1968 Edwards agreed to become a consultant to UNCTAD to outline new projects for UN involvement in the control of RBPs.[75] The subject of restrictive business practices is obviously too important to be ignored internationally in the age of the multinational corporation. And the United States was and is too dedicated to antitrust law and too expert in it to play any international role short of leadership. Such leadership will be crucial to ensure that the UN RBP Code and the permanent committee of experts function in neutral, procompetitive ways.

It seems likely that some suspicion about UN rules will persist in American business circles. The NAM and the Chamber of Commerce led the opposition to the codes, but eventually came to support the RBP Code as finally adopted. Originally, U.S. business organizations expressed concern that any UN antitrust agreement would involve undue exceptions or preferences for developing country and state enterprises, would not sufficiently recognize the reasons for parent company control of subsidiaries, would so embrace development goals as to lose its identity as a competition code, and would be so vague as to be open to changing and abusive interpretations.[76] It was also argued that the exclusion of intergovernmental agreements—such as OPEC—from the code would vitiate its usefulness.

Many of these criticisms were important in shaping a final text that the United States and multinational companies could support. Some of the objections, however, appear in retrospect to have been excessive or unfounded. There was undoubtedly reason for concern that wholesale acceptance of the Group of 77's initial positions in the transfer of technology and RBP negotiations would have threatened the procompetitive rationale of antitrust regulation and might have involved endorsement of discriminatory treatment of Western enterprises, with the long-run effect of discouraging foreign licensing, trade, and investment rather than facilitating them on more acceptable terms. But the outcome of the negotiations has been strongly conservative of basic antitrust positions. The logic of the discipline almost always triumphed over hastily improvised efforts to graft investment and development politics upon established antitrust doctrines. More importantly, early recognition in these negotiations that control of RBPs is much more a problem of disputes between governments about when and how to prevent, allow, or even encourage RBPs than a problem simply relating to enterprise behavior led to a careful balance in the texts between rules for states and rules for companies.

In late 1974, the developing countries pushed a "Charter of Economic Rights and Duties" through the UN General Assembly, over the reservation of the United States, the United Kingdom, the Federal Republic of

Germany, and a few other Western states, in an attempt to create a new principle of international law legitimizing unfettered national sovereignty over natural resources and foreign investment.[77] As Oscar Schachter has perceptively pointed out, the effect, paradoxically, was just the opposite: The very recourse to international declarations strengthened the principle that economic regulation by nations is indeed subject to international rules, however permissive those may be in a given document.[78] The transfer of technology and RBP exercises have carried forward this trend in a much more obvious way. Developing countries have won the principles that enterprises have no more right to engage in RBPs against weak states than against strong ones, and that all states have the right to enact and enforce legislation in this field. The price for these principles has been agreement to rules that tend to establish what is acceptable commercial conduct as much as what is unacceptable, and to rules that specify such duties as fair treatment and respect for confidentiality that states owe to foreign enterprises involved in RBP disputes. These tough, specialized negotiations in the UNCTAD forum have eroded much of the *carte blanche* for arbitrary regulation contained in the Charter of Economic Rights and Duties.

The relation of the UNCTAD RBP principles to the legitimization of commodity cartels like OPEC is somewhat more complex. The Charter of Economic Rights and Duties stated unequivocally that producer cartels are good and that no state should interfere with them. Significantly, the Western alternative to this text was not a condemnation of such cartels but rather a demand that consumer countries should be included in the negotiation of any such "stabilization agreements." The UNCTAD RBP principles largely bypass the OPEC issue by providing that restrictive business practices are practices by enterprises, not by states themselves, and by exempting intergovernmental agreements. The possibility that OPEC needs the cooperation of enterprises to function and that the RBP text on exemptions based on state approval may be read to require the approval of consumer states might justify discussions or consultations about OPEC or similar cartels in an UNCTAD RBP forum, but there seems no likelihood that such requested consultation would even be accepted, much less cause modification of a major commodity cartel among producer governments.

International antitrust rules are justified not only by free market or free trade principles, but also by the concept that restraint or cartelization of international markets is a sovereign prerogative and therefore that private enterprises may not engage in such activities except under rules set down by states. This concept reflects fundamental American conceptions of the separation of private and state economic activity. Condemning restrictive business practices by enterprises in an antitrust code while leaving the issue of OPECs to state-to-state diplomatic relations is entirely consistent with this approach.

In the long run, UN antitrust principles, combined with continuing international work and study in the antitrust field, may help to create a climate unfavorable to OPECs, much as U.S. antitrust principles justified the fight to de-regulate American industries cartelized in the 1930s.[79]

During this active period of formulation of RBP principles at the international level, it is too early to make a final assessment or prediction about the value of what has been or will be achieved. Some successes are evident. Controlling restrictive business practices has been accepted as an international goal, justified largely on the basis of a free market rationale. Discrimination against foreign enterprises has been avoided, while the principle of fair treatment has been firmly established. The seeds for useful institutional work internationally at the expert level have been planted.

In regard to the larger issues, measurement of success will turn on the modesty of one's conception of what is presently possible. Final codification of a body of law like antitrust that varies widely and does not exist in many countries is almost certainly not feasible. Direct international investigation and punishment of individual restrictive practices seems equally unlikely in the near future, given nations' insistence on sovereignty and the diversity, even conflict, of their interests. But increased international publicity about, and a subsequent reduction in, certain types of RBPs seems more attainable as a positive result of these exercises. Transforming grievances about multinational enterprises from political rhetoric into specific issues about which experts can analyze facts and negotiate rules can be a significant step in reducing North-South tensions and improving the climate for investment. All in all, there seem to be good grounds for judging the work of the last five years as being a success.

NOTES

1. Edwards' writings include *Economic and Political Aspects of International Cartels,* U.S. Congress, Senate, A Study for the Subcommittee on War Mobilization of the Committee on Military Affairs, 78th Cong., 2d Sess. (Washington, D.C.:

Government Printing Office, 1944); *Maintaining Competition: Requisites of a Governmental Policy* (New York: McGraw-Hill, 1949); *Big Business and the Policy of Competition* (Cleveland: Western Reserve University Press, 1956).

2. Public letter, Franklin D. Roosevelt to Cordell Hull, Sept. 1944, quoted by Edwards in his article, "The Possibilities of an International Policy Toward Cartels," in *A Cartel Policy for the United Nations* (New York: Columbia University Press, 1945), p. 97.

3. Edwards' work in Japan is described in Eleanor M. Hadley, *Antitrust in Japan* (Princeton: Princeton University Press, 1970), pp. 125–26.

4. Title V of *Havana Charter for an International Trade Organization,* Department of State Publication no. 3206, Commercial Policy Series no. 114 (Washington, D.C.: Government Printing Office, 1948). The negotiation is described in Dale Furnish, "A Transnational Approach to Restrictive Business Practices," *International Lawyer* (1970), 4:322–27.

5. See U.S. Congress, House, Hearings before the Committee on Foreign Affairs, 81st Cong., 2d Sess., on H.R. Res. 236 (Washington, D.C.: Government Printing Office, 1950), p. 564. See also *ibid.,* p. 419.

6. See Sigmund Timberg, "Restrictive Business Practices as an Appropriate Subject for United Nations Action," *Antitrust Bulletin* (1955), 1:410.

7. Report of the Ad Hoc Committee on Restrictive Business Practices, ECOSOC, Official Records, 16th Sess., Supp. no. 11, UN Doc. E/2380 (1953), pp. 12–18.

8. See Corwin D. Edwards, *Control of Cartels and Monopolies* (Dobbs Ferry, New York: Oceana, 1967), pp. 234–35.

9. UN Doc. E/2612/Add.2 (1955), p. 5. See Furnish, "Restrictive Business Practices," p. 327.

10. The ECSC rules are discussed in Edwards, *Cartels and Monopolies,* pp. 243–79. The Common Market rules are examined, e.g., in James A. Rahl, "European Common Market Antitrust Laws," *Antitrust Law Journal* (1971), 40:810.

11. Edwards, *Cartels and Monopolies,* pp. 325–26.

12. *Ibid.,* p. 327.

13. UNCTAD Res. 73 (III), May 19, 1972, discussed in L. Robert Primoff, "International Regulation of Multinational Corporations and Business—the United Nations Takes Aim," *Journal of International Law and Economics* (1976), 11:288–89.

14. See Fritz Machlup, "The Nature of the International Cartel Problem," in *A Cartel Policy,* pp. 11–12.

15. See Ben W. Lewis, "The Status of Cartels in Post-War Europe," in *ibid.,* pp. 25–46.

16. Detlev Vagts, "The Multinational Enterprise: A New Challenge for Transnational Law," *Harvard Law Review* (1970), 83:739.

17. *The Impact of Multinational Corporations on the Development Process and on International Relations* (New York: United Nations, 1974, Sales no. E.74.II.A.5).

18. *Ibid.,* p. 69.

19. *Ibid.,* p. 111.

20. *Ibid.*, p. 143.

21. OECD, *Restrictive Business Practices of Multinational Enterprises* (Paris: OECD, 1977).

22. *Ibid.*, p. 58, paras. 193 and 194.

23. *Ibid.*, pp. 59 and 63, paras. 200 and 212.

24. UN Doc. TD/B/C.2/119/Rev.1 (1974).

25. See UNCTAD, Report of the Second Ad Hoc Group of Experts on Restrictive Business Practices (Geneva: United Nations, 1976, TD/B/C.2/AC.5/6); UNCTAD, Report of the Third Ad Hoc Group of Experts on Restrictive Business Practices on its Sixth Session (Geneva: United Nations, 1979, TD/B/C.2/AC.6/20).

26. OECD, *International Investment and Multinational Enterprises* (Paris: OECD, 1976), discussed in Joel Davidow, "Some Reflections on the OECD Competition Guidelines," *Antitrust Bulletin* (1977), 12:441.

27. The background of these conferences is discussed in Mark R. Joelson, "The Proposed Codes of Conduct as Related to Restrictive Business Practices," *Law and Policy in International Business* (1977), 8:857–61. See also UNCTAD Res. 89(iv) (1976), and UNCTAD Res. 103(v) (1979).

28. See generally Marcus B. Finnegan, "Code: A Panacea or Pitfall?" *Les Nouvelles* (June 1978), pp. 74–75.

29. See generally Joel Davidow, "U.S. Antitrust Laws and International Transfers of Technology: The Government View," *Fordham Law Review* (1975), 43:733; Marcus B. Finnegan, "The Burgeoning Development of the Common Market Competition Rules and its Impact on International Licensing," *Mercer Law Review* (1976), 27:519.

30. See Pugwash Code, UN Doc. TD/B/AC.11/L.12 (1974); Surendra Patel, "Transfer of Technology and Developing Countries," *Foreign Trade Review* (January–March 1972), 6:387.

31. See J. D. Gribbin, rev. of OECD, *Export Cartels,* Report of the Committee of Experts on Restrictive Business Practices, 1974, *Antitrust Bulletin* (Summer 1976), 21(2):343–44.

32. One such study is UNCTAD, Major Issues Arising from the Transfer of Technology to Developing Countries, UN Doc. TD/B/AC.11/10/Rev.1 (1974).

33. UNCTAD Res. 113(v), June 3, 1979.

34. UNCTAD, The Set of Multilaterally Agreed Equitable Principles and Rules for the Control of Restrictive Business Practices, UN Doc. TD/RBP/CONF/10 (April 1980) (hereinafter referred to as RBP Code), Scope of Application, provision 4.

35. See UNCTAD, Draft International Code of Conduct on the Transfer of Technology, UN Doc. TD/CODE TOT/20 (1979) (hereinafter cited as TOT Code), provision 1.4 and n.6.

36. Mannington Mills v. Congoleum Corp., 595 F.2d 1278, 1296 (3d Cir. 1979); Timberlane Lumber Co. v. Bank of America, 549 F.2d 597, 612 (9th Cir. 1976).

37. See Note, "Discovery of Documents Located Abroad in U.S. Antitrust Lit-

igation: Recent Developments in the Law Concerning the Foreign Illegality Excuse for Non-production," *Virginia Journal of International Law* (1974), 14:747; International Law Association, *Report of the Fifty-first Conference Held at Tokyo* (London: ILA, 1965) (collection of diplomatic protests), pp. 565–92.

38. One such matter was the *Hoffman-La Roche Vitamins* case. Hoffman objected that the Commission was using this information obtained through a breach of the Swiss Criminal Code, but this contention was rejected in a decision of the Commission (76/642/EEC of June 9, 1976). The informant was prosecuted *in absentia* by the Swiss Government, discussed in Jeremy Lever, "Aspects of Jurisdictional Conflict in the Field of Discovery," in *Proceedings of Fifth Annual Fordham Corporate Law Institute on International Antitrust* (New York: Harcourt, Brace, Jovanovich, 1979), p. 358.

39. This distinction would approximate the present state of U.S. law, under which national export cartels are exempted by the Webb-Pomerene Act of 1918, 15 U.S.C. §§61–66 (1976); but cartel agreement between a U.S. export cartel and a foreign one is not permitted. United States v. United States Alkalai Export Ass'n, 86 F.Supp. 59 (S.D.N.Y. 1949).

40. See Don C. Piper, "On Changing or Rejecting the International Legal Order," *International Lawyer* (1978), 12:293.

41. TOT Code, provision 3.1.

42. Illustrative of the highly factual nature of this determination are Zenith Radio Corp. v. Matsushita Elec. Inc. Co., 402 F.Supp. 262 (E.D. Pa. 1975) (parent-sub treated as an entity); and Williams v. Canon, Inc., 432 F.Supp. 376 (C.D. Cal. 1977) (insufficient contacts found between parent and sub). See generally, OECD, *Restrictive Business Practices,* pp. 40–54; Joseph Griffen, "The Power of Host Countries Over the Multinational: Lifting the Veil in the European Economic Community and the United States," *Law and Policy in International Business* (1974), 6:375.

43. This practice would violate U.S. antitrust law. *See, e.g.,* Albrecht v. Herald Co., 390 U.S. 145 (1968). However, it is almost never attacked by the Justice Department or the Federal Trade Commission. The rule is criticized in Philip Elman, " 'Petrified Opinions' and Competitive Realities," *Columbia Law Review* (1966), 66:625.

44. Chicago Board of Trade v. United States, 246 U.S. 231 (1918).

45. *See, e.g.,* United States v. American Society of Anesthesiologists, Inc., 473 F.Supp. 147 (E.D. Pa. 1979).

46. United States v. Aluminum Co. of America, 148 F.2d 416, 426 (2d Cir. 1945). See Laurens H. Rhinelander, "The Roche Case: One Giant Step for British Antitrust," *Virginia Journal of International Law* (Fall 1974), 15:34–35.

47. See Rhinelander, "The Roche Case" pp. 34–35. United Brands Co., [1975–2] Comm. Mkt. Rep. (CCH) ¶9800; Corwin D. Edwards, "American and German Policy Toward Conduct by Powerful Enterprises: A Comparison," *Antitrust Bulletin* (1978), 23:100.

48. See Edwards, "American and German Policy," pp. 93–94; Kurt Markert, "The New German Antitrust Reform Law," *Antitrust Bulletin* (1974), 19:135; Val-

entine Korah, "Interpretation and Application of Article 86 of the Treaty of Rome: Abuse of a Dominant Position within the Common Market," *Notre Dame Lawyer* (1978), 53:768.

49. See Treaty Establishing European Economic Community, *United Nations Treaty Series,* 298:11, Art. 86, March 25, 1957; European Economic Commission, *Report by the Commission on the behavior of the oil companies in the Community during the period from October 1973 to March 1974* (Brussels: European Communities, 1977), pp. 154–55. Under German law, see section 22 of the German Law Against Restraints of Competition, July 27, 1957; see also Kurt Markert, "The Control of Abuses by Market-Dominating Enterprises Under German Antitrust Law," *Cornell International Law Journal* (Summer 1978), 11:275.

50. See Edward H. Levi, "The Antitrust Laws and Monopoly," *University of Chicago Law Review* (1947), 14:153; Richard A. Posner, "Oligopoly and the Antitrust Laws: A Suggested Approach," *Stanford Law Review* (1969), 21:1562; W. T. Stanbury and G. B. Reschenthaler, "Oligopoly & Conscious Parallelism: Theory, Policy & Canadian Cases," *Osgoode Hall Law Journal* (1977), 15:617–700.

51. In the United States, the Robinson-Patman Act prohibits price discrimination by any seller. See Corwin D. Edwards, *The Price Discrimination Law* (Washington, D.C.: Brookings Institution, 1959). Tying arrangements are also condemned by U.S. law whenever the party using them has sufficient economic power in the tying product to appreciably restrain competition. Northern Pac. Ry. v. United States, 356 U.S. 1 (1958). The Treaty of Rome, Article 85(d) and (e), condemns price discrimination and tying arrangements by parties whenever those practices have as their object or effect the restraint of competition, and regardless of whether the parties have a dominant position cognizable under Article 86.

52. See generally, OECD, *Restrictive Business Practices relating to Trademarks* (Paris: OECD, 1978). *See also* the EEC cases Grundig-Consten, [1966] E.C.R. 299, and Sirena, [1971] E.C.R. 69.

53. *See* United States v. Guerlain Inc. 155 F.Supp. 77 (S.D.N.Y.), *dismissed,* 172 F.Supp. 107 (S.D.N.Y. 1959); 19 C.F.R. §133.21(b) and (c).

54. United States v. Everest & Jennings Intl., Civ. No. 77–1648 R (C.D. Cal. 1977), [1979–1] Trade Cases (CCH) ¶62508, at 76,961 (Feb. 5, 1979).

55. For instance, the OECD Guidelines on International Investment and Multinational Enterprises ("Competition Guidelines") provide in guideline 5 on general policies that MNEs should "allow their component entities freedom to develop their activities and to exploit their competitive advantage in domestic and foreign markets, consistent with the need for specialization and sound commercial practice." This provision is not treated as an antitrust principle, but as an investment policy. No analogous principle has yet been proposed in the UN Centre's code on TNEs. The Competition Guidelines are an annex to the OECD Declaration on International Investment and Multinational Enterprises of June 21, 1976.

56. In the OECD Guidelines for Multinational Enterprises, the second taxation guideline warns against use of "transfer pricing which does not conform to an arms length standard" to violate national laws.

57. The relevant OECD text is Competition Guideline 1(e). Two U.S. antitrust

cases, Gottesman v. General Motors Corp., 310 F.Supp. 1257 (S.D.N.Y. 1970), *aff'd,* 436 F.2d 1205 (2d Cir. 1971), and Trans World Airlines v. Hughes, 449 F.2d 51 (2d Cir. 1971), *rev'd on other grounds,* 409 U.S. 363 (1973), suggest that tying arrangements by a parent company to "bleed" an affiliate may be actionable under the antitrust laws at the behest of minority stockholders.

58. *See* Brulotte v. Thys Co., 379 U.S. 29 (1964), and A.O.I.P. v. Beyrard, 17 Comm. Mkt. L.R. D14 (1976) (condemning restrictions after expiration); Lear, Inc. v. Adkins, 395 U.S. 653 (1969), and Davidson Rubber, 11 Comm. Mkt. L.R. D52 (1972) (condemning "no-challenge" clauses); Transparent Wrap Mach. Corp. v. Stokes & Smith Co., 329 U.S. 637 (1947), and Raymond-Nagoya, [1973] Comm. Mkt. Rep. (CCH) §9513 (applying a rule of reason to grant-back clauses). See generally Mark R. Joelson, "United States Law and the Proposed Code of Conduct on the Transfer of Technology," *Antitrust Bulletin* (1978), 23:835.

59. *Compare* United States v. National Lead Co., 332 U.S. 319 (1947), and United States v. Imperial Chem. Indus., 100 F.Supp. 504 (S.D.N.Y. 1951) (condemning cross-licensing international cartels) *with* Brownell v. Ketchum Wire & Mfg. Co., 211 F.2d 121 (9th Cir. 1954), and Dunlop Co., Ltd. v. Kelsey-Hayes Co., 484 F.2d 407 (6th Cir. 1973) (upholding export restrictions on one-way licenses).

60. *See* Foundry Services Inc. v. Beneflux Corp., 110 F.Supp. 857 (S.D.N.Y. 1953), Shin Nippon Koki Co. v. Irvin Industries, Inc., [1975–1] Trade Cases (CCH) ¶60,347, 66,438 (N.Y. Sup. Ct. 1975); U.S. Department of Justice, *Antitrust Guide for International Operations* (Washington, D.C.: Government Printing Office, 1977), pp. 28–32.

61. *Compare* Consten and Grundig-Verkaufs GmbH v EEC Comm'n, [1966] Comm. Mkt. Rep. (CCH) ¶7618, and Centrafarm B.V. v. Sterling Drug, Inc., 14 Comm. Mkt. L.R. 480 (1974) *with* Raymond-Nagoya, [1973] Comm. Mkt. Rep. (CCH) ¶9513 (1973).

62. See UNCTAD, The Role of the Patent System in the Transfer of Technology to Developing Countries, UN Doc. TD/B/AC.11/19/Rev.1 (1975), pp. 47–52.

63. *See* United States v. Westinghouse Elec. Corp., 471 F.Supp. 532 (N.D. Cal. 1978), *appeal filed,* No. 794109 (9th Cir. 1979). See generally, Miles W. Kirkpatrick and Steven P. Mahinka, "Antitrust and the International Licensing of Trade Secrets and Know-How: A Need for Guidelines," *Law and Policy in International Business* (1977), 9:725.

64. TOT Code, provision (viii).

65. *See* United States v. General Elec. Co., 272 U.S. 476 (1926), discussed in Lawrence A. Sullivan, *Handbook of the Law of Antitrust* (St. Paul: West, 1977), ¶185, pp. 541–54.

66. Aronson v. Quick Point Pencil Co., 99 S.Ct. 1096 (1979), *rev'g* 567 F.2d 757 (8th Cir. 1977).

67. See Sullivan, *Antitrust,* ¶186, pp. 554–62.

68. TOT Code, preamble, provision 11, p. 2.

69. *Ibid.,* provision 13.

70. This can be seen in the Group of 77's insistence that codes be enforced by national, not international, means, and that granting exemptions should be the right of national officials.

71. Roger Blanpain, *The Badger Case and the OECD Guidelines for Multinational Enterprises* (Amsterdam: Kluwer-Deventer, 1977).

72. OECD, Report on the Operation of the 1967 Council Recommendation Concerning Cooperation Between Member Countries on Restrictive Business Practices Affecting International Trade During the Period 1967–1975, reprinted in *Antitrust Bulletin* (Summer 1977), 22:459–85.

73. See UNCTAD, International Consultation and Conciliation Procedures Aimed at Facilitating Control of Restrictive Business Practices, UN Doc. TD/B/C.2/AC.5/3 (1975); Joel Davidow and Lisa Chiles, "The United States and the Issue of the Binding or Voluntary Nature of Codes of Conduct Regarding Restrictive Business Practices," *American Journal of International Law* (April 1978), 72:265–68.

74. See OECD, *Restrictive Business Practices*, pp. 35–45.

75. Edwards was a principal author of a paper entitled "Study of Certain Restrictive Business Practices Adopted by Private Enterprises of Developed Countries," UN Doc. TD/B/C.2/54 (1968). This study was made pursuant to Resolution 25(II) of the second UNCTAD Conference.

76. U.S. industry's position is reviewed in David G. Gill, "The UNCTAD Restrictive Business Practices Code: A Code for Competition?" *International Lawyer* (1979), 13:607.

77. See Charles N. Brower and John B. Tepe, "The Charter of Economic Rights and Duties of States: A Reflection or Rejection of International Law," *International Lawyer* (1975), 9:295.

78. Oscar Schachter, "The Evolving International Law of Development," *Columbia Journal of Transnational Law* (1976), 15:16.

79. See chapter 4, "Participation of Competition Officials in the Formulation and Implementation of Regulatory Regimes and Programs" in OECD, *Competition Policy in Regulated Sectors* (Paris: OECD, 1979).

Appendix

❖

THE SET OF MULTILATERALLY AGREED EQUITABLE PRINCIPLES AND RULES FOR THE CONTROL OF RESTRICTIVE BUSINESS PRACTICES

The United Nations Conference on Restrictive Business Practices,

Recognizing that restrictive business practices can adversely affect international trade, particularly that of developing countries, and the economic development of these countries,

Affirming that a Set of Multilaterally Agreed Equitable Principles and Rules for the control of restrictive business practices can contribute to attaining the objective in the establishment of a New International Economic Order to eliminate restrictive business practices adversely affecting international trade and thereby contribute to development and improvement of international economic relations on a just and equitable basis,

Recognizing also the need to ensure that restrictive business practices do not impede or negate the realization of benefits that should arise from the liberalization of tariff and non-tariff barriers affecting international trade, particularly those affecting the trade and development of developing countries,

Considering the possible adverse impact of restrictive business practices, including among others those resulting from the increased activities of transnational corporations, on the trade and development of developing countries,

Convinced of the need for action to be taken by countries in a mutually reinforcing manner at the national, regional and international levels to eliminate or effectively deal with restrictive business practices, including those of transnational corporations adversely affecting international trade, particularly that of developing countries, and the economic development of these countries.

Convinced also of the benefits to be derived from a universally applicable

set of multilaterally agreed equitable principles and rules for the control of
restrictive business practices and that all countries should encourage their
enterprises to follow in all respects the provisions of such a set of multilaterally agreed equitable principles and rules,

Convinced further that the adoption of such a set of multilaterally agreed
equitable principles and rules for the control of restrictive business practices will thereby facilitate the adoption and strengthening of laws and
policies in the area of restrictive business practices at the national and
regional levels and thus lead to improved conditions and attain greater efficiency and participation in international trade and development, particularly that of developing countries and to protect and promote social welfare
in general, and in particular the interests of consumers in both developed
and developing countries;

Affirming also the need to eliminate the disadvantages to trade and development which may result from the restrictive business practices of
transnational corporations or other enterprises, and thus help to maximize
benefits to international trade and particularly the trade and development
of developing countries;

Affirming further the need that measures adopted by States for the control
of restrictive business practices should be applied fairly, equitably, on the
same basis to all enterprises and in accordance with established procedures
of law; and for States to take into account the principles and objectives of
the Set of Multilaterally Agreed Equitable Principles and Rules,

Hereby agrees on the following Set of Principles and Rules for the control
of restrictive business practices, which take the form of recommendations:

SECTION A—*Objectives*

Taking into account the interests of all countries, particularly those of
developing countries, the Set of Multilaterally Agreed Equitable Principles
and Rules are framed in order to achieve the following objectives:

1. To ensure that restrictive business practices do not impede or negate
    the realization of benefits that should arise from the liberalization of
    tariff and non-tariff barriers affecting world trade, particularly those
    affecting the trade and development of developing countries.
2. To attain greater efficiency in international trade and development,
    particularly that of developing countries, in accordance with national
    aims of economic and social development and existing economic
    structures, such as through:

(a) The creation, encouragement and protection of competition;

(b) Control of the concentration of capital and/or economic power;

(c) Encouragement of innovation.

3. To protect and promote social welfare in general and, in particular, the interests of consumers in both developed and developing countries.

4. To eliminate the disadvantages to trade and development which may result from the restrictive business practices of transnational corporations or other enterprises, and thus help to maximize benefits to international trade and particularly the trade and development of developing countries.

5. To provide a Set of Multilaterally Agreed Equitable Principles and Rules for the control of restrictive business practices for adoption at the international level and thereby to facilitate the adoption and strengthening of laws and policies in this area at the national and regional levels.

SECTION B—Definitions and scope of application

For the purpose of this set of Multilaterally Agreed Equitable Principles and Rules

(i) *Definitions*:

1. "Restrictive business practices" means acts or behaviour of enterprises which, through an abuse or acquisition and abuse of a dominant position of market power, limit access to markets or otherwise unduly restrain competition, having or being likely to have adverse effects on international trade, particularly that of developing countries, and on the economic development of these countries, or which through formal, informal, written or unwritten agreements or arrangements among enterprises have the same impact.

2. "Dominant position of market power" refers to a situation where an enterprise, either by itself or acting together with a few other enterprises, is in a position to control the relevant market for a particular good or service or group of goods or services.

3. "Enterprises" means firms, partnerships, corporations, companies, other associations, natural or juridical persons, or any combination thereof, irrespective of the mode of creation or control or ownership, private or State, which are engaged in commercial activities, and includes their branches, subsidiaries, affiliates, or other entities directly or indirectly controlled by them.

(ii) *Scope of application*:

4. The Set of Principles and Rules apply to restrictive business prac-

tices, including those of transnational corporations, adversely affecting international trade, particularly that of developing countries and the economic development of these countries. They apply irrespective of whether such practices involve enterprises in one or more countries.

5. The "principles and rules for enterprises, including transnational corporations" apply to all transactions in goods and services.

6. The "principles and rules for enterprises, including transnational corporations" are addressed to all enterprises.

7. The provisions of the Set of Principles and Rules shall be universally applicable to all countries and enterprises regardless of the parties involved in the transactions, acts or behaviour.

8. Any reference to "States" or "Governments" shall be construed as including any regional groupings of States, to the extent that they have competence in the area of restrictive business practices.

9. The Set of Principles and Rules shall not apply to intergovernmental agreements, nor the restrictive business practices directly caused by such agreements.

SECTION C—*Multilaterally agreed equitable principles for the control of restrictive business practices*

In line with the objectives set forth, the following principles are to apply:

(i) *General principles*

1. Appropriate action should be taken in a mutually reinforcing manner at national, regional and international levels to eliminate, or effectively deal with, restrictive business practices, including those of transnational corporations, adversely affecting international trade, particularly that of developing countries and the economic development of these countries.

2. Collaboration between governments at bilateral and multilateral levels should be established, and where such collaboration has been established, it should be improved to facilitate the control of restrictive business practices.

3. Appropriate mechanisms should be devised at the international level and/or the use of existing international machinery improved to facilitate exchange and dissemination of information among governments with respect to restrictive business practices.

4. Appropriate means should be devised to facilitate the holding of multilateral consultations with regard to policy issues relating to the control of restrictive business practices.

5. The provisions of the Set of Principles and Rules should not be construed as justifying conduct by enterprises which is unlawful under applicable national or regional legislation.

(ii) *Relevant factors in the application of the Set of Principles and Rules*

6. In order to ensure the fair and equitable application of the Set of Principles and Rules, States, while bearing in mind the need to ensure the comprehensive application of the Set of Principles and Rules, should take due account of the extent to which the conduct of enterprises, whether or not created or controlled by States, is accepted under applicable legislation or regulations, bearing in mind that such laws and regulations should be clearly defined and publicly and readily available, or is required by States.

(iii) *Preferential or differential treatment for developing countries*

7. In order to ensure the equitable application of the Set of Principles and Rules, States, particularly of developed countries, should take into account in their control of restrictive business practices the development, financial and trade needs of developing countries, in particular the least developed countries, for the purposes especially of developing countries in:

   (a) promoting the establishment or development of domestic industries and the economic development of other sectors of the economy; and

   (b) encouraging their economic development through regional or global arrangements among developing countries.

SECTION D—Principles and Rules for enterprises, including transnational corporations

1. Enterprises should conform to the restrictive business practices laws, and the provisions concerning restrictive business practices in other laws, of the countries in which they operate, and in the event of proceedings under these laws should be subject to the competence of the courts and relevant administrative bodies therein.

2. Enterprises should consult and co-operate with competent authorities of countries directly affected in controlling restrictive business practices adversely affecting the interests of those countries. In this regard, enterprises should also provide information, in particular details of restrictive arrangements, required for this purpose, including that which may be located in foreign countries to the extent that in the latter event such production or disclosure is not prevented by applicable law or established public polity. Whenever the provision of in-

formation is on a voluntary basis, its provision should be in accordance with safeguards normally applicable in this field.

3. Enterprises, except when dealing with each other in the context of an economic entity wherein they are under common control, including through ownership, or otherwise not able to act independently of each other, engaged on the market in rival or potentially rival activities, should refrain from practices such as the following when, through formal, informal, written or unwritten agreements or arrangements, they limit access to markets or otherwise unduly restrain competition, having or being likely to have adverse effects on international trade, particularly that of developing countries, and on the economic development of these countries:
    (a) agreements fixing prices including as to exports and imports;
    (b) collusive tendering;
    (c) market or customer allocation arrangements;
    (d) allocation by quota as to sales and production;
    (e) collective action to enforce arrangements—e.g., by concerted refusals to deal;
    (f) concerted refusal of supplies to potential importers;
    (g) collective denial of access to an arrangement, or association, which is crucial to competition.

4. Enterprises should refrain from the following acts or behaviour in a relevant market when, through an abuse* or acquisition and abuse of a dominant position of market power, they limit access to markets or otherwise unduly restrain competition, having or being likely to have adverse effects on international trade, particularly that of developing countries, and on the economic development of these countries:
    (a) predatory behaviour towards competitors, such as using below cost pricing to eliminate competitors;

* Whether acts or behaviour are abusive or not should be examined in terms of their purpose and effects in the actual situation, in particular with reference to whether they limit access to markets or otherwise unduly restrain competition, having or being likely to have adverse effects on international trade, particularly that of developing countries, and on the economic development of these countries, and to whether they are:

(a) appropriate in the light of the organizational, managerial and legal relationship among the enterprises concerned, such as in the context of relations within an economic entity and not having restrictive effects outside the related enterprises;
(b) appropriate in light of special conditions or economic circumstances in the relevant market such as exceptional conditions of supply and demand or the size of the market;
(c) of types which are usually treated as acceptable under pertinent national or regional laws and regulations for the control of restrictive business practices;
(d) consistent with the purpose and objectives of these principles and rules.

(b) discriminatory (i.e. unjustifiably differentiated) pricing or terms or conditions in the supply or purchase of goods or services, including by means of the use of pricing policies in transactions between affiliated enterprises which overcharge or undercharge for goods or services purchased or supplied as compared with prices for similar or comparable transactions outside the affiliated enterprises;

(c) mergers, takeovers, joint ventures or other acquisitions of control, whether of a horizontal, vertical or a conglomerate nature;

(d) fixing the prices at which goods exported can be resold in importing countries;

(e) restrictions on the importation of goods which have been legitimately marked abroad with a trademark identical or similar to the trademark protected as to identical or similar goods in the importing country where the trademarks in question are of the same origin, i.e., belong to the same owner or are used by enterprises between which there is economic, organizational, managerial or legal interdependence and where the purpose of such restrictions is to maintain artificially high prices;

(f) when not for ensuring the achievement of legitimate business purposes, such as quality, safety, adequate distribution or service:

   (i) partial or complete refusals to deal on the enterprise's customary commercial terms;

  (ii) making the supply of particular goods or services dependent upon the acceptance of restrictions on the distribution or manufacture of competing or other goods;

 (iii) imposing restrictions concerning where, or to whom, or in what form or quantities goods supplied or other goods may be re-sold or exported;

 (iv) making the supply of particular goods or services dependent upon the purchase of other goods or services from the supplier or his designee.

SECTION E—*Principles and rules for States at national, regional and subregional levels*

1. States should, at the national level or through regional groupings, adopt, improve and effectively enforce appropriate legislation and implementing judicial and administrative procedures for the control of restrictive business practices, including those of transnational corporations.

2. States should base their legislation primarily on the principle of eliminating or effectively dealing with acts or behaviour of enterprises which, through an abuse or acquisition and abuse of a dominant position of market power, limit access to markets or otherwise unduly restrain competition, having or being likely to have adverse effects on their trade or economic development, or which through formal, informal, written or unwritten agreements or arrangements among enterprises have the same impact.

3. States in their control of restrictive business practices should ensure treatment of enterprises which is fair, equitable, on the same basis to all enterprises, and in accordance with established procedures of law. The laws and regulations should be publicly and readily available.

4. States should seek appropriate remedial or preventive measures to prevent and/or control the use of restrictive business practices within their competence when it comes to the attention of States that such practices adversely affect international trade and particularly the trade and development of the developing countries.

5. Where, for the purposes of the control of restrictive business practices, a State obtains information from enterprises containing legitimate business secrets, it should accord such information reasonable safeguards normally applicable in this field, particularly to protect its confidentiality.

6. States should institute or improve procedures for obtaining information from enterprises, including transnational corporations, necessary for their effective control of restrictive business practices, including in this respect details of restrictive agreements, understandings and other arrangements.

7. States should establish appropriate mechanisms at the regional and sub-regional levels to promote exchange of information on restrictive business practices and on the application of national laws and policies in this area, and to assist each other to their mutual advantage regarding control of restrictive business practices at the regional and sub-regional levels.

8. States with greater expertise in the operation of systems for the control of restrictive business practices should, on request, share their experience with, or otherwise provide technical assistance to, other States wishing to develop or improve such systems.

9. States should, on request, or at their own initiative when the need comes to their attention, supply to other States, particularly of developing countries, publicly available information, and, to the extent consistent with their laws and established public policy, other information necessary to the receiving interested State for its effective control of restrictive business practices.

SECTION F—*International measures*

Collaboration at the international level should aim at eliminating or effectively dealing with restrictive business practices, including those of transnational corporations, through strengthening and improving controls over restrictive business practices adversely affecting international trade, particularly that of developing countries, and the economic development of these countries. In this regard, action should include:

1. Work aimed at achieving common approaches in national policies relating to restrictive business practices compatible with the Set of Principles and Rules.
2. Communication annually to the Secretary-General of UNCTAD of appropriate information on steps taken by States and regional groupings to meet their commitment to the Set of Principles and Rules, and information on the adoption, development and application of legislation, regulations and policies concerning restrictive business practices.
3. Continued publication annually by UNCTAD of a report on developments in restrictive business practices legislation and on restrictive business practices adversely affecting international trade, particularly the trade and development of developing countries, based upon publicly available information and as far as possible other information, particularly on the basis of requests addressed to all member States or provided at their own initiative and, where appropriate, to the United Nations Centre on Transnational Corporations and other competent international organizations.
4. Consultations:
    (a) Where a State, particularly of a developing country, believes that a consultation with another State or States is appropriate in regard to an issue concerning control of restrictive business practices, it may request a consultation with those States with a view to finding a mutually acceptable solution. When a consultation is to be held, the States involved may request the Secretary-General of UNCTAD to provide mutually agreed conference facilities for such a consultation;

(b) States should accord full consideration to requests for consultations and upon agreement as to the subject of and the procedures for such a consultation, the consultation should take place at an appropriate time;

(c) If the States involved so agree, a joint report on the consultations and their results should be prepared by the States involved and, if they so wish with the assistance of the UNCTAD secretariat, and be made available to the Secretary-General of UNCTAD for inclusion in the annual report on restrictive business practices.

5. Continued work within UNCTAD on the elaboration of a model law or laws on restrictive business practices in order to assist developing countries in devising appropriate legislation. States should provide necessary information and experience to UNCTAD in this connexion.

6. Implementation within or facilitation by UNCTAD, and other relevant organizations of the United Nations system in conjunction with UNCTAD, of technical assistance, advisory and training programmes on restrictive business practices particularly for developing countries:

(a) Experts should be provided to assist developing countries, at their request, in formulating or improving restrictive business practices legislation and procedures;

(b) Seminars, training programmes or courses should be held, primarily in developing countries, to train officials involved or likely to be involved in administering restrictive business practices legislation and, in this connexion, advantage should be taken, *inter alia,* of the experience and knowledge of administrative authorities especially in developed countries in detecting the use of restrictive business practices;

(c) A handbook on restrictive business practices legislation should be compiled;

(d) Relevant books, documents, manuals and any other information on matters related to restrictive business practices should be collected and made available, particularly to developing countries;

(e) Exchange of personnel between restrictive business practices authorities should be arranged and facilitated;

(f) International conferences on restrictive business practices legislation and policy should be arranged;

(g) Seminars for an exchange of views on restrictive business practices among persons in the public and private sectors should be arranged.

7. International organizations and financing programmes, in particular the United Nations Development Programme, should be called upon

to provide resources through appropriate channels and modalities for the financing of activities set out in paragraph 6 above. Furthermore, all countries are invited, in particular the developed countries, to make voluntary financial and other contributions for the above-mentioned activities.

SECTION G—*International institutional machinery*

(i) *Institutional arrangements*

1. An Intergovernmental Group of Experts on Restrictive Business Practices operating within the framework of a Committee of UNCTAD will provide the institutional machinery.
2. States which have accepted the Set of Principles and Rules should take appropriate steps at the national or regional levels to meet their commitment to the Set of Principles and Rules.

(ii) *Functions of the Intergovernmental Group*

3. The Intergovernmental Group shall have the following functions:
    (a) To provide a forum and modalities for multilateral consultations, discussion and exchange of views between States on matters related to the Set of Principles and Rules, in particular its operation and the experience arising therefrom;
    (b) To undertake and disseminate periodically studies and research on restrictive business practices related to the provisions of the Set of Principles and Rules, with a view to increasing exchange of experience and giving greater effect to the Set of Principles and Rules;
    (c) To invite and consider relevant studies, documentation and reports from relevant organizations of the United Nations system;
    (d) To study matters relating to the Set of Principles and Rules and which might be characterized by data covering business transactions and other relevant information obtained upon request addressed to all States;
    (e) To collect and disseminate information on matters relating to the Set of Principles and Rules to the over-all attainment of its goals and to the appropriate steps States have taken at the national or regional levels to promote an effective Set of Principles and Rules, including its objectives and principles;
    (f) To make appropriate reports and recommendations to States on matters within its competence, including the application and implementation of the Set of Multilaterally Agreed Equitable Principles and Rules;

(g) To submit reports at least once a year on its work.

4. In the performance of its functions, neither the Intergovernmental Group nor its subsidiary organs shall act like a tribunal or otherwise pass judgement on the activities or conduct of individual Governments or of individual enterprises in connexion with a specific business transaction. The Intergovernmental Group or its subsidiary organs should avoid becoming involved when enterprises to a specific business transaction are in dispute.

5. The Intergovernmental Group shall establish such procedures as may be necessary to deal with issues related to confidentiality.

(iii) *Review procedure*

6. Subject to the approval of the General Assembly, five years after the adoption of the Set of Principles and Rules, a United Nations Conference shall be convened by the Secretary-General of the United Nations under the auspices of UNCTAD for the purpose of reviewing all the aspects of the Set of Principles and Rules. Towards this end, the Intergovernmental Group shall make proposals to the Conference for the improvement and further development of the Set of Principles and Rules.

Commentary

◆

Timothy Atkeson

It is a pleasure to read Joel Davidow's piece. His mastery of the subject, his historical perspective, and his candor lead one easily past his warning at the beginning that Americans who have sought to extend new and better freedoms to the whole world "have tended to die with their dreams unfulfilled, if not totally frustrated." One is moved to join in the hope expressed at the end that he and his colleagues will indeed make progress in transforming North-South grievances about multinational enterprises from political rhetoric into tension-reducing analysis of facts and useful negotiation of rules on restrictive business practices.

Yet, if we are to find out whether in this "Quixotic Quest" Davidow is himself playing the role of Don Quixote [1] or is in reality more like the simple but astute squire, Sancho Panza, we must press him on his ideas about whether this quest will actually produce at this time a world competition code that we could support or whether our goal must be more modest. Davidow himself cites the conclusion reached by Corwin Edwards in 1967 after a life's career working toward building an international antitrust consensus: "[I]nternational collaboration to control restrictive business practices cannot be global. It cannot succeed if it includes countries that are widely divergent in their legal and political systems or in the place that they give to private enterprise. . . . Comprehensive collaboration, such as was contemplated by those who drafted the ITO charter and the ad hoc committee's report, is not now practicable."

Since Edwards reached this conclusion over a decade ago, there has indeed been a remarkable spread of national anti-restrictive business practice legislation. But during the seventies there have also been some important negative developments. Led by OPEC and the producers of bauxite, and including a long list of aspirants to building new governmental cartels to wield monopoly power over primary exports, the Group of 77 in the UNCTAD discussions is willing to focus only on the restrictive business practices of private entities. Furthermore, the Group of 77 countries envision this exercise as being mainly directed at what they term the restrictive business practices of multinational enterprises from the developed countries, with the developing countries being left free to sanction exceptions or differential treatment of their own state-owned or private enterprises where this seems desirable. Third, there appears to be a growing debate in the United States about the proper targets of antitrust enforcement policy. We are ourselves in the midst of a debate over whether "big is bad." The McLaren suits to stop conglomerate mergers have for the most part been turned back in the courts, and the debate has shifted to Congress and such proposals as S. 600 to curtail such mergers. The energy crisis produced an interesting debate between the Antitrust Division and the Senate Judiciary Committee as to whether horizontal or vertical divestiture in the oil industry would be a blow for freedom or a shot in the foot. Now, however, the Senate Judiciary Committee and the Antitrust Division have joined in recommending some versions of S. 1246, which would impose a ban on all acquisitions of $100 million or more by major oil companies without regard to any advance showing of adverse effects on competition—and incidentally would be applied abroad to acquisitions by foreign subsidiaries without any requirement for a showing of effects on the United States.

In this problematic environment it is not surprising that the American business community has raised questions whether we should proceed now to subscribe to broad new global statements on restrictive business practices. They ask whether such codes in the UNCTAD context will find their principal use in discriminatory and anticompetitive actions against our multinational enterprises; and they wonder about the inclusion of complex and controversial concepts such as abuse of a dominant position of market power and shared monopoly (Davidow with some understatement describes the latter on page 383 as "involv[ing] a more controversial point" under U.S. than under West German or EEC antitrust law), about provisions that pose questions concerning intraenterprise transactions and technology export restrictions considered to be permissible under U.S. law, and about the lack of assurances on nondiscriminatory treatment. In the State Department's Advisory Committee on International Investment, Technology and Development, as the prospect of diplomatic negotiations in the next twelve months on the UNCTAD Codes on Restrictive Business Practices and Transfer of Technology and on a UN Code for Transnational Corporations becomes imminent, such questions as the following are increasingly being asked: How should the United States or the other Group B countries respond if the Group of 77 decides to press ahead with codes of conduct for multinational corporations or codes on restrictive business practices that we cannot accept? If our own fundamental concerns for fair and nondiscriminatory treatment and application of international law norms to our enterprises abroad cannot win acceptance at this time from the Group of 77, how should we handle this problem? What course of action serves our national interests best, given the remaining points of difference in the various UN and UNCTAD code projects?

Let us consider some of the answers to questions about our national interest in seeking a world competition code that Davidow suggests in his paper or has mentioned on other occasions. One is that by participating in good faith negotiations the United States and other developed countries can avoid the political isolation that might result from nonparticipation. There is certainly some truth in this and, as long as our representatives are as knowledgeable and persuasive as Davidow in support of an aggressive antitrust policy, it is clear we will not be politically isolated in the restrictive business practice negotiations themselves. But we have learned at the most recent UNCTAD meeting in Manila and the Havana Conference of Nonaligned Nations that broader political decisions by the Group of 77 to take a hard line on the "New International Economic Order" have a rhythm of their own, apparently without relation to how forthcoming the United States has been or the reasonableness of either our positions or our negotiators.

Another point made by Davidow is that U.S. participation in the search for international competition codes helps to defuse the political rhetoric about multinational enterprises and to reduce this cause of North-South tension. Today, in contrast to the mid-1970s when global codes of conduct for multinationals seemed a pressing need, the *actual* conduct of our multinational enterprises and the *actual* sense of need in the developing countries for capital and technology seem far more important than any codes in determining the climate in which multinationals operate. So far as codes are concerned, the 1976 OECD declaration furnishes sound guidance for OECD multinational corporations and its Competition Guidelines appear adequate. It seems doubtful that any likely UN Code on Transnational

Corporations or UNCTAD Codes on Restrictive Business Practices or Technology Transfer will make multinational enterprises less a target of criticism. Indeed, codes with vague and broad prohibitions would seem more likely to arm critics of such enterprises than dispel their complaints.

Finally, it has been suggested that, given our expertise in antitrust matters, our participation will produce more rational codes and more moderate national laws on restrictive business practices and that, if we abstain, the Group of 77 and Group D countries will go ahead and adopt worse codes and laws. This sometimes happens even if we participate fully, as Davidow recognizes. Even with our close participation in the UNCTAD project to develop a code on restrictive business practices, for example, the model national law proposed by the UNCTAD Secretariat remains unsatisfactory. It is at least arguable that with respect to well-drafted national laws we will achieve more through technical assistance to individual national governments of developing countries than we will ever achieve through bloc negotiations with the Group of 77 in the United Nations or UNCTAD.

In his conclusion Davidow tells us that conservative forces in American business mistakenly opposed meaningful progress toward a world competition code: "The subject of restrictive business practices is obviously too important to be ignored internationally in the age of the multinational corporation. And the United States was and is too dedicated to antitrust law and too expert in it to play any international role short of leadership. . . . It seems likely that some suspicion about UN rules will persist in American business circles."

The questions posed by the American business community about the Draft UN Code on Restrictive Business Practices, however, were not unreasonable. Consider, for example, the recommendations of the United States Council of the International Chamber of Commerce with respect to this code:

> It is therefore recommended that the Group B countries should avoid taking any actions in the forthcoming diplomatic negotiating conference that would encourage the Group of 77 and Group D countries to assume that the proposed principles will be accepted in their present form, without the amendments presently sought by Group B and certain additional clarifications. Specifically, the following amendments and clarifications should be obtained:
>
> (1) The code should be expressed as a nonbinding, voluntary set of principles and recommendations.

(2) Transactions bwtween affiliated entities should be expressly excluded from the coverage of the code.

(3) The attempt to extrapolate the principles to cover "shared monopoly" should be abandoned. A possible compromise might be reached by requiring as added elements specific identified acts of abusive behavior or agreeing with other enterprises, in both instances to limit competition from third parties.

(4) The definition of "restrictive business practices" in both Sections B and D must be appropriately clarified to limit the ambiguities, particularly the "open-ended" dangers which have been criticized. In particular, every effort must be made to prevent the standard of "adverse effects" on development from becoming a source of additional "offenses."

(5) Efforts to tilt the code's provisions against transnational enterprises and in favor of national companies and state-owned enterprises should be firmly opposed, and Group B should make it clear that the provisions are equally applicable to all groups.

It is fair to ask, if we cannot satisfactorily resolve these significant remaining issues, why we should not put off any final decision. The United States has taken the laboring oar on so many past international projects in order to arrive at some agreement, however, that we tend to neglect the alternative of viewing the continuing discussion process as itself the goal if fundamental differences remain. The U.S. representatives should be candid about their constituents' concerns over what are perceived as broad and vague descriptions of restrictive business practices which go beyond U.S. doctrines or which could be used in a discriminatory way. There appears to be little advantage in papering over differences in order to achieve a UN consensus statement on restrictive business practices by any particular date.

These doubts and second thoughts are not limited to "the recalcitrant in the developed world." Davidow himself has laid their foundation in many of his own observations. But like the Man of La Mancha, he may be tempted to invite us to dream what may be the impossible dream for the present. Davidow states that "[i]t now appears certain that by the end of 1980 global antitrust principles will be adopted."* Let us ask him and his colleagues at the forthcoming Geneva negotiations on the UN Code on Restrictive Business Practices to play a Sancho Panza role, remembering that there are no such time deadlines, that the discussion and clarification

---

* This phrase appeared in Davidow's paper as originally devliered (ed.).

process itself may be our goal for the time being, and that real progress on international antitrust issues will be measured much more by national and regional practice over the next decade than by flawed global declarations.

NOTE

1. "An amiable elderly gentleman addicted to reading romances of chivalry [who] goes out of his mind and sets out as a doughty knight errant in search of adventure and to redress the wrongs in the world, as though it were really the world of his storybooks." *The Penguin Companion to European Literature* (Harmondsworth, Eng.: Penguin, 1971), p. 176.

Commentary

◆

Samuel Wex

INTRAENTERPRISE TRANSACTIONS
AND MARKET ALLOCATION

The problem of intraenterprise market allocation appears to have been characterized by Joel Davidow as the type of issue that is not really an antitrust problem, but instead should be seen as a management strategy that is inconsistent with national development goals (p. 367). He warns us that it is the intermixture of this type of issue with conventional antitrust questions that has delayed and complicated UNCTAD RBP and transfer of technology negotiations.

Intraenterprise transactions, and in particular market allocation arrangements, may be treated as an RBP on the theory of (1) abuse of dominant position, or (2) intraenterprise conspiracy. Group B does not object to dealing with intraenterprise transactions as a possible abuse of dominant position, depending upon the facts of each case. Under proposed Canadian legislation, any subsidiary accounting for 25 percent or more of the Canadian market that substantially restricts exports from Canada (or imports) for the purpose of protecting price levels may be ordered to cease such activity. The Underlying theory for this provision is ambiguous. There are elements of intraenterprise conspiracy ("agreement or arrangement with an affiliate") and abuse of dominant position (25 percent of the market and the Canadian subsidiary is prevented from importing so that higher prices are maintained in Canada or prevented from exporting so that higher prices are maintained outside Canada). It is inherent in intraenterprise activities that there will be an "agreement," "arrangement," "directive," "Instruction," "intimation of policy," or other "communication" to bring about the activity and, thus, one might assume some sort of communication. (Query: is it the communication or the activity that is to be prohibited? If the latter, why burden the Government's case with the necessity to prove a conspiracy?) Rather, it would appear that it is the abuse of dominant position that the provision is diected at, as in the Zoja case. There is potential to build from this provision to deal with excesses of intraenterprise activities in general.

Any consideration of treating intraenterprise market allocation as a conspiracy (cartel) is the object of Davidow's concern. Thus, quoting from the OECD experts (p. 369), he noted: "In no case have arrangements within the same legal entity, such as between branches or operating divisions of the same company, been held to be unlawful. Even in cases involving separate legal entities under common control, findings of illegality have been rare and have been based upon exhaustive factual analysis of the particular cases."

What this quotation refers to is the fact that there have been cases under U.S. jurisprudence upholding the intraenterprise conspiracy theory, but, as I understand it, only where there has been an autonomous relationship between parent and subsidiary.[1] Why is the principle enunciated in these cases inappropriate to the international scene?

To suggest that intraenterprise market allocation is beyond the pale of RBP concern (if this is not overstating Davidow's position) runs counter to the very legitimate concerns expressed by the Group of Eminent Persons and seems to be inconsistent with the agreed-upon Objectives of the Rules and Principles on RBPs.

Among the objectives is that of attaining greater efficiency through the encouragement of innovation (section A, paragraph 2 (c)). This objective applies to parent-subsidiary transactions. Sigmund Timberg also spoke of the role of innovation as a development goal. The goal of innovation and the problem of market allocation are inextricably linked. Without the location by the parent of responsibility for certain product innovation in the host country, that host country cannot hope to become innovative in the products of that enterprise and eventually capture export markets. In other words, if the parent retains its entire innovative capability at home, it will not encourage innovation in the subsidiary, and thus will prevent the subsidiary from attaining greater efficiency through innovation. That is why the Group of Eminent Persons recommended "that governments should agree to prohibit the market allocation of exports by multinational corporations—*except* when such allocations secure other benefits for the countries concerned." The principal benefit that a rational market allocation can bring to the host country is an equitable sharing in the innovative capacity of the MNC.

To secure an equitable sharing in innovation within the MNC may not be entirely within the domain of RBP legislation. In this regard, Davidow's caution is appropriate. To turn to the intraenterprise conspiracy theory could wreak havoc in determining an equitable allocation of innovative capability between the parent and its subsidiary. (But to ignore theories and compel the subsidiary to engage in R&D leading to export markets should secure an equitable sharing of innovative capability.) The problem of encouraging export performance by foreign-controlled firms requires a multidirected approach. The statistics show that in Canada, for example, foreign-controlled firms generally export relatively less than Canadian-controlled firms. The question remains as to what policy instruments would be most appropriate to "encouraging" the parent company to allocate innovative capability in certain products to the subsidiaries so as to attain greater efficiency for host countries and greater opportunity for exports, and thereby secure benefits for these countries. This is an issue in which not only the LDCs have a vital interest.

PREFERENTIAL TREATMENT BASED ON NATIONALITY

One of the most controversial issues facing the group of experts until the final stages of the negotiations was the question of preferential treatment for domestic enterprises of developing countries.[2] Group B accepted that any "special" treatment for enterprises should turn on their lack of size and market power, not their nationality. This is not special treatment; it is accepted, as a general rule, that noncomparability is a ground for differential treatment. What would entitle the host country to invoke preferential treatment for its domestic enterprises would be noncomparability based on size, but could it not also look at noncomparability in terms of the very nature of the TNC? That is to say, by the very nature of the TNC— foreign decision making, diffuse marketing, and manufacturing—it may be different from the domestic enterprise (that is not itself an MNC).

Increased attention should be directed at how to determine "unlike situations" (OECD Guidelines) or noncomparable situations. In Latin America, we are told, national and foreign firms are treated differently under RBP legislation. Rather than insisting upon principles of nondiscrimination, Group B should, in my opinion, be exploring the limits of noncomparable situations and principles of "fairness and reasonableness" that should be applied in those cases. Moreover, procedures for reporting exceptions to "national treatment" to some central machinery should be considered.

NOTES

1. Milton Handler, Harlan M. Blake, and Robert Pitofsky, *Cases and Materials on Trade Regulation* (Mineola, N.Y.: Foundation, 1975), pp. 473 et seq.
2. As Davidow points out, this was resolved in the 1980 approved text.

Discussion

◆

LOUIS T. WELLS, JR.: There have been allusions to antitrust as a kind of regulation. However, I think antitrust and regulation are opposites. "Regulation" is a substitute for competition. It's a way of handling a situation where competition does not exist. "Antitrust" is just the opposite. It's a way of making sure that competition does exist. I think if one moves toward de-regulation, one should also move toward stronger antitrust.

JOEL DAVIDOW: I join Louis Wells in his point that antitrust, properly written and administered, is not regulatory. My antitrust rationale is that private parties should not regulate an industry. If regulation by government is bad, regulation by people who aren't responsible to the public is even worse. So I think antitrust is strongly antiregulative.

TIMOTHY ATKESON: I certainly recognize that the tradition of antitrust is "antiregulatory." But it seems to me that, under the antitrust banner, we are increasingly moving into a regulatory mode. You're familiar with the comments of the previous panel on the terms of mergers. I think that is an extensive regulatory exercise. In a bill now before the Senate Judiciary Committee, S. 1246, there is a proposal that major oil companies may not make any acquisition of assets over $100 million unless they go through a clearance process with the Antitrust Division. That seems to me a major substitution of governmental decision making for what used to be decision making by the private sector.

DAVIDOW: Touché.

ATKESON: The precepts advocated here may lead us to an automatic, self-functioning system. I expect, however, that they will instead lead to even larger bureaucracies that will screen even more actions of multinational corporations.

DAVID G. GILL: What is Group B's position regarding a code provision on transfer pricing between affiliated enterprises?

DAVIDOW: There is some disagreement as to whether we should say anything about transfer pricing in an antitrust code. Some people think it is just a tax problem, not an antitrust problem; others point out that transfer pricing can be used to injure an outside firm. We have been looking at some formulations that would cover abuse of dominant position by transfer pricing when there was injury to an outside firm. We're still uncomfortable with it. Group B clearly supports the idea that arm's-length transfer pricing is proper behavior for a multinational corporation.

SEYMOUR J. RUBIN: Assuming that the objective of the "New International Economic Order" is the transfer of resources from North to South, will the codes effect that? Any code will be filled with ambiguities and will not have a single interpretive body to resolve them. There will be no body to decide particular controversies. Will the codes then have any substantial importance?

K. VENKATA RAMAN: To an extent what you say is true: the New International Economic Order may have more procedural than substantive importance. But I believe the codes will give developing countries some additional bargaining position in negotiations with transnational corporations.

DAVIDOW: On the broad question of the codes' significance, I've learned a lot from the expert in my family, my wife, who's a political scientist. Her message is that the New International Economic Order, realistically viewed, is procedural, not substantive; that it has no serious chance of changing the substantive basis of world economic power. But it may change the procedural way in which rules are written.

It may be less important what the codes say than the fact that the developing countries set the agenda and that they participated fully in writing the rules for world commerce. Their main attack on international law has been: "It was written when we weren't participating." Their participation in the formulation of international economic principles is a political victory for the developing countries.

Contributors

◈

ATKESON, TIMOTHY B. Partner, Steptoe & Johnson, Washington, D.C.; General Counsel, Asian Development Bank, 1967–1969.

BLOOM, L. H. President, Unilever United States, Inc.

DAVIDOW, JOEL. Partner, Mudge, Rose, Guthrie & Alexander; formerly Director of Policy Planning, Antitrust Division, U.S. Department of Justice; U.S. Delegate to the UN Conference on Restrictive Business Practices and on Transfer of Technology, 1975–1980; U.S. Delegate to the OECD Committee of Experts on Restrictive Business Practices, 1974–1980. Published works include articles on domestic and international antitrust matters and regulation of international trade.

GILL, DAVID G. Member, Law Department, Exxon Corporation; Adviser to U.S. Delegation to the UN Conference on Restrictive Business Practices, 1980. Publications include articles on international antitrust questions.

GLASS, WALTER H. Counsel, General Electric Company, New York.

GREER, DOUGLAS F. Professor of Economics, California State University; Consultant, UN Conference on Trade and Development, 1969–1976, 1979; Research economist, Federal Reserve Board of Governors, May 1973–July 1975. Published works include articles on patents, international restrictive business practices, and antitrust policy.

HELLAWELL, ROBERT. Professor of Law, Columbia University; Codirector, Investment Negotiation Center, 1973–the present; formerly Peace Corps Director, East Africa. Editor of *United States Taxation and Developing Countries* (Columbia University Press, 1980); other publications include articles on taxation, law, and development.

HELLEINER, G. K. Professor of Economics, University of Toronto; Consultant, UN Centre on Transnational Corporations (on intrafirm trade) and UN Conference on Trade and Development (on the impact of floating exchange rates on developing countries), 1980–1981. Publications include *International Economic Disorder, Essays in North-South Relations* (University of Toronto, 1981) and *Intra-firm Trade and the Developing Countries* (St. Martin's Press, 1981).

HUFBAUER, G. C. Deputy Director, International Law Institute, Georgetown Law Center; Counsel, Chapman, Duff & Paul; Deputy Assistant Secretary for International Trade and Investment Policy, U.S. Department of the Treasury, 1977–1980; Director, International Tax Staff, U.S. Department of the Treasury, 1974–1977. Has written extensively on international trade and international taxation.

JOELSON, MARK R. Partner, Wald, Harkrader & Ross, Washington, D.C.; formerly Consultant, UN Conference on Trade and Development; Member, Department of State Advisory Committee on International Investment, Technology and Development. Coauthor of *An International Antitrust Primer* (Macmillan, 1974) and coeditor of *Enterprise Law of the 80's* (American Bar Association, 1980).

MARKERT, KURT. Chairman, Federal Cartel Office, Federal Republic of Germany; Professor of Law, Free University of Berlin; Member, OECD Committee of Experts on Restrictive Business Practices, 1964–1970 and EEC Consultative Antitrust Committee, 1970–1973; Antitrust Consultant to UNCTAD, 1969–1971. Publications include articles on international antitrust questions in both European and U.S. periodicals.

MUELLER, W. F. Vilas Research Professor, Agricultural Economics, Economics and Law, University of Wisconsin, 1969–the present; Executive Director, President's Cabinet Committee on Price Stability, 1968–1969; Chief Economist and Director, Bureau of Economics, Federal Trade Commission, 1961–1968. Has written extensively on industrial organization and antitrust policy.

RAHL, JAMES A. Owen L. Coon Professor of Law, Northwestern University; Counsel, Chadwell, Kayser, Ruggles, McGee & Hastings; Member, White House Task Force on Antitrust Policy, 1967–1968, and Attorney General's National Committee to Study the Antitrust Laws, 1953–1955; U.S. Delegate to UNCTAD Ad Hoc Group of Experts on International Restrictive Trade Practices, 1973. Editor of *Common Market and American Antitrust: Overlap and Conflict* (McGraw Hill, 1970); other publications include articles on international antitrust questions.

SCHACHTER, OSCAR. Hamilton Fish Professor of International Law and Diplomacy, Columbia University; Coeditor in Chief, *American Journal of International Law;* past President, American Society of International Law; Director, Legal Division, United Nations, 1952–1966. Publications include *Sharing the World's Resources* (Columbia University Press, 1977) and other books and articles on international law and institutions.

SMITH, ROBERT E. Professor of Economics and Business Administration, University of Oregon; formerly Chief, Restrictive Business Practices Section, Manufactures Division, UN Conference on Trade and Development (UNCTAD); Economic Advisor to Commissioner Mary Gardiner Jones, Federal Trade Commission. Publications include articles on cartels and international competition policy.

TIMBERG, SIGMUND. Member of the District of Columbia and New York Bars; formerly Special Assistant to the Attorney General and Chief, Judgments and Judgment Enforcement Section, Antitrust Division, U.S. Department of Justice; Secretary, UN Committee on Restrictive Business Practices. Publications include numerous articles on antitrust questions, international law, patents, trademarks and copyrights.

WALTER, INGO. Professor of Economics and Finance and Chairman, International Business, Graduate School of Business Administration, New York University; has served as Consultant to UN Conference on Trade and Development (Geneva), UN Centre on Transnational Corporations (New York), and the Organisation for Economic Co-operation and Development (Paris). Publications include *Multinationals Under Fire* (Wiley, 1980) and *International Economics,* 3d ed. (Wiley, 1981).

WANG, N. T. Adjunct Professor of Business and Director, China-International Business Project, Columbia University; formerly Director, Information Analysis Division, UN Centre on Transnational Corporations; Team Leader, UN Missions to Jamaica and Eastern Africa. Publications include *Taxation and Development* (Praeger, 1976); editor of *Business with China: An International Reassessment* (Pergamon Press, 1980).

WELLS, LOUIS T., JR. Professor of Business Administration, Graduate School of Business Administration, Harvard University; Consultant on foreign investment to the Government of Indonesia, 1970–the present. Publications include *Negotiating Third World Mineral Agreements* (with David N. Smith, Ballinger, 1976) and *The Acquisition of Technology from Multinational Corporations by Developing Countries* (with Walter Chudson, UN Department of Economic and Social Affairs, 1974).

Contributors

Wex, Samuel.   Legal Adviser, International Joint Commission, Canadian Section; Adjunct Professor, Carleton University School of of International Affairs; Auxiliary Professor, McGill University, Faculty of Law. Publications include international antitrust article on code of conduct, vol. XV, *The Canadian Yearbook of International Law* (1977); *International Business Practices* (Canadian Council on International Law, 1979).

Index

◇

ACP countries, 215

Act of state doctrine, 264–65, 267, 278, 280

Adaptation restrictions, in technology transfer, 97, 108–9, 141, 386

Agricultural industries, 195, 197, 211

Alcoa case, 74, 255, 381

Alkali Export case, 173

Allocation function of market process, 203, 213, 218, 222

Aluminum industry, 220

American Law Institute *Restatement of Foreign Relations Law*, 255, 257, 279

Andean Common Market (ANCOM), 73, 107

Antidumping laws, 193

Antitrust Guide for International Business Operations (U.S. Justice Department), 255, 262, 265, 341

Antitrust laws and policies, 29, 35, 172, 209–10, 426; decriminalization of antitrust activities, 286–88; enforcement of, and disappearance of cartels, 249; European Economic Community, 251–54, 256–57, 260, 263, 265–67; exclusive dealing, 113–14; impact and weaknesses, 250–59; international, 175, 226; price fixing, 114–15; and technology transfer, 74, 162, 166–67; tie-in restrictions, 112–13; United States, 3, 9, 245–47, 335–43; *see also* specific laws and specific aspects and violations of the law

Argentina, 29, 71

Arm's-length transactions, 8, 31, 144

Association of Natural Rubber Producing Countries, 223, 225

Attorney General (U.S.), 347

Automobile industry, 148, 169

Bain-Sylos Postulate, 188–89, 194

Bargaining: host country and transnational corporation, 17–18; power of developing countries, 104; in technology transfer, 143, 160–61

Barrier theory of market power, 185–94

Basic regulatory agreement, of cartels, 211–12

Bayer/Allied Chemical case, 317

Bechtel case, 280

Below-cost pricing, 6

Blockaded entry to market power, 186, 194

Blocking statutes, 259, 265

Brazil, 51, 62, 168–69

Brazilian Coffee Institute, 223

Break-even point, 198, 200

Brown Shoe case, 348

CA, *see* Commodity agreement

Canada, 422–24

Cantor v. Detroit Edison Co., 264

Capacity, and short-run market power, 194, 197, 200–2

Capital goods, differential pricing of, 34

Capital-intensive firms and facilities, 148–49

Cartels and cartel-like activities, 4–5, 11–12, 29, 34–37, 74; *Alkali* case, 173–74; antitrust laws, impact and weaknesses of, 250–59; blocking provision, 259; conduct control, 67; coordinating techniques, 181; definition of, 179–80, 242; development of, 211–13; economic and political characteristics, 179–239; economic sanctions in response to, 286; external politics, 226–31; goals, 180–81; government action or intervention, 259–66; incidence of, 244–50, 366; internal politics, 225; market power determinants,

Cartels and cartel-like activities (*Cont.*) 182–222; operational techniques, 181; planning agreement, 212; regulation, 240–76; restrictions, in international codes, 118–20, 370, 377, 379–80

Celler-Kefauver Act of 1950 (U.S.), 348–49

Central American Coffee Producers' Federation, 223

Chamber of Commerce (U.S.), 363, 395, 419–20

Charter of Economic Rights and Duties of States, 395–96

Chemical industries, 54, 169, 200

CICO industries, 197

Clayton Act (U.S.), 74, 245, 336, 339, 346, 356

Coal industry, 294, 310, 344

Cocoa, 223–24

Cocoa Marketing Board (Ghana), 223

Cocoa Producers' Alliance, 223

Codes, international, *see* Restrictive business practice codes; Technology transfer code

Coffee, 223

Collusion: collusive tendering, 5; in interfirm internalization, 207–10; and short-run market power, 200

Colombia, 69

Colonial and semi-colonial territories, 11

Comity principle, in antitrust policy, 255, 260, 267, 375

Commercial knowledge, 42

Commission for the Review of Antitrust Laws and Procedures (U.S.), 3

Commodity agreement (CA), 213–15, 222–25, 228–29, 241

Common Fund for Commodities, 228–29

Communist countries' antitrust laws, 250–51

Compensatory financing, 216

Competition, 175; foreign, in U.S. domestic markets, 175; in long-run market power, 188–94; and price stabilization, 197–98; restraint of, 5 (*see also* Restrictive business practices); technology transfer, 47, 49, 52–56, 61, 100, 162–63, 169, 171–73; world competition code, search for, 361–405

Competition Commission (France), 301–2, 314, 345–46

Competitive bidding, in technology transfer, 72, 105, 161

Computer industry, 53, 65, 168–69

Conduct control, 44–45, 63–64, 66–70, 160, 162–64, 172; *see also* Restrictive business practice codes; Technology transfer code

Conference on International Economic Cooperation (1977), 241

Conglomerate mergers, 307, 338–39, 348–50, 356, 417

Conglomerates, intrafirm internalization in, 221

Consumer protection, 12, 96, 203

Continental Can case, 298, 344

Continuous input, continuous output (CICO) industries, 197

Contract law, 89, 109

Conventional technology, 48

Cooperative joint venture, 308

Coordination function of market process, 203–7, 217, 222

Copper industry, 212

Core technology, 43

Corporate entity doctrine re subsidiaries, 103

Cost-push inflation, 200

Costs: reduction of, by internalization process, 202; and short-run market power, 194, 197–202; stabilization of, by internalization process, 220; transaction, 206–7, 209–10, 213, 217–18, 227

Crisis cartels, 254

Cross-licenses, 387

Customer allocation arrangements, 5

Defense industries, 17

Demand: fluctuations in, 197; and intrafirm internalization, 218; and short-run market power, 194, 196–201

Developed countries: technology transfers between, 58; view of transnational's activities in developing countries, 11–12; *see also* Group B countries

Developing countries: antitrust protection, 251; bargaining, 35–36; cartels, 266; Charter of Economic Rights and Duties, 395; discriminatory treatment of transnationals, 13; exports, restrictions on, 12; home countries' view of transnational policies in, 11–12; information base, strengthening of, 104–6; innovation, interest in, 165; joint ventures, 355; Lomé Convention, 215;

multi-layered bargains, 98, 100; national regulation of restrictive business practices, 28–29; New International Economic Order, 228–29; pure competition, infeasibility of, 14, 16; raw materials cartels, 247; repackaging of foreign direct investment, 17; restrictive business practices, scope of, 6–7; skills and information, availability of, 163; technology transfer, 41–84, 91–92, 143; transnational corporations, view of restrictive business practices of, 12–14; *see also* Group of 77 countries

Differential treatment of foreign enterprise, 168, 170

Direct investment, foreign, *see* Foreign direct investment

Discriminatory pricing, 6

Distribution pattern, in technology transfer, 98, 113–17

du Pont-ICI case, 139, 259

Düsseldorf agreement (1939), 245, 247

Dyestuffs cartel, 253, 256, 258

East Germany (German Democratic Republic), 263

Economic and Social Council (ECOSOC), United Nations, 119, 363

Economic sanctions, in response to cartels, 286

ECOSOC, 119, 363

ECSC, *see* European Coal and Steel Community

Edwards, Corwin, viii–ix, 221, 244, 247, 248, 361–65, 372, 394, 416

EEC, *see* European Economic Community

Effects doctrine, in antitrust law, 255–56, 265

Efficiency, at global level, 27

EFTA, 226

Electrical industry, 34–35, 139, 289–90

Electronics industry, 148

European Coal and Steel Community (ECSC), 294, 296–97, 310, 314, 316, 344, 347, 364

European Economic Community (EEC), 12, 119–20, 123–24, 226, 364; antitrust policy, 251–54, 256–57, 260, 263, 265–67; cartel control, 240; export restrictions, 116; extraterritorial application of antitrust law, 376; Lomé Convention, 215; merger control

law, 293–94, 296–99, 303, 310–11, 314, 344, 347

European Free Trade Association (EFTA), 226

Everest and Jennings wheelchair company case, 384

Excessive pricing, 382

Exclusive dealing arrangements, 113–15, 167

Exploitative option, in short-run market power, 195

Export cartels, 12, 29, 34–36, 74, 249–51, 261–62, 268, 290, 377

Exporting governments and groups: commodity agreements, 215, 222–25; orderly marketing agreements, 225

Exports: in barrier theory of market power, 193; earnings, stabilization of, 196; price fixing, 5; restrictions, 9–10, 12, 69, 115–17, 386–87

Extraterritorial application of antitrust laws, 254–57, 267–68, 277–79, 376, 391

Fairness limitation, in act of state and foreign sovereign compulsion defenses, 280

Fair Trading Act of 1973 (United Kingdom), 299–300, 315, 344–45

Federal Cartel Office (West Germany), 295–96, 305–9, 317, 345–46; Guidelines on Domestic Effects, 332–34

Federal Maritime Commission (U.S.), 287

Federal Trade Commission (U.S.), 245, 335–36, 339–40, 348

Firm specific technology, 43

Food industry, 148

Foreign direct investment, 10, 15, 170; Japan, 50; repackaging, 17, 25–26; technology transfer, 50, 52

Foreign sovereign compulsion defense, 264–65, 267, 278, 280–81

Foreign Sovereign Immunities Act of 1976 (U.S.), 263

France: merger control law, 301–3, 314–16, 345–47, 354, 356; spheres of influence, 162; technology transfers, 62

Friedman, Milton, 201

General Agreement on Tariffs and Trade (GATT), 32–34, 226, 231

General Electric case, 114–15

General Electric Company in Canada, 171
General Services Administration (U.S.), 214
General technology, 43
German Democratic Republic, *see* East Germany
Germany, Federal Republic of, *see* West Germany
Germany, Nazi, 245, 247
Ghana, 223
Government acquiescence and involvement in restrictive business practices, 226–31, 241–42, 246, 259–67, 277–78, 288; commodity agreements, 222–25; orderly marketing agreements, 225–26; principles for, in world codes, 375–78
Grand jury proceedings, secrecy of, 289
Grant-back provisions, in licensing arrangements, 106–7
Great Britain, *see* United Kingdom
Group B countries, 23, 31, 365, 389–90, 392–93; restrictive business practice codes, 375–77, 382–83, 385; technology transfer code, 374, 378, 385, 387–88
Group D countries, 84, 365, 374, 378, 387
Group of 77 countries, 23, 37, 365–66, 390–92; restrictive business practice codes, 365–66, 373, 375–77, 382–84, 390–92, 417; technology transfer code, 84, 122–23, 369–72, 374, 378, 385–88, 390–92

Haindl/Holzmann case, 306
Hart-Scott-Rodino Antitrust Improvements Act of 1976 (U.S.), 340
Havana Charter (International Trade Organization), 119, 362–63
High technology industries, 17, 48–49, 148, 248
Hong Kong, 165
Horizontal mergers, 337–38, 348–49
Hunt v. Mobil Oil Corporation, 281

IBM, 53, 74, 156, 168–69
ICA, 228–29
ICP, *see* Integrated Commodity Programme
Illinois Brick case, 264
IMF, 216
Implementation agreement, of cartels, 212
Import cartels, 29

Imports: and barrier theory of market power, 193–94; commodity agreements, 222, 224–25; concerted refusal of supplies to importers, 5; orderly marketing agreements, 214–15, 225–26; price fixing, 5–6; United States, origin of, 31
Income stabilization, 196–97
Industrial property rights, 110–11, 118, 371, 387; *see also* Patents; Trademarks
Inflation, 200–1
Innovation, 90, 98, 165, 171, 423–24
Institute for Scientific and Technological Cooperation (U.S.), 26
Integrated Commodity Programme (ICP), 213, 216, 228–30
Interfirm internalization, 202–16, 222
Internalization, as market power strategy, 202–22, 284
International Association of Machinists and Aerospace Workers suit against OPEC, 264
International Chamber of Commerce, 363
International codes, *see* World competition codes
International commodity agreement (ICA), 228–29
International Electrical Association, 34–35
International Monetary Fund (IMF), 216
International regulation, 30–33; *see also* World competition codes
International Telephone and Telegraph cases, 287, 349
International Tin Agreement, 214
International Trade Organization (ITO), 33, 119, 362–63
Intrafirm transactions, 8, 31–32, 34, 37, 144; internalization for cost reduction and benefit realization, 202–4, 216–22; market allocation, 369, 422–23; and transfer pricing, 68, 139
Invention, 90–91
Inventory regulation, 195–97, 218–21
Investment barrier to technology transfer, 97
Italy, 70
ITO, 33, 119, 362–63

Japan: export cartels, 225, 261; patents, 70; royalty rates on technology, 58; technology transfers, 50–53, 65, 141, 162

Joint ventures, 6, 9, 175, 293, 355; technology transfer, 53, 101; United States law, 339–41; West German control, 308–9

Jurisdiction, in antitrust law, 254–58; *see also* Extraterritorial application of antitrust laws

Justice, Department of (U.S.), 255–56, 260, 262–63, 265, 279, 287, 289; merger control, 335–37, 340–41, 348

Karstadt (German firm), 309

Know-how, in technology transfer, 86, 88–92, 387–89

Korea, 165

Kronstein, Heinrich, 179–80, 211–13, 243–44, 249

Labor-intensive component manufacturing, 52

Less-developed countries (LDCs), *see* Developing countries

Liberal International Economic Order (LIEO), 228

Licensing practices: technology transfers, 52–53, 84–88, 92, 95, 101–2, 105–18; trademarks, 96; world competition codes, 385–89

LIEO, 228

Limited goods, 41

Local adaptation barrier, in technology transfer, 97

Local personnel, use of, in technology transfer, 102–3, 141

Lomé Convention, 196, 215–16, 230

Long-run market power, 182–94, 202–3, 207

Machlup, Fritz, 207–8, 210–11, 244

McLaren, Richard W., 349

Malaysia, 165, 223

Mandatory package licensing, 113

Mannington Mills case, 265, 278

Market allocation arrangements, 5, 8–9, 367–69, 422–24

Market domination, 293–94, 346, 348, 381–83; EEC merger control law, 298; German merger control law, 295–96, 305–9, 345

Market-extension mergers, 338

Market power: of cartels, 179–80, 182–222; components of, 183; developing countries' concern with, 36

MCNs, *see* Multinational corporations

Merger Guidelines (U.S. Department of Justice), 337–38

Mergers and merger control, 6, 74, 293–331, 353; EEC, 293–94, 296–99, 303, 310–11, 314, 344, 347; France, 301–3, 314–16, 345–47, 354, 356; international policy aspects of control, 318–20; statutory merger law, 314–18; United Kingdom, 299–301, 303, 311–15, 344–47, 350; United States, 335–43, 346–51; West Germany, 294–96, 302–10, 315–18, 345–48, 352–54

Mexico, 51; technology transfer, 44–45, 62, 66, 104–5

MFA, 214

Monopolies, 176, 185–86, 348, 370; technology transfer, 47, 53–55, 61

Monopolies and Mergers Commission (United Kingdom), 299–301, 311, 315, 345, 347

Multi-Fibre Agreement (MFA), 214

Multi-layered bargain, 87, 97–100

Multinational (transnational) corporations, 7; antitrust enforcement, problems of, 258–59; assertiveness of, 145–51; bargaining with host country, 17–18; and cartels, 248–49; cooperativeness of, 145–46, 151–53; discriminatory treatment of, by developing countries, 13; foreign ties, and competitive edge at home, 175; future of, 18–19; global view of, 25; home country's view of, 11–12; host country's view and regulation of, 12–14, 24; innovative capability, 171; insurance, 149; interest interdependence of, 151–52; international regulation, 30; intrafirm trading practices, 31–32; national regulation, 28–30; normal versus restrictive practices, 8; in OECD code, 370; parent-subsidiary relations, 242–43, 368–69, 384–85, 423; positivist approach to, 16–18, 25; power position, 149–51; principles and rules for, in world competition codes, 378–89; rationale for, 9; restrictive business practices, 3–37, 366–68; technology transfer, 50–53, 99–104, 143–57; United Nations report by Eminent Persons, 367–68

National Association of Manufacturers (NAM), 363, 395

National Commission for the Review of Antitrust Laws and Procedures (U.S.), 262
Nationality, preferential treatment based on, 424–25
National regulations, 24, 28–30, 44–45, 393; *see also* specific countries
Natural resource industries, 148
Neckermann (German firm), 309
Neo-mercantilism, 12
New International Economic Order (NIEO), 85, 142, 213, 228–30, 278, 370, 372, 427
Newly industrialized countries (NICs), 35, 165
NIEO, *see* New International Economic Order
Nonrenewable resources, industries involving, 17
Nontariff trade barriers, 226

OECD, *see* Organisation for Economic Co-operation and Development
Offshore assembly, 52
Oil industry, 417; price increases, impact of, 200, 284
Oligopoly, 55–56, 101, 205–6
OMA, *see* Orderly marketing agreement
One-tier cartel, 225
OPEC, *see* Organization of Petroleum Exporting Countries
Orderly marketing agreement (OMA), 203, 214–15, 225–26, 241
Organisation for Economic Co-operation and Development (OECD), 35, 226, 320; declaration of 1976, 392, 418; export cartels, 261; export restrictions, 116–17; international application of antitrust law, 376; multinational enterprises, 368–70; resolution of 1967, 393; technology transfer code, 84–85, 122–23
Organization of Petroleum Exporting Countries (OPEC), 4, 228–31, 241, 246, 263, 396–97; shadow OPEC, 230; suit against, by machinists and aerospace workers, 264

Package deals, in technology transfers, 69
Pakistan, 58
Pareto efficiency, 27, 29
Paris Union Convention of 1883, 86–87, 92–95

Parker v. Brown, 264
Patents, 70–71, 87–88, 92–95, 371; in barrier theory of market power, 193; grant-back provisions, 107; in technology transfer, 161; and unpatented know-how, 86, 88–92; validity, challenges to, 107–8, 117–18
Penn-Olin Chem Co. case, 339
Percentage effect, in market power theory, 186, 188, 190–91, 193–94
Personnel, use of, in technology transfer, 102–3, 109, 386
Petrochemicals, 52, 58, 65
Pharmaceutical industry, 58, 70–71, 91, 148, 161
Philadelphia National Bank case, 337
PIPO, 195–96
Point-input, point-output (PIPO) production process, 195–96
Portugal, 58
Prices and pricing behavior, 382, 384–85; in barrier theory of market power, 187–94; below-cost pricing, 6; cartels' effect on, 34–35; and commodity agreements, 223–24; discriminatory pricing, 6; elasticity, in technology transfers, 59; in oligopolistic market, 205–6; price fixing, 5–6, 114–15, 287, 379–80; price supports, 224; price stabilization, 194, 196–201, 218, 224; in technology transfers, 42, 54, 63, 67–69; transfer pricing, 6–8, 68–69, 139, 218, 384–85, 427
Private companies, resentment of government protection, 168–70
Product-extension mergers, 338
Production cutbacks, in market stabilization, 197–202, 218–19
Production volume, right of licensing company to restrict, 113
Profits: of collusive firms, 210; and intrafirm internalization, 220; in long-run market power model, 187–94; in short-run market power model, 194, 197, 199–201
Promotional techniques, and technology transfers, 98
Property rights, industrial, *see* Industrial property rights
Protectionism, 241; orderly marketing agreements, 225–26; private companies' resentment of, 168–70

Public interest standard, in merger law, 346–47, 350, 356

Publicity restrictions, in technology transfer licensing, 117

Purely concentrative joint venture, 308–9

Quality controls, in technology transfer, 95–96

Queue model of investment, 187, 194

Quickpoint Pencil case, 142

Quinine cartel, 246, 252–53, 258

Quotas: lifting of, after World War II, 226; as market stabilization technique, 195–96; United States Trade Act of 1974, 226

R&D, *see* Research and development

Raw materials, price increases, 200

Recession, and orderly marketing agreements, 225–26

Research and development (R&D), 48–49, 55–56, 141, 171; innovation, 91; licensing restrictions on, 108–9; subsidy of, 73

Restatement (Second) of Foreign Relations Law of the United States (American Law Institute), 255, 257, 279

Restraints of Competition, Act Against (West Germany), 294–95, 304, 308, 315, 317, 345

Restrictive business practice codes:

——*Economic and Social Council* (ECOSOC), 119, 124–26, 363

——*United Nations Conference on Trade and Development* (UNCTAD), 30–31, 354, 365–72, 395–97, 417–19; general principles and objectives, 374–75; legal nature and implementation, 389–92; principles and rules for enterprises, 378–85; principles for governments, 375–77; scope of application of, 373–74; text of, 404–15; United States business community's attitude toward, 419–20

Restrictive business practices, 5–7, 23, 37, 42, 373; consultation procedures to remedy, 393–94; global view of, 11, 14–15; impact on trade and development, 3–37; International Trade Organization's Charter, 362; national view of, 11–14; national regulation of, 28–29; positivist approach to, 16–18; in technology transfer, 84–138; *see also* Government acquiescence and involvement in restrictive business practices

Reynolds Metal case, 349

Rival-oriented market power, 183, 217–18

Role of the Patent System in the Transfer of Technology to Developing Countries, The (UN report), 112

Rome Treaty, 23, 119–20, 123, 226, 253, 256

Roosevelt, Franklin D., 361–62

Royalties, in technology transfer, 67–68, 91–92, 99

Rubber, 223–25

Sachs/GKN case, 307, 310

Scale economies, 13–14; and intrafirm internalization, 217; and long-run market power, 185, 188–89, 193

Semiconductor industry, 74

Sherman Act (U.S.), 120, 245, 252, 254–56, 258, 262–64, 268, 336, 346, 348

Shipping industry, 287, 289

Short-run market power, 182–84, 188, 194–202, 207

Singapore, 165

Socialist countries, 117, 172, 373, 382; *see also* Group D countries

Sovereignty, national: and antitrust enforcement, 263–65, 267; natural resources and foreign investment, 396

Spain, 58

Stabex Fund, 215–16

Stabilization options: from intrafirm internalization, 218–20; in short-run market power, 194–202

Stagflation, 201

State action concept, 264

Steel industry, 294, 310

Stop-go policy sequence, 200

Storage of products, 196

Subject matter jurisdiction, in cartel control, 254–57, 264–65

Subsidiaries, 101–4, 242–43, 368–69, 384–85, 423

Sugar cartel, 253

Supply: fluctuations in, 197; restrictive control of, 6; and short-run market power, 194–99

Supply contracts, long-term, 213

Swiss Watch case, 260
System specific technology, 43

Taiwan (Formosa), 165
Takeovers, 6
Tariffs, 226
Tax issues, and commodity agreements, 223
Technical knowledge, forms of, 43
Technology transfer, 95, 99–104; bargaining, 58–60, 143; barriers to, 97–98; conduct control, 44–45, 63–64, 66–70, 160; conflict management and, 156–57; costs, 49–50, 57–58; cost-time trade-off, 49, 55–56; export restrictions, 69–70; financial mechanisms, 168; ideal policy on, 44; of inappropriate technology, 140; incentives, 140–41; institutional comparative advantage, 144–47; intercountry cooperation, 73; and international patent system, 92–95; intrafirm, 218; market, 42, 46, 51, 54; methods of, 43–44; multi-layered bargain, 97–99; onerous terms and restraints, 61–63; packaged transfer, 52; payment after expiration of property rights, 118; prices, 63, 67–69; recipients' information base, strengthening of, 104–6; research and development expenditures, 48; restrictive business practices in, 84–138; royalty rate ceilings, 67–68; structural approach to, 45–46, 64–66, 70–75, 160–61, 167–68; terms and conditions for, 41–83; tie-ins and packages, 69; time, 49–50; trademarks and quality controls, 95–96; transferees, 56–60, 87–88; transferors, 46–56; unpatented resources and innovation, 88–92, 97–99
Technology transfer code, 75, 84
——*United Nations Conference on Trade and Development* (UNCTAD), 23, 30, 85–86, 95, 99, 369–72; implementation of international consensus, 120–27; international cartel arrangements, 118–20; legal nature and implementation, 389–93; licensing restrictions, 105–18; local personnel, use of, 102–3; principles and rules for enterprises, 385–89; principles for governments, 376, 378; respect of supplier for policies and priorities of importing country, 103; scope of application of, 374; special treatment for developing countries, 375; subsidiaries,
conduct of, 101–4; unpackaging objectives, 105
Territorial allocation of goods, 6
Textile industry, 214
Third Ad Hoc Group of Experts on Restrictive Business Practices (United Nations), 5–6, 240
Third World, *see* Developing countries
Thyssen/Hüller case, 306
Tie-in clauses, 69, 111–13
Tie-out clauses, 113–17
Timberlane case, 265, 278–80
Tin industry, 214, 224
TNEs (transnational enterprises), *see* Multinational corporations
Tort law, and unpatented know-how, 89
Trade, international, *see* Developing countries; Exports; Imports; Multinational corporations; Technology transfer
Trade, intrafirm, 31–32, 34
Trade Act of 1974 (U.S.), 226
Trademarks, 71–72, 95–96, 161, 193, 381–83
Transaction costs, 206–7, 209–10, 213, 217–18; government's effect on, 227
Transfer pricing, 6–8, 68–69, 139, 218, 384–85, 427
Transnational corporations, *see* Multinational corporations
Two-tier cartel, 225

Unbundling, 167–68
UNCTAD, *see* United Nations Conference on Trade and Development
Unemployment, 201
United Kingdom: antitrust policy, 258–59; cartels, incidence of, 245; export cartels, 261; merger control law, 299–301, 303, 311–15, 344–47, 350
United Nations, 3–4, 23, 372; *see also* specific agencies
United Nations Conference on Trade and Development (UNCTAD), 23, 29–31, 33; Integrated Commodity Programme, 213, 216, 228; Third Ad Hoc Group of Experts on Restrictive Business Practices, 5–6, 240; *see also* Restrictive business practice codes; Technology transfer code
United States: antitrust policy, 3, 74, 113, 245–47, 251–54, 258–59, 264–68, 278–81,

417; cartels, 119–20, 244–46; export cartels, 35–36, 261–62; export restrictions, 116; extraterritoriality doctrine, in application of antitrust laws, 254–57, 341, 376; government acquiescence in cartel activities, 260–63; imports, origin of, 31; International Trade Organization Charter, 362–63; know-how licensing, 389; license fees and royalties from abroad, 95; loss of market share in developing countries, 174; loss of technological leadership, 141–42; mergers and acquisitions, 335–43, 346–51; orderly marketing agreements, 226; payment of royalties after expiration of patents, 118; petrochemical sales, 58; pharmaceutical sales, 58; price fixing, 114–15; protectionist policies, 241; restrictive business practice codes, 362–64, 395, 418–20; restrictive business practices, regulation of, 35–37; rule of reason, 122–23; sovereign states, immunity of, 263; technology transfers, 50, 52, 62–63; technology transfers received, 58; tie-in restrictions, 111–12; trade deficit, 171; trademarks and quality control, 87, 95–96

Unlimited goods, 41
Unpackaging of technology, 105, 111–13
Unpatented know-how, 86, 88–92
Unpatented technology, 142, 161
Uranium cartel, 246, 258, 280, 288–89

Validity of patents and other protection, challenges to, 107–8, 117–18
VAW/Kaiser Aluminium case, 310
Vertical mergers, 338, 348
Voluntary export restraint, 214
Von's Grocery Co. case, 337, 348

Webb-Pomerene Act (U.S.), 35–36, 116, 162, 245–46, 256, 261–62, 268
Welfare economics, 203, 222
West Germany (Federal Republic of Germany): antitrust policy, 256, 287–88; export cartels, 261; merger control law, 293–96, 302–10, 315–18, 345–48, 352–54; technology transfers, 62
World competition codes, 30–33, 361–403; *see also* Restrictive business practice codes; Technology transfer code
World War II, cartels and, 247